Sovereignty, International Law, and the Princely States of Colonial South Asia

THE HISTORY AND THEORY OF INTERNATIONAL LAW

General Editors

In the past few decades the understanding of the relationship between nations has undergone a radical transformation. The role of the traditional nation-state is diminishing, along with many of the traditional vocabularies that were once used to describe what has been called, ever since Jeremy Bentham coined the phrase in 1780, 'international law'. The older boundaries between states are growing ever more fluid, new conceptions and new languages have emerged that are slowly coming to replace the image of a world of sovereign independent nation-states that has dominated the study of international relations since the early nineteenth century. This redefinition of the international arena demands a new understanding of classical and contemporary questions in international and legal theory. It is the editors' conviction that the best way to achieve this is by bridging the traditional divide between international legal theory, intellectual history, and legal and political history. The aim of the series, therefore, is to provide a forum for historical studies, from classical antiquity to the twenty-first century, that are theoretically informed and for philosophical work that is historically conscious, in the hope that a new vision of the rapidly evolving international world, its past and its possible future, may emerge.

PREVIOUSLY PUBLISHED IN THIS SERIES

The World Bank's Lawyers
The Life of International Law as Institutional Practice
Dimitri Van Den Meerssche

Preparing for War
The Making of the Geneva Conventions
Boyd van Dijk

The Invention of Custom
Natural Law and the Law of Nations, ca. 1550–1750
Francesca Iurlaro

The Right of Sovereignty
Jean Bodin on the Sovereign State and the Law of Nations
Daniel Lee

Jews, Sovereignty, and International Law
Ideology and Ambivalence in Early Israeli Legal Diplomacy
Rotem Giladi

Crafting the International Order
Practitioners and Practices of International Law since c.1800
Marcus M. Payk, Kim Christian Priemel

The Justification of War and International Order
From Past to Present
Lothar Brock, Hendrik Simon

Sovereignty, International Law, and the Princely States of Colonial South Asia

PRIYASHA SAKSENA

OXFORD
UNIVERSITY PRESS

OXFORD
UNIVERSITY PRESS

Great Clarendon Street, Oxford, OX2 6DP,
United Kingdom

Oxford University Press is a department of the University of Oxford.
It furthers the University's objective of excellence in research, scholarship,
and education by publishing worldwide. Oxford is a registered trade mark of
Oxford University Press in the UK and in certain other countries

First Edition published in 2023

Published in the United States of America by Oxford University Press
198 Madison Avenue, New York, NY 10016, United States of America

British Library Cataloguing in Publication Data

Data available

Library of Congress Control Number: 2023936694

ISBN 978–0–19–286658–5

DOI: 10.1093/oso/9780192866585.001.0001

Printed and bound by CPI Group (UK) Ltd, Croydon, CR0 4YY

For my parents, Pranjul and Rajendra Saksena

Series Editor's Preface

Ultimately every discussion over the range, authority, and the very identity of international law comes up against the question of sovereignty. Ever since it emerged in the sixteenth century sovereignty has been what the philosopher W. B. Gallie famously described in 1955 as an 'essentially contested'—or in Priyasha Saksena's word—'polysemic'—concept. At the centre of this contestation there has always been the question of the necessary indivisibility of sovereign power. For the writers of the sixteenth and seventeenth centuries, who first defined the term—most notably Jean Bodin and Thomas Hobbes—if sovereignty was to achieve what it was primarily intended to achieve, namely an end to civil war and the protection of the state against outsiders, it could only ever be, in Hobbes' words, 'immortal . . . incommunicable and inseparable'. But that supposed the existence of what it was trying to create; namely an homogenous, territorially bounded nation-state. In the relationship between states, however, in the domain of the international, there simply was no 'Common Power to keep them in awe'. Therefore, as Henry Maine, jurist, historian, pioneer anthropologist, and Law Member of the Viceroy of India's Council, put it bluntly in 1887, 'indivisibility of Sovereignty . . . Does not belong in International Law'. Beyond the limits of the heavily centralized—at least after 1648—European state system, argued Maine, 'The powers of sovereigns'

> are a bundle or collection of powers that may be separated from one another. Thus a ruler may administer civil and criminal justice, may make laws for his subjects and for his territory, may exercise power over life and death and may levy taxes and dues, but nevertheless he may be debarred from making war and peace, and from having foreign relations with any authority outside his territory.

The distinction that Maine was making here between what were called 'internal' and 'external' spheres of legislation had already been placed firmly on the British imperial agenda by Benjamin Franklin's famous three-hour testimony before the House of Commons in February 1776. In America where the colonists were still British subjects, however, a distinction of this kind made no constitutional sense. British India was another matter. Here as Maine argued,

> the 'Native Princes of India'—self-governing polities within what was perceived to be a British territory—offered, in Maine's view a model for a new species of colonialism in which 'no attempt [is] made to annex the land, to found a colony in the old sense of the word, but the local tribes are forbidden all foreign relations

> except those permitted by the protecting state.' Most nineteenth and twentieth-century European colonial societies operated with some distinction of this kind. It was, however, by no means as simple as Maine seems to suggest, and its implications, as Priyasha Saksena demonstrates in her remarkable book, reach well beyond the final days of most forms of colonial rule.

The British empire of the late nineteenth century was what Priyasha Saksena calls 'legally plural'. It contained within itself a bewildering number of different legal regimes: dominions, colonies, protectorates, protected states, and, after 1919, mandates. 'I know of no example of it either in ancient or modern history,' wrote Benjamin Disraeli in 1878, 'No Caesar or Charlemagne ever presided over a dominion so peculiar.' Of all these, the princely states were perhaps the most peculiar, in that they were the only ones in which sovereignty was clearly divided between the 'external' and 'internal', something that made them at once both subject to what was known vaguely as British 'paramountcy' and at the same time, and on their own understanding, 'allies' in the imperial project.

Little wonder, then, that it should have been the princes who were initially at least strongly in favour of the creation of a federal state in post-imperial India as one in which they would be able to retain their sovereign status and their attachment to the Crown, while at the same time, also being able to create for themselves a measure of international status. Federation, however, like the concept of shared or divided sovereignty on which it rests, can also be a heavily contested concept, and there were many within Britain who saw it not as a means of granting full independence from imperial rule but instead as a way of surreptitiously preserving it. Above all it could be used to fend off the spectre of 'self-determination' and the democratic institutions that would necessarily accompany it. As Samuel Hoare, Secretary of State for India, put it bluntly, federation presented 'an opportunity of avoiding democracy in the central government', and of providing a means to 'retain in our hands the realities and verities of British control'.

The struggles over the nature and the possible role the princes might have in any future independent, or quasi-independent India, the disputes over the kind, and extent of the powers of sovereignty that might exist within a federation—or a confederation—staggered on, until finally all the princely states acceded to either India or Pakistan. The principle of divisible (or shared) sovereignty which had been at the heart of all the debates over the future of India—and of the entire British empire since the late nineteenth century—finally ceded to an earlier more monist, more Hobbesian, understanding of the nature of the state, and the limits of its powers.

This remarkable book is at once a rigorous and far-reaching examination of the implications of the concept of 'shared' or 'divisible' sovereignty, a history of the complex negotiations between the British and the princes in the latter's bid to remain, in effect, the rulers of fully independent states, and of the impact that this was to have on the constitution of what would, in the end, become the modern Indian nation-state. But its implications also reach far beyond the Indian context. As Priyasha Saksena rightly concludes, the struggle over the nature and the limits of 'sovereignty were and continue to be, a reflection of broader discussions over where the realms of the national and the international lie, i.e., they are debates over the boundaries of the international'.

Anthony Pagden

Acknowledgements

This book has been a decade in the making. I have been tremendously fortunate to have been supported by numerous institutions and individuals along the way, and it is a pleasure to be able to thank the teachers, colleagues, friends, and family who have helped to make this book possible.

The encouragement of my doctoral supervisors at Harvard, where this book was born as a dissertation, was key to making it a reality. David Kennedy patiently mentored me through the vicissitudes of the graduate student experience. His probing questions made me think more deeply about the issues with which I chose to engage and he was ineffably considerate about the many turns that my research underwent. Samuel Moyn was exceptionally generous in sharing his insights into the art of writing history and continually pushed me to be more imaginative and to think about this project in broader terms. Sunil Amrith deftly guided me through debates in South Asian history and helped me to connect economic and political context with the numerous legal arguments that I examine. All three have been inspirational advisors and teachers, have been magnanimous with their time, and have been tolerant of my many shortcomings; I cannot thank them enough. I also had the privilege of working with a number of other people during my Harvard years—Duncan Kennedy, Mark Wu, and Sugata Bose—this study has benefitted enormously from their acumen. I am grateful to the Harvard Law School Graduate Program—particularly Bill Alford, Jeanne Tai, Nancy Pinn, Catherine Peshkin, and Naomi Schaffer—for their support. Special thanks to Jane Bestor, who often had more faith in this project than I have had myself. My fellow graduate students—Carolina Silva-Portero, Erum Sattar, Farida Mortada, Kibrom Teweldebirhan, Mohammad Hamdy, Oteng Acheampong, Pieter-Augustijn Van Malleghem, Rabiat Akande, Rana Elkawahgy, and Svitlana Starosvit—provided me with the intellectual atmosphere and the personal friendship that is essential to sustain any dissertation effort. Afroditi Giovanopoulou read portions of the manuscript at various stages, her own research has shaped my thinking, and our continued conversations have provided a constant source of encouragement. I am incredibly grateful to be able to count her as a friend.

I have been warmly welcomed by my colleagues at Leeds, which has provided me with a new home. Marie-Andrée Jacob and Henry Yeomans have been pivotal in helping me navigate the early years of life in academia and have furnished critical insights to sharpen my research. Ilias Trispiotis and Rebecca Moosavian provided feedback on parts of the manuscript. Much of critical transition from dissertation to book was completed during the pandemic, during which the support of my co-workers was invaluable for balancing teaching commitments, administrative responsibilities, and research aims—thanks to Adam Baker, Amrita Mukherjee, Carrie Bradshaw, Ilaria Zavoli, Imogen Jones, Konstantinos Stylianou, Luke Clements, Michael Cardwell, Mitch Travis, Or Brook, Rachael O'Connor, and Stuart Wallace, for providing conversation and camaraderie. I am also grateful to Alastair Mullis, Joan Loughrey, and Louise Ellison for their leadership and for making me feel a part of the Leeds community.

I was fortunate to be able to spend a year at the Max Planck Institute for Legal History and Legal Theory, where I wrote an initial draft of the final chapter of the book. I am grateful to Stefan Vogenauer for providing me with this opportunity and to Donal Coffey, Emily Whewell, Justine Collins, Rahela Khorakiwala, and Victoria Barnes for making my stay there both enjoyable and intellectually enriching.

I have also been lucky to gather support from beyond the numerous institutions with which I have been affiliated. I have benefitted enormously from the exciting South Asian legal history scholarship that has flourished over the past couple of decades; thanks to Mitra Sharafi and Rohit De for showing the way and for their interest in my work. Angma Jhala, Nehal Bhuta, and Dylan Lino generously read and commented on several draft chapters. Thanks also to Abhinav Sekhri and Sarath Pillai, who provided keen insights. Amita Gupta Katragadda taught me how to be a professional during the two years that I spent at Amarchand Mangaldas; I will always be grateful for all her advice. My undergraduate education at the National Law School of India University was key to shaping my thinking, with V. S. Elizabeth demonstrating the innovative ways in which history can be taught and written. I would also like to express my thanks to my very first teacher, Sultana Shaheen Moidu, who taught me how to read and whose life is still an inspiration.

This research was made possible by the unstinting support of librarians and archivists across the world. I would like to thank the staff of the Harvard University libraries (particularly Aslihan Bulut and the FRIDA staff), the University of Leeds libraries, the Central Library at Goethe University, the Max Planck Institute for Legal History and Legal Theory library, the Asian and African Studies Reading Room at the British Library in London, the National Archives of India (in New Delhi and at the regional office in Bhopal), the Nehru Memorial Museum and Library in New Delhi, and the Balliol College Archives in Oxford. Without their help, I would never have managed to grasp the rich historical material that is the basis of this book.

A number of different institutions provided grants to support archival research. Thanks to the Harvard Law School Graduate Program and International Legal Studies, the Lakshmi Mittal and Family South Asia Institute at Harvard University, the Weatherhead Center for International Affairs at Harvard University, and the University of Leeds School of Law Research and Scholarship Fund.

I have presented parts of this book at various forums over the years, where audiences asked searching questions and provided perceptive comments to help me refine its central arguments: the Institute for Global Law and Policy workshop in Madrid; the Workshop on Protectorates and Semi-Colonialisms in Comparison at the Inter-Asia Initiative at Yale University; the Conference on International Law and Decolonization at Princeton University; the Empire, International Law, and History webinar series at the Centre for International Legal Studies, Jindal Global Law School; the Max Planck Institute for Legal History and Legal Theory; the Edinburgh Centre for Global and International Law; the annual conferences of the Socio-Legal Studies Association in York and Cardiff; the British Legal History Conference sessions in Belfast and London; the Law and Social Sciences Research Network conference in New Delhi; and the annual meeting of Law and Society Association in New Orleans.

At Oxford University Press, Merel Alstein, Jack McNichol, Jordan Burke, Kim Vollrodt, and the rest of the production team provided invaluable support during the publication process. The final manuscript has been greatly improved by the careful reading of Edward J. Kolla and three other reviewers. An earlier version of chapter three was published as 'Jousting Over Jurisdiction: Sovereignty and International Law in Late Nineteenth-Century South Asia', *Law and History Review*, 38/2 (2020), 409–457; thanks to the editor, Gautham Rao, and three anonymous reviewers for their comments, and to Cambridge University Press for permission to republish. An earlier version of chapter six was published as 'Building the Nation: Sovereignty and International Law in the Decolonisation of South Asia', *Journal of the History of International Law*, 23/1 (2021), 52–79; thanks to two anonymous reviewers for their comments and to Brill for permission to republish.

My friends and family have made the often solitary research and writing process easier. I have been very fortunate to maintain the friendship of the formidable women I met on my first day in law school in Bangalore all those years ago. Aditi Srivastava, Sangita John, Shubhangi Bhadada, and Surya Sreenivasan have kept me company ever since, despite my many moves across continents. They have listened to me talk about this project and about life, they have opened their homes to host me, and they have been unstinting in their support. Thanks to them for being my kindred spirits. Gowthaman Ranganathan, Madhav Kanoria, and Vikram Hegde have supplied me with enough good humour to pass even the darkest hours. Eashan Ghosh's warm-hearted friendship has provided the emotional shelter to sustain me through several arduous years. I have learnt so much from his work ethic and professional commitment and he has always been at hand to give me encouragement. It is only thanks to his relentless efforts that we have managed to become better friends in the years we have spent apart than when we were living in the same city. I was blessed to have my brother, Pulkit Saksena, as my companion while growing up. He was my first influence and I have only managed to write this book by taking inspiration from him. Although we have both relocated several times over the years, he continues to be a bedrock of support from afar; I am immensely thankful for his love and understanding.

My deepest thanks go to my parents, whose love and support have been unwavering. I was able to set across on my scholarly journey because of my father, Rajendra Saksena, who has had firm faith in me. And there are no words that I can use to express my gratitude to my mother, Pranjul Saksena. I am incredibly lucky to be her daughter and I can only hope that one day I might be more like her. My parents' commitment and sacrifice have made me the person I am today and they remain my closest confidantes and most important role models. This book is dedicated to them, with all my love.

Leeds
November 2022

Contents

List of Abbreviations

AGG	Agent to the Governor-Ggeneral
AISPC	All India States' Peoples' Conference
BBCIR	Bombay, Baroda, and Central India Railway
EIC	English East India Company
GoI Act	Government of India Act 1935
ILO	International Labour Organization
IoAs	Instruments of Accession
RTC	Round Table Conference
UN	United Nations

Chapter One
Introduction

Defining Sovereignty

In 1911, George Wellington Statham filed a petition in the Probate, Divorce, and Admiralty Division of the High Court in London seeking a dissolution of his marriage with Beatrix Alice Statham on the ground of her adultery.[1] What made this petition unusual was the co-respondent: Statham claimed that his wife had committed adultery with Sayajirao Gaekwad III,[2] the *maharaja* (ruler) of Baroda, one of the six hundred-odd 'princely states' that covered about two-fifths of the area and one-third of the population of South Asia under British rule.[3] The princely states were ruled by indigenous rulers who were 'advised' by British officials on issues of governance. The government of India also exercised certain functions, such as defence and external affairs, on behalf of the states.[4]

Despite being subject to British 'influence', Sayajirao refused to submit to the jurisdiction of an English court. He claimed that as 'a reigning sovereign' he was not subject to the court's jurisdiction in accordance with 'the rules of international law'.[5] To support his position, he produced a certificate issued by the British government[6] that stated: '... But, though His Highness is thus not independent, he

[1] *Statham* v. *Statham and His Highness the Gaekwar of Baroda*, [1912] P 92.

[2] This wasn't Sayajirao's only run-in with colonial authorities. See Ian Copland, 'The Dilemmas of a Ruling Prince: Maharaja Sayaji Rao Gaekwar and "Sedition"', in Peter Robb and David Taylor, eds., *Rule, Protest, Identity: Aspects of Modern South Asia* (London: Curzon Press, 1978), 28–48; Charles W. Nuckolls, 'The Durbar Incident', *Modern Asian Studies*, 24/3 (1990), 529–559; Stephen Bottomore, '"Have You Seen the Gaekwar Bob?": Filming the 1911 Delhi Durbar', *Historical Journal of Film, Radio and Television*, 17/3 (1997), 309–345; and Manu Bhagavan, *Sovereign Spheres: Princes, Education, and Empire in Colonial India* (Oxford: Oxford University Press, 2003), 47–69. On Sayajirao's life more generally, see Philip W. Sergeant, *The Ruler of Baroda: An Account of the Life and Work of the Maharaja Gaekwar* (London: John Murray, 1928); Stanley Rice, *Life of Sayaji Rao III Maharaja of Baroda*, 2 vols (London: Oxford University Press, 1931); Fatehsinhrao Gaekwad, *Sayajirao of Baroda: The Prince and the Man* (London: Sangam, 1989); Barbara Ramusack, 'Gaikwar [Gaekwar], Sayaji Rao, maharaja of Baroda (1863–1939)', in David Cannadine, ed., *Oxford Dictionary of National Biography*, online edn (Oxford: Oxford University Press, 2004), https://doi.org/10.1093/ref:odnb/30613, accessed 19 October 2020; and Uma Balasubramaniam, *Sayajirao Gaekwad III: The Maharaja of Baroda* (New Delhi: Rupa Publications, 2019).

[3] These statistics exclude Burma and Ceylon. The exact number of princely states varied over time and the very category of 'princely state' remained contested. See Ian Copland, *The Princes of India in the Endgame of Empire, 1917–1947* (Cambridge: Cambridge University Press, 1997), 8; and Barbara Ramusack, *The Indian Princes and their States* (Cambridge: Cambridge University Press, 2004), 2.

[4] Ramusack, *The Indian Princes and their States*, (n 3) 53.

[5] *Statham*, (n 1) 93.

[6] I use the term 'British government' to refer to various levels of British authority with respect to South Asia, including the Crown, the East India Company, the secretary of state for India, the India

Sovereignty, International Law, and the Princely States of Colonial South Asia. Priyasha Saksena, Oxford University Press.
 DOI: 10.1093/oso/9780192866585.003.0001

exercises as ruler of his State various attributes of sovereignty, including internal sovereignty ... subject, however, to the suzerainty of His Majesty the King of England ....'[7]

By relying on his allegedly sovereign status, Sayajirao transformed the divorce suit into an exploration of the legal status of the princely states and the nature and extent of the powers exercised by the princes and the British government. Henry Bargrave Deane, the presiding judge, attempted to decipher the meaning of 'suzerainty' by relying on international law treatises written by Hugo Grotius and Emer de Vattel. He concluded that Sayajirao was incapable of being made a co-respondent in the suit.[8]

Sayajirao's case was not an isolated one; issues of the states' legal status remained deeply controversial and heavily debated throughout colonial rule. What was the nature of the relationship among the state of Baroda, the government of India, and the British Crown? What rights did the *maharaja* enjoy within his own territory, in British India, and in Britain? Conversely, what powers did the British exercise within Baroda territory and over the *maharaja* himself? What law governed the relationship between the princely states and the British government—national, imperial, or international law? The colonial archives are littered with details of incidents that raised similarly tangled questions of sovereignty, of empire, and of international law.

This book traces how the language of sovereignty became the discourse for debating the legal status of the princely states and, in this way, mediated the exercise of political power in colonial South Asia.[9] I argue that the doctrine of sovereignty came to structure political imagination in South Asia and consequently the framework of the modern Indian state. Focusing on the period between the mid-eighteenth and mid-twentieth centuries, I examine how international lawyers, British politicians, colonial officials, rulers and bureaucrats of princely states,

Office in London, the government of India, the viceroy and governor-general of India, the governments of various British Indian provinces, and British political officers in the princely states.

[7] *Statham*, (n 1) 95.

[8] ibid 95–96.

[9] I follow Rande Kostal in arguing that law was the language in which disputes over the exercise of political power were conducted across the British empire. See R. W. Kostal, *A Jurisprudence of Power: Victorian Empire and the Rule of Law* (Oxford: Oxford University Press, 2005). I also build on Lauren Benton's work on the significance of sovereignty for deliberations over the legal status of the princely states. See Lauren Benton, *A Search for Sovereignty: Law and Geography in European Empires, 1400–1900* (Cambridge: Cambridge University Press, 2010), 222–278. Law was not, however, the only language in which these debates were carried out; other discourses, such as religion, were also significant for constructing political alternatives and demonstrating princely sovereignty. See Mridu Rai, *Hindu Rulers, Muslim Subjects: Islam, Rights, and the History of Kashmir* (Princeton, NJ: Princeton University Press, 2004); Aya Ikegame, *Princely India Re-imagined: A Historical Anthropology of Mysore from 1799 to the Present* (London: Routledge, 2013); and Carla Bellamy, 'Alternative Kingdoms: Shrines and Sovereignty in Jaora', *Comparative Studies of South Asia, Africa and the Middle East*, 40/3 (2020), 444–453.

and anticolonial nationalists continually defined and redefined the concept of sovereignty in South Asia. Assertions of sovereignty enabled these players to rely on the vocabulary of international law to resolve questions of legal status, the extent of rights, and the proper exercise of powers, as well as to construct a political order that was in line with their interests and aspirations. British authorities relied on the divisibility of sovereignty to justify their incursions into the internal affairs of the princely states and cement the authority of the colonial state. The states variously defined sovereignty as territorial and divisible to defend themselves from unnecessary interference by colonial authorities and anticolonial nationalists and simultaneously build productive relationships with each other and with the broader world. Anticolonial nationalists described sovereignty as territorial to create a unified state space over which centralized authority could be exercised after independence while also tackling the challenges posed by subnational movements to their developmentalist project. By invoking the vernacular of sovereignty in contrasting ways to support their differing visions of world order, these actors also attempted to reconfigure the boundaries among the spheres of the national, the imperial, and the international.

Exploring the legal debates over the princely states is, I argue, key to understanding the history of sovereignty, the construction of the modern Indian nation-state, and the scope and stakes of international law itself. Colonial South Asia was rife with jurisdictional disputes and debates over whether the princely states could be considered to be 'sovereign states' or if they were simply 'hollow crowns'.[10] These discussions took place in a wide range of spaces and were conducted in and through legal opinions, memos, and texts; official and personal letters; diplomatic petitions; political speeches, pamphlets, and propaganda material; governmental and committee reports; and generalist writings. Instead of being confined to the pages of international law treatises, debates over the legal status

[10] In an early influential study, Nicholas Dirks argued that British colonialism preserved only the appearance of the pre-colonial regime, while there was a total collapse of earlier political structures and processes. The crown, he contended, was 'hollow' and the princely states were reduced to 'theatre states' obsessed with the symbols of past glory. See Nicholas Dirks, *The Hollow Crown: Ethnohistory of an Indian Kingdom* (Cambridge: Cambridge University Press, 1987). For a more recent study making a similar argument, see Bhangya Bhukya, 'The Subordination of the Sovereigns: Colonialism and the Gond Rajas in Central India, 1818–1948', *Modern Asian Studies*, 47/1 (2013), 288–317. Other histories have more complicated notions of indigenous agency, the state, and sovereignty. Some scholars argue that the princely states provided the quintessential example of indigenous resistance to colonialism. See Hira Singh, *Colonial Hegemony and Popular Resistance: Princes, Peasants, and Paramount Power* (New Delhi: Sage Publications, 1998). Another stream of scholarship focuses on the construction of 'alternative modernities' in the princely states through the centralization of power and describe the attempts of several states to manoeuvre the partial autonomy they enjoyed in the colonial context. See Shail Mayaram, *Resisting Regimes: Myth, Memory and the Shaping of a Muslim Identity* (New Delhi: Oxford University Press, 1997); Bhagavan, *Sovereign Spheres*, (n 2); Rai, *Hindu Rulers, Muslim Subjects*, (n 9); Janaki Nair, *Mysore Modern: Rethinking the Region under Princely Rule* (Minneapolis, MN: University of Minnesota Press, 2011); and Eric Lewis Beverley, *Hyderabad, British India, and the World: Muslim Networks and Minor Sovereignty, c. 1850–1950* (Cambridge: Cambridge University Press, 2015).

of the princely states occupied a prominent place in colonial politics.[11] I focus on five controversies—discussions over British intervention into state affairs, jurisdictional disputes between the states and the British government, hearings before the Indian States Committee, negotiations over a possible federation of British India and the states, and deliberations over the transfer of power during the process of decolonization—to demonstrate how the princes and their advisors relied on iterations of sovereignty to recast the states' relations with British India, the British Crown, and the wider world. Despite their astonishingly rapid erasure from the postcolonial political map of South Asia, the princely states were, for nearly two centuries, at the heart of discussions over what sovereignty meant and how it could be defined.

By placing the princely states at the centre of this study, I illustrate the key role of sub-imperial polities[12] in the historical debates over the 'boundaries of the international'[13] that continue to haunt international law even today. Contemporary international lawyers, for example, still argue over the entities that constitute the proper subjects of international law, including questions such as whether indigenous peoples are to be recognized as peoples entitled to self-determination.[14] Scholars have focused on the constitutive role played by colonialism in this process

[11] In emphasizing the importance of exploring colonial legal politics, I follow Lauren Benton and Lisa Ford who assert that international legal language was intricately linked to the everyday administration of the British empire. See Lauren Benton and Lisa Ford, *Rage for Order: The British Empire and the Origins of International Law, 1800–1850* (Cambridge, MA: Harvard University Press, 2016). In recent years, there has been considerable scholarly debate on the appropriate methodology for the writing of international legal histories, particularly on the need to discuss the broader 'context' within which legal arguments were made in the past. See Valentina Vadi, 'International Law and Its Histories: Methodological Risks and Opportunities', *Harvard International Law Journal*, 58/2 (2017), 311–352; Lauren Benton, 'Beyond Anachronism: Histories of International Law and Global Legal Politics', *Journal of the History of International Law*, 21/1 (2019), 7–40; Jean d'Aspremont, 'Critical Histories of International Law and the Repression of Disciplinary Imagination', *London Review of International Law*, 7/1 (2019), 89–115; Jacob Katz Cogan, 'A History of International Law in the Vernacular', *Journal of the History of International Law*, 22/2–3 (2020), 205–217; Kate Purcell, 'On the Uses and Advantages of Genealogy for International Law', *Leiden Journal of International Law*, 33/1 (2020), 13–35; and Anne Orford, *International Law and the Politics of History* (Cambridge: Cambridge University Press, 2021). Given the key role of the princely states in colonial legal politics, I believe that it is essential to examine this broader context to fully understand the way legal concepts like sovereignty were deployed in these debates.

[12] Numerous scholars have focused on the role of semi-sovereign entities in international law. See Prabhakar Singh, 'Of International Law, Semi-colonial Thailand, and Imperial Ghosts', *Asian Journal of International Law*, 9/1 (2019), 46–74; Ali Hammoudi, 'The International Law of Informal Empire and the "Question of Oman"', *Third World Approaches to International Law Review*, 1 (2020), 121–151; and Yuan Yi Zhu, 'Suzerainty, Semi-Sovereignty, and International Legal Hierarchies on China's Borderlands', *Asian Journal of International Law*, 10/2 (2020), 293–320. This book adds the princely states to the list of such semi-sovereign actors.

[13] I borrow this term from Jennifer Pitts, *Boundaries of the International: Law and Empire* (Cambridge, MA: Harvard University Press, 2018).

[14] See the discussions in Matthew Craven and Rose Parfitt, 'Statehood, Self-Determination, and Recognition', in Malcolm D. Evans, ed., *International Law* (5th edn, Oxford: Oxford University Press, 2018), 177–226; and James Crawford, *Brownlie's Principles of Public International Law*, 9th edn (Oxford: Oxford University Press, 2019), 105–133.

of delimiting the extent of international law.[15] Antony Anghie, for instance, has explored how nineteenth-century international lawyers relied on a dichotomy between 'civilized' European states and the 'uncivilized' non-European 'other' to define sovereignty so as to exclude non-Europeans.[16] However, demarcating the border between the imperial and the international has also been a sharply contested affair in view of the deep internal divisions within European political thought on the international status of non-Europeans.[17] Historians have suggested that interrogating the jurisdictional politics of empire is critical to understanding the creation of the modern state-dominated international legal order.[18] As highlighted by *Statham*, sub-imperial entities such as the princely states posed particularly vexing questions for actors trying to define the scope of the international because of their disputed sovereign status.[19] Although recent scholarship has taken the controversy over the sovereignty of the princely states seriously, it has often focused on internal British discussions about the legal status of the states,[20] with legal arguments made by the states remaining unevenly mapped.[21]

[15] Early scholarship on the relationship between international law and empire focused on the role played by international law in the subordination of non-European peoples. See C. H. Alexandrowicz, *An Introduction to the History of the Law of Nations in the East Indies (16th, 17th and 18th Centuries)* (Oxford: Clarendon Press, 1967); T. O. Elias, *Africa and the Development of International Law* (Leiden: A. W. Sijthoff, 1972); and R. P. Anand, *New States and International Law* (New Delhi: Vikas Publications, 1972). Starting with Antony Anghie, *Imperialism, Sovereignty and the Making of International Law* (Cambridge: Cambridge University Press, 2005), the focus of critical scholarship has shifted to examining the effect that colonialism has had on the construction of international law doctrines like sovereignty. See Duncan Bell, ed., *Victorian Visions of Global Order: Empire and International Relations in Nineteenth-Century Political Thought* (Cambridge: Cambridge University Press, 2007); Benton, *A Search for Sovereignty*, (n 9); Arnulf Becker Lorca, *Mestizo International Law: A Global Intellectual History, 1842–1933* (Cambridge: Cambridge University Press, 2014); Benton and Ford, *Rage for Order*, (n 11); Luis Eslava, Michael Fakhri, and Vasuki Nesiah, eds., *Bandung, Global History, and International Law: Critical Pasts and Pending Futures* (Cambridge: Cambridge University Press, 2017); and Pitts, *Boundaries of the International*, (n 13).

[16] Anghie, *Imperialism, Sovereignty and the Making of International Law*, (n 15) 33–35.

[17] See Andrew Fitzmaurice, 'Liberalism and Empire in Nineteenth-Century International Law', *American Historical Review*, 117/1 (2012), 122–140; Robert Travers, 'A British Empire by Treaty in Eighteenth-Century India', in Saliha Belmessous, ed., *Empire by Treaty: Negotiating European Expansion, 1600–1900* (Oxford: Oxford University Press, 2015), 132–160; and Pitts, *Boundaries of the International*, (n 13).

[18] In her pioneering work on jurisdictional disputes in legally diverse empires, Lauren Benton argues that plural legal orders in which individual litigants attempted to take advantage of imperial fragmentation gave way in the nineteenth century to a state-dominated order since engagement with the state's legal institutions reinforced the authority of the colonial state itself. See Lauren Benton, *Law and Colonial Cultures: Legal Regimes in World History, 1400–1900* (Cambridge: Cambridge University Press, 2002), 148–149.

[19] See Lauren Benton, 'From International Law to Imperial Constitutions: The Problem of Quasi-Sovereignty, 1870–1900', *Law and History Review*, 26/3 (2008), 595–619; Stephen Legg, 'An International Anomaly? Sovereignty, the League of Nations and India's Princely Geographies', *Journal of Historical Geography* 43 (2014), 96–110; and Beverley, *Hyderabad, British India, and the World*, (n 10) 54–72.

[20] Scholars have focused on arguments among colonial officials or those between British officials and critics arguing for colonial reform. See Ian Copland, *The British Raj and the Indian Princes: Paramountcy in Western India, 1857–1930* (Bombay: Orient Longman, 1982), 211–221; Copland, *The Princes of India in the Endgame of Empire*, (n 3) 19–20; Ramusack, *The Indian Princes and their States*, (n 3) 92–97; Benton, 'From International Law to Imperial Constitutions'(n 19); and Zak Leonard, 'Law of Nations Theory and the Native Sovereignty Debates in Colonial India', *Law and History Review*, 38/2 (2020), 373–407.

[21] Scholars have usually alluded to the views of the states briefly or have focused on specific states (such as Hyderabad) or incidents (such as the federation debates) rather than engaging in a

The fluidity of the boundary between the spheres of the imperial and the international facilitated the attempts of the princely states to redefine their legal status and construct a political order that was more conducive to their concerns. The principal tool in their arsenal was the polysemic concept of sovereignty, a legal idea that is capable of being defined in multiple ways.[22] Sovereignty has gained manifold meanings and justifications over time, as a variety of players have used, manipulated, cannibalized, reimagined, and structured the idea in different ways to give shape to their often-conflicting visions of an ideal global order. The princely states were no exception. Rulers of the states, their advisors, and their bureaucrats engaged deeply with international law concepts, particularly that of sovereignty, and developed their own legal vocabularies to shape the destiny of the states.

Princely conceptions of sovereignty were closely linked to their ever-changing political projects. In the early years of their interaction with British officials, the princes defined sovereignty as 'territorial' to claim that there was a single sovereign authority in state territory. This conceptualization aided them in their attempts to minimize colonial interference in internal state affairs and build centralized administrations that could undermine the efforts of local rivals to challenge monarchical authority. By the turn of the twentieth century, the princes became more ambitious and sought to carve out a more significant role for themselves in imperial and global affairs while also defending themselves against the demands of political reformers who had built links with anticolonial nationalists in British India. With this turn of events, the princes redefined sovereignty as 'divisible'; this definition enabled them to maintain loose relationships with the Crown and British India

comprehensive overview. See Andrew Muldoon, *Empire, Politics and the Creation of the 1935 India Act* (Farnham: Ashgate, 2009); Benton, *A Search for Sovereignty*, (n 9) 265; Eric Lewis Beverley, 'Frontier as Resource: Law, Crime, and Sovereignty on the Margins of Empire', *Comparative Studies in Society and History*, 55/2 (2013), 241–272; Priya Naik, 'The Case of the "Other India" and Indian IR Scholarship', *Third World Quarterly*, 35/8 (2014), 1496–1508; Kavita Saraswathi Datla, 'The Origins of Indirect Rule in India: Hyderabad and the British Imperial Order', *Law and History Review*, 33/2 (2015), 321–350; Sarath Pillai, 'Fragmenting the Nation: Divisible Sovereignty and Travancore's Quest for Federal Independence', *Law and History Review*, 34/3 (2016), 743–782; Rama Sundari Mantena, 'Anticolonialism and Federation in Colonial India', *Ab Imperio*, 3 (2018): 36–62; Kavita Saraswathi Datla, 'Sovereignty and the End of Empire: The Transition to Independence in Colonial Hyderabad', *Ab Imperio*, 3 (2018). 63–88; Sunil Purushotham, 'Federating the Raj: Hyderabad, Sovereign Kingship, and Partition', *Modern Asian Studies*, 54/1 (2020), 157–198; Prabhakar Singh, 'Indian Princely States and the 19th-century Transformation of the Law of Nations', *Journal of International Dispute Settlement*, 11/3 (2020), 365–387; Thomas Blom Hansen, 'Sovereignty in a Minor Key', *Public Culture*, 33/1 (2021), 41–61; and Devika Shankar, 'A Slippery Sovereignty: International Law and the Development of British Cochin', *Comparative Studies in Society and History*, 64/3 (2022), 820–844.

[22] Hent Kalmo and Quentin Skinner, for instance, argue that sovereignty is a highly ambiguous concept that has been 'amenable to numerous, often directly contradictory, uses'. See Hent Kalmo and Quentin Skinner, 'Introduction: A Concept in Fragments', in Hent Kalmo and Quentin Skinner, eds., *Sovereignty in Fragments: The Past, Present and Future of a Contested Concept* (Cambridge: Cambridge University Press, 2010), 8.

to benefit from economic and infrastructural links while also defending state autonomy in the exercise of other sovereign functions. Throughout colonial rule, the princes often took approaches different to those taken by other actors, including international lawyers and colonial officials, since international law, despite its apparently universal nature, means different things to different people in different places.[23]

In the course of deliberations over the legal status of the princely states, the concept of sovereignty became both the tool and the terrain of legal and political struggle between British and South Asian actors.[24] These debates recast the relationship among the domestic, the imperial, and the international spheres; examining them can help us to unravel the transition of South Asia from a colonial web of overlapping sovereignties to a postcolonial world of nation-states. By focusing on this particular narrative, this book aims to unravel the complex history of sovereignty—especially of its multiple definitions—to better appreciate the work that international law performed in the colonial context as well as its continued significance as a language that is used by peoples and entities seeking international recognition and subnational movements negotiating their relationships with the nation-state.

The Princely States in the British Empire

To explore the ways in which the princely states relied on the language of sovereignty, it is critical to map out the distinctive position of the states within the broader, legally diverse, British empire.[25] By the early twentieth century, when the empire reached its greatest extent, its territories included dominions, colonies, protectorates, protected states, and mandates.[26] The British exercised different levels of sovereign power in these disparate polities, with the empire's legal structures remaining dynamic and changing over time. The slow transformation

[23] David Kennedy, 'The Disciplines of International Law and Policy', *Leiden Journal of International Law*, 12/1 (1999), 17.

[24] I am influenced by E. P. Thompson's idea of law constituting a site of conflict where the aristocracy and the plebians engaged in battles to redefine the nature of property rights. See E. P. Thompson, *Whigs and Hunters: The Origin of the Black Act* (London: Allen Lane, 1975), 261–269.

[25] The British empire's legal diversity is not unusual. Plural legal orders were the dominant mode of political organization in the early modern period, with layered notions of sovereignty generating legal disputes. See Sugata Bose, *A Hundred Horizons: The Indian Ocean in the Age of Global Empire* (Cambridge, MA: Harvard University Press, 2006); Benton, *A Search for Sovereignty*, (n 9); Jane Burbank and Frederick Cooper, *Empires in World History: Power and the Politics of Difference* (Princeton, NJ: Princeton University Press, 2011); Lauren Benton and Richard J. Ross, eds., *Legal Pluralism and Empires, 1500–1850* (New York, NY: New York University Press, 2013); and Lauren Benton and Adam Clulow, 'Protection Shopping Among Empires: Suspended Sovereignty in the Cocos-Keeling Islands', *Past & Present*, 257 (2022), 209–247.

[26] For an overview of the differences in the legal positions of these entities, see A. B. Keith, *The Governments of the British Empire* (London: Macmillan and Co., 1935).

in the position of the dominions (Australia, Canada, New Zealand, South Africa, and the Irish Free State) provides a useful illustration. A mainstay of imperial law was the principle that laws made by colonial legislatures would be invalid if they were 'repugnant' to those made by the imperial parliament, which effectively made the dominions (like other colonies) subordinate to Britain.[27] With demands for increased autonomy by the dominions after the First World War, the 1926 imperial conference confirmed that the United Kingdom and the dominions were 'autonomous communities within the British Empire, equal in status, in no way subordinate one to another in any aspect of their domestic or external affairs, though united by a common allegiance to the Crown and freely associated as members of the British Commonwealth of Nations'.[28] By strengthening the position of the dominions in the sphere of foreign affairs, these developments put pressure on the notion that the British empire was a single unit for the purposes of international law and highlighted the contested nature of the boundary between the imperial and the international.[29]

Even within this legally plural empire, the princely states posed particularly acute questions for the division between the imperial and the international spheres because of the lengthy debates over their legal status. Governed by local rulers, the states remained legally separate from directly-ruled British India, a distinction that was pictorially represented in colonial maps of South Asia that coloured British India pink and depicted the princely states in yellow.[30] British India was first administered by the English East India Company (referred to as 'the EIC' or 'the Company') and later by the British Crown through the viceroy and governor-general, who was the executive head of the government of India and subject to the control of parliament through the secretary of state for India, a member of the British cabinet. In contrast to directly-administered British India, the relationship between the states and the British government was mediated by political officers who were posted at the states' courts to advise the princes on how to rule, with the government of India exercising only specific functions, such as defence and foreign affairs, for the princes.[31]

While the states are often considered to exemplify 'indirect rule', this concept is capacious and merits closer interrogation. Indirect rule is ordinarily understood as a system in which colonial administrators 'incorporated indigenous political institutions into their imperial administrations'.[32] Although the princely states

[27] The repugnancy clause was, however, ambiguous and the subject of many legal disputes. See Philip Stern, 'Bundles of Hyphens', in *Legal Pluralism and Empires*, (n 25) 29.

[28] *Imperial Conference: Summary of Proceedings* (1926), 12.

[29] For a discussion of these developments, see Keith, *The Governments of the British Empire*, (n 26) 30–33, 86–100.

[30] Copland, *The British Raj and the Indian Princes*, (n 20) 2.

[31] Ramusack, *The Indian Princes and their States*, (n 3) 53.

[32] Michael H. Fisher, *Indirect Rule in India: Residents and the Residency System, 1764–1858* (Delhi: Oxford University Press, 1991), 1.

provided the inspiration for legal structures that were utilized in other parts of the empire, including the Persian Gulf states, the Malay states, Uganda, and northern Nigeria,[33] colonial officials also adapted general ideas to suit specific contexts. The broad category of indirect rule, therefore, encompassed several different structures of governance. The Malay states and northern Nigeria, for instance, ended up being under greater direct supervision of British officials than the princely states ever were.[34] As a result, the princely states were considered to be *sui generis*, both by British[35] and state officials.[36]

Although the term 'princely states' implies a degree of homogeneity, the states were, in fact, quite diverse in terms of size, social composition, administration, and politics. The state of Hyderabad, for instance, covered an area of over 200,000 square kilometres and had a population of over eleven million in 1901,[37] while there were several states in the Kathiawar region of western India that were less than three square kilometres in area and had populations of fewer than two hundred people.[38] The princes themselves were divided by religion and caste, with perceived differences in status often being a cause of friction among them.[39] The category of 'princely state' itself remained heavily contested. Only forty states had a treaty relationship with the British (either with the Company or its successor, the Crown); relations of the rest were mapped out in *sanads* (British decrees offering protection to a prince) or letters of understanding.[40] On account of the varied basis of these relationships, British administrators struggled to classify entities as princely states, with many South Asian elites claiming to be rulers of states rather than landholders or revenue-collectors. A long running dispute in the

[33] See Copland, *The British Raj and the Indian Princes*, (n 20) 298; and Fisher, *Indirect Rule in India*, (n 32) 459. Lauren Benton notes that nineteenth-century international lawyers and colonial officials also drew comparisons between the princely states and Native American tribes that were considered to be 'domestic dependent nations' within the United States; however, she also concedes that the histories of these two types of polities were quite different. See, Benton, *A Search for Sovereignty*, (n 9) 271–276.

[34] Fisher, *Indirect Rule in India*, (n 32) 461–477; and Thomas Metcalf, *Imperial Connections: India in the Indian Ocean Arena, 1860–1920* (Berkeley, CA: University of California Press, 2007), 32–45. In fact, Mahmood Mamdani argues that there was little difference between direct and indirect rule in Africa. See Mahmood Mamdani, *Citizen and Subject: Contemporary Africa and the Legacy of Late Colonialism* (Princeton, NJ: Princeton University Press, 1996); and Mahmood Mamdani, *Define and Rule: Native as Political Identity* (Cambridge, MA: Harvard University Press, 2012).

[35] In correspondence with the Colonial Office, India Office officials repeatedly noted that the princely states' rulers exercised far more sovereign powers than other rulers like the Malay *sultans*. See Simon C. Smith, *British Relations with the Malay Rulers from Decentralization to Malayan Independence, 1930–1957* (Kuala Lumpur: Oxford University Press, 1995), 51–53. See also *Report of the Indian States Committee* (1929), para 43.

[36] K. M. Panikkar, *An Introduction to the Study of the Relations of Indian States with the Government of India* (London: Martin Hopkinson, 1927), xix.

[37] *The Imperial Gazetteer of India*, iv: *The Indian Empire, Administrative* (Oxford: Clarendon Press, 1909), 92.

[38] Ramusack, *The Indian Princes and their States*, (n 3) 3.

[39] Copland, *The Princes of India in the Endgame of Empire*, (n 3) 10.

[40] Ramusack, *The Indian Princes and their States*, (n 3) 51–52.

late nineteenth century, for example, related to whether the area known as Cooch Behar was to be termed a 'state' or an 'estate'; the issue was significant since a state was legally separate from British India while an estate was not.[41] These controversies contributed to the drastic changes in the number of princely states over time; *The Imperial Gazetteer of India* listed 693 states in 1909 but only 562 were recorded in the *Report of the Indian States Committee* published two decades later.[42]

Despite this diversity, the British treated the states as a class by choosing to handle their relations with them through the Political Department of the government of India,[43] whose officials were recruited from the Indian army and the Indian Civil Service.[44] Apart from having different personnel, the Political Department was also structurally different from other government departments. Unlike the secretaries of the others, who reported to members of the viceroy's council, the most senior civil servant of the Political Department, the political secretary (at times also known as the foreign secretary), reported directly to the viceroy, who was the representative of the British Crown in India after 1858.[45] Political officers were located at the Political Department's offices in the British Indian capital, Calcutta (later relocated to New Delhi), at provincial capitals like Bombay or Madras, or at the courts of individual states, where they were known variously as residents, political agents, or agents to the governor-general. Even within the confines of British officialdom in South Asia, the political service tended to attract those with a conservative outlook; its recruits were deeply sceptical of political developments in British India and viewed the 'traditional' rule of the *rajas* to be more suitable to Indian conditions.[46] Both the peculiar position of the Political Department within the overall colonial administrative structure and the conventional ideology of its

[41] After years of wrangling, the government of Bengal concluded that Cooch Behar was a princely state to which British legislation could not be extended. See Letter from the Under-Secretary, Government of Bengal to the Commission to Cooch Behar, 20 February 1873, Proceedings of the Government of India in the Foreign Department, Political, June 1873, no. 213, IOR/P/769; Letter from the Foreign Secretary, Government of India to the Political Secretary, Government of Bengal, 29 May 1873, Proceedings of the Government of Bengal in the Political Department, June 1873, no. 42, IOR/P/262; Letter from the Political Secretary, Government of Bengal to the Foreign Secretary, Government of India, 12 July 1880, Proceedings of the Government of India in the Foreign Department, Political, October 1881, no. 19, IOR/P/1744.

[42] See *The Imperial Gazetteer of India*, (n 37) iv, 92–103; and *Report of the Indian States Committee*, para 11.

[43] The name and organization of the department changed significantly over time. In 1843, it was named the Foreign Department; in 1914, it was renamed the Foreign and Political Department; and in 1937, it was renamed Political Department. Overviews can be found in Terence Creagh Coen, *The Indian Political Service: A Study in Indirect Rule* (London: Chatto & Windus, 1971); and William Murray Hogben, 'The Foreign and Political Department of the Government of India, 1876–1919: A Study in Imperial Careers and Attitudes', PhD thesis, University of Toronto, 1973. For uniformity, I will refer to the department as the Political Department.

[44] L. S. S. O'Malley, *The Indian Civil Service, 1601–1930* (2nd edn, London: Frank Cass, 1965), 160.

[45] Hogben, 'The Foreign and Political Department of the Government of India', (n 43) vi.

[46] Ian Copland, 'The Other Guardians: Ideology and Performance in the Indian Political Service', in Robin Jeffrey, ed., *People, Princes and Paramount Power: Society and Politics in the Indian Princely States* (Delhi: Oxford University Press, 1973), 290.

officers played significant roles in reinforcing the division between British India and the states.

While remaining legally distinct from British India, the states continued to be subject to British influence through the malleable concept of 'paramountcy'. As I will describe in more detail in chapter two, the idea of paramountcy can be traced to treaties that the East India Company signed with some rulers in the early nineteenth century. Many of these treaties involved an acknowledgement by the states of British overlordship (for instance, a cession of the right to engage in diplomacy with foreign powers to the Company) in return for a measure of state autonomy. Later, this idea of overlordship found expression in the doctrine of paramountcy, which became the basis of British relations with all princely states regardless of whether a treaty had been signed. By virtue of being the self-declared 'paramount power' in South Asia, the British claimed to possess both the right and responsibility to take decisions on issues such as defence and external affairs as well as the right to interfere in the internal affairs of the states to maintain peace in the region.[47]

Although the doctrine of paramountcy became the basis for increasing British interference in state affairs, its effect on the sovereignty of the princely states was ambiguous, with the exercise of political power being 'far from a one-sided contest'.[48] British political officers were, in Barbara Ramusack's words, 'janus-faced functionaries' since they formulated and implemented British policy as well as represented the views of the princes to the British government. These dual functions 'spawned continual disagreements within the British hierarchy' that are particularly visible in the numerous contestations over the states' legal status.[49] In addition, as Ian Copland has argued, '[t]he mediocrity of the Political Service, its dependence on corrupt subordinates, the physical isolation of the political agencies, and the astuteness of *darbaris* … combined to thwart the intrusion of British power and allowed the states to pursue their dynastic objectives almost unfettered by the imperial connection'.[50]

On behalf of the princely states, a range of different actors were involved in harnessing the concept of sovereignty to contest British claims of paramountcy, including the princes themselves, bureaucrats and state officials, as well as external legal advisors who were often well-paid British Indians or foreigners. Since the states were largely absolutist monarchies,[51] the positions taken by their rulers were of prime importance. Monarchs such as Sayajirao Gaekwad of Baroda, Ganga

[47] Michael H. Fisher, 'Diplomacy in India, 1526–1858', in H. V. Bowen, Elizabeth Mancke, and John G. Reid, eds., *Britain's Oceanic Empire: Atlantic and Indian Ocean Worlds, c. 1550–1850* (Cambridge: Cambridge University Press, 2012), 251, 260–264.

[48] Copland, *The British Raj and the Indian Princes*, (n 20) 311.

[49] Ramusack, *The Indian Princes and their States*, (n 3) 105.

[50] Copland, *The British Raj and the Indian Princes*, (n 20) 311–312.

[51] A few states experimented with limited forms of popular representation in the twentieth century. See Copland, *The Princes of India in the Endgame of Empire*, (n 3) 9.

Singh of Bikaner, Bhupinder Singh of Patiala, Hamidullah Khan of Bhopal, and Osman Ali Khan of Hyderabad were relentless in their efforts to create the legal and political space for the states to thrive. But since managing the states' relations with the British government was a formidable and delicate task, rulers also sought and obtained broader support. The *diwan* (chief minister) was often a state's principal official and the relative autonomy of a princely state ensured that an outsized role was played by bureaucrats, administrative officials, and legal advisors.[52] Princely arguments on the legal status of the states were, therefore, shaped by the extensive work of state officials such as T. Madhava Rao, K. N. Haksar, K. M. Panikkar, Akbari Hydari, and Mirza Ismail, as well as external advisors such as Tej Bahadur Sapru, Leslie Scott, Walter Monckton, William Wadhams, and Hersch Lauterpacht. Lured by high salaries,[53] many of these men ultimately formed 'an all-India cadre that circulated through several Indian states'.[54] The Oxford-educated Panikkar, for instance, started out as an advisor to the *maharaja* of Kashmir, was then appointed as the secretary to the Chamber of Princes, after which he was named the foreign minister of Patiala, and rounded out his princely state career by serving as the prime minister of Bikaner.[55]

Legal ideas, including ways of defining sovereignty, travelled with these advisors across state borders alongside efforts to build alliances among the states. In the early years of British paramountcy, states largely engaged in individual disputes with colonial authorities on the scope and extent of British authority in their internal affairs. These included debates over whether British colonial authorities could intervene in or annex states as well as jurisdictional conflicts over persons, activities, and infrastructure within princely state territory. Although such individual disputes continued to exist, there was a marked change in these legal controversies by the turn of the twentieth century. As I describe in chapter four, the establishment of institutions such as the Chamber of Princes in 1921 provided a forum for the states to engage with each other as well as build coalitions for defending their political interests as a class. In later years therefore, princely arguments focused on shared projects such as persuading the British government to limit paramountcy, developing appropriate constitutional structures during the federal negotiations, and fashioning alternatives to the territorial nation-state after the demise of British colonial power in South Asia. Over the course of two centuries, the princes and their advisors excavated the language of international law, and particularly the doctrine of sovereignty, to redefine the relationship of the states with the British

[52] Nair, *Mysore Modern*, (n 10) 14.

[53] K. M. Panikkar admitted that he agreed to serve in the states for 'freedom from financial worry'. See K. M. Panikkar, *An Autobiography*, trans. K. Krishnamurthy (Madras: Oxford University Press, 1977), 70.

[54] Ramusack, *The Indian Princes and their States*, (n 3) 184.

[55] Details of Panikkar's work in each of these positions can be found in Panikkar, *An Autobiography*, (n 53).

government, with Indian anticolonial nationalists, and ultimately with the wider world; their individual and collective efforts to do so lie at the heart of this book.

The Narrative and Organization of the Book

The book adopts a chronological approach to parse through the distinctive legal status of the princely states and the ways in which the princes and their advisors harnessed legal arguments over sovereignty to carve out a space for themselves in the struggle for political power. Chapter two explores the legal construction of British paramountcy during the late eighteenth and early nineteenth centuries by analysing the implications of the extensive treaty-making between the East India Company and South Asian rulers. Scholars have noted that eighteenth-century European political thinkers were deeply ambivalent about relations with non-Europeans, as demonstrated in the tension between a universalist notion of the law of nations and the idea that treaties with non-Europeans existed in a separate legal space.[56] In line with this view, British jurists such as William Manning and Robert Phillimore argued that international law principles would apply to relations between European and non-European communities, albeit in a less stringent manner than amongst European nations. I extend this analysis of the partial incorporation of non-Europeans into the realm of the international to the princely states. The chapter documents the fraught nature of the Company's claims of paramountcy because of deep unease within the British state with the extent of power exercised by a private corporation and amidst repeated efforts to regulate the Company's activities. Assertions of British paramountcy also ran up against the recognition of the princes as sovereign rulers by English courts and the jurisdictional claims of the states themselves. Focusing on two key controversies—over whether British subjects could be extradited for trial in the princely states of Pudukkottai and Hyderabad and over the situations in which colonial authorities could intervene in the internal affairs of states such as Bharatpur and Awadh—I argue that interactions between the Company and the princely states took place within the context of intense competition for the exercise of sovereign power. In this atmosphere, international law provided backing for arguments favouring extensive British imperial authority because of the alleged superiority of European civilization as well as assertions of the binding nature of treaties with South Asian rulers. Despite sweeping claims of British paramountcy by the middle of the nineteenth century, legal debates over princely state sovereignty continued to proliferate.

[56] See Jennifer Pitts, 'Empire and Legal Universalisms in the Eighteenth Century', *American Historical Review*, 117/1 (2012), 92–121; and Travers, 'A British Empire by Treaty in Eighteenth-Century India', (n 17) 156.

Chapter three transitions to the latter half of the nineteenth century to focus on the changes in strategy of the British government and the princely states in the aftermath of the rebellion of 1857. International lawyers of the period, such as John Westlake, Thomas Lawrence, and William Edward Hall, relied on the 'standard of civilization'[57] to limit the applicability of international law to 'civilized', primarily European states and relegate the governance of the princely states to imperial constitutional law. Colonial officials in South Asia, however, treated the 'civilizing mission' with scepticism and attributed the uprising to the Company's adoption of interventionist modes of rule that included the annexations of princely states that allegedly failed to provide 'good government' to their subjects. After the revolt, the Company's territories in South Asia were vested in the Crown,[58] which embarked on a new mode of governance that capitalized on relationships with local rulers. I argue that an explicit theory of sovereignty was key to this change in imperial ideology. Henry Maine, the law member in the council of the viceroy and governor-general of India, conceived of sovereignty as 'divisible' and 'a question of fact'. His thesis enabled the British to entrench their supremacy by claiming that the princely states were both subject to British paramountcy and allies in the imperial project. Political officials such as Charles Aitchison, Charles Lewis Tupper, and William Lee-Warner relied on Maine's theory of divisible sovereignty to build a system of precedent through which decisions made by the British government in relation to a single state were made generally applicable to all states. The princely states, however, conceived of a different version of sovereignty altogether. In two jurisdictional disputes—the attempts by Travancore and Baroda to exercise criminal jurisdiction over European British subjects in the state and over telegraph lines traversing state territory respectively—the princes and their advisors such as T. Madhava Rao and Kazi Shahabuddin claimed that sovereignty was 'absolute', 'exclusive', and 'territorial'. Despite existing within the system of British paramountcy, they argued in favour of a single sovereign authority—the princely state itself—exercising jurisdiction over all persons and actions within state territory. This conceptualization of sovereignty served a dual purpose: it was an attempt to defend the existence of the states against the increasingly intrusive nature of British colonialism and a bid to forge centralized bureaucracies to curb the power of local aristocrats who undercut the authority of the princes within their states.

These opposing interpretations of sovereignty as 'divisible' and 'territorial' remained influential till the end of the first decade of the twentieth century. Chapter four charts the changes in definitions of sovereignty put forth by British and princely officials during and after the First World War, which, for many international lawyers, revealed the deficiencies of an approach that focused on the

[57] Gerrit Gong, *The Standard of 'Civilization' in International Society* (Oxford: Clarendon Press, 1984).
[58] See Government of India Act 1858, s 1.

unfettered will of sovereign states.[59] Interwar jurists such as Hersch Lauterpacht, James Brierly, and Robert Cecil instead relied on the notion that sovereignty was 'divisible' to advance political programmes that ranged from the establishment of dispute settlement mechanisms that would discipline state actions to the foundation of international institutions such as the Mandate System of the League of Nations that had the power to intervene in the internal affairs of non-European societies. I focus on the similar manner in which the common vocabulary of divisible sovereignty became the bedrock of different political projects in the first few decades of the twentieth century in South Asia. British political officers such as Harcourt Butler justified the division of sovereign rights based on 'the interests of empire' to buttress a laissez-faire attitude towards the states that was necessitated by the need to procure princely support in response to the pressures of anticolonial nationalism. I illustrate how this definition of sovereignty furnished a renewed legal basis for the British to claim the authority to intervene in the internal affairs of the states without being bound by precedent. Although this approach increased princely protests about British arbitrariness, the princes also sought to use their relationship with the British to defend themselves from critiques by anticolonial nationalists. Rulers such as Ganga Singh of Bikaner and Bhupinder Singh of Patiala and bureaucrats and advisors such as Leslie Scott, K. M. Panikkar, and K. N. Haksar redefined sovereignty as 'divisible' but focused on 'state consent' as a mechanism to divide sovereign powers. Envisaging sovereignty as divisible enabled the states to claim a 'semi-international' status, in terms of which they asserted a direct relationship with the British Crown through the viceroy while being bound to British India through economic and infrastructural links. The princes also hoped that the focus on state consent would limit arbitrary British interference into state affairs. The key clash of these two versions of divisible sovereignty came before the Indian States Committee, which was appointed in 1927 to investigate the relationship between the states and the British government, and which ultimately delivered a report favouring the colonial conception of sovereignty as being divided based on imperial interests.

Chapter five focuses on the strategies adopted by the princes after the debacle before the Indian States Committee, specifically engaging with their varied positions during the 1930s negotiations over the establishment of a federation of British India and the princely states. This proposal drew on late nineteenth-century debates over imperial federation,[60] while anticipating the global move

[59] See the discussions on the need to renew international law on account of the effects of war in Manley O. Hudson, 'The Prospect for International Law in the Twentieth Century', *Cornell Law Quarterly*, 10/4 (1925), 419–459; and Alejandro Alvarez, 'The New International Law', *Transactions of the Grotius Society* 15 (1929), 35–51.

[60] Duncan Bell, *The Idea of Greater Britain: Empire and the Future of World Order, 1860–1900* (Princeton, NJ: Princeton University Press, 2007).

towards federalism after the Second World War.[61] Federations are structured around the divisibility of sovereignty and the malleability of federalism, as Merve Fejzula argues, made it the ideal language for advancing imperial interests as well as for overcoming them.[62] I examine the South Asian federal debates to elucidate the ways in which British and princely state officials defined sovereignty to redraw the boundaries among the domestic, the imperial, and the international spheres. Political officers such as Francis Wylie and Conrad Corfield along with politicians such as Samuel Hoare considered federation to be a means to extend British authority over South Asia in the face of anticolonial protests. Other British officials, including Conservative politicians such as Winston Churchill, claimed federation to be a disastrous policy that would result in a loss of imperial territory. The princes emerged even more divided about federal proposals. Although they regarded the divisibility of sovereignty in federal arrangements to be a useful mechanism to allow the states to maintain their autonomy while cultivating relationships with the Crown and with British India, they disagreed on the implications of federation for state sovereignty. Federationists such as Ganga Singh of Bikaner, Hamidullah Khan of Bhopal, K. N. Haksar, and K. M. Panikkar argued that the federal structure would 'legalize' the existing mechanism of paramountcy by minimizing British (and nationalist) interference in state affairs to issues that were specifically set out in negotiated constitutional documents. Others in the princely camp were less sanguine about being constitutionally united with British India, fearing the radicalism of anticolonial nationalism. Consequently, anti-federationists like Udaibhan Singh of Dholpur, Osman Ali Khan of Hyderabad, Akbar Hydari, and John Hartman Morgan favoured the looser model of confederation with British India together with the provision of imperial guarantees for the protection of state affairs from nationalist interference. I examine three key moments in the federal debates—the birth of federation, the fracas over the adoption of a federal or confederal model, and the final federal offer to the princes—to trace the varied political projects that were supported by articulations of divisible sovereignty.

Chapter six excavates the role that ideas of sovereignty played in the decolonization of South Asia. Although the federal project of the 1930s was a failure, political players continued to rely on the language of sovereignty to imagine the future of South Asia after the British withdrawal from the region. In recent years, scholars have challenged narratives of the inexorable move from empire to nation-state in the middle of the twentieth century by examining the way numerous actors

[61] See Michael Collins, 'Decolonisation and the "Federal Moment"', *Diplomacy and Statecraft*, 24/1 (2013), 21–40; Frederick Cooper, *Citizenship between Empire and Nation: Remaking France and French Africa, 1945–1960* (Princeton, NJ: Princeton University Press, 2014); Gary Wilder, *Freedom Time: Negritude, Decolonization and the Future of the World* (Durham, NC: Duke University Press, 2015); and Adom Getachew, *Worldmaking After Empire: The Rise and Fall of Self-Determination* (Princeton, NJ: Princeton University Press, 2019), 107–141.

[62] Merve Fejzula, 'The Cosmopolitan Historiography of Twentieth-Century Federalism', *The Historical Journal*, 64/2 (2021): 477–500.

grappled with a variety of visions of how to transform empire.[63] Although international law scholarship of the period was broadly focused on international institutions rather than decolonization, the language of sovereignty played a key role in the creation of new states. Focusing on the political upheaval of 1940s South Asia, I trace the way a particular conception of sovereignty—that of exclusive, absolute territoriality, aimed at creating centralized economic units—became dominant in the years of decolonization, while drowning out visions of alternative political orders. Many plans for the devolution of power were predicated on divisible sovereignty and advanced frameworks with multiple layers of authority, such as, for instance, proposals for a loose confederation of the British Indian provinces and the princely states. Even after the partition of British India into the dominions of India and Pakistan, the states continued to seek independence or broad association agreements with the new entities. These political possibilities were, however, abandoned in favour of the 'integration'[64] of the states into postcolonial India because of the demands to centralize sovereign authority that were imposed by 'developmentalism' on the new political order. To illustrate this process, I rely on the arguments made by Indian and Hyderabad state officials before the United Nations in relation to a dispute over the state's legal status and its invasion by the Indian army in 1948. After the withdrawal of Hyderabad's petition, the princely states disappeared as separate political entities from the South Asian landscape, with the articulation of territorial sovereignty playing a key role in the construction of a unified Indian state space.

In the epilogue, I examine some of the contemporary implications of this long history of sovereignty debates, both for the postcolonial Indian state and for the history of international law. Tracing the princely states' use of legal argumentation demonstrates the complexity of the relationship between law and power: law can restrain power, but it can also manage power and act as a vocabulary for power.[65] The language of international law, therefore, was all-encompassing and was (and continues to be) capable of being deployed by multiple actors for a variety of purposes.[66] In the international sphere, the terminology of sovereignty plays a role

[63] See Burbank and Cooper, *Empires in World History*, (n 25); and Manu Goswami, 'Imaginary Futures and Colonial Internationalisms', *American Historical Review*, 117/5 (2012), 1461–1485.

[64] The use of the term 'integration' to describe the often-violent process by which many of the princely states were made to join the Indian union can be traced to a book written by one of the principal protagonists in the affair, V. P. Menon, who was the secretary to the Ministry of States, and in charge of persuading the princes to sign instruments of accession to India. See V. P. Menon, *The Story of the Integration of the Indian States* (New York: Macmillan, 1956).

[65] This typology can be found in David Kennedy, 'Speaking Law to Power: International Law and Foreign Policy—Closing Remarks', *Wisconsin International Law Journal*, 23/1 (2005), 173–182.

[66] Relying on the idea of linguistic indeterminacy, American legal realists have long argued that law is mutable, a product of human will, and a means to achieve social goals. See the overview in Hugh Collins, 'Law as Politics: Progressive American Perspectives', in James Penner, David Schiff, and Richard Nobles, eds., *Introduction to Jurisprudence and Legal Theory: Commentary and Materials* (London: LexisNexis Butterworths, 2002), 279–333.

in shaping the political projects of actors ranging from indigenous peoples to Palestine, while in the South Asian context, it is significant for subnational movements seeking to redefine their relations with an increasingly centralized and authoritarian Indian state. Given the continued import of the vocabulary of sovereignty, it is critical to remember the alternative possibilities demonstrated by the history of sovereignty in South Asia, a history of the various ways in which people have thought about organizing the world and their relationships with each other.

Chapter Two
Setting the Stage
The Legal Construction of British Paramountcy

The East India Company and the Princely States

In a letter written in May 1821, David Newall, the British resident at Travancore, questioned the ability of the Supreme Court of the British Indian province of Madras to issue writs for the arrest of British subjects residing in the princely states.[1] The advocate-general of the government of Madras dismissed his concerns, arguing that 'the jurisdiction of the Supreme Court of Judicature extends to all British subjects resident within any of the Dominions of the Native Princes in India in alliance with our Government'.[2] Others, however, were not so sanguine, with the East India Company's (EIC's or the Company's) court of directors in London admitting that the practice of extending the jurisdiction of British courts into princely state territory could cause 'political inconvenience'.[3] The directors were supported by the Crown's law officers who asserted that

> Courts of Judicature in the East Indies established by the charters ... can have no legal authority to cause writs or process of any kind issued against European born British subjects or Natives of the British Territories in the service of the East India Company to be executed by arrest of persons, seizure of property or any other compulsory method within the Dominions of Native Princes in alliance with the British Government in India.[4]

The advocate-general of Madras was asked to communicate this opinion to the Madras judges;[5] he reported that they would not issue further process to be

[1] Letter from the Resident in Travancore and Cochin to the Chief Secretary to the Government of Madras, no. 30, 3 May 1821, IOR/F/4/881/23024.

[2] Letter from James Minchin, the Solicitor to the East India Company to the Chief Secretary to the Government of Madras, 1 June 1821, IOR/F/4/881/23024.

[3] Despatch of the Court of Directors to the Government of Bengal, Political Department, 9 January 1822, IOR/F/4/881/23024.

[4] Opinion of Robert Gifford, John Singleton Copley, and J. B. Bosanquet on the Case for the East India Company, 16 February 1821, IOR/F/4/881/23024.

[5] The directors asked the government of India to communicate this opinion to the judges of the Supreme Court 'in the most delicate way possible, and of avoiding the slightest appearance of an endeavour to interfere officially with the powers delegated by law to the discretion of the Bench'. See Despatch from the Court of Directors to the Government of Bengal, Political Department, 9 January 1822, IOR/F/4/881/23024.

Sovereignty, International Law, and the Princely States of Colonial South Asia. Priyasha Saksena, Oxford University Press.
 DOI: 10.1093/oso/9780192866585.003.0002

executed within princely territory before an opportunity was granted to the British government to contest jurisdiction.[6]

Even after providing this assurance, and over the specific objections of the advocate-general,[7] the Madras Supreme Court continued to issue writs for the arrest of British subjects residing in the princely states.[8] Alarmed Madras officials claimed that Supreme Court's jurisdiction was 'ill defined and capable by misapplication of becoming dangerous'.[9] The advocate-general of the government of India agreed, arguing that since the British government was incapable of erecting courts 'in a foreign sovereignty without the assent of the sovereign power of such country', it was also 'incapable of directing the execution of any description of judicial power or process within such country unless with the direct assent of the ruling power there'.[10] Relying on this opinion, the government of India started to refuse to intervene to seek the execution of such writs in princely state territory.[11] To clarify the messy situation, the advocate-general sought an appeal in the Privy Council but admitted that there were concerns about standing.[12] Perhaps on account of these questions, no appeal was ever filed. By the latter half of the nineteenth century, writs issued by British courts began to be executed in state territory through local courts rather than through pressure placed by British residents on the states. However, disputes continued over whether and to what extent there could be reciprocal execution of writs issued by princely courts in British territory.[13]

To some extent, the differing opinions offered by Madras Supreme Court judges and EIC officials can be traced to the complex court system in late eighteenth- and early nineteenth-century South Asia. The EIC had been granted the power to mete out justice in its charter and had set up a series of Company courts starting 1764. Since these courts proved to be inadequate for people with complaints against the Company itself, the Supreme Court at Calcutta was established by the Regulating Act of 1773.[14] A similar state of affairs prevailed in the other two presidencies of

[6] Letter from the Advocate-General to the Chief Secretary to the Government of Madras, 28 January 1823, IOR/F/4/1754/71727.

[7] Letter from the Advocate-General to the Chief Secretary to the Government of Madras, 5 April 1836, IOR/F/4/1754/71727.

[8] See, for instance, Letter from Attorney to the Chief Secretary to the Government of Madras, 10 March 1836, IOR/F/4/1754/71727; and Letter from the Resident at Hyderabad to the Secretary of the Government of India, 20 July 1840, IOR/F/4/1925/82621.

[9] Letter from the Secretary to the Government of Madras to the Secretary to the Government of India, Military Department, no. 1318, 26 April 1836, IOR/F/4/1754/71727.

[10] Opinion of the Officiating Advocate General, 1 July 1840, IOR/F/4/1925/82621.

[11] Letter from the Officiating Secretary to the Government of India to the Resident at Hyderabad, 20 July 1840, IOR/F/4/1925/82621; and Letter from the Officiating Secretary to the Government of India to the Resident at Hyderabad, no. 355, 27 July 1840, IOR/F/4/1925/82621.

[12] Opinion of the Officiating Advocate General, 1 July 1840, IOR/F/4/1925/82621.

[13] See the discussion on the complicated practices around the execution of writs and processes in the second half of the nineteenth century in Charles Lewis Tupper, *Indian Political Practice: A Collection of the Decisions of the Government of India in Political Cases*, iii (Calcutta: Office of the Superintendent of Government Printing, India, 1895; repr., Delhi: B. R. Publishing, 1974), 104–122.

[14] Mithi Mukherjee, *India in the Shadows of Empire: A Legal and Political History, 1774–1950* (New Delhi: Oxford University Press, 2010), 48–49.

Bombay and Madras, with Company courts continuing to exist after the establishment of Supreme Courts by royal charter.[15] Scholars have explored the jurisdictional struggles between the Supreme Courts and the law courts of the Company in the late eighteenth century; the Supreme Court's willingness to hear suits against Company employees proved to be a particular bone of contention.[16] These disputes epitomized larger struggles between the British state and the Company over the exercise of political power in South Asia.

The Supreme Court's claims of jurisdiction in the princely states added another layer of complexity to the already messy map of sovereignties in South Asia. Although this was a period in which the Company's territorial holdings in South Asia expanded, many princely states maintained their separate legal existence, raising questions about the extent of British authority over the states. What did the EIC's military and political stranglehold over South Asia mean for the princely states? What was the nature of the relationship between the Company and the states? What legal ideas underpinned the discussions around the status of the states?

The legal bases and implications of imperial expansion at the turn of the nineteenth century have attracted significant scholarly attention. About half a century ago, Charles Henry Alexandrowicz argued that the move from natural law to positivism ushered in an era in which non-Europeans were excluded from conceptions of the international.[17] More recent scholarship has, however, emphasized that positivism and naturalism co-existed for much of the nineteenth century.[18] And in her careful revision of Alexandrowicz's account, Jennifer Pitts has described how eighteenth-century European scholars were deeply ambivalent about relations with non-Europeans. Pitts uses the lens of European relations with the Ottoman empire to make a broader argument about the eighteenth-century characterization of non-European, particularly Muslim, societies as lawless despotisms lying outside the European state system. Alongside tracing these exclusionary ideas, Pitts also charts the 'critical legal universalism' of the period, in which political thinkers relied on treaty relations with non-Europeans to critique the conduct of European imperialism.[19]

[15] Rahela Khorakiwala, *From the Colonial to the Contemporary: Images, Iconography, Memories, and Performances of Law in India's High Courts* (Oxford: Hart Publishing, 2019), 109–112, 163–167.

[16] Lauren Benton, 'Colonial Law and Cultural Difference: Jurisdictional Politics and the Formation of the Colonial State', *Comparative Studies in Society and History*, 41/3 (1999), 566–574; Robert Travers, *Ideology and Empire in Eighteenth-Century India: The British in Bengal* (Cambridge: Cambridge University Press, 2007), 181–206; and Mukherjee, *India in the Shadows of Empire*, (n 14) 50–55.

[17] C. H. Alexandrowicz, 'Mogul Sovereignty and the Law of Nations', in David Armitage and Jennifer Pitts, eds., *The Law of Nations in Global History* (Oxford: Oxford University Press, 2017), 62–68; and C. H. Alexandrowicz, 'Some Problems in the History of the Law of Nations in Asia', in *The Law of Nations in Global History*, 76–82.

[18] Casper Sylvest, 'International Law in Nineteenth-Century Britain', *British Year Book of International Law*, 75 (2005), 12.

[19] Jennifer Pitts, *Boundaries of the International: Law and Empire* (Cambridge, MA: Harvard University Press, 2018), 17, 28–67, 92–117. The fluidity of the legal discourse during the period also

Company officials in late-eighteenth and early-nineteenth century South Asia were similarly conflicted when it came to defining relations with the princely states. As the varied opinions on the execution of writs issued by British courts within princely state territory demonstrate, some Company officials continued to recognize the sovereignty of the states, at least over their own territory. The Company's political and military supremacy in South Asia, therefore, did not necessarily translate into the exercise of full jurisdiction within the princely states or the deprivation of the states of all sovereign powers. In fact, the scope of the Company's authority over the states remained unclear, with new legal concepts such as 'paramountcy' being coined but remaining ill-defined. In particular, the relationship between British paramountcy and princely state sovereignty was heavily debated.

In this chapter, I examine the long roots of the slippery concept of paramountcy, which was key to British indirect rule in South Asia. First, I trace the conflict within the work of British international lawyers in the early nineteenth century on the question of relations with non-European peoples. Since these jurists emphasized the Christian basis of international law, they claimed the discipline's principles would have to be 'diluted' in their application to non-Europeans. This qualified incorporation of non-Europeans also extended to the princely states; I examine the complicated relationship between the British state, the Company, and the princely states in late eighteenth- and early nineteenth-century South Asia to elucidate how the expansion of Britain's imperial ambitions pushed legal conceptions of statehood to breaking point. Although the Company claimed to be the 'paramount power' in South Asia by the early decades of the nineteenth century, English courts continued to recognize the princely states as sovereign entities. By parsing through the different legal positions taken by the Company and princely officials in two key controversies—over the extradition of British subjects to the princely states and over intervention in the princely states—I argue that the early nineteenth century was a period in which exclusionary legal ideas based on the superiority of European civilization co-existed with arguments about the need to consider treaties with South Asian rulers as binding. The implications of British paramountcy for princely state sovereignty, therefore, remained unclear, creating a fertile space for legal argumentation, with the language of international law simultaneously being the basis for increasing interference in state affairs and a limitation on Company authority.

enabled other actors, such as Native American nations, to rely on the language of international law to defend their sovereignty. See Gregory Ablavsky, 'Species of Sovereignty: Native Nationhood, the United States, and International Law, 1783–1795', *Journal of American History*, 106/3 (2019), 591–613.

International Law and Non-European Peoples at the Turn of the Nineteenth Century

Late eighteenth- and early nineteenth-century scholars were remarkably prolific in their works on international legal thought. This was the period in which the term 'international law', coined by the utilitarian philosopher Jeremy Bentham, began to replace the 'law of nations' as the most popular descriptor of the legal system governing inter-state relations.[20] But utilitarianism also posed a challenge for international law after the jurist John Austin relegated the entire discipline to the class of 'law improperly so called' since it did not fit within the description of commands issued by a sovereign and backed by a sanction but rather constituted 'opinions current amongst nations'.[21] Despite facing an existential crisis in the face of Austin's provocation, international lawyers used the rapid expansion of the British empire as fodder for generating new ideas about relations among different polities, albeit not in a completely consistent fashion.[22]

Although there was a 'treaty-making revolution' in the nineteenth century,[23] international legal language continued to encapsulate conflicting views about relations with non-European peoples.[24] Early nineteenth-century international law texts written in Britain often emphasized the specifically Christian basis of the law of nations.[25] William Manning,[26] the author of the first introductory text on international law published by an English author, claimed that Christian principles provided 'a general system of morality' for the law of nations although 'the application to the details of practice is left to be discovered by human reason'.[27] Despite this focus on Christian nations, Manning's work did not limit legal subjecthood based on the possession of 'civilization', a move made by lawyers later in the century.[28]

Manning's emphasis on morality was reaffirmed by Robert Phillimore,[29] who published the first of his volumes on international law in 1854. Phillimore argued that international law was 'enacted by the will of God' and was 'expressed in the

[20] Pitts, *Boundaries of the International*, (n 19) 118.

[21] John Austin, *The Province of Jurisprudence Determined* (London: John Murray, 1832), 146–147.

[22] Lauren Benton and Lisa Ford, *Rage for Order: The British Empire and the Origins of International Law, 1800–1850* (Cambridge, MA: Harvard University Press, 2016).

[23] Edward Keene, 'The Treaty-Making Revolution of the Nineteenth Century', *The International History Review*, 34/3 (2012), 475–500.

[24] Pitts, *Boundaries of the International*, (n 19) 118–122.

[25] Sylvest, 'International Law in Nineteenth-Century Britain', (n 18) 10–29.

[26] Manning was not trained as a lawyer. See G. Le G. Norgate, 'Manning, William Oke (1809–1878)', rev. Catherine Pease-Watkin, in David Cannadine, ed., *Oxford Dictionary of National Biography*, online edn (Oxford: Oxford University Press, 2004), https://doi.org/10.1093/ref:odnb/17980, accessed 29 July 2021.

[27] William Oke Manning, *Commentaries on the Law of Nations* (London: S. Sweet, 1839), 65.

[28] Martti Koskenniemi, *To the Uttermost Parts of the Earth: Legal Imagination and International Power, 1300–1870* (Cambridge: Cambridge University Press, 2021), 691.

[29] Phillimore's views were influenced by his civil and ecclesiastical law training. See Norman Doe, 'Phillimore, Sir Robert Joseph, baronet (1810–1885)', in *Oxford Dictionary of National Biography*, https://doi.org/10.1093/ref:odnb/22138, accessed 29 July 2021.

consent, tacit or declared, of Independent Nations'. On account of the influence of the law of nature on international law, it was 'not confined in its application to the intercourse of Christian nations' or only to 'European nations'. Instead, it subsisted 'between Christian and Heathen, and even between two Heathen nations, though in a vaguer manner and less perfect condition than between two Christian communities'. International law, then, was simultaneously universal and peculiarly Christian. Phillimore relied on this dual nature of international law to draw out concrete implications for European relations with non-European peoples. Although he admitted that non-European communities could be recognized as 'states', he claimed that 'they are perhaps in some points entitled to a relaxed application of the principles of International Law, derived exclusively from European custom'.[30]

By arguing for the 'relaxed' application of international law to certain peoples, Phillimore implied that fundamental aspects of the discipline could be suspended in the case of non-Europeans. A key example related to state jurisdiction. Ordinarily, Phillimore noted, a state had 'absolute and uncontrolled power of jurisdiction over all Persons, and over all Things, *within* her territorial limits, and, ... in certain specific cases, *without* them'. However, one of the principal exceptions related 'to the *status* of Christians in Infidel countries' such as the Ottoman empire, in terms of which 'Christian nations trading with the territories subject to that power, obtained from it ... a concession of exclusive authority over their own subjects'. This 'departure from the strict rule of Territorial Jurisdiction' was justified on account of '[t]he vital and ineradicable differences which must always separate the Christian from the Mahometan or Infidel, the immiscible character which their religion impresses upon their social habits, moral sentiments, and political institutions'. Consequently, 'the Consuls of Christian Powers residing in Turkey, and the Mahometan countries of the Levant, exercise an exclusive Criminal and Civil Jurisdiction over their fellow-countrymen'.[31]

Phillimore extended this analysis to other non-European communities such as the princely states. Since 'the *principles* of international justice do govern, or *ought* to govern, the dealings of the Christian with the Infidel community', they were 'binding ... upon Great Britain, in her intercourse with the native powers of India'. He relied on the existence of treaties between European nations (like Britain and France) and South Asian powers (such as Mysore) as well as on the evidence of Edmund Burke's speeches during the impeachment of Warren Hastings to buttress this view about the applicability of international law to the states.[32] But Phillimore

[30] Robert Phillimore, *Commentaries Upon International Law*, i (Philadelphia, PA: T&JW Johnson, 1854), v, 59, 93, 97.

[31] ibid, 261–262, 271–272.

[32] ibid, 60–61. Jennifer Pitts also focuses on the closing arguments made by Edmund Burke at the impeachment of Warren Hastings to argue that some European actors maintained that 'the British were bound by the law of nations in their dealings with powers in India'. See Pitts, *Boundaries of the International*, (n 19) 93.

immediately qualified his position on international law's universality by claiming that 'the obligations of International Law attach with greater precision, distinctness, and accuracy to Christian States in their commerce with each other'.[33] In the South Asian context, international law's uneasy embrace of non-Europeans, as exemplified by Phillimore, was put under additional pressure by the Company's rapidly changing relationship with the princely states.

Law and British Imperial Expansion in South Asia

The period between 1757 and 1858 was one of enormous change in South Asia. With the decline of the Mughal empire in the early eighteenth century, regional powers such as the Marathas, Hyderabad, and Mysore as well as European traders such as the EIC and the French East India Company began to gain influence.[34] As trade grew more profitable and competitive, these companies began to intervene in local politics to ensure that their favoured leaders attained power and provided them with commercial privileges.[35] The French and the English backed rival claimants to the throne in the southern states of Arcot and Hyderabad, with the EIC gaining the upper hand by the end of the Seven Years' War in 1763.[36] After military victories at Palashi and Buxar, the Company won the right of *diwani* (revenue collection) for the eastern provinces of Bengal, Bihar, and Orissa in return for the payment of tribute to the Mughal emperor.[37] In later years, Company officials represented the *diwani* as foundational to the establishment of British sovereignty in South Asia.[38] Although the treaties granting the *diwani* retained references to the dwindling Mughal empire, they also bound the *nawab* of the province of Awadh in a mutual defence pact with the Company, thereby marking a transition from the Mughal-centric political landscape of South Asia. The treaties, therefore, 'concretis[ed] the emerging yet ill-defined claims of provincial sovereignty and

[33] Phillimore, *Commentaries Upon International Law*, (n 30) 61.

[34] C. A. Bayly, *Indian Society and the Making of the British Empire* (Cambridge: Cambridge University Press, 1990), 7–26; Barbara D. Metcalf and Thomas R. Metcalf, *A Concise History of Modern India* (2nd edn, Cambridge: Cambridge University Press, 2006), 29; and Sugata Bose and Ayesha Jalal, *Modern South Asia: History, Culture, Political Economy* (4th edn, London: Routledge, 2018), 42–46.

[35] Metcalf and Metcalf, *A Concise History of Modern India*, (n 34) 49; and Bose and Jalal, *Modern South Asia*, (n 34) 51.

[36] Bayly, *Indian Society and the Making of the British Empire*, (n 34) 45; and Rajmohan Gandhi, *Modern South India: A History from the 17th Century to Our Times* (New Delhi: Aleph Book Company, 2018), 34–49.

[37] Bayly, *Indian Society and the Making of the British Empire*, (n 34) 46; Metcalf and Metcalf, *A Concise History of Modern India*, (n 34) 51–53; and Bose and Jalal, *Modern South Asia*, (n 34) 51–52.

[38] Robert Travers, 'A British Empire by Treaty in Eighteenth-Century India', in Saliha Belmessous, ed., *Empire by Treaty: Negotiating European Expansion, 1600–1900* (Oxford: Oxford University Press, 2015), 146–147. A copy of the Mughal *firman* granting the *diwani* is extracted as 'Firman from the Mughal Emperor to the East India Company, 17 August 1765', in Adrian Sever, ed., *Documents and Speeches on the Indian Princely States*, i (Delhi: B. R. Publishing, 1985), 75–76.

statehood in mid-century imperial discourse' and laid the groundwork for British supremacy by 'recasting Hindustan as an empire of independent "states"'.[39]

The legal instrument of the treaty was also used to cement the Company's relationships with these newly powerful regional states. The Company relied on treaties to give legal sanction to military conquests, formalize alliances with local rulers, and impose tribute payments on such rulers.[40] As Jane Burbank and Frederick Cooper note, reliance on intermediaries was an important strategy of imperial expansion; since colonial rulers were rarely able to directly govern every part of the realm, they often depended on indigenous elites.[41] Treaties with local rulers were particularly significant in the complex landscape of late eighteenth-century South Asia where the EIC was only one of several significant political players; the Maratha confederacy and Mysore emerged as strong challengers.[42] The Company was also involved in a long-running dispute with the British state over the nature and exercise of its powers, leading to the passage of the India Act of 1784 through which it was subjected to ministerial control.[43] To counter the influence of rival powers, the Company entered into alliances with local rulers such as the *nizam* of Hyderabad.[44]

Despite this proliferation of treaties, their meaning and import remained deeply contested within British political thought because of the persistent belief that 'Asian countries had no laws or property, and hence its peoples no rights'.[45] These 'entrenched stereotypes of lawless Asiatic despots' were linked to 'a persistent rhetoric of "native" faithlessness and barbarity'; consequently, Company officials claimed that treaties with South Asian rulers could only be effective if 'backed by the fear of overwhelming British force'.[46] By relegating these treaties to 'a distinct legal universe',[47] British colonial officials brought into focus the simultaneously universal and parochial nature of international law, as theorized by scholars such as Robert Phillimore. Although considered to be binding, these treaties were often the means to carve out additional privileges for Company officials.

[39] Nicholas J. Abbott, 'A Mulk of One's Own: Languages of Sovereignty, Statehood, and Dominion in the Eighteenth-Century "Empire of Hindustan"', *Itinerario*, 44/3 (2021), 487–488.

[40] Travers, 'A British Empire by Treaty in Eighteenth-Century India', (n 38) 132.

[41] Jane Burbank and Frederick Cooper, *Empires in World History: Power and the Politics of Difference* (Princeton, NJ: Princeton University Press, 2011), 13–14.

[42] Bose and Jalal, *Modern South Asia*, (n 34) 55.

[43] Robert Travers, 'Constitutions, Contact Zones, and Imperial Ricochets: Sovereignty and Law in British Asia', in H. V. Bowen, Elizabeth Mancke, and John G. Reid, eds., *Britain's Oceanic Empire: Atlantic and Indian Ocean Worlds, c. 1550–1850* (Cambridge: Cambridge University Press, 2012), 109; Philip Stern, 'Company, State, and Empire: Governance and Regulatory Frameworks in Asia', in *Britain's Oceanic Empire*, 147–148; and Koskenniemi, *To the Uttermost Parts of the Earth*, (n 28) 764–777.

[44] Travers, 'Constitutions, Contact Zones, and Imperial Ricochets', (n 43) 103.

[45] Thomas Metcalf, *Ideologies of the Raj* (Cambridge: Cambridge University Press, 1995), 7.

[46] Travers, 'A British Empire by Treaty in Eighteenth-Century India', (n 38) 137.

[47] Jennifer Pitts, 'Empire and Legal Universalisms in the Eighteenth Century', *American Historical Review*, 117/1 (2012), 103.

As the Company became the dominant military and political power in South Asia, its treaties with local rulers became increasingly unequal.[48] The power imbalance between the parties was exemplified in the 1800 treaty with Hyderabad.[49] The preamble noted the treaty to be one of 'general defensive alliance' for the 'reciprocal protection of their respective territories' with the text of the treaty providing that an act of hostility against either of the parties would require them to 'proceed to concert and prosecute such further measures as the case shall appear to demand'. Despite the initial claim of an alliance, later provisions in the treaty clarified that Hyderabad would have to host a permanent garrison of British troops in its territory; this military support would be paid for through a cession of territory to the Company. The *nizam* also pledged 'never to commit any act of hostility or aggression against any power whatever', thereby effectively giving up the sovereign right to wage war. The treaty further required the *nizam* to refrain from commencing or pursuing negotiations with any foreign power without consulting the Company.[50] The diplomatic isolation of the states through extensive control over their foreign relations became a significant element of the Company's system of alliances.[51]

Key to British domination over the states was the figure of the resident, the Company's main representative in the states. During the early years of the Company's presence in South Asia, its envoys used a range of diplomatic techniques, including petitions and embassies, to interact with the Mughal empire.[52] This was in keeping with the Mughal-centred diplomatic practices of early modern South Asia, in which subordinate rulers stationed their representatives, known as *vakils*, in the Mughal emperor's court. These *vakils* submitted *nazr* (an offering of submission) to the emperor and gathered information from the imperial centre for their employers. Once the Company became influential towards the end of the eighteenth century, it replaced the existing system of exchanging reciprocal *vakils* with 'a new system of British political agents who resided at Indian courts'.[53] Since the legal authority of the Company to appoint ambassadors was contested, it decided to adopt the term 'resident' for its political representatives in the Mughal court and the courts of other regional powers. The establishment of residencies in

[48] Travers, 'A British Empire by Treaty in Eighteenth-Century India', (n 38) 156.

[49] For a discussion of the role played by diplomatic intermediaries in the transformation of British-Hyderabadi relations through the 1800 treaty, see Tanja Bührer, 'Intercultural Diplomacy at the Court of the Nizam of Hyderabad, 1770–1815', *The International History Review*, 41/5 (2019), 1039–1056.

[50] The text of the treaty can be found in 'Treaty with the Nizam—1800', in Charles U. Aitchison, ed., *A Collection of Treaties, Engagements and Sanads Relating to India and Neighbouring Countries*, ix (Calcutta: Superintendent Government Printing, India, 1909), 67–73.

[51] This system can be seen as a consolidation of earlier, more piecemeal efforts by the Company to exert control over the states. For a discussion of these attempts in relation to the state of Hyderabad, see Kavita Saraswathi Datla, 'The Origins of Indirect Rule in India: Hyderabad and the British Imperial Order', *Law and History Review*, 33/2 (2015), 321–350.

[52] Guido van Meersbergen, 'The Diplomatic Repertoires of the East India Companies in Mughal South Asia, 1608–1717', *The Historical Journal*, 62/4 (2019), 875–898.

[53] Michael H. Fisher, 'Diplomacy in India, 1526–1858', in *Britain's Oceanic Empire*, (n 43) 251, 255–256.

large, powerful states such as Awadh, Hyderabad, and Mysore starting in 1798 dramatically expanded Company influence even though it continued to acknowledge the nominal sovereignty of the Mughal emperor until 1858.[54]

Although dependant on the work of local intermediaries to navigate the complex linguistic, cultural, and diplomatic protocols of South Asia, residents soon began to monitor and control them to cement their own position and promote Company interests.[55] The rulers initially treated British residents like they had treated *vakils* sent to their courts by other South Asian powers; they also sent their own *vakils* to British Indian presidencies. Even after the institution of British attempts to exert control over the states' external relations, some rulers 'sustained an underground exchange of wakils despite the efforts by Residents to detect and preclude it'. Others frustrated the efforts of British residents to intervene in matters that they considered to be internal to the state. Michael Fisher details an instance from 1814 when the resident told off the *nizam* of Hyderabad 'for acting—by British standards—despotically'; in response, the *nizam* simply said, '"... the Country is mine, and the Troops are mine, and I have the right to do what I choose with them both"'.[56] Some rulers exploited divisions within Company officialdom to their own advantage. The Bombay government, for instance, exercised relatively independent control over nearly 300 states in western India;[57] its policies were often different from those of other presidency governments, 'leading to confusion and Residents working at cross-purposes with each other'.[58] Company officials then 'deliberately blurred the real differences among rival British authorities and policies in India and in London' to establish an increasingly monopolistic system of diplomacy with an ever-growing number of states.[59] By the end of the governor-generalship of Lord Hastings,[60] the EIC had concluded treaties with major Maratha rulers, effectively ending the last major challenge to Company authority.[61]

After suppressing the Marathas, EIC officials began to refer to the British as the 'paramount power' in South Asia. Edward Thompson claims that the first use of

[54] Michael Fisher, *Indirect Rule in India: Residents and the Residency System, 1764–1858* (Bombay: Oxford University Press, 1991), 48–49, 56; and Travers, *Ideology and Empire in Eighteenth-Century India*, (n 16) 20.

[55] Callie Wilkinson, 'Weak Ties in a Tangled Web? Relationships between the Political Residents of the English East India Company and their Munshis, 1798–1818', *Modern Asian Studies*, 53/5 (2019), 1574–1612.

[56] Fisher, *Indirect Rule in India*, (n 54) 269–273, 277, 393.

[57] Ian Copland, *The British Raj and the Indian Princes: Paramountcy in Western India, 1857–1930* (Bombay: Orient Longman, 1982), 52.

[58] Fisher, *Indirect Rule in India*, (n 54) 137.

[59] Fisher, 'Diplomacy in India', (n 53) 256.

[60] Hastings was appointed governor-general in 1813 and served till 1823. See Roland Thorne, 'Hastings, Francis Rawdon, first marquess of Hastings and second earl of Moria (1754–1826)', in *Oxford Dictionary of National Biography*, https://doi.org/10.1093/ref:odnb/12568, accessed 24 June 2021). For an overview of the policies of Hastings with respect to the states, see Mohan Sinha Mehta, *Lord Hastings and the Indian States* (Bombay: D. B. Taraporevala Sons & Co., 1930).

[61] Barbara Ramusack, *The Indian Princes and their States* (Cambridge: Cambridge University Press, 2004), 76–80.

the term 'paramount' was in an 1820 letter from David Ochterlony,[62] the resident at Delhi, to Charles Metcalfe,[63] then the resident at Hyderabad.[64] A year later, John Malcolm, who had been involved in the negotiations with the various Maratha rulers,[65] explicitly referred to the Company as the 'paramount power' of the region, noting that '[t]he Princes and Chiefs of India may, in different degrees, be said to be all dependent on the British Government: many have little more than the name of that power they before enjoyed; but they seem, as they lose the substance, to cling to the forms of station'.[66] The slippery concept of 'paramountcy' became key to the British legitimation of their authority over the princely states. Although built on the foundations of the Company's military superiority, paramountcy was also shaped by early nineteenth-century theoretical insights into alleged 'civilizational differences' between Britain and South Asia, which, for many officials justified interference in the states to 'protect' peoples living under Indian rulers from 'misgovernment'.[67]

The scope and extent of British paramountcy in South Asia would, however, remain contested throughout colonial rule. Did British paramountcy, for instance, imply the extinguishment of the sovereignty of the princely states? Although John Malcolm appeared to suggest that princely sovereignty existed only on paper, several states continued to exercise significant sovereign rights including 'the collection of revenues and legal jurisdiction over [their] subjects within [their] territories'.[68] Company officials also worked hard to exclude princes as well as local chiefs from the jurisdiction of British courts in South Asia, complicating professions of British authority.[69] The states themselves claimed to be sovereign and

[62] Ochterlony was an EIC military official. See A. P. Coleman, 'Ochterlony, Sir David, first baronet (1758–1825)', in *Oxford Dictionary of National Biography*, https://doi.org/10.1093/ref:odnb/20492, accessed 5 November 2021.

[63] Metcalfe spent much of his career in the princely states. See John William Kaye, *The Life and Correspondence of Charles, Lord Metcalfe*, 2 vols (London: Smith, Elder & Co., 1858); Edward Thompson, *The Life of Charles, Lord Metcalfe* (London: Faber and Faber, 1938); and C. A. Bayly, 'Metcalfe, Charles Theophilus, Baron Metcalfe (1785–1846)', in *Oxford Dictionary of National Biography*, https://doi.org/10.1093/ref:odnb/18617, accessed 26 June 2021.

[64] Edward Thompson, *The Making of the Indian Princes* (London: Oxford University Press, 1943), 283–284.

[65] See John William Kaye, *The Life and Correspondence of Major-General Sir John Malcolm*, 2 vols (London: Smith, Elder & Co., 1856); and Robert Eric Frykenberg, 'Malcolm, Sir John (1769–1833)', in *Oxford Dictionary of National Biography*, https://doi.org/10.1093/ref:odnb/17864, accessed 28 June 2021. For an overview of Malcolm's intellectual contributions to the formation of British India, see Jack Harrington, *Sir John Malcolm and the Creation of British India* (Basingstoke: Palgrave Macmillan, 2010).

[66] 'Instructions to Officers Serving under Sir John Malcolm, 28 June 1821', in *Documents and Speeches on the Indian Princely States*, (n 38) i, 136.

[67] Partha Chatterjee, *The Black Hole of Empire: History of a Global Practice of Power* (Princeton, NJ: Princeton University Press, 2012), 190.

[68] Ramusack, *The Indian Princes and their States*, (n 61) 63.

[69] Haruki Inagaki has described the differing approaches of Company officials and the King's Court when it came to jurisdiction over princes and local chiefs during the 1820s. See Haruki Inagaki, 'The Rule of Law and Emergency in Colonial India: The Conflict between the King's Court and the Government in Bombay in the 1820s', PhD thesis, King's College, London, 2016, 179–217.

this assertion was often affirmed by courts in England. Prabhakar Singh has described a series of 'kingly litigations' in the first half of the nineteenth century in which English courts concluded that the actions of the EIC in annexing territories in South Asia constituted 'acts of state' that were outside the purview of the courts rather than the confiscation of property by a private actor.[70] While legitimating the expansion of Company territory, many of these cases also confirmed that the princely states themselves were sovereign actors that were subject only to the law of nations rather than any municipal law.

By engaging in an uneasy embrace of the princely states, akin to the work of international lawyers such as William Manning and Robert Phillimore, these courts enabled the spread of the British empire. In one of the earliest cases filed by a South Asian ruler in an English court, the *nawab* of Arcot sued the Company to repay excess revenues that had been assigned to it in discharge of a debt. The Company's initial plea of sovereign status was dismissed for technical reasons[71] but was upheld two years later, with the court holding '… where one sovereign is dealing with another sovereign upon matters of sovereignty, no cause of action can arise from those transactions'.[72] A series of later cases also acknowledged that the EIC exercised sovereign powers.[73]

Even after the Company's multiple proclamations of paramountcy over the whole of South Asia, English courts continued to recognize the princes as sovereign. For instance, the *raja* of Coorg was described as possessing 'absolute power' over his 'independent State', albeit rendering 'the British Government, as the supreme ruling power in India, an acknowledgement of fidelity'.[74] The *raja* of Tanjore was similarly described as 'an independent Sovereign of territories undoubtedly small, and bound by Treaties to a powerful neighbour, which left him, practically, little power of free action; but he did not hold his territory, such as it was, as a fief of the British Crown, or of the East India Company'.[75] While legitimating the expansion of Company territory, these courts failed to clarify the effect of British paramountcy over princely state sovereignty. This complexity in the legal position of the states was exemplified by two controversies in the early nineteenth century: extradition between the princely states and Company territory and British intervention in the princely states.

[70] Prabhakar Singh, 'Indian Princely States and the 19th-century Transformation of the Law of Nations', *Journal of International Dispute Settlement*, 11/3 (2020), 381–384.
[71] *Nabob of Arcot* v. *The East India Company*, 29 ER 544, 552–553.
[72] *Nabob of Arcot* v. *The East India Company*, 29 ER 841, 847.
[73] See, for instance, *The East India Company* v. *Syed Ally*, 19 ER 417.
[74] *The Ex-Rajah of Coorg (Veer Rajunder Wadeer)* v. *The East India Company*, 54 ER 642.
[75] *The Secretary of State in Council of India* v. *Kamachee Boye Sahaba*, 19 ER 388, 408.

Pudukkottai, Hyderabad, and the Extradition of Offenders between Princely and Company Territory

The early nineteenth century saw a spate of extradition treaties that attempted to combat the easy movement of offenders across borders using new means of transport such as railways and steamships.[76] While intra-European treaties emphasized reciprocity and established formal procedures for extradition,[77] western states often extended their police jurisdiction within foreign states to project their power and expand their informal empire.[78] Extradition was also a complicated affair within the British empire as colonies struggled to reconcile local agreements and procedures with statutes passed by the imperial parliament in London.[79] The problems were particularly acute in South Asia, where the uniform exercise of British jurisdiction was disrupted by the continued existence of pockets of French and Portuguese territory as well as the princely states.[80] Even after declaring themselves to the paramount power in the region, British officials engaged in lengthy discussions over extradition policy, as exemplified by the cases of the southern states of Pudukkottai and Hyderabad.

Although never an entirely reciprocal affair, the extradition of 'native' British subjects (i.e. those born in British India rather than in Britain) for offences committed in the princely states was not uncommon in the early nineteenth century. In 1833, for example, Pudukkottai officials successfully obtained the extradition of two native British subjects from Trichinopoly in the Madras presidency to stand trial for a robbery committed in state territory.[81] A year later however, the government of Madras raised questions about the legitimacy of the extradition based on Regulation II of 1829, which provided that British subjects apprehended in British territory after committing crimes in non-British territories could be tried

[76] Mark Condos, 'The Indian "Alsatia": Sovereignty, Extradition, and the Limits of Franco-British Colonial Policing', *The Journal of Imperial and Commonwealth History*, 48/1 (2020), 104.

[77] William Magnuson, 'The Domestic Politics of International Extradition', *Virginia Journal of International Law*, 52/4 (2012), 849.

[78] For the argument that extraordinary rendition was a means for the extension of American empire at the turn of the nineteenth century, see Katherine Unterman, *Uncle Sam's Policemen: The Pursuit of Fugitives Across Borders* (Cambridge, MA: Harvard University Press, 2015).

[79] Condos, 'The Indian "Alsatia"', (n 76) 105. On the imperial politics of extradition across the Canada-United States border in the long nineteenth century, see Bradley Miller, *Borderline Crime: Fugitive Criminals and the Challenge of the Border, 1819–1914* (Toronto: University of Toronto Press, 2016). For a discussion of the complicated politics of the enforcement of extradition laws between Hong Kong and China in the mid-nineteenth century, see Jenny Huangfu Day, 'The Enigma of a Taiping Fugitive: The Illusion of Justice and the "Political Offence Exception" in Extradition from Hong Kong', *Law and History Review*, 39/3 (2021), 415–450.

[80] On the way the French territory of Chandernagore became a haven for Indian anticolonial nationalists seeking to escape arrest from British colonial authorities, see Condos, 'The Indian "Alsatia"', (n 76).

[81] Letter from the Resident at Tanjore to the Magistrate of Trichinopoly, 1 August 1833, IOR/F/4/1533/60788.

in British courts.[82] Although the text of the Regulation did not make the jurisdiction of British courts exclusive, the Madras government instructed the resident at Tanjore to seek the return of the extradited British subjects, claiming that their extradition had been illegal since British subjects apprehended in British territory were amenable only to British courts.[83]

The British resident at Tanjore took the Madras government's instructions to imply reciprocity, i.e. he considered the Company and the princely states to have jurisdiction over their own subjects no matter where they were apprehended. So a few months later, he refused to apply for the extradition of two Pudukkottai subjects who had allegedly committed assault in British territory.[84] Both the government of Madras and the government of India, however, denied that extradition could be reciprocal. According to them, British subjects were amenable to princely state courts for crimes committed in state territory only if they were apprehended there while princely state subjects were subject to the jurisdiction of British courts for crimes committed in British India regardless of where they were apprehended. This distinction was, according to the government of Madras, 'a proper prerogative of the paramount power'.[85] Concurring with this view, the government of India argued that reciprocity could only be 'fairly expected where the state of the Laws and of civilization in the different countries to which the rule applies has attained the same degree of perfection'.[86]

The issue was also brought to the attention of the Company's court of directors in London, which, in an 1836 despatch, commended the government of Madras for the new rules, claiming that '[t]he views which you adopted upon the questions of international law . . . are entirely conformable not only to the provisions of Regulation II, 1829, but also to expediency and the ends of justice'. Like the government of India, the directors also emphasized the 'inequality in the state of civilization and of jurisprudence under the British Government and that of native states' to justify the lack of reciprocity on extradition.[87] On the face of it, therefore, the Company's extradition policy was shaped by the discourse around civilizational differences that had permeated the consciousness of early nineteenth-century colonial officials and moulded the concept of paramountcy as the power of British authorities to interfere in state affairs to ensure good government.

[82] Letter from the Officiating Secretary to the Government of Madras to the Acting Magistrate of Trichinopoly, no. 355, 12 May 1834, IOR/F/4/1533/60788.

[83] Order of the Government of Madras, Judicial Department, 27 May 1834, IOR/F/4/1533/60788.

[84] Letter from the Resident at Tanjore to the Magistrate of Trichinopoly, 10 July 1834, IOR/F/4/1533/60789.

[85] Letter from the Officiating Secretary to the Government of Madras to the Officiating Chief Secretary to the Government of India, no. 763, 19 September 1834, IOR/F/4/1533/60789.

[86] Letter from the Officiating Chief Secretary to the Government of India to the Officiating Secretary to the Government of Madras, no. 807, 9 October 1834, IOR/F/4/1533/60789.

[87] Despatch of the Court of Directors to the Government of Madras, Judicial Department, no. 3, 1 June 1836, Judicial Despatches to Madras (February 1835–December 1837), IOR/L/PJ/3/1388.

Despite relying on British paramountcy to strip the princely states of jurisdiction over crimes committed within their territory, these rules did include one curiosity. Colonial officials agreed that British subjects apprehended in princely state territory for a crime committed there were subject to state courts.[88] How exactly did the distinction between British subjects apprehended within and outside princely state territory make sense considering this emphasis on the paramountcy of the Company and the alleged civilizational differences between Britain and South Asia? The court of directors admitted that British subjects apprehended in princely state territory for crimes committed there had to be left to the jurisdiction of local courts as a means of 'guarding against the plea of being a British subject, which every person accused might otherwise set up'.[89] In spite the rhetoric of civilizational differences and the alleged lack of the rule of law in the states, therefore, practical considerations of governance remained significant in determining British policy on extradition to the states. Continual assertions of British paramountcy did not eliminate the exercise of sovereign powers, such as criminal jurisdiction, by the princely states, with the scope of both British paramountcy and princely state sovereignty remaining open to question.

Despite the policy endorsed by the court of directors, some British officers started to claim that all British subjects were subject to British courts regardless of where they were apprehended. As a result, they demanded the surrender of British subjects who had been arrested in state territory for trial in Company courts. These stipulations caused significant problems for the princely states. The *raja* of Pudukkottai sent several representations to the resident, complaining that his subjects were forced to travel to Company territory to prosecute cases or appear as witnesses; since most could not afford to do so, the alleged criminals remained unpunished. The operation of British jurisdictional regulations, the *raja* argued, 'weakened his authority among his own people', thereby affecting the sovereignty of the state more broadly.[90] The resident agreed with this assessment of the situation and recommended that the power to try all persons accused of crimes within state territory should lie with the *raja*.[91] He also noted that his proposal had the support of British magistrates in the presidency's border districts, all of whom had expressed concern at the increase in crime and the difficulty of prosecution

[88] Letter from the Officiating Secretary to the Government of Madras to the Officiating Chief Secretary to the Government of India, no. 763, 19 September 1834, IOR/F/4/1533/60789; Letter from the Officiating Chief Secretary to the Government of India to the Officiating Secretary to the Government of Madras, no. 807, 9 October 1834, IOR/F/4/1533/60789; and Despatch of the Court of Directors to the Government of Madras, Judicial Department, no. 3, 1 June 1836, Judicial Despatches to Madras (February 1835–December 1837), IOR/L/PJ/3/1388.

[89] Despatch of the Court of Directors to the Government of Madras, Judicial Department, no. 3, 1 June 1836, Judicial Despatches to Madras (February 1835–December 1837), IOR/L/PJ/3/1388.

[90] The resident referred to these representations in Letter from the Resident at Tanjore to the Chief Secretary to the Government of Madras, 22 December 1835, IOR/F/4/1811/74611.

[91] Letter from the Resident at Tanjore to the Chief Secretary to the Government of Madras, 22 December 1835, IOR/F/4/1811/74611.

because of a lack of witnesses.[92] The magistrate at Tanjore went as far as calling the new rules tantamount to 'a denial of justice to the subjects of His Excellency', and sought a return to reciprocity as he was not aware of a 'shade of difference' between British and princely territory with regard to civilization.[93]

Under pressure, the government of Madras clarified that British subjects apprehended in foreign territory were not solely subject to British courts.[94] The government of India went even further, arguing that Regulation II of 1829 did 'not prescribe that a Native subject of the British Government charged with a crime committed out of the British provinces and found within the British territory is amenable only to the Company's Courts but merely that such offender may be tried in the Company's Courts'. Since the jurisdiction of Company courts was permissive rather than exclusive, there was 'nothing in the ... Regulation to prevent the British Government from making over the offender to be dealt with according to the laws of the country wherein he committed the offence in any instance where such course of proceeding may be deemed expedient'. Consequently, the government of India saw no objection in permitting the magistrates of border districts to extradite native British subjects to Pudukkottai for trial for offences committed there.[95]

Only a few months after non-reciprocal rules on extradition between Company territories and the princely states had been approved, the Madras government confirmed that native British subjects could, in fact, be extradited to Pudukkottai for offences committed in state territory.[96] Even in the case of a small state such as Pudukkottai, therefore, a combination of princely opposition and the disapproval of its own officials forced the Company to accept the possibility of extraditing British subjects for trial in the princely states. With this position, the Company returned to prior practice that was structured around reciprocity, at least in the case of the extradition of native British subjects and princely state subjects for crimes committed in territory that was foreign to them.

Even after this clarification, Company officials continued to face jurisdictional questions, largely because the rules on reciprocity did not conform with established practice in some areas. For instance, when the local collector of Masulipatnam

[92] Letter from the Magistrate of Madura to the Resident at Tanjore, 5 November 1835, IOR/F/4/1811/74611; and Letter from the Magistrate of Trichinopoly to the Resident at Tanjore, 13 November 1835, IOR/F/4/1811/74611.

[93] Letter from the Magistrate of Tanjore to the Resident at Tanjore, 2 November 1835, IOR/F/4/1811/74611.

[94] Letter from the Chief Secretary to the Government of Madras to the Secretary to the Government of India, no. 80, 2 February 1836, IOR/F/4/1811/74611.

[95] Letter from the Secretary to the Government of India to the Chief Secretary to the Government of Madras, no. 12, 22 February 1836, IOR/F/4/1811/74611. In reaching this conclusion, the government received support from the judges of the local criminal court. See Letter from the Register to the Faujdari Adalat to the Chief Secretary to the Government of Madras, no. 67, 31 March 1836, IOR/F/4/1811/74611.

[96] Despatch from the Government of Madras, Judicial Department to the Court of Directors, no. 12, 8 November 1836, IOR/F/4/1811/74611; and Despatch from the Government of Madras, Judicial Department to the Court of Directors, no. 5, 16 May 1837, IOR/F/4/1811/74611.

sought the extradition of Hyderabadi subjects for trial in British courts in relation to crimes committed in British territory, the government of India opposed the plea, claiming that the recently-decided jurisdiction rules were only applicable to 'petty chiefs' like the *raja* of Pudukkottai; Hyderabad, however, could try its own subjects even for crimes committed in British territory.[97] In the case of large states then, the Company seemed to adopt the position that sovereign polities (i.e. the Company and the state) would each try their own subjects if apprehended in their territory regardless of where the crime was committed. Since states like Hyderabad were significant powers whose support was often necessary for the stability of Company authority, colonial officials seemed more flexible when it came to the recognition of their sovereign authority.

This flexibility bred further confusion. When the resident for Travancore and Cochin advocated a similar position for those states,[98] local Company officials complained about the problems posed by the jurisdiction rules for British subjects forced to travel to the princely states to act as witnesses.[99] The government of Madras supported its officials, arguing that 'it would be preferable that crimes by which the public peace and security are violated, either by British subjects or the subjects of Native States, should be tried according to the laws of the country whether they are committed, where also evidence of the real facts of the case can be more satisfactorily procured, and the benefit of example which is there most wanted, be at the same time secured'.[100] Even after the declaration of British paramountcy over South Asia, some colonial officials advocated for the exercise of territorial jurisdiction by the various political powers in the region rather than vesting jurisdiction solely or primarily with British courts.

Faced with a dilemma, the government of India simply refused to draw up 'fixed rules of universal application' on extradition. While acknowledging that British subjects might suffer hardships in having to travel to foreign lands for criminal trials, it noted that the opposite rule would lead to 'great hardship which would be inflicted upon a person accused of an offence by being removed for trial beyond the reach of his own friends and resources and being tried by laws with which he is unacquainted and having to bring his witnesses from their own to a foreign country'.[101] In this situation, the government of India's concern with civilizational

[97] Letter from the Secretary to the Government of India to the Officiating Resident at Hyderabad, 29 May 1837, IOR/F/4/1653/66009.

[98] Letter from the Resident of Travancore and Cochin to the Joint Magistrate in Charge of Coimbatore, no. 1418, 5 August 1837, IOR/F/4/1653/66009; and Letter from the Resident of Travancore and Cochin to the Magistrate of Malabar, 15 August 1837, IOR/F/4/1653/66009.

[99] See, for instance, Letter from the Joint Magistrate in Charge of Coimbatore to the Secretary to the Government of Madras, Judicial Department, 23 August 1837, IOR/F/4/1653/66009; and Letter from the Magistrate of Malabar to the Chief Secretary to the Government of Madras, no. 27, 18 August 1837, IOR/F/4/1653/66009.

[100] Letter from the Chief Secretary to the Government of Madras to the Secretary to the Government of India, 13 July 1837, IOR/F/4/1653/66009.

[101] Letter from the Secretary to the Government of India to the Chief Secretary to the Government of Madras, no. 8, 2 October 1837, IOR/F/4/1653/66009.

differences implied that all persons, whether British or South Asian, had the right to be tried by familiar legal systems instead of being used as a basis to carve out exceptional privileges for British subjects. Although colonial officials considered that the state of Hyderabad and the Company were equally entitled to try their own subjects for crimes committed outside their territory, they remained resistant to the idea of reciprocity more generally. For many states, the government of India continued to claim that the paramount power had the right to demand the surrender of state subjects while refusing to give up its own. In the case of Hyderabad though, it insisted that justice would be served by leaving the trial of princely state subjects to state authorities.[102] The court of directors sanctioned the modification of the rules for Hyderabad.[103]

The government of India's policy change for the state of Hyderabad led to further uncertainty, with the government of Madras seeking a clarification on whether the new approach would also apply to states such as Travancore and Cochin, which could claim like status.[104] Although the government of India did not agree to change existing practice for these other states, it also did not offer any clear rationale for drawing this distinction between the states.[105] Additional confusion was caused by the government of India's explanation that the policy change for Hyderabad was an exception to the general lack of reciprocity on extradition between the princely states and the Company. In light of the Company's disclaimer of reciprocity more generally, the government of Madras also sought to understand whether the reciprocity that had been extended to Pudukkottai a year earlier was still valid.[106] After much discussion, it finally decided that the Pudukkottai position had not been superseded by later instructions, although no reasoning was offered for this conclusion.[107]

Even the policy permitting Hyderabad to exercise jurisdiction over its own subjects for crimes committed in Company territory was reversed a few months

[102] Letter from the Secretary to the Government of India to the Chief Secretary to the Government of Madras, no. 8, 2 October 1837, IOR/F/4/1653/66009. See also Minute by Lord Auckland, Governor-General of India in Council, 23 September 1837, IOR/F/4/1653/66009. However, one member of the council offered a different view, arguing that reciprocity was the only fair rule, and ought to always be followed 'when there is a reasonable assurance that the accused will be acquitted if he is innocent and punished only if he is proved to be guilty'. Therefore, he favoured allowing the state where the offenders were apprehended to try them, regardless of their nationality. See Minute by H. Shakespear, 5 September 1837, IOR/F/4/1653/66009.

[103] Despatch from the Court of Directors to the Government of India, Judicial Department, no. 7, 10 July 1837, IOR/F/4/1811/74609.

[104] Minutes of Madras Judicial Consultations, 3 November 1837, IOR/F/4/1811/74614; and Letter from the Chief Secretary to the Government of Madras to the Secretary to the Government of India, no. 1027, 3 November 1837, IOR/F/4/1811/74614.

[105] Letter from the Officiating Secretary to the Government of India to the Chief Secretary to the Government of Madras, no. 132, 2 July 1838, IOR/F/4/1811/74609; and Despatch from the Government of India, Judicial Department to the Court of Directors, no. 10, 30 July 1838, IOR/F/4/1811/74609.

[106] Letter from the Register of the Faujdari Adalat to the Chief Secretary to the Government of Madras, no. 404, 3 December 1837, IOR/F/4/1811/74614.

[107] Minutes of Madras Judicial Consultations, 12 December 1837, IOR/F/4/1811/74614.

later when the government of India discovered that its understanding of existing practice was incorrect; extraditions of British subjects to Hyderabad for crimes committed in state territory, however, remained common.[108] Much like in the case of Pudukkottai then, the Company accepted the necessity of extraditing its subjects to Hyderabad in the name of following existing practice, putting claims of paramountcy or civilizational differences on the backburner. And Hyderabad itself continued to contest British claims over its subjects and was a reluctant extradition partner even later in the nineteenth century.[109]

The repeated changes in Company policy on extradition to the princely states reveal the difficulties that British officials faced in drawing up a uniform understanding of the princely states. In some instances, the states were considered Company allies that retained significant sovereign authority, and therefore had the legal authority to try British subjects who could be extradited there. In other situations, the states were classified as uncivilized dependencies that were subject to British paramountcy and to which British subjects could not be extradited. The lack of a coherent position on extradition was reflective of the broader confusion around the scope of British paramountcy and its effect on the legal status of the states. Since there was no consistent understanding of the scope of paramountcy or a cogent explanation of how the doctrine applied to different states, colonial officials adopted a piecemeal approach to developing extradition policy in ways that entangled with the power politics of the period and relied on the maintenance of different types of relations with different states to entrench British authority. This debate over the relationship between British paramountcy and princely state sovereignty was only intensified when it came to intervening in the internal affairs of the states.

Bharatpur, Awadh, and British Intervention in the Princely States

The early nineteenth century was a period of intense reform in British India. Under the influence of utilitarian philosophers and evangelical thinkers, Company officials embarked on a series of legal codification projects to introduce the 'rule of law' in a region that they claimed had been subject to the degradations of 'Oriental despotism';[110] somewhat paradoxically, these reforms were entwined with increasing

[108] Letter from the Officiating Secretary to the Government of India to the Chief Secretary to the Government of Fort St. George, no. 132, 2 July 1838, IOR/F/4/1811/74609.

[109] For a discussion of the legal contestations along the Hyderabad-British India frontier in the last two decades of the nineteenth century, see Eric Lewis Beverley, 'Frontier as Resource: Law, Crime, and Sovereignty on the Margins of Empire', *Comparative Studies in Society and History*, 55/2 (2013), 241–272.

[110] Metcalf, *Ideologies of the Raj*, (n 45) 28.

colonial autocracy.[111] Several British officials also desired administrative changes in the princely states but faced the roadblock of the Company's network of treaties that limited intervention in state affairs. Consequently, some reformers advocated the annexation of states that, in their view, had failed to provide 'good government' to their subjects.[112]

This expansionist outlook led to a tremendous increase in the Company's territorial possessions in the early nineteenth century,[113] but the question of intervention into the internal affairs of states remained intensely contested, with officials often changing their approach over time. The philosopher and Company administrator John Stuart Mill, for instance, initially considered indirect rule via the states to be a mistake that propped up extravagant rulers. By the 1830s, he became more sympathetic towards local customs, often criticizing British political officers for being overly interventionist.[114] Some of the hesitation around intervention came from concerns around the consequences. In his classic text on the Malwa region, the political officer John Malcolm advised the Company to 'avoid the minute and vexatious interference, which counteracts the purpose for which we maintain them in existence, by lessening their power, and consequently their utility', but also warned against 'a blind support to their authority, however ruinous its measures to the prosperity of the country and the happiness of its inhabitants'.[115] Other Company officials had broader concerns about intervening in the states. The governor-general, Lord Hastings, claimed that if states were permitted to intervene in the affairs of others on account of misgovernment, 'a powerful State would never want a colour for subjugating a weak neighbour'; the consequences were 'so obvious that no principle in the law of nations leaves room for acting on such a presumption'.[116] Principles of international law, therefore, still seemed to provide a framework for considering relations between the Company and the princely states, with the implications of British paramountcy for princely sovereignty being unclear.

Two minutes written by the EIC administrator Charles Metcalfe a decade apart exemplify the tensions within British political thought. The first memo related to the state of Bharatpur, whose ruler, Baldeo Singh, died in 1825, leaving a minor

[111] Nasser Hussain, *The Jurisprudence of Emergency: Colonialism and the Rule of Law* (Ann Arbor, MI: University of Michigan Press, 2004).

[112] Thomas Metcalf, *The Aftermath of Revolt: India, 1857–1870* (Princeton, NJ: Princeton University Press, 1964), 30–31.

[113] The Company annexed approximately 50,000 square kilometres of territory every year during the governor-generalship of Lord Wellesley (1798–1805); annexations continued in later years, reaching approximately 85,000 square kilometres a year during the governor-generalship of Lord Dalhousie (1848–1856). See Chatterjee, *The Black Hole of Empire*, (n 67) 190, 197.

[114] Lynn Zastoupil, 'J. S. Mill and India', *Victorian Studies*, 32/1 (1988), 42–49.

[115] John Malcolm, *Memoir of Central India*, ii (2nd edn, London: Kingsbury, Parbury, and Allen, 1824), 266.

[116] 'Letter—Government of India to the Resident at Hyderabad, 20 December 1822', in *Documents and Speeches on the Indian Princely States*, (n 38) i, 144.

son, Balwant Singh. The young prince was acknowledged as the heir-apparent by the Company but his right to succeed was disputed by his uncle, Durjan Sal, who imprisoned him. The Company initially refused to intervene in the state to support Balwant Singh, triggering the resignation of David Ochterlony from his position as the resident at Delhi.[117] As his replacement, Charles Metcalfe wrote a detailed memo in which he admitted that the 'general principle' that had been 'enjoined by the repeated orders of the Court of Directors' was that 'we ought not to interfere in the internal affairs of other States'. However, he also noted that 'we are continually compelled to deviate from this rule, which is found untenable in practice; and the deviation is generally sanctioned, and sometimes directed, by the same authority'. After acknowledging that the Company had 'by degrees become the paramount State of India', he argued that it had become 'an established principle of our policy to maintain tranquillity among all the States of India, and to prevent the anarchy and misrule which were likely to disturb the general peace'. Given this authority to maintain peace in the region, Metcalfe concluded, '[w]ith respect, therefore, to all States over which our supremacy extends, our duty requires that we should support the legitimate succession of the Prince, while policy seems to dictate that we should, as much as possible, abstain from any further interference in their affairs'.[118]

In Metcalfe's view, the doctrine of paramountcy implied that the Company had the right to intervene in the internal affairs of the states although he attempted to draw a line between legitimate and illegitimate interventions. In reality, of course, such a distinction was difficult to implement. Even apart from practical concerns, some Company officials were wary of intervening in the states altogether. The court of directors in London was unimpressed with Metcalfe's minute, noting that he had 'endeavored to establish the necessity and propriety of British interference in the succession and internal concerns of independent native powers to an extent in which we cannot concur'. They also explicitly rejected the view that British paramountcy had 'in any degree extended our right of interference in the internal concerns of other states, except in so far as that right has been established by treaty'.[119] Although the directors' missive was too late to stop the Company from sending troops to support Balwant Singh's claim to the throne,[120] the debate raised questions about the scope of British paramountcy and the legal status of the princely states as sovereign entities. Bharatpur survived as a princely state, but Metcalfe's

[117] Kaye, *The Life and Correspondence of Charles, Lord Metcalfe*, (n 63) ii, 135–137.

[118] Charles Metcalfe, 'General Question of Interference in the Concerns of Other States', in John William Kaye, ed., *Selections from the Papers of Lord Metcalfe* (London: Smith, Elder & Co., 1855), 122, 124.

[119] 'Letter from the Secret Committee to Governor-General in Council, 26 March 1826', in Kaye, *The Life and Correspondence of Charles, Lord Metcalfe*, (n 63) ii, 141.

[120] The British massacred about eight thousand people within the fort where Balwant Singh was being held and proceeded to plunder the area. See Thompson, *The Life of Charles, Lord Metcalfe*, (n 63) 246, 249–251.

minute cemented Company claims of the right to intervene in—and even annex—states on account of being the paramount power in the region.

By the time Metcalfe became acting governor-general in 1835, he appeared to be more circumspect about intervening in the affairs of the states. He noted that some treaties with the states made them 'with respect to external relations, dependent and under our protection' but admitted that they were 'still independent in internal affairs'. He also warned against twisting the Company's 'obligation of protection against enemies into a right to interference in the internal affairs of protected States' by noting that no such right was provided by any of the treaties with the states, except in situations where 'the legitimate sovereign' required support 'against usurpation or dethronement, in the event of his not having merited the disaffection of his subjects'. However, he immediately qualified his claim of the Company's limited power to intervene in the states by noting that there were 'undoubtedly, extreme cases in which the interference of the protecting power may be unavoidable'; these included '[i]nstances of prolonged anarchy, affecting others under our protection'.[121] Company officials, therefore, reaffirmed the importance of treaty provisions while simultaneously claiming the right to intervene in state affairs based on paramountcy.

Succession in the princely states was a ripe moment for intervention since the British asserted 'the right to determine who was the legitimate heir' and contested the right of rulers' to adopt heirs.[122] Under the so-called 'doctrine of lapse', the Company annexed states where an Indian ruler died without leaving a legitimate (in the judgement of the Company) male heir.[123] The doctrine was hugely controversial and often justified by the avowal of British paramountcy. It was also useful for the intensification of the policy of annexation under the governor-generalship of Lord Dalhousie,[124] becoming the basis for the high-profile annexations of the states of Satara, Nagpur, and Jhansi.[125]

Dalhousie's expansionist rhetoric did not apply equally to all states, as demonstrated by his response to the 1851 proposal by the British resident, Hastings Fraser, that the Company directly administer the state of Hyderabad.[126] Dalhousie

[121] Charles Metcalfe, 'Duty Towards Native States—Interference and Non-Interference', in *Selections from the Papers of Lord Metcalfe*, (n 118) 241, 239.

[122] Ramusack, *The Indian Princes and their States*, (n 61) 138.

[123] Fisher, *Indirect Rule in India*, (n 54) 257.

[124] Dalhousie was appointed governor-general in 1848 and served till 1856. For details on his controversial Indian career, see William Lee-Warner, *The Life of the Marquis of Dalhousie*, 2 vols (London: Macmillan and Co., 1904); and David J. Howlett, 'Ramsay, James Andrew Broun, first marquess of Dalhousie (1812–1860)', in *Oxford Dictionary of National Biography*, https://doi.org/10.1093/ref:odnb/23088, accessed 30 June 2021.

[125] 'Minute by Lord Dalhousie, 30 August 1848', in *Documents and Speeches on the Indian Princely States*, (n 38) i, 198; and 'Minute by Lord Dalhousie, 28 January 1854', in *Documents and Speeches on the Indian Princely States*, (n 38) i, 212. In the case of Jhansi, the doctrine was supplemented by allegations of misgovernment. See Ramusack, *The Indian Princes and their States*, (n 61) 84.

[126] Lee-Warner, *The Life of the Marquis of Dalhousie*, (n 124) ii, 113.

strongly opposed this suggestion. He admitted that '[t]he acknowledged supremacy of the British power in India gives to it the right, and imposes upon it the duty, of maintaining by its influence, and (if need be) compelling by its strength, the continuance of general peace'. The Company's paramountcy, in other words, 'entitles it to interfere in the administration of native princes, if their administration tends unquestionably to the injury of the subjects or of the allies of the British Government'. It did not, however, 'confer upon it the right, of deciding authoritatively on the existence of native independent sovereignties, and of arbitrarily setting them aside, whenever their administration may not accord with its own views, and although their acts in no way affects the interests or security of itself or its allies'.[127]

Dalhousie relied on the Company's treaties with Hyderabad to reach his conclusions on the limits of British authority over the states. For him 'the acknowledged supremacy of the British Government in India' could not be used to 'justify its rulers in disregarding the positive obligations of international contracts, in order to obtrude on native Princes and their people a system of subversive interference, which is unwelcome alike to people and prince'. Since the *nizam* was acknowledged as 'an independent Prince', the Company was 'bound by the solemn obligations of a treaty to abstain from all interference in his Highness's internal affairs' and had 'no just right to enter upon a system of direct interference in the internal affairs of his Highness's kingdom, which is explicitly forbidden by the positive stipulations of treaty, which would be utterly repugnant to the wishes of the Sovereign our ally, and is unsought by the people over whom he rules'.[128]

By taking this position on Hyderabad, Dalhousie seemed to draw a distinction between 'independent' states that were not subordinate to the paramount power and 'dependent' states that were subject to British paramountcy.[129] The effect of British paramountcy on princely state sovereignty, therefore, appeared to depend on the type of the state in question. Dalhousie's sympathetic biographer, William Lee-Warner, admitted that 'the line between independence and dependence' was 'difficult to fix'; Karauli, for instance, was described as 'in some sort a dependent state'.[130]

The incoherence came to a head during debates over the annexation of Awadh, one of the richest territories in nineteenth-century South Asia. In 1801, the *nawab*, Saadat Ali Khan, was forced to conclude a treaty with the Company in which he agreed to cede half of Awadh's territory and establish 'a system of administration "conducive to the prosperity of his subjects"'.[131] However, he soon found his

[127] 'Minute by Lord Dalhousie, 27 May 1851', in *Documents and Speeches on the Indian Princely States*, (n 38) i, 204.
[128] ibid, 204–205.
[129] Ramusack, *The Indian Princes and their States*, (n 61) 83.
[130] Lee-Warner, *The Life of the Marquis of Dalhousie*, (n 124) ii, 112.
[131] Metcalf, *The Aftermath of Revolt*, (n 112) 34.

government to be 'crippled by the constant interference of the British resident'.[132] By the time Wajid Ali Shah acceded to the throne, British officials admitted that the state had sunk 'into a state of anarchy' for which they themselves were 'at least partially responsible'.[133]

Under pressure from the evangelical movement, which pushed for the annexation of states on the basis that 'the Indian nobility was immoral and incapable of good government',[134] Dalhousie declared that '[t]he Government of Oude has been notorious for its abuse of power, for gross misrule, and for the oppression of its subjects'. Despite this, he argued that '[t]he reform of the administration of the province may be wrought, and the prosperity of the people may be secured, without resorting to so extreme a measure as the annexation of the territory, and the abolition of the throne'. Instead of annexation, he recommended that the *nawab* 'be required to vest the exclusive administration of the civil and military government of Oude and its dependencies in the hands of the Company', a step that required '[t]he King's consent'.[135]

Dalhousie's rather cautious plan faced opposition from other members of his council and officials in London.[136] James Dormin simply claimed that the Company ought to 'assert the right of the Government of India, as paramount power, to adopt its own system of government in respect to any portion of the Indian Empire that is hopelessly ground to the dust by the oppression of its native rulers'.[137] John Peter Grant was equally dismissive of Dalhousie's conclusion that the *nawab*'s consent was necessary for the Company to take over Awadh's administration.[138] Taking these dissenting views into account, the court of directors instructed the government of India to seek the *nawab*'s consent only if 'his acceptance of the Treaty proposed to be tendered to him' was 'a matter of virtual certainty'. If there was any doubt, the directors were prepared to authorize 'the only other course by which our duties to the People of Oude can be fulfilled, that of assuming authoritatively the powers necessary for the permanent establishment of good government throughout the country'.[139]

[132] Chatterjee, *The Black Hole of Empire*, (n 67) 201.
[133] Metcalf, *The Aftermath of Revolt*, (n 112) 35.
[134] Chatterjee, *The Black Hole of Empire*, (n 67) 202.
[135] 'Minute by the Governor-General of India, 18 June 1855', in *Parliamentary Papers: Papers Relating to Oude* (London: Harrison and Sons, 1856), 150, 184–185, 187.
[136] Metcalf, *The Aftermath of Revolt*, (n 112) 36.
[137] 'Minute by James Dorin, 11 July 1855', in *Parliamentary Papers: Papers Relating to Oude*, (n 135) 192.
[138] 'Minute by John Peter Grant, 7 August 1855', in *Parliamentary Papers: Papers Relating to Oude*, (n 135) 215.
[139] 'Letter from the Court of Directors of the East India Company to the Governor-General of India in Council, 21 November 1855', in *Parliamentary Papers: Papers Relating to Oude*, (n 135) 236.

Dalhousie decided to ask Wajid Ali Shah to execute a treaty to cede control over Awadh to the Company.[140] When faced with this ultimatum, the *nawab* wrote of his distress, arguing that any change in policy towards the state would be 'assuredly contrary to Treaties' and 'opposed to all the amicable relations which have hitherto existed'.[141] He also declined to sign the new treaty, claiming that the 'all-powerful' British government had reduced him to a 'helpless position', making any agreement between them illogical since '[t]reaties are necessary between equals only'.[142] A few days later, British troops entered the Awadh capital and the British resident, James Outram, issued a proclamation that announced Wajid Ali Shah's removal and the assumption of power by the Company. Scholars such as Partha Chatterjee have argued that the tortured discussions among Company officials were only 'a show ... for the sanctity of treaty obligations'. In his view, the Awadh annexation exemplifies 'the effective erasure in the nineteenth century, under British imperial auspices, of the law of nations from the territorial space of the Indian subcontinent', with 'empire's law' replacing 'the classical law of nations'.[143]

The language of international law remained key to the Awadh debates, albeit in rather contradictory ways. Dalhousie's initial rejection of the annexation path was based on the claim that forcing the *nawab* to execute 'a new treaty or to assume the government of his country' would not be 'in accordance with international law' and would instead 'be either conquest or usurpation of the powers of Government by force of arms'.[144] He gathered support from Barnes Peacock, the legal member of the governor-general's council and future chief justice of both the Supreme Court and Calcutta High Court. Peacock agreed that the *nawab*'s consent was necessary for the state to cede administrative authority but concluded that the Company had the right to proceed against the *nawab* even if such consent was not obtained. His analysis was based on a reading of how international law dealt with the breach of treaties. Drawing on Vattel, he argued that 'if a Treaty entered into by two nations be broken by one of them, the injured nation has the option either to consider the Treaty at an end, or to uphold it, and insist upon the performance of it, and, if necessary, to resort to force for that purpose'. In the 1801 treaty with the Company, the *nawab* had 'engaged to establish in his dominions such a system of administration, to be carried into effect by his own officers, as should be conducive to the prosperity of his subjects, and calculated to secure the lives and property of the

[140] 'Letter from the Governor-General of India to the King of Oude, 23 January 1856', in *Parliamentary Papers: Papers Relating to Oude*, (n 135) 244–251; and 'Draft of Treaty between the East India Company and the King of Oude', in *Parliamentary Papers: Papers Relating to Oude*, (n 135) 251–253.

[141] 'Letter from the King of Oude to Major-General Outram, 1 February 1856', in *Parliamentary Papers: Papers Relating to Oude*, (n 135) 283.

[142] 'Note of an interview which took place between the King of Oude and Major-General Outram, 4 February 1856', in *Parliamentary Papers: Papers Relating to Oude*, (n 135) 288.

[143] Chatterjee, *The Black Hole of Empire*, (n 67) 211, 208, 196.

[144] 'Letter—Dalhousie to Couper, 15 December 1855', in *Documents and Speeches on the Indian Princely States*, (n 38) i, 228.

inhabitants'; however, he had 'utterly violated the obligation'. With this breach, the Company, which had 'obtained a perfect right to have such a Government maintained', was 'justly authorised to resort to force to obtain a just satisfaction for the past, and a reasonable security for the future'.[145] The vocabulary of international law, therefore, provided both the means of opposing annexations and of justifying them. Although princely treaties were binding, they were interpreted in a manner to justify state annexations, exemplifying the uneasy embrace of non-European political entities by international law.

Much like in the case of extradition, British policy on intervening in the internal affairs of the princely states changed rapidly over the course of the first half of the nineteenth century. Some Company officials remained circumspect about intervening in state affairs since they considered them to be sovereign polities whose rights had to be respected. Other officials pushed for the annexation of states that allegedly failed to provide government, claiming that the Company obtained a right to do so on account of being the paramount power in the region. Parsing through these debates demonstrates the lack of a coherent view on the effect of British paramountcy on princely state sovereignty and the varied attempts to categorize the states depending on their relations with the Company. Instead of straightforward assertions of British supremacy, therefore, Company officials often relied on the language of international law itself, particularly the binding nature of treaties, to expand their authority in South Asia.

Conclusion

By the turn of the nineteenth century, debates over extradition policy and the power of the Company to intervene in or annex princely states appeared to overwhelm many colonial officials. At a time when the Company's authority and territorial possessions in South Asia were expanding at a rapid pace, colonial administrators struggled to come up with a coherent understanding of newly developed terminology such as 'paramountcy' or an explanation of its scope, its operation, and its effects on the exercise of sovereign powers by the numerous princely states that continued to exist in the region. In some disputes, Company officials admitted that the states were sovereign entities to which British subjects could be extradited and in whose internal affairs the British could not interfere. In other instances, administrators relied on expansive notions of British paramountcy and particular interpretations of treaty obligations to claim the right to intervene in and annex states that did not provide good government to their subjects or to refuse to extradite

[145] 'Minute by Barnes Peacock, 22 August 1855', in *Parliamentary Papers: Papers Relating to Oude*, (n 135) 228–233.

British subjects for trial in the states while claiming the right to try princely state subjects.

Even by the middle of the nineteenth century, Company officials lacked a cogent theory of sovereignty that would enable them to claim that British paramountcy in South Asia extinguished all sovereign authority of the princely states. The Company also continued to recognize the nominal sovereignty of the Mughal emperor and repeatedly clashed with the British state in relation to the exercise of political power in South Asia. Company officials struggled to specify the scope of their authority over the states even though some of them, such as Lord Dalhousie, attempted to create a framework for the exercise of British authority by distinguishing between 'dependent' and 'independent' states. On account of these continually shifting understandings of sovereignty, the overall picture remained in flux. As David Kennedy notes, the early nineteenth century was a period when 'many sovereigns and many types of sovereignty' co-existed and 'overlapped unproblematically'. In a world in which the term 'sovereignty' simply 'described the capacity and powers of a variety of actors' as it 'had not yet been consolidated',[146] chartered companies, European states, and South Asian rulers of various shapes and sizes all jostled to exercise power.[147]

In this fluid situation, the language of international law continued to play a significant role in the South Asian context. On some occasions, this vernacular was used to underline the fact that the princely states were sovereign entities, as seen in references to important states such as Hyderabad. However, despite the best efforts of states such as Pudukkottai and Hyderabad to carve out a space for themselves, the vocabulary of international law was often the basis for the annexation of polities that had allegedly failed to comply with the terms of binding treaties, as in the case of Awadh. As Priya Satia argues (albeit in the context of the relationship between the Company and the Crown), it was 'the very absence of legal clarity' that 'abetted colonialism by extending deniability about it'.[148] As I argue in the next chapter, although the incoherence over sovereign rights enabled annexations, it was also one of the triggers of the 1857 revolt, and led to the development of a distinct theoretical approach to sovereignty that treated it as a bundle of rights that could be divided among a number of actors. This approach was key to the post-1857 British strategy of moulding the princes into loyal allies who would play a role in maintaining the stability of the empire, while also creating the legal space for the use of the concept of sovereignty by the princely states to defend their rights.

[146] David Kennedy, 'International Law and the Nineteenth Century: History of an Illusion', *Quinnipiac Law Review*, 17/1 (1997), 122–123.

[147] Robert Travers has made this argument for late eighteenth-century South Asia. See Travers, 'A British Empire by Treaty in Eighteenth-Century India', (n 38) 137. I would argue that it can be extended to early nineteenth-century South Asia as well.

[148] Priya Satia, 'Risking a Colonial Anticolonialism', *European Journal of International Law*, 32/3 (2021), 1024.

Chapter Three
Jousting Over Jurisdiction
Sovereignty Debates in the Aftermath of the 1857 Rebellion

Sovereignty and Jurisdictional Questions

In 1879, the government of India passed the Elephants' Preservation Act mandating that individuals acquire a government-issued licence to engage in the capture of wild elephants.[1] A year later, it promulgated a set of rules to make the British Indian legislation applicable to the Orissa Tributary Mahals, the collective name for a number of princely states in eastern India.[2] Dhanurjai Narayan Bhanj Deo, the *maharaja* of Keonjhar, one of those states, was vociferous in his protests against this move, arguing that he had an 'absolute' right to capture elephants found within his territory without requiring a licence issued by a British Indian authority. British Indian legislation, he contended, did not apply to the princely states because of their separate legal status; any extension of such laws would breach the treaties made by the British with his predecessors and the *sanads* issued to him.[3]

We can read this vignette in a number of ways: as an anecdote about the decadent lives of the Indian princes, obsessed with activities like hunting and typecast as 'Oriental despots' by the British; as a tale of defiance by a high-minded *maharaja* against the might of the British empire; or as an account of a contretemps between a princely state and the British government over crucial natural resources.[4] The dispute, however, became entangled with broader questions about the legal status of the princely states. The controversy was exacerbated by a Calcutta High Court decision in which a majority of the judges held that the state of Mayurbhanj, one of

[1] Elephants' Preservation Act 1879, s 5.

[2] Letter from the Superintendent, Orissa Tributary Mahals to the Political Secretary, Government of Bengal, 15 May 1882, Proceedings of the Government of Bengal in the Political Department, June 1883, no. 26, IOR/P/2034.

[3] Letter from the *maharaja* of Keonjhar to the Superintendent, Orissa Tributary Mahals, 4 January 1882, Proceedings of the Government of Bengal in the Political Department, June 1883, no. 26, IOR/P/2034.

[4] For a discussion of the economic significance of elephants, see Vijaya Ramadas Mandala, 'The Raj and the Paradoxes of Wildlife Conservation: British Attitudes and Expediencies', *The Historical Journal*, 58/1 (2015), 101–109. The regulation of elephant hunting itself became an important source of revenue for the British government. See Geetashree Singh, 'Colonising Elephant Hunting in Assam (1826–1947)', *Indian Historical Review*, 47/2 (2020), 313–329.

Sovereignty, International Law, and the Princely States of Colonial South Asia. Priyasha Saksena, Oxford University Press.
 DOI: 10.1093/oso/9780192866585.003.0003

the other Orissa princely states, was not part of British India;[5] the same logic could be extended to Keonjhar.

Although the *maharaja* was finally 'permitted' to carry on with the practice of capturing wild elephants in his territory, the government of India made it clear that this decision could be revisited.[6] As the Keonjhar controversy demonstrates, late nineteenth-century colonial and princely officials struggled to define the scope of rights and the degree of powers of the states and the British government in a series of jurisdictional disputes.[7] Even a seemingly innocuous dispute over elephants raised persistent questions about the legal status of the princely states and over the situations in which the British could intervene in state affairs. As a result, schemas of sovereignty became particularly significant in defining the relationship between the princely states and the British government.

The concept of sovereignty also lay at the heart of the attempts of the international legal profession to come to terms with European colonialism. During the 'age of empire',[8] many international lawyers envisaged a world composed of states that were recognized as 'civilized' by those already part of the international community. Late nineteenth-century international law, then, distinguished between 'civilized' Europe and 'uncivilized' non-Europeans to define sovereignty so as to exclude the latter.[9] As Lauren Benton notes, this conceptualization did not clarify how sub-imperial polities like the princely states, which both exercised sovereign powers and were subject to imperial authority, fitted within the broader configuration. Benton argues that when faced with this problem, British colonial officials such as Henry Maine and Charles Lewis Tupper created a new jurisprudence of

[5] *Empress* v. *Keshub Mahajan*, [1882] 8 Cal 985. A copy of the judgment can also be found in Proceedings of the Government of India in the Foreign Department, Internal, Political, August 1884, no. 103, IOR/P/2335.

[6] Letter from the Junior Under-Secretary to the Government of India, Foreign Department to the Chief Secretary to the Government of Bengal, no. 3282I, 19 July 1887, Proceedings of the Government of India in the Foreign Department, Internal, July 1887, no. 350, IOR/P/3039.

[7] Lauren Benton provides an overview of the struggles of British officials to classify the princely states by analysing a late nineteenth-century crisis in the state of Baroda. See Lauren Benton, 'From International Law to Imperial Constitutions: The Problem of Quasi-Sovereignty, 1870–1900', *Law and History Review*, 26/3 (2008), 595–619. She also discusses these endeavours, linking them with the discourse about the backwardness of hill regions, in Lauren Benton, *A Search for Sovereignty: Law and Geography in European Empires, 1400–1900* (Cambridge: Cambridge University Press, 2010), 222–278. Eric Lewis Beverley traces jurisdictional conflicts along the border between the state of Hyderabad and Bombay in British India as well as Hyderabadi attempts to assert sovereignty over urban spaces in Eric Lewis Beverley, *Hyderabad, British India, and the World: Muslim Networks and Minor Sovereignty, c. 1850–1950* (Cambridge: Cambridge University Press, 2015), 186–255. Beyond the princely states, there is also work on the disputes generated by the lumpiness of sovereignty in the frontier regions of British India. See Christoph Bergmann, 'Confluent Territories and Overlapping Sovereignties: Britain's Nineteenth-Century Indian Empire in the Kumaon Himalaya', *Journal of Historical Geography* 51 (2016), 88–98; and Reeju Ray, 'Interrupted Sovereignties in the North East Frontier of British India, 1787–1870', *Modern Asian Studies*, 53/2 (2019), 606–632.

[8] I borrow this term from Eric Hobsbawm, *The Age of Empire: 1875–1914* (New York: Pantheon Books, 1987).

[9] Antony Anghie, *Imperialism, Sovereignty and the Making of International Law* (Cambridge: Cambridge University Press, 2005), 33–35.

'imperial law' with distinctive qualities; it was 'a hybrid of municipal law and international law that could encompass divided sovereignty'. In this scheme, '[r]ather than signifying a quality that a state either possessed or failed to retain, sovereignty could be held by degrees, with full sovereignty reserved for the imperial power'.[10] The construction of 'imperial law', however, did not resolve questions of sovereignty or the significance of international law for the princely states. Instead, the legal wrangle over their international status continued into the twentieth century.[11]

Amidst these jurisdictional tangles, scholars have traced British attempts to define sovereignty in a manner that would enable paramountcy to ultimately reside with the colonial state. Ian Copland and Barbara Ramusack describe how the legal manoeuvres of late nineteenth-century colonial officials stripped the princely states of much of their sovereignty.[12] Lauren Benton argues that the British advocacy of 'divisible' sovereignty often occasioned the 'outright suspension of law';[13] quasi-sovereign entities such as the princely states, therefore, were examples of 'anomalous legal spaces, where imperial law applied differently—and sometimes not at all'.[14] These views, however, capture only one side of the legal debates; the states' responses to the endeavours of colonial officials, although sometimes alluded to, remain largely unmapped. Benton, for instance, touches on legal arguments made by the states but does not explore them in depth.[15] Legal language, however, was a feature of arguments made by both the British and the princes in these jurisdictional conflicts.

This all-round reliance on legal language was facilitated by the lack of a clear boundary between the imperial and international spheres, which, as seen in the previous chapter, had plagued colonial administrators in the early nineteenth century and which continued into the latter half of the century. The consequences of this fluidity were significant: it enabled a variety of interested players, including international lawyers, British politicians, colonial officials, rulers of princely states, and their advisors, to appropriate international legal language in different ways during jurisdictional disputes. Specifically, these actors articulated differing

[10] Benton, *A Search for Sovereignty*, (n 7) 238, 294, 245. For the argument that sovereignty was consolidated, albeit only for the 'last five minutes' of the nineteenth century, into an abstract idea in terms of which it was absolute, exclusive within its territory, excluding other, overlapping authorities, and thereby an 'on/off affair', see David Kennedy, 'International Law and the Nineteenth Century: History of an Illusion', *Quinnipiac Law Review*, 17/1 (1997), 99–138.

[11] Eric Beverley makes this point in relation to the state of Hyderabad. See Beverley, *Hyderabad, British India, and the World*, (n 7) 54–72. See also Oliver Godsmark, 'Fragmented Sovereignty, *Ḍakaitī* (Banditry), and "Criminal Tribe" in a "Minor" State of Late Colonial India', *The Historical Journal*, 66/2 (2023), 435–458.

[12] Ian Copland, *The British Raj and the Indian Princes: Paramountcy in Western India, 1857–1930* (Bombay: Orient Longman, 1982), 211–221; Ian Copland, *The Princes of India in the Endgame of Empire, 1917–1947* (Cambridge: Cambridge University Press, 1997), 19–20; and Barbara Ramusack, *The Indian Princes and their States* (Cambridge: Cambridge University Press, 2004), 92–97.

[13] Benton, *A Search for Sovereignty*, (n 7) 241.

[14] Benton, 'From International Law to Imperial Constitutions', (n 7) 600.

[15] Benton, *A Search for Sovereignty*, (n 7) 265.

versions of the idea of sovereignty to resolve questions surrounding the legal status of the princely states and the scope of the powers exercised by the states and the British government. In the process of 'jousting over jurisdiction',[16] therefore, both the princely states and the British government considered the concept of sovereignty to be the tool and the terrain of legal and political struggle.

To trace these varied iterations of sovereignty, I examine legal texts authored by nineteenth-century British international lawyers and colonial officials as well as imperial legal practice, using the arguments made in two jurisdictional disputes between the princely states and the British government as a fulcrum for analysis. By analysing colonial legal arguments and princely state responses, we can see that there were two opposing conceptions of sovereignty articulated in late nineteenth-century South Asia. British colonial officials, influenced by Henry Maine, argued that sovereignty was 'divisible', 'flexible', and a 'question of historical fact'. This understanding allowed the British to rely on the separate legal status of the princely states to maintain them as 'allies' in the imperial project, while also affirming the right to intervene in the internal affairs of the states. However, on account of the capacity of sovereignty to be defined in multiple ways, the princely states were able to weigh in with their own contentions in response to British legal arguments. State representatives argued that sovereignty was 'absolute' and 'territorial' to defend the states' jurisdiction from British interference and to consolidate control in the effort to construct powerful, centralized administrations; these endeavours were successful to a limited extent. Princes, their political advisors, and state bureaucrats, therefore, played a significant role in negotiating relations between the states and the British colonial power.

In this chapter, I trace the way international law, and the doctrine of sovereignty in particular, became the common language of choice to conduct deliberations over the legal status of the princely states. First, I discuss the significance of sovereignty in late nineteenth-century international law, tracing the different approaches taken by scholars in the period to the legal status of entities such as the princely states. In particular, I focus on the work of Henry Maine to trace the theoretical basis of the conception of 'divisible' sovereignty, which became the legal foundation of the turn in British imperial ideology towards working with local rulers rather than annexing territory. Then, I study the way three colonial officials in the Political

[16] This is inspired by Lauren Benton's use of the term 'jurisdictional jockeying'. She uses it to describe both the competition among colonial authorities to gain jurisdiction over disputes and the strategic use of institutional gaps by litigants in their own favour. See Lauren Benton, *Law and Colonial Cultures: Legal Regimes in World History, 1400–1900* (Cambridge: Cambridge University Press, 2002), 2–33. I prefer to use 'jurisdictional jousting' to provide a clearer focus on the competition among state authorities (i.e. the princely states and the British government) over jurisdiction rather than actions of forum shopping in which a number of low-level participants engaged in the imperial world. Mitra Sharafi also takes inspiration from Benton but chooses to use the term 'jurisdictional jostling' to describe forum shopping in order to emphasize 'the often clumsy nature of these moves', as in her view, the term 'jockeying' implies 'a certain amount of skill'. See Mitra Sharafi, 'The Marital Patchwork of Colonial South Asia: Forum Shopping from Britain to Baroda', *Law and History Review*, 28/4 (2010), 981.

Department of the government of India (Charles Aitchison, Charles Lewis Tupper, and William Lee-Warner) adapted Maine's theory of divisible sovereignty and developed a system of precedent to expand British authority over the princely states. After analysing the British understanding of sovereignty, I move toward exploring the approach taken by the princely states. Specifically, I review the princely state conception of 'territorial' sovereignty by examining the legal arguments made by state officials in two jurisdictional disputes: the dispute between Travancore and the British government over criminal jurisdiction over European British subjects and the dispute between Baroda and the British government over jurisdiction over telegraph lines. By examining these historical debates, we can better appreciate the crucial role played by the doctrine of sovereignty in the construction of imperial and global legal structures in the latter half of the nineteenth century.

The Princely States, Sovereignty, and Late Nineteenth-Century International Law

Much like their contemporary counterparts, late nineteenth-century international lawyers were engaged in fierce debates on the scope and limits of 'the international'. More specifically, they sought to demarcate the frontiers of the spheres of national, imperial, and international law during a period when empire loomed large[17] over the newly developing field of international law.[18]

While international lawyers in the first half of the nineteenth century had emphasized the simultaneously universal and particularly Christian nature of international law, many late-nineteenth century jurists relied on the narrower idea of the 'standard of civilization' to draw these boundaries, which limited the applicability of international law to 'civilized', primarily European states.[19] For instance,

[17] For instance, John Westlake dedicated three of the eleven chapters of his international law textbook to colonial issues, including an entire chapter to 'The Empire of India'. See John Westlake, *Chapters on the Principles of International Law* (Cambridge: Cambridge University Press, 1894). Scholars have noted that 'the British rarely lost sight of the commanding ambitions of their Empire, which seemed particularly to condition their attitudes to any international juristic order'. See William Cornish, 'International Law', in William Cornish et al., eds., *The Oxford History of the Laws of England*, xi: *1820–1914: English Legal System* (Oxford: Oxford University Press, 2010), 263.

[18] The late nineteenth century is often seen as a formative period in the history of international law. For some, this is because of the 'professionalization' of international law through the establishment of associations and chairs at universities. See Martti Koskenniemi, *The Gentle Civilizer of Nations: The Rise and Fall of International Law, 1870–1960* (Cambridge: Cambridge University Press, 2001), 11–97; and Casper Sylvest, 'International Law in Nineteenth-Century Britain', *British Year Book of International Law*, 75 (2004), 9–70. For others, it is because of changes in doctrine rather than the structures of the profession. See Anghie, *Imperialism, Sovereignty and the Making of International Law*, (n 9) 32–33; and C. H. Alexandrowicz, 'Some Problems in the History of the Law of Nations in Asia', in David Armitage and Jennifer Pitts, eds., *The Law of Nations in Global History* (Oxford: Oxford University Press, 2017), 79–80.

[19] The most comprehensive analysis of the effect of the idea of the 'standard of civilization' on the construction of the doctrine of sovereignty in nineteenth-century international law is in Anghie, *Imperialism, Sovereignty and the Making of International Law*, (n 9) 32–114.

John Westlake, one of the most influential British international lawyers of the time,[20] argued that international society was geographically limited to European and American states, and 'a few Christian states in other parts of the world'. This was because international law was 'social' and had to be 'well adapted to the character and circumstances of the men who are to observe it'.[21] Westlake's contemporary, the English lawyer William Edward Hall,[22] also thought that international law was 'a product of the special civilisation of modern Europe, and forms a highly artificial system of which the principles cannot be supposed to be understood or recognised by countries differently civilised'.[23] This view was shared by Thomas Joseph Lawrence, a lawyer and clergyman[24] who argued that international law was a body of rules that 'grew up in Christian Europe, though some of its roots may be traced back to ancient Greece and ancient Rome', and then spread to 'all civilized communities outside the European boundaries'.[25] In the eyes of these scholars, international law was 'based on the possession by states of a common and in that sense an equal civilization'.[26]

On account of the 'civilized/uncivilized' dichotomy, these scholars drew relatively sharp distinctions between the international and imperial spheres. Instead of following his predecessor Robert Phillimore's view that international law applied in a more relaxed manner to the princely states, Westlake argued that the relationship between the princely states and the British government had 'shifted from an international to an imperial basis',[27] relegating the governance of princely states to imperial constitutional law.[28] Lawrence also claimed that the princely states were 'not even part-sovereign' and thereby not subjects of international law.[29] Hall shared this view, noting that entities such as the princely states 'are of course not subjects of international law'.[30] These jurists then proceeded to devise a series of techniques to 'civilize the uncivilized' in order to bring non-European peoples into the realm

[20] Westlake was appointed Whewell Professor of International Law at Cambridge in 1888. See Nathan Wells, 'Westlake, John (1828–1913)', in David Cannadine, ed., *Oxford Dictionary of National Biography* (online edn, Oxford: Oxford University Press, 2004), https://doi.org/10.1093/ref:odnb/36840, accessed 23 May 2019.

[21] Westlake, *Chapters on the Principles of International Law*, (n 17) 80–81.

[22] T. E. Holland, 'Hall, William Edward (1835–1894)', rev. Catherine Pease-Watkin, in *Oxford Dictionary of National Biography*, https://doi.org/10.1093/ref:odnb/11997, accessed 23 May 2019.

[23] William Edward Hall, *International Law* (Oxford: Clarendon Press, 1880), 34.

[24] A. Pearce Higgins, 'The Late Doctor T. J. Lawrence', *British Year Book of International Law*, 1 (1920–21), 233.

[25] T. J. Lawrence, *The Principles of International Law* (Boston, MA: D. C. Heath & Co., 1895), 4–5, 26.

[26] Westlake, *Chapters on the Principles of International Law*, (n 17) 102–103.

[27] ibid 204.

[28] Lauren Benton argues that Westlake continued to regard international law as having 'the power of analogy' in relation to the princely states despite relegating them to the 'imperial' field. See Benton, *A Search for Sovereignty*, (n 7) 239. However, Westlake's contemporaries in South Asia were more circumspect of his views on the princely states and his advocacy of a constitutional tie between the states and the British government; see, for instance, the discussion on William Lee-Warner below.

[29] Lawrence, *The Principles of International Law*, (n 25) 68.

[30] Hall, *International Law*, (n 23) 23 n. 2.

of international law. The ideological basis of this approach was, as Antony Anghie argues, the idea of expanding European empires for the purpose of educating and improving the lives of the colonized peoples.[31]

In the second half of the nineteenth century, however, justifications of imperial rule based on the idea of the 'civilizing mission' were undergoing a broad critique in South Asia, largely on account of the events of 1857. This was the year in which almost the whole of northern India broke out in a widespread and violent revolt, the intensity of which left a deep impression on British administrators. There was broad participation in the revolt, which included a military mutiny, peasant uprisings, and rebellions led by deposed rulers and landlords. The British repressed the revolt after a long and violent siege and transferred control over territories in South Asia from the East India Company to the Crown.[32] Karuna Mantena notes that prior to the rebellion, 'liberal' imperial administrators inspired by the 'civilizing mission' had engaged in deeply interventionist modes of rule to radically reconstruct 'native societies'.[33] As I described in the previous chapter, this project included the annexation of princely states that, in the opinion of British administrators, had failed to provide 'good government' to their subjects. Allegations of misgovernment were brought to justify the annexations of Jhansi and Awadh,[34] both of which became centres of the uprising in 1857. Consequently, Conservative politicians in Britain and colonial officials attributed the revolt to the 'Evangelical zeal of the liberals'. The second half of the nineteenth century was, therefore, dominated by an imperial ideology that focused on rule through local rulers, chiefs, and power brokers.[35] The increasingly dominant view within the British establishment was that the rulers of the princely states were 'traditional' or 'natural' leaders who commanded the respect, loyalty, and obedience of the Indian masses who were immune to earlier projects of reform.[36] However, the language of 'good

[31] Anghie, *Imperialism, Sovereignty and the Making of International Law*, (n 9) 96.

[32] On the revolt, see Barbara D. Metcalf and Thomas R. Metcalf, *A Concise History of Modern India* (2nd edn, Cambridge: Cambridge University Press, 2006), 92–114; Ian Talbot, *A History of Modern South Asia: Politics, States, Diasporas* (New Haven, CT: Yale University Press, 2016), 75–89; and Sugata Bose and Ayesha Jalal, *Modern South Asia: History, Culture, Political Economy* (4th edn, London: Routledge, 2018), 77–84.

[33] Karuna Mantena, *Alibis of Empire: Henry Maine and the Ends of Liberal Imperialism* (Princeton, NJ: Princeton University Press, 2010), 1–2.

[34] Ramusack, *The Indian Princes and their States*, (n 12) 81–84.

[35] Partha Chatterjee, *The Black Hole of Empire: History of a Global Practice of Power* (Princeton, NJ: Princeton University Press, 2012), 212. For further discussion of the causes and consequences of the revolt, see Thomas Metcalf, *The Aftermath of Revolt: India, 1857–1870* (Princeton, NJ: Princeton University Press, 1964), 219–227; Copland, *The British Raj and the Indian Princes*, (n 12) 88–98; and Mantena, *Alibis of Empire*, (n 33) 1–7. For a discussion of the reactions of Conservative politicians in metropolitan Britain, see Matthew Stubbings, 'British Conservatism and the Indian Revolt: The Annexation of Awadh and the Consequences of Liberal Empire, 1856–1858', *Journal of British Studies*, 55/4 (2016), 728–749.

[36] Michael H. Fisher, 'Diplomacy in India, 1526–1858', in H. V. Bowen, Elizabeth Mancke, and John G. Reid, eds., *Britain's Oceanic Empire: Atlantic and Indian Ocean Worlds, c. 1550–1850* (Cambridge: Cambridge University Press, 2012), 265; and Mantena, *Alibis of Empire*, (n 33) 52.

government' and 'progress' continued to be employed to rank and rate these rulers.[37]

This change in imperial ideology was facilitated by Henry Maine's nuanced critique of the liberal view of empire. Maine was a leading Victorian jurist; between 1862 and 1869 he was also a prominent member of Britain's colonial administration in India as law member in the Council of the Viceroy and Governor-General of India. On his return to England, he was appointed Corpus Professor of Jurisprudence at Oxford; in 1871, he became a member of the secretary of state's Council of India in London;[38] in 1887, he was elected Whewell Professor of International Law at Cambridge.[39]

As Karuna Mantena notes, Maine was a central figure in the late nineteenth-century reconfiguration of ideas about modernity and progress. He constructed a binary model: ancient societies were based around communities and fractured on contact with imperial rule by societies that had reached later stages of evolution and were focused on the individual. But rather than advocating the end of imperialism, he contended that only the British empire's dominance could prevent a further dissolution of 'traditional' societies. To avert fresh episodes of rebellion that would threaten the stability of the empire, he argued in favour of 'the preservation and incorporation of native institutions into imperial power structures'.[40] The princely states were the archetype of such 'native' institutions. Since maintaining alliances with entities such as the princely states necessitated their legal recognition in some form, it also required reinterpreting the concept of sovereignty and the nature of the boundary between imperial and international law, drawn so sharply by international law scholars like Westlake, Hall, and Lawrence. Key to this change was Maine's conceptualization of sovereignty as 'divisible'.[41]

[37] Manu Bhagavan, *Sovereign Spheres: Princes, Education, and Empire in Colonial India* (Oxford: Oxford University Press, 2003), 3–4.

[38] R. C. J. Cocks, 'Maine, Sir Henry James Sumner (1822–1888)', in *Oxford Dictionary of National Biography*, https://doi.org/10.1093/ref:odnb/17808, accessed 23 May 2019.

[39] Maine had considered standing for the Whewell professorship as early as 1867, with a view to having a settled position after his upcoming return to England from India. See George Feaver, *From Status to Contract: A Biography of Sir Henry Maine 1822–1888* (London: Longmans, 1969), 109–110, 255–257.

[40] Mantena, *Alibis of Empire*, (n 33) 57, 177, 171.

[41] Two decades ago, Carl Landauer pointed out that Maine's multiple biographers rarely paid attention to his ideas on international law. See Carl Landauer, 'From Status to Treaty: Henry Sumner Maine's *International Law*', *Canadian Journal of Law and Jurisprudence*, 15/2 (2002), 221. This has changed in recent years, with scholars considering Maine's conception of sovereignty within the context of trends in Victorian international law, in social thought, or in imperial legal practice. See Michael Lobban, 'English Approaches to International Law in the Nineteenth Century', in Matthew Craven, Malgosia Fitzmaurice, and Maria Vogiatzi, eds., *Time, History and International Law* (Leiden: Martinus Nijhoff Publishers, 2007), 65–90; Benton, 'From International Law to Imperial Constitutions', (n 7) 603–607; Casper Sylvest, *British Liberal Internationalism, 1880–1930: Making Progress?* (Manchester: Manchester University Press, 2009), 61–100; Benton, *A Search for Sovereignty*, (n 7) 246–250; Mantena, *Alibis of Empire*, (n 33) 113–118; and Jennifer Pitts, *Boundaries of the International: Law and Empire* (Cambridge, MA: Harvard University Press, 2018), 148–184.

Maine first discussed the concept of sovereignty in an 1855 paper that he delivered before the Juridical Society. There he regretted the tendency of 'the great majority of contemporary writers on International Law [to] tacitly assume that the doctrines of their system, founded on the principles of equity and common sense, were capable of being readily reasoned over in every stage of modern civilization' when, in fact, the explanation behind the doctrines was 'entirely historical'.[42] This historical approach contrasted with what he considered to be the abstract and ahistorical analytical school of jurisprudence, which was predominant in England at the time and was exemplified in the work of John Austin. In Maine's view, Austin's definition of law as 'the command of the sovereign' placed an overwhelming emphasis on the coercive power of a sovereign as the source of legal obligation. This position, he argued, was the outcome of abstraction, which neglected 'the entire mass of its historical antecedents, which in each community determines how the Sovereign shall exercise or forbear from exercising his irresistible coercive power'. The result was that law, as defined by analytical jurisprudence, was exclusively the product of coercive force and required the backing of a sanction.[43] Maine argued instead that the link between coercive force and legal obligation was not a logically necessary one but rather was the product of particular historical and social processes. He contended that sovereignty in Europe was linked to legislative activity on account of the influence of the Roman empire, which had both legislated and levied taxes. The result of the Roman legacy was the modern social organization of western Europe: highly centralized, actively legislating, territorially sovereign nation-states.[44] This position, however, was historically exceptional since other ancient empires had raised revenues and armies but had interfered only minimally in the civil and religious life of their subjects.[45] Consequently, other empires had not developed along the lines of centralized western European states. Maine even doubted the status of the United States and the German empire, whose constituent states exercised significant sovereign powers.[46]

Relying on the claim of a radical difference between 'traditional' societies that were based around local communities (rather than a distant ruler) and 'modern', centralized western European states, Maine rejected the analytical school's insistence on the indivisibility of sovereignty. Instead, he contended that '[t]he powers of sovereigns are a bundle or collection of powers, and they may be separated one from another'.[47] Maine sharpened this idea of the 'divisibility' of sovereignty in the

[42] Henry Sumner Maine, 'The Conception of Sovereignty and Its Importance in International Law', *Papers of the Juridical Society* (1855), 40.

[43] Henry Sumner Maine, *Lectures on the Early History of Institutions* (London: John Murray, 1875), 360, 363.

[44] Mantena, *Alibis of Empire*, (n 33) 116.

[45] Maine, *Lectures on the Early History of Institutions*, (n 43) 383, 389–393.

[46] Maine, 'The Conception of Sovereignty and Its Importance in International Law', (n 42) 40–45.

[47] Henry Sumner Maine, *International Law* (London: John Murray, 1888), 58.

context of theorizing the relationship between the princely states and the British government.

In 1864, Maine wrote what was to become a tremendously influential minute on the sovereignty of Kathiawar, the collective name for several small princely states in the peninsular region of western India.[48] Before the arrival of the British, the rulers of the Kathiawar states had recognized the supremacy of a succession of overlords, including the *sultans* of Delhi, the Mughals, and the Marathas, through the payment of tribute. In 1820, after a series of agreements, the East India Company obtained the right of tribute over the region.[49] In the 1830s, Company interventions in Kathiawar affairs increased; for instance, it took over criminal jurisdiction in the states. Despite these developments, on several occasions Company officials stated clearly that Kathiawar was not part of British territory, indicating their recognition of the separate legal status of the princely states.[50]

A rather innocuous attempt to transfer jurisdiction over the state of Bhavnagar from Ahmedabad authorities (in British India) to the Kathiawar political agent (a British representative in princely state territory) set the stage for Maine's minute.[51] This process ran into trouble when the Finance Department of the government of India questioned whether Kathiawar was part of British territory. If Kathiawar was foreign territory, then the proposed transfer could not be done by legislation. It would require a properly ratified treaty of cession since the change would not merely reorganize territory but transfer it to a foreign sovereign.[52]

The members of the Council of the Government of Bombay, a province in British India, unanimously decided that Kathiawar was British territory,[53] with the governor, Henry Bartle Frere, contending that the Kathiawar rulers' minimal rights, such as jurisdiction over their own subjects, could not be called rights of

[48] As the key theoretical basis of the British understanding of princely state sovereignty, Maine's minute has received considerable scholarly attention. It is extracted as one of the main documents defining the relationship between the princely states and the British government in Adrian Sever, ed., *Documents and Speeches on the Indian Princely States*, i (Delhi: B. R. Publishing, 1985). Both princely state historians and legal historians have discussed it. See Ramusack, *The Indian Princes and their States*, (n 12) 94–96; Benton, 'From International Law to Imperial Constitutions', (n 7) 604–607; and Benton, *A Search for Sovereignty*, (n 7) 247–250. For a discussion of the Kathiawar dispute more generally, see Copland, (n 12) *The British Raj and the Indian Princes*, 98–112.

[49] John McLeod, *Sovereignty, Power, Control: Politics in the States of Western India, 1916–1947* (Leiden: Brill, 1999), 14–19.

[50] In 1858, the East India Company's court of directors wrote, 'We cannot, however, dismiss the correspondence which has arisen out of these questions of jurisdiction, without expressing our surprise that an officer in the high political position occupied by Major Davidson (Resident at Baroda), should have declared his opinion that "the whole province of Kattyawar, with the exception of the districts belonging to the Gaekwar is British territory and its inhabitants are British subjects"'. See Despatch of the Court of Directors, no. 8, 31 March 1858, IOR/L/PS/6/532.

[51] Minute by Governor of Bombay, 22 July 1860, IOR/L/PS/6/532; and Letter from the Under-Secretary, Government of India to the Government of Bombay, no. 3174, 12 July 1861, IOR/L/PS/6/532.

[52] Extract from the Proceedings of the Finance Department, Government of India, 10 February 1862, IOR/L/PS/6/532.

[53] Letter from the Chief Secretary, Government of Bombay to the Government of India, no. 119, 17 October 1863, IOR/L/PS/6/532.

sovereignty.[54] Henry Mortimer Durand, the foreign secretary of the government of India, agreed with the Bombay Council, arguing that the Kathiawar rulers had the status of dependents. He dismissed the East India Company's earlier declaration of Kathiawar as foreign territory, arguing that it had been a confidential expression of views, and not a formal and publicly promulgated renunciation of British sovereign rights.[55] The matter was referred to the Council of the Viceroy and Governor-General of India, of which Maine was the law member.

In his minute, Maine defined sovereignty as

> ... a term which, in International Law, indicates a well ascertained assemblage of separate powers or privileges. The rights which form part of the aggregate are specifically named by publicists, who distinguish them as the right to make war and peace, the right to administer civil and criminal justice, the right to legislate, and so forth. A sovereign who possesses the whole of this aggregate of rights is called an independent sovereign, but there is not, nor has there ever been, anything in International Law to prevent some of these rights being lodged with one possessor and some with another. Sovereignty has always been regarded as divisible.[56]

He went on to note, '"sovereignty" is divisible, but "independence" is not'. In his view, the British government was the only independent sovereign in India but there also existed numerous other sovereigns, i.e. the princely states, which were not independent.[57]

Maine also argued that sovereignty, for the purposes of international law, was a 'question of fact' that had to be separately decided in each case and to which 'no general rules' applied. Treaties often contained the way sovereign rights were to be divided, but when there were no written documents or when the documents were ambiguous, jurists could determine this distribution from the *de facto* relations of the states with the British government. Maine proceeded to conduct a factual analysis of the situation and concluded that the principal right the Kathiawar states enjoyed was immunity from foreign laws; other rights included the exercise of limited civil and criminal jurisdiction and the right to coin money. He therefore approved of British interference for the improvement in administration so long as it did not disturb the unqualified immunity of the states from foreign laws. However, he also admitted that the Kathiawar states enjoyed some limited degree of sovereignty, and hence were foreign territory, so international rules and conceptions applied to them 'in some sense'.[58]

54 Minute by Henry Bartle Frere, the Governor of Bombay, 21 March 1863, IOR/L/PS/6/532.
55 Note by Henry Mortimer Durand, Foreign Secretary, Government of India, 13 April 1864, IOR/L/PS/6/532.
56 Minute by Henry Sumner Maine, 22 March 1864, IOR/L/PS/6/532.
57 ibid.
58 ibid.

Another Council member, H. B. Harington, agreed, and quoted the work of the American international lawyer Henry Wheaton to argue that the exercise of some rights by the British did not mean that the Kathiawar chiefs had lost all their rights of sovereignty. Like Maine, however, he argued that this did not prevent the British, as the 'paramount power', from intervening to improve the peace.[59] The viceroy, John Lawrence, also expressed his support for the divided nature of Kathiawar sovereignty, contending that 'although Kattywar is British Territory in the sense that its Chiefs and people owe allegiance to the sovereignty of the British Crown, yet it is not British Territory in the sense of its being subject to British Laws, Regulations, and Administration'; hence, British laws could not be extended to the region.[60]

Maine's views received a stamp of approval when the secretary of state for India, Charles Wood, recognized the 'modified form of sovereignty' of the region. Wood argued that although the British government had intervened in Kathiawar for the maintenance of order, it had never imposed British laws since official policy was not aimed at undermining the authority and independence of local chiefs, but rather to work through the agency of these rulers.[61]

The Kathiawar minute exemplified Maine's historical approach to legal concepts such as sovereignty, with the idea that the princely states possessed only certain sovereign rights (the remainder being exercised by the British government) fitting within his broader understanding of 'native' societies as radically different from 'modern' centralized European nation-states. By arguing that sovereignty was divisible, and thereby that the Kathiawar rulers were both sovereign and not sovereign, Maine softened the boundary between imperial and international law and advocated the application of international law to the states 'in some sense', for instance, in the case of treaty interpretation or sovereign immunity, but not in others.[62] Like Maine's thought in general, this conceptualization of the fuzzy frontiers of national, imperial, and international law enabled the British to entrench their paramountcy in South Asia by providing the legal basis of the post-1857 imperial ideology of the recognition of the princely states and their simultaneous incorporation into the broader imperial hierarchy.[63] Consequently, the British abandoned their earlier policy of princely state annexation, and replaced it with a strategy of providing support to the princes to maintain them as 'junior allies' in the imperial project. Maine's approach proved to be an inspiration for the Political Department of the

[59] Minute by H. B. Harington, 16 March 1864, IOR/L/PS/6/532.

[60] Minute by the Viceroy and Governor-General and President of the Council of India, 23 February 1864, IOR/L/PS/6/532.

[61] Despatch of the Secretary of State for India to the Government of India, no. 79, 16 December 1864, IOR/L/PS/6/597.

[62] Lauren Benton, however, argues that Maine distanced the princely states from international law. See Benton, *A Search for Sovereignty*, (n 7) 249.

[63] As Jennifer Pitts notes, the 'inclusion' of certain entities into the international community on unequal terms was often the basis for the dispossession and subjugation of indigenous peoples. See Pitts, *Boundaries of the International*, (n 41) 8–10.

government of India, influencing successive generations of British political officers in the late nineteenth century.[64] These political officials interpreted Maine in different ways and drew on his ideas to develop a coherent approach to understanding the relationship between the princely states and the British government.

Divisible Sovereignty and the Indian Political Department

Officials of the Political Department of the government of India played a key role in managing British relations with the princely states. Around seventy per cent of serving political officers had an army background. Although Ian Copland claims that the preference for military men meant that the Political Department 'became a byword for intellectual mediocrity',[65] the most influential members of the department were civil servants who had passed competitive examinations for their place.[66] Political officers did not have any special administrative or diplomatic training and relied largely on learning through experience.[67] Internal Political Department texts and manuals, therefore, became particularly significant in guiding officials in their work. Consequently, understanding the nuances of these texts is crucial for analysing the British colonial view of princely state sovereignty and the nature of the relationship between the states and the British government.[68]

One of the first of the Political Department treatises was an 1875 tract titled *The Native States of India*,[69] written by Charles Aitchison, a political officer who spent much of his career in Punjab and rose to become the foreign secretary of the government of India.[70] Although he did not specifically acknowledge Maine's Kathiawar minute (he did, however, cite *Ancient Law*[71]), Aitchison emphasized the divisibility of sovereignty by arguing that sovereignty was 'an assemblage of powers

[64] Maine's influence is unsurprising as his texts were required reading for members of the Indian Civil Service. See Mantena, *Alibis of Empire*, (n 33) 155.

[65] Ian Copland, 'The Other Guardians: Ideology and Performance in the Indian Political Service', in Robin Jeffrey, ed., *People, Princes and Paramount Power: Society and Politics in the Indian Princely States* (Delhi: Oxford University Press, 1973), 287.

[66] The first annual open competitive examination for recruitment to the Indian Civil Service was held in 1855; men recruited in the early decades of open competition were referred to as 'competition wallahs'. See Takehiko Honda, 'Competition wallahs (*act.* 1855–1891)', in *Oxford Dictionary of National Biography*, https://doi.org/10.1093/ref:odnb/95501, accessed 23 May 2019.

[67] Ramusack, *The Indian Princes and their States*, (n 12) 101.

[68] For other analyses of these texts, see Copland, *The British Raj and the Indian Princes*, (n 12) 211–221; Copland, *The Princes of India in the Endgame of Empire*, (n 12) 19–20; Ramusack, *The Indian Princes and their States*, (n 12) 92–97; Benton, 'From International Law to Imperial Constitutions', (n 7) 600–607; and Benton, *A Search for Sovereignty*, (n 7) 242–250.

[69] Charles U. Aitchison, *The Native States of India: An Attempt to Elucidate a Few of the Principles which Underlie their Relations with the British Government* (2nd edn, Calcutta: Office of the Superintendent of Government Printing, 1881).

[70] A. J. Arbuthnot, 'Aitchison, Sir Charles Umpherston (1832–1896)', rev. Ian Talbot, in *Oxford Dictionary of National Biography*, https://doi.org/10.1093/ref:odnb/253, accessed 23 May 2019.

[71] Henry Sumner Maine, *Ancient Law* (London: John Murray, 1861).

or attributes which may either be all concentrated in one possessor or shared with another'. With respect to the princely states, he noted that sovereignty was shared between the British government and the princes in varying degrees. The princely states enjoyed sovereign power 'more or less imperfect' but did not possess 'international life'. Although Aitchison argued that international law did not apply to the relations between the British government and the princely states, he noted that it could be a useful guide for the settlement of disputes to the extent that it was 'an embodiment of principles of natural equity, or of usages which independent nations have found it convenient or for their common advantage to agree upon regulating their intercourse with each other'.[72]

Aitchison's enduring contribution to the Political Department did not lie in the treatise but rather in his work on the compilation of treaties between the princely states and the British government.[73] He built on the idea that he first developed in his monograph, where he had outlined general principles drawn from a series of disputes between the states and the British government; these principles, he argued, sustained British relations with the states. This was the first indication of the development of precedent to define the relationship. In the compilation, Aitchison listed the treaties state-wise, and prefaced each one with a detailed historical narrative,[74] arguing that the treaties had to be interpreted based on the evolution of the relationship between the states and the British government.[75] Aitchison's successors in the Political Department built upon this insight to argue that 'decisions' in later 'cases' or disputes could be used to override specific provisions in the treaties, most often at the expense of the states.

One of these successors was Charles Lewis Tupper, also a man who spent much of his official life in Punjab.[76] Tupper freely admitted his intellectual debt to Maine, noting that 'his pregnant suggestions have constantly guided my work in India, and throughout my life have chiefly inspired my studies'.[77] In 1893, Tupper published an unofficial text, *Our Indian Protectorate*,[78] in which he provided an outline of 'Indian political law', a term he used to refer to the law that governed the relationship between the princely states and the British government. For Tupper, one of the

[72] Aitchison, *The Native States of India*, (n 69) 34, 6, 2.

[73] Charles U. Aitchison, ed., *A Collection of Treaties, Engagements and Sanads Relating to India and Neighbouring Countries*, 14 vols (5th edn, Calcutta: Government of India Central Publication Branch, 1929–1933). The first volume was published in 1862; eleven volumes appeared by 1892 and the Political Department continued to update the collection after Aitchison's retirement. See Arbuthnot, 'Aitchison, Sir Charles Umpherston', (n 70).

[74] Arbuthnot, 'Aitchison, Sir Charles Umpherston', (n 70).

[75] Copland, *The Princes of India in the Endgame of Empire*, (n 12) 19.

[76] Katherine Prior, 'Tupper, Sir (Charles) Lewis (1848–1910)', in *Oxford Dictionary of National Biography*, https://doi.org/10.1093/ref:odnb/36577, accessed 23 May 2019.

[77] Charles Lewis Tupper, 'India and Sir Henry Maine', *Journal of the Society of Arts*, 46/2365 (1898), 390.

[78] Charles Lewis Tupper, *Our Indian Protectorate: An Introduction to the Study of the Relations between the British Government and its Indian Feudatories* (London: Longmans, Green and Co., 1893).

basic principles underlying Indian political law was the divisibility of sovereignty; he quoted extensively from Maine's Kathiawar minute to support this contention. He described the princely states as 'autonomous states, enjoying various degrees of sovereignty, levying their own taxes, administering their own laws, and possessing territory which is, for purposes of internal administration, foreign territory, and has not been annexed to the dominions of the British Crown'. The states, however, did not have the right to external relations and were politically subordinate to the British government, and so, could not be subjects of international law.[79] Despite this assertion, Tupper, like Aitchison, did not entirely dismiss the application of international law to the princely states.[80] The states had immunity from foreign law, the British government concluded treaties with the states, and questions arose relating to boundary disputes, extraterritorial jurisdiction, and the extradition of offenders. In all these cases, Tupper argued that international law could be used to resolve the issue.[81]

Tupper's views proved to be influential and the government of India invited him to update *Leading Cases*, a textbook on Indian political practice written by Mortimer Durand.[82] The result was Tupper's four-volume *Indian Political Practice*,[83] a survey of major cases from which he drew the main principles governing the relationship between the British government and the princely states. The treatise became a reference manual for the Political Department, and was kept confidential.[84] Tupper included treaties with the princely states, provisions in British Indian statutes, and court decisions as sources of the principles, but noted that the most important source was the actual practice of the British government in its dealings with the states—what he dubbed 'usage'.[85] Tupper essentially

[79] ibid 6, 2, 4–5.

[80] Ian Copland and Barbara Ramusack both argue that Tupper considered the relationship between the princely states and the British government to be a feudal one. See Copland, *The British Raj and the Indian Princes*, (n 12) 218; and Ramusack, *The Indian Princes and their States*, (n 12) 96–97. Lauren Benton contends that Tupper rejected the use of the term 'international' in favour of the term 'political' law. See Benton, *A Search for Sovereignty*, (n 7) 244 n. 67.

[81] Tupper, *Our Indian Protectorate*, (n 78) 7–9.

[82] Henry Mortimer Durand was a former foreign secretary of the government of India. See H. V. Lovett, 'Durand, Sir (Henry) Mortimer (1850–1924)', rev. S. Gopal, in *Oxford Dictionary of National Biography*, https://doi.org/10.1093/ref:odnb/32941, accessed 23 May 2019. Tupper's first revision of *Leading Cases* was titled *Political Law and Policy* and although it was acknowledged as a brilliant piece of legal theorizing, it was considered insufficiently practical for the men in the field. Hence, Tupper was seconded to the government of India to enable him to produce his second version. See Prior, 'Tupper, Sir (Charles) Lewis', (n 76); and Copland, *The British Raj and the Indian Princes*, (n 12) 217–218.

[83] Charles Lewis Tupper, *Indian Political Practice: A Collection of the Decisions of the Government of India in Political Cases*, 4 vols (Calcutta: Office of the Superintendent of Government Printing, India, 1895; repr., Delhi: B. R. Publishing, 1974).

[84] William Murray Hogben, 'The Foreign and Political Department of the Government of India, 1876–1919: A Study in Imperial Careers and Attitudes', PhD thesis, University of Toronto, 1973, 194–197. By way of an example, the legal counsel representing the princes before the Indian States Committee in 1928 was denied access to copies of *Indian Political Practice* on account of its confidential nature. See Copland, *The Princes of India in the Endgame of Empire*, (n 12) 70.

[85] Tupper, *Our Indian Protectorate*, (n 78) 10.

produced a manual of case law to guide political officers in their work in relation to the princely states. The emphasis, building on Aitchison's work, was on historical practice to determine the way sovereign rights were divided between the princely states and the British government.[86] Tupper's work extended the idea that principles developed in the case of a single state were applicable in relation to all states; unsurprisingly, then, 'usage' formed the basis of British claims of more extensive sovereign powers, thereby strengthening British authority over the states.

The final architect of the legal understanding of the relations between the states and the British government was William Lee-Warner, who was largely based in the Bombay presidency through his career, and was Tupper's competitor in 'the realm of ideas, and for official favour'.[87] Lee-Warner also cited Maine to argue that sovereignty was divisible; in the case of the princely states, the distribution of sovereign powers was a question of fact to be determined by the evidence of treaties or usage. Of the two, he emphasized the role of usage; like Tupper, he argued that practice in relation to some states could constitute a precedent that was applicable against other states as well.[88] He first tried to promote his views in an 1886 manuscript titled *Elementary Treatise on the Conduct of Political Relations with Native States*; however, the government of India chose Tupper over him to compile a textbook on political practice.[89] In 1894, therefore, Lee-Warner published the work as a private individual, under the title *Protected Princes of India*, a revised version of which appeared in 1910 as *The Native States of India*.[90]

In comparison with Tupper and Aitchison, Lee-Warner was a much stronger proponent of the international status of the princely states.[91] He relied on the idea of divisible sovereignty to argue that the princely states were semi-sovereign since they possessed some (though not all) powers of a sovereign. He admitted that the tie between the princely states and the British government was not 'strictly' international since the states were not equal powers and had restrictions placed on both external relations and internal government. Despite this, he argued that it was possible to conceive of a sovereignty that, 'although wanting in completeness in every

[86] Parallels can perhaps be drawn with Tupper's other great work of the period, a multi-volume treatise titled *Punjab Customary Law*, which was an attempt to codify local unwritten customs into usable precedent. I am grateful to an anonymous reviewer for the *Law and History Review* who pointed out the compatibility of these two projects.

[87] Copland, *The British Raj and the Indian Princes*, (n 12) 217.

[88] William Lee-Warner, *The Native States of India* (London: Macmillan and Co., 1910), 30–34.

[89] Ian Copland and Barbara Ramusack claim that Tupper was chosen over Lee-Warner as he was willing to characterize the relationship between the princely states and the British government as a feudal rather than a constitutional one. See Copland, *The British Raj and the Indian Princes*, (n 12) 218; and Ramusack, *The Indian Princes and their States*, (n 12) 97.

[90] F. H. Brown, 'Warner, Sir William Lee- (1846–1914)', rev. Katherine Prior, in *Oxford Dictionary of National Biography*, https://doi.org/10.1093/ref:odnb/34472, accessed 23 May 2019.

[91] Ian Copland claims that Lee-Warner considered the tie between the states and the British government to be a constitutional one. See Copland, *The British Raj and the Indian Princes*, (n 12) 218. Lauren Benton also argues that Lee-Warner considered international law to be inapplicable to the states. See Benton, 'From International Law to Imperial Constitutions', (n 7) 602 n. 24.

respect, was a sure defence against annexation'. Combined with the argument that international law regulated, to a limited extent, the relations of 'communities of an analogous character with independent states', Lee-Warner argued that the princely states could claim the shelter of international law.[92]

Lee-Warner specifically criticized John Westlake, for being 'the strongest advocate' of the argument in favour of a constitutional tie between the princely states and the British government.[93] Westlake noted that the states 'had no international existence' as foreign states could not engage with them without the acquiescence of the British government. Hence, he argued that the ties between the states and the British government could only be 'constitutional'.[94] Lee-Warner, however, relied on Maine's Kathiawar minute to argue that the loss of one facet of sovereignty, i.e. the right to external relations, did not destroy the international status of the princely states.[95] He noted that even 'if we officially avoid speaking of [states] as sovereigns we constantly apply to them conceptions of sovereignty, and are guided in many our negotiations with them by the spirit or the conceptions of international law'.[96] He pointed out that the British parliament had accepted princely states' treaties as binding, while British courts had consistently treated the treaties as international obligations, with international law principles being used for their interpretation. He also described situations where the princely states were not treated as a constitutional part of British India, including, for instance, the exclusion of princely states from obligations under commercial treaties and from British Indian law.[97]

For Lee-Warner, the break in the constitutional tie signified that international law could be the only law applicable to the relationship, even if the states lacked complete independence or even internal autonomy. Instead, the crucial tests were, first, whether there was 'common subjection to a common legislature, capable of making municipal laws binding upon the consenting states and their subjects', and secondly, the existence of 'a conflict of rights and interests which the states concerned could not in the absence of international law settle otherwise than by appeal to force'. The lack of a common legislature for British India, the princely states, and other parts of the British empire, together with the existence of disputes led him to argue that peaceful adjustment was needed by legal methods, leaving the field open for international law.[98]

Lee-Warner argued that Maine himself had envisaged such a view. In his Kathiawar minute, Maine had relied on the assumption that international law

[92] Lee-Warner, *The Native States of India*, (n 88) 390, 399–400.

[93] ibid 397.

[94] Westlake, *Chapters on the Principles of International Law*, (n 17) 213–214, 223–224.

[95] William Lee-Warner, 'The Native States of India: A Rejoinder', *Law Quarterly Review*, 27/1 (1911), 84.

[96] Letter from William Lee-Warner to John Westlake, 14 April 1898, William Lee-Warner Papers, Mss Eur F92/3.

[97] Lee-Warner, 'The Native States of India', (n 95) 86–87.

[98] ibid 85.

applied 'in some sense' to the case to argue that the British government was bound, with regard to international rules, by its earlier disclaimer of sovereignty over Kathiawar. If international rules were applied, then rulers of princely states would be entitled, Lee-Warner argued, to 'the respect and independence which the idea of international law so powerfully secures'. Since the states were foreign territory, if the British government wished to obtain an attribute of sovereignty within the realm of the state, such as railway jurisdiction, then it had to obtain a concession from the state; it could not simply use the constitutional mechanism of enacting a law to obtain the jurisdiction.[99]

A review of the writings of Aitchison, Tupper, and Lee-Warner reveals the two basic principles that guided British political officers in late nineteenth-century South Asia. The first was the idea of 'divisible sovereignty', developed through Henry Maine's powerful influence. Sovereign powers were divided between the princely states and the British government; as a result, the states were both sovereign and not so, blurring the boundary between imperial and international law. Maine and his cohort in the Political Department all thought that international law had some part to play in defining the relationship between the states and the British government, although each of them had a different answer as to the precise nature of this role. Since boundaries between imperial and international law were hazy, colonial bureaucrats were able to argue in favour of extensive British extraterritorial jurisdiction, while also maintaining the princely states as 'allies'.

Interlinked with the first principle of divisible sovereignty was the second, the idea of 'precedent'.[100] Since colonial officials agreed that sovereign powers were divided among several entities, they were concerned with the question of how such powers were distributed. Instead of deducing answers from an abstract idea of sovereignty, they relied heavily on history and political practice. This led to the development of precedent in the context of princely state relations, exemplified in the reliance on manuals of case law like *Indian Political Practice*, and the official claim that general principles drawn from cases in relation to one state could be applied in similar cases in other states. Much like the concept of divisible sovereignty, the idea of political precedent enabled the British to entrench their paramountcy by expanding their own sovereign powers at the expense of the princely states through the mechanism of relying on case law to override specific provisions in British treaties with the states.

The twin principles of 'divisible sovereignty' and 'precedent' formed the core legal repercussions of the shift in British imperial ideology in the aftermath of the

[99] See Lee-Warner's comments on Tupper, 'India and Sir Henry Maine', (n 77) 400–401.

[100] For other discussions of precedent in the context of the states, see Copland, *The British Raj and the Indian Princes*, (n 12) 215; Copland, *The Princes of India in the Endgame of Empire*, (n 12) 19–20; and Ramusack, *The Indian Princes and their States*, (n 12) 96. Lauren Benton, however, argues that 'indeterminacy' was the core of British policy as officials relied on imperial prerogatives rather than the systematization of political relations. See Benton, *A Search for Sovereignty*, (n 7) 250–260.

turmoil of 1857. Inspired by Henry Maine's understanding of radical differences between 'traditional' Asian and 'modern' European societies, this new philosophy of colonialism relied on the incorporation of local rulers into the imperial hierarchy to provide stability to colonial rule after a period of rebellion. As a result, entities such as the princely states were recognized as 'somewhat' sovereign junior allies albeit within the broader enterprise of entrenching British paramountcy.

The softening of the boundaries between the imperial and the international, however, also had other consequences. Specifically, it led to the saturation of the South Asian landscape with the language of international law, and sovereignty in particular. In addition to British officials, princely state representatives also appropriated international legal language to argue about the legal status and sovereign powers of the states. Colonial civil servants considered jurisdiction to be one of the powers exercised by a sovereign; since sovereign powers were divided between the British government and the princely states, they argued that the British government exercised some jurisdiction within a state, while the remainder was with the state itself. Therefore, disputes over jurisdiction were rife, and the states and the British government continually argued over the appropriate way jurisdictional powers were divided.[101] The princely states had their own conceptions of sovereignty that they articulated in these disputes, at times with some success. Two such conflicts exemplify the situation: a dispute between Travancore and the British government over jurisdiction over European British subjects who committed crimes within the territory of princely states and a dispute between Baroda and the British government over jurisdiction over telegraph lines within state territory.

Travancore and Jurisdiction over European British Subjects

In the second half of the nineteenth century, the British government began to expand its jurisdictional claims over its subjects who resided in the princely states.[102]

[101] Lauren Benton also argues that disputes continued to fester between the princely states and the British government but contends that they were often settled through the claim that the suspension of law was a core feature of imperial law itself. See Benton, *A Search for Sovereignty*, (n 7) 241, 250. I consider the articulation of divisible sovereignty to result in a deeper engagement with the language of law by the parties.

[102] This jurisdiction can be traced to seventeenth-century agreements between the East India Company and Mughal emperors that permitted the English to adjudicate internal disputes in their factories. In the latter half of the nineteenth century, however, the British government started to claim more expansive jurisdiction. See M. P. Jain, *Outlines of Indian Legal History* (5th edn, Bombay: N. M. Tripathi, 1990), 8. In general, there is extensive literature on extraterritorial jurisdiction claimed by European empires in non-European territories. See Benton, *Law and Colonial Cultures*, (n 16) 201–252; Anghie, *Imperialism, Sovereignty and the Making of International Law*, (n 9) 85–86; Turan Kayaoğlu, *Legal Imperialism: Sovereignty and Extraterritoriality in Japan, the Ottoman Empire, and China* (Cambridge: Cambridge University Press, 2010); Pär Kristoffer Cassel, *Grounds of Judgment: Extraterritoriality and Imperial Power in Nineteenth-Century China and Japan* (Oxford: Oxford University Press, 2012); Arnulf Becker Lorca, *Mestizo International Law: A Global Intellectual History, 1842–1933* (Cambridge: Cambridge University Press, 2014), 76–97; Li Chen,

While early nineteenth-century disputes were largely over the extradition of British and princely subjects who committed crimes and then escaped to territory that was foreign to them, by the latter half of the century, the British government also claimed jurisdiction over its subjects who were apprehended in princely state territory. The states resisted these claims as they considered British extraterritorial jurisdiction to be highly intrusive. A case in point was the long-running dispute between Travancore and the British government over jurisdiction over European British subjects[103] who committed crimes in Travancore territory.[104]

The dispute was triggered in September 1868 by John Liddell's petition to the governor of the British Indian province of Madras, seeking relief from an alleged unlawful detention by the authorities of the state of Travancore.[105] Liddell had been convicted of theft by a Travancore court,[106] but claimed that as a European British subject, he was subject only to the jurisdiction of British Indian courts. He argued, therefore, that his trial and subsequent conviction had been illegal.[107] To support his claim, he adduced the governor-general's proclamation (dated 10 January 1867) that provided:

> ... The Governor-General in Council is ... pleased to declare ... that original criminal jurisdiction over European British subjects of Her Majesty being Christians residing in the Native States and Chiefships below named, shall ... be exercised by, and distributed among, the several High Courts ... as follows:
>
> ...
>
> By the High Court of Madras in Mysore, Travancore, and Cochin.[108]

Chinese Law in Imperial Eyes: Sovereignty, Justice, and Transcultural Politics (New York, NY: Columbia University Press, 2015); Jessica M. Marglin, 'Extraterritoriality and Legal Belonging in the Nineteenth-Century Mediterranean', *Law and History Review*, 39/4 (2021), 679–706; and Ivan Lee, 'From Reciprocity to Territoriality: Extradition, the Opium War, and the Idea of British Sovereignty in Hong Kong, 1842–44' *Law and History Review*, 40/3 (2022), 437–458.

[103] The term 'European British subjects' was defined in section 71 of the Code of Criminal Procedure 1872 as, '(1) All subjects of Her Majesty, born, naturalized, or domiciled in the United Kingdom of Great Britain and Ireland or in any European, American, or Australian Colonies or possessions of Her Majesty, or in the Colony of New Zealand, or in the Colony of the Cape of Good Hope or Natal. (2) The children or grandchildren of any such person by legitimate consent'.

[104] Lauren Benton briefly discusses the Liddell case to argue that indeterminacy was core to the British articulation of divisible sovereignty. See Benton, *A Search for Sovereignty*, (n 7) 257–258.

[105] Petition from John Liddell to the Governor in Council, Madras, 3 September 1868, Proceedings of the Government of Madras in the Political Department, October 1868, no. 1, IOR/P/441/6.

[106] A copy of the witness statements as well as the appellate court judgment in the case can be found in Papers on Prosecution in *Sadr* Court of John Liddell, Late Commercial Agent at Alleppey, referred by the *maharaja* of Travancore for disposal by this Court, IOR/L/PJ/5/405.

[107] Petition from John Liddell to the Governor in Council, Madras, 3 September 1868, Proceedings of the Government of Madras in the Political Department, October 1868, no. 1, IOR/P/441/6.

[108] Notification in the Madras Gazette, no. 221, 10 January 1867, Proceedings of the Government of Madras in the Political Department, August 1870, no. 1, IOR/P/441/8.

The advocate-general of the Madras government opined that Liddell's trial was illegal, arguing that '[t]he criminal jurisdiction over European British subjects hitherto exercised by the Travancore Courts does not appear to rest upon any treaty, but to have been ceded by courtesy and comity', and that it had ended with the 1867 proclamation that conferred such jurisdiction on the Madras High Court.[109] The Madras government, therefore, asked Travancore for Liddell's release.[110]

In response, T. Madhava Rao,[111] the *diwan* of Travancore, launched a strong defence of Travancore's exercise of criminal jurisdiction over European British subjects. He cited from international law treatises by Henry Wheaton and Emer de Vattel to argue that jurisdiction was 'an inherent right of sovereignty',[112] and that 'the jurisdiction of the nation within its own territory is necessarily exclusive and absolute.... All exceptions, therefore, to the full and complete power of a nation within its own territories must be traced up to the consent of the nation itself.'[113] He also noted that Travancore had not agreed to cede jurisdiction over European British subjects; in fact, on several previous occasions, the British government had recognized Travancore's right to try Europeans residing in its territory. Finally, he argued that the 1867 proclamation, being British Indian municipal law, could not affect the inherent rights of foreign states, which were subjects of international law.[114] For Madhava Rao, sovereign powers were linked with the control of territory and jurisdiction was a right exercised by the territorial sovereign, in this case, the *maharaja* of Travancore.

Travancore also sought additional support to buttress its case, taking the opinion of J. D. Mayne, a well-respected member of the Madras bar and former advocate-general of the Madras government.[115] Mayne first discussed the situation in the Ottoman empire and China, both of which had entered into treaties for the cession of jurisdiction over foreigners. In comparison, none of Travancore's treaties contemplated such a renunciation. And in support of Madhava Rao, Mayne also

[109] Opinion of the Advocate-General, Government of Madras, 28 September 1868, Proceedings of the Government of Madras in the Political Department, October 1868, no. 2, IOR/P/441/6.

[110] Letter from the Resident at Travancore to the *diwan* of Travancore, no. 776, 12 October 1868, Proceedings of the Government of India in the Foreign Department, Judicial, October 1874, no. 24, IOR/P/752.

[111] For discussions of Madhava Rao's life and service in various princely states, see G. Paramaswaran Pillai, 'Raja Sir T. Madava Row', in *Representative Men of Southern India* (Madras: Price Current Press, 1896), 33–48; and 'Raja Sir T. Madhav Rao', in *Indian Statesmen: Dewans and Prime Ministers of Native States* (Madras: G. A. Natesan & Co., 1927), 193–224.

[112] Letter from the *diwan* of Travancore to the Resident at Travancore, 19 October 1868, Proceedings of the Government of India in the Foreign Department, Judicial, September 1870, no. 18, IOR/P/438/18.

[113] Letter from the *diwan* of Travancore to the Resident at Travancore, 20 October 1868, Proceedings of the Government of India in the Foreign Department, Judicial, September 1870, no. 18, IOR/P/438/18.

[114] Letter from the *diwan* of Travancore to the Resident at Travancore, 23 October 1868, Proceedings of the Government of India in the Foreign Department, Judicial, October 1874, no. 24, IOR/P/752.

[115] Charles Edward Buckland, *Dictionary of Indian Biography* (London: Swan Sonnenschem & Co., 1906), 280.

insisted that the government of India's 1867 proclamation would be inoperative against Travancore since 'Parliament is as incapable of taking away the powers of a court in Travancore as it is of dealing with the courts of France'.[116]

On the strength of these arguments, a majority of the members of the Council of the Government of Madras agreed with Travancore's claim. The dissenter, H. D. Phillips, claimed that the British government was bound by the 1867 proclamation and denied that Travancore could claim the privileges of international law since it was a 'feudatory' state.[117] However, the governor of Madras, Francis Napier, conceded that no treaty was necessary to confer jurisdiction on Travancore, as it was 'a right which is inherent in free and absolute sovereignty'. He denied that Travancore had the right to appeal to international law, which regulated the relations of independent and equal European states, since the position of the British as the 'paramount power' deprived the princely states of some of their sovereign rights. In this specific case, however, he argued that it was inappropriate to deny Travancore the exercise of criminal jurisdiction.[118] A. J. Arbuthnot, the final member of the Council, agreed with Napier and emphasized the need for a state's explicit consent for the cession of jurisdiction.[119] As a result, the government of Madras revoked its previous resolution seeking Liddell's release.[120]

When the government of India intervened in the situation, the Law Member, Henry Maine, admitted that Travancore 'theoretically' had jurisdiction to try European British subjects for offences committed within its boundaries since it was not a part of British India. He also agreed with J. D. Mayne that the 1867 notification could not take away Travancore's inherent jurisdiction, any more than English statutes could take away the rights of France or Prussia to try British subjects committing offences in their territories. Being politically astute, however, he argued that without denying Travancore's abstract right to try European British subjects, the British government ought to point out that there were reasons for Europeans to be committed to Madras for trial, including the importance of trying them by a procedure to which they were accustomed and the problems of native prisons.[121]

[116] Opinion by J. D. Mayne on the Liddell case, 11 November 1868, Proceedings of the Government of India in the Foreign Department, Judicial, September 1870, no. 18, IOR/P/438/18.

[117] Minute by H. D. Phillips, Member of the Council of the Government of Madras, 13 November 1868, Proceedings of the Government of Madras in the Political Department, December 1868, no. 25, IOR/P/441/6.

[118] Minute by Francis Napier, President of the Council of the Government of Madras, 15 November 1868, Proceedings of the Government of Madras in the Political Department, December 1868, no. 24, IOR/P/441/6.

[119] Minute by A. J. Arbuthnot, Member of the Council of the Government of Madras, 21 November 1868, Proceedings of the Government of Madras in the Political Department, December 1868, no. 26, IOR/P/441/6.

[120] Resolution of the Government of Madras, no. 274, 14 December 1868, Proceedings of the Government of Madras in the Political Department, December 1868, no. 30, IOR/P/441/6.

[121] Henry Maine, 'Trial of European British Subjects under Jurisdiction Assumed by Native States', in Montstuart Elphinstone Grant Duff, *Sir Henry Maine: A Brief Memoir of his Life, with Some of his Indian Speeches and Minutes*, ed. Whitley Stokes (New York: Henry Holt & Co., 1892), 400–401.

This was a practical application of Maine's enunciation of divisible sovereignty; here he argued that the British could exercise jurisdiction over some persons within princely state territory while the state would retain jurisdiction over everyone else.

In August 1871, the government of India laid down a categorical rule, stating, 'No Native State can be allowed to try a European British subject according to its own forms of procedure and punish him according to its own laws'. It admitted that in theory, every state that had independent internal administration had the right to deal with persons resident within its jurisdiction according to its own laws. However, it claimed that there was a universal exception to this: extraterritoriality, which had been applied by Christian states in Muslim and 'heathen' countries 'out of necessity' on account of the differences in 'religion, education, social habits, laws and judicial institutions'. Underlining the role of historical facts in determining the division of powers, the government of India also built upon earlier claims relating to extradition, asserting that the British had never surrendered European British subjects for trial by princely state courts. Since full reciprocity between the British and the princely states had never been accepted practice in the past, the government of India argued the princely states could not be permitted to try European British subjects apprehended in princely state territory; instead, they were to be tried by justices of the peace appointed by the British government and committed to courts in British India.[122]

After the 1871 resolution, the government of India passed the Foreign Jurisdiction and Extradition Act 1872, which provided for the appointment of justices of the peace in the princely states to commit European British subjects to trial and barred the extradition of European British subjects to the states. The Act did not, however, explicitly provide that the princely states could not try European British subjects. The government of India then issued a notification delegating jurisdiction over European British subjects in Travancore to the resident, appointed the resident as a justice of the peace, and directed that the resident commit European British subjects to the Madras High Court for trial.[123]

Travancore lodged a protest, with A. Sashiah Shastri,[124] Madhava Rao's successor as *diwan*, referring to his predecessor's arguments in the Liddell case. He questioned the notification since it related to European British subjects, but not to other Europeans or Americans or the subjects of Indian or Asian sovereigns.[125] Surprisingly, the British resident at Travancore supported Sashiah Shastri; he

[122] Resolution of the Government of India in the Foreign Department, Judicial, no. 158J, 8 August 1871, Proceedings of the Government of India in the Foreign Department, Judicial, August 1871, no. 24, IOR/P/748.

[123] Notification of the Government of India, Foreign Department, no. 8J, 9 January 1874, Proceedings of the Government of India in the Foreign Department, Judicial, January 1874, no. 12, IOR/P/752.

[124] For a description of Sashiah Shastri's life, see B. V. Kamesvara Aiyar, *Sir A. Sashiah Shastri, An Indian Statesman: A Biographical Sketch* (Madras: Srinivasa, Varadachari & Co., 1902).

[125] Letter from the *diwan* of Travancore to the Resident at Travancore, 13 April 1874, Proceedings of the Government of India in the Foreign Department, Judicial, October 1874, no. 24, IOR/P/752.

contended that European British subjects had voluntarily chosen to settle under the sovereignty of a princely state and that residency records did not show any complaints against the exercise of jurisdiction by state authorities. He proposed a compromise: Christian judges in Travancore courts, who could be arranged to be European British subjects, could be appointed justices of the peace with powers to try petty cases, with serious offences committed to the Travancore Sadr Court. He suggested that the appointment of the justices of the peace not be done by a unilateral act of the British government but rather through an arrangement with Travancore.[126] The Madras government described the compromise as one deserving the 'most attentive consideration'.[127]

The government of India consented to the resident's alternative proposal on account of the 'special circumstances affecting the States of Travancore and Cochin, and more particularly of the enlightened and progressive principles which have been followed by those States in their judicial administration'.[128] The secretary of state for India also approved of the general principles governing criminal jurisdiction over European British subjects as well as the compromise in the Travancore case. However, he did not consider that Liddell, who had been released by Travancore after the completion of his sentence, had suffered any hardship because of his conviction, and so refused to ask Travancore to pay any compensation.[129] As a result of this decision, princely states were required to consult the political officer posted at their court in the trial of European British subjects and were bound by his advice.

The Travancore case is an example of a dispute over the exercise of extraterritorial jurisdiction by European colonial empires. Such jurisdiction is often considered to be based on the idea of a 'civilizational difference' between Europeans and non-Europeans that required special privileges for Europeans. In the case of the princely states, the idea of such a difference was complicated by multiple factors: the British both did not claim jurisdiction over certain Europeans and did claim jurisdiction over those who were not European. Perhaps the most curious was the position of Americans and Europeans who were not British subjects. The government of India admitted that the same concerns of 'heathen' laws applied,

[126] Memorandum of the Resident at Travancore on criminal jurisdiction over European British subjects, 25 April 1874, Proceedings of the Government of India in the Foreign Department, Judicial, October 1874, no. 25, IOR/P/752.

[127] Letter from the Acting Chief Secretary, Government of Madras to the Foreign Secretary, Government of India, no. 252/3, 24 June 1874, Proceedings in the Government of India in the Foreign Department, Judicial, October 1874, no. 22, IOR/P/752.

[128] Letter from the Foreign Secretary, Government of India to the Chief Secretary, Government of Madras, no. 189J, 12 October 1874, Proceedings of the Government of India in the Foreign Department, Judicial, October 1874, no. 30, IOR/P/752.

[129] Despatch from the Secretary of State for India to the Government of India, no. 99, 14 August 1873, Proceedings of the Government of India in the Foreign Department, Judicial, September 1873, no. 16, IOR/P/752; and Despatch from the Secretary of State for India to the Government of India, no. 97, 23 July 1874, Proceedings of the Government of India in the Foreign Department, Judicial, October 1874, no. 28, IOR/P/752.

yet it did not include these subjects in its considerations. This was because of concerns about the legality of extending British Indian laws to foreign subjects in a foreign state. On several occasions, the British government claimed jurisdiction over Americans and Europeans who were not British subjects on the ground of being the 'paramount power' and to prevent 'awkward diplomatic incidents' but admitted that the question was controversial.[130] A later memo clarified that Americans and Europeans who were not British subjects or in the service of the Crown did not have the right to be tried by British Indian courts. Instead, the princely states exercised jurisdiction over them subject to the control of British political officers who had the responsibility to ensure that foreigners received a fair trial since the British government was responsible for the external affairs of the states.[131] The states also retained jurisdiction over those European British subjects who were charged under state laws for acts that were not offences under British law; these included, for instance, offences against revenue laws.[132] European British subjects in the service of princely states were also usually left to the jurisdiction of state courts.[133] Another exception followed on account of the difficulty in determining what constituted a criminal case, with the British contending that 'technical' criminality (such as trespass)[134] existed on the boundary of civil and criminal questions and could be dealt with by princely state courts.[135] Further complicating the idea of a 'civilizational difference' was the fact that the British also claimed jurisdiction over persons who were not European British subjects. Most prominently, they claimed the right to exercise jurisdiction over British Indian subjects who were in the service of the Crown (i.e. those who were government personnel); these would include, for instance, postal or railway employees who were stationed in the princely states.[136]

[130] Jurisdiction of the Nizam over Europeans, 1895, IOR/R/2/81/188; Letter from the Political Secretary, Government of India to Manley O. Hudson, Harvard University, 23 February 1927, NAI, Foreign and Political Department, 567-Internal, 1926; and Trial of Europeans and Americans not in the service of the Nizam, 1940, IOR/R/1/1/4810.

[131] Political Department Note clarifying the present position in regard to the exercise of jurisdiction over Europeans and Americans and British Indians in Indian States, 8 October 1937, IOR/R/2/901/416.

[132] Despatch from the Government of India to the Secretary of State for India, no. 3, 1 September 1873, Proceedings of the Government of India in the Foreign Department, Judicial, September 1873, no. 9, IOR/P/752; and Letter from the Foreign Secretary, Government of India to the Chief Secretary, Government of Madras, no. 175J, 29 August 1873, Proceedings of the Government of India in the Foreign Department, Judicial, September 1873, no. 34, IOR/P/752.

[133] Circular from the Foreign Secretary, Government of India to the Governments of Madras, Bombay, and Bengal, no. 188J, 12 October 1874, Proceedings of the Government of India in the Foreign Department, Judicial, October 1874, no. 29, IOR/P/752.

[134] Although trespass is primarily a civil wrong, British Indian legislation also criminalized trespass under certain circumstances. See Indian Penal Code 1860, ss 441–447.

[135] Letter from the Foreign Secretary, Government of India to the Chief Secretary, Government of Madras, no. 9J, 9 January 1874, Proceedings of the Government of India in the Foreign Department, Judicial, January 1874, no. 13, IOR/P/752.

[136] Political Department Note on Jurisdiction to be exercised over British Indian subjects and servants of Government for offences committed in the territory of Indian States, NAI, Foreign and Political Department, 808-Internal (Secret), 1926.

As these complexities demonstrate, the notion of a 'civilizational difference' could not fully encompass British claims to jurisdiction within entities like the princely states, which straddled the boundaries of the imperial and the international. In the Travancore case, the British government argued that it possessed some (though not all) sovereign rights within the territory of princely states. By defining sovereignty as divisible, it was able to claim jurisdiction not only over European British subjects (on most occasions, at least) but also over British Indian subjects who oversaw critical infrastructure works (such as railways and the postal service) in the states, while admitting that the states retained jurisdiction over most other people present in their territory. The idea of divisible sovereignty, therefore, enabled the British to establish and expand their control over the states, a position that was further facilitated by the notion of political precedent.

The British buttressed their claim to jurisdiction over European British subjects apprehended in state territory by building on earlier decisions where the government of India had refused to extradite European British subjects who were apprehended in British territory.[137] Initially, this strategy of expanding British sovereign powers by building on earlier affirmations ran into a problem since Madhava Rao specifically pointed[138] to an 1837 government of India statement that provided, 'Europeans residing in the territory of Native States, not being servants of the British Government, must be held in all respects, and in all cases, civil and criminal, subject to the law of the country in which they reside.'[139] Consequently, the government of India chose to engage in a move familiar in the common law: it distinguished the cases, arguing that earlier (unnamed) difficulties in the British exercise of jurisdiction in the states had been removed by legislation; the question, therefore, 'was placed on a different footing from that on which it formerly rested'.[140] The Liddell case then became the basis for British claims to jurisdiction over European British subjects in other princely states. Tupper, for instance, included it in *Indian Political Practice* as a precedent to be relied on.[141] Several later Political Department notes also relied on the case to articulate the general principle

[137] Resolution of the Government of India in the Foreign Department, Judicial, no. 158J, 8 August 1871, Proceedings of the Government of India in the Foreign Department, Judicial, August 1871, no. 24, IOR/P/748.

[138] Letter from the *diwan* of Travancore to the Resident at Travancore, 19 October 1868, Proceedings of the Government of India in the Foreign Department, Judicial, September 1870, no. 18, IOR/P/438/18.

[139] This statement was made in a letter from the government of India and was issued after a query from the resident at Travancore seeking clarifications about the extent of British jurisdiction over Europeans in the princely states. See Letter from the Secretary, Government of India to the Secretary, Government of Madras, no. 24, 12 June 1837, IOR/F/4/1811/74609.

[140] Letter from the Foreign Secretary, Government of India to the Chief Secretary, Government of Madras, no. 175J, 29 August 1873, Proceedings of the Government of India in the Foreign Department, Judicial, September 1873, no. 34, IOR/P/752.

[141] Tupper, *Indian Political Practice*, (n 83) iii, 8–11.

that princely states could not exercise criminal jurisdiction over European British subjects.[142]

Travancore's *diwans*, Madhava Rao and Sashiah Shastri, sought to challenge this vision of divisible sovereignty and the significance of precedent, and thereby also the British colonial claim to powers of intervention in the states. In this, they relied on the idea of 'territorial sovereignty'. Both argued that there was a single entity that exercised jurisdiction over a particular piece of territory, in this case, Travancore. Therefore, they argued that the Travancore state had jurisdiction over everyone (regardless of nationality) within its territory, and hence, had the jurisdiction to try European British subjects who committed offences in state territory. Since jurisdiction was vested in a single entity, all jurisdictional powers were vested in the Travancore state, with other entities like the British government being excluded from exercising jurisdiction in Travancore territory. This focus on a unified notion of sovereignty lent support to the efforts of the princely states to maintain their separate existence and limit British interference in their internal affairs through extraterritorial jurisdiction. Madhava Rao, in particular, had expressed his concerns about the pre-1857 British policy of annexation of states, and argued that 'native administrators' had a duty to defend the princely states and ensure their survival.[143]

One of the most significant ways to minimize colonial interference, Madhava Rao realized, was to develop the kind of administration that would win British approval.[144] The product of an English education, Madhava Rao 'knew what the British wanted, and he was able to give it to them; he played them successfully at their own game'.[145] Even though colonial control was established largely on the basis of divisible sovereignty and precedent, the British did rely on the idea of 'civilization' in a secondary manner: they used it as the basis for an elaborate system of classification of the princely states whereby 'more' civilized states enjoyed the exercise of broader powers than 'less' civilized states.[146] States that wished to defend

[142] Jurisdiction of the Nizam over Europeans, 1895, IOR/R/2/81/188; Political Department Note on Jurisdiction to be exercised over British Indian subjects and servants of Government for offences committed in the territory of Indian States, NAI, Foreign and Political Department, 808-Internal (Secret), 1926; and Political Department Note, 30 April 1928, NAI, Foreign and Political Department, 243-Internal, 1928.

[143] Koji Kawashima, *Missionaries and a Hindu State: Travancore, 1858–1936* (Delhi: Oxford University Press, 1998), 37–38.

[144] In a lecture delivered to the *maharaja* of Baroda when he was *diwan* of the state, Madhava Rao argued the best means for a prince to ensure his state's survival was to 'govern his state well'. See T. Madhava Rao, *Minor Hints: Lectures Delivered to the Maharaja Gaekwar, Sayaji Rao* (Bombay: British India Press, 1881), 285–289.

[145] Robin Jeffrey, *The Decline of Nayar Dominance: Society and Politics in Travancore, 1847–1908* (London: Chatto & Windus for Sussex University Press, 1976), 74.

[146] An example of these distinctions can be seen in the complicated eight-tier classification of the jurisdiction of the Kathiawar states developed by the political agent, Richard Keatinge, and allegedly based on the 'progress' of the states. The categories ranged from 'first class' (full civil and criminal jurisdiction, except over European British subjects) through to 'seventh class' (very limited criminal and no civil jurisdiction) to non-jurisdictional chiefs who were not placed in any class. The classification was not watertight; states argued for increases in their jurisdictional powers, while the British argued

their sovereignty were, therefore, compelled to conform to British ideals of governance. During his tenure as *diwan*, Madhava Rao instituted a range of reform measures, including the establishment of a plantation economy and fiscal reforms to improve the finances of the state, the improvement of both the English and vernacular education systems of the state, the institution of competitive examinations for government jobs, and the construction of a wide-ranging public works system.[147] One of the rationales for the institution of these projects was to enable Travancore to take advantage of the colonial scheme of classification, but although the measures impressed the British, as Robin Jeffrey points out, they only 'sought to "improve" society as a whole, not to adjust relationships among its members'.[148] Rather than resulting in any meaningful social engineering, the reforms simply resulted in the development of a centralized, bureaucratic, efficient state that was capable of intervening more deeply in the lives of its citizens. The articulation of absolute, territorial sovereignty in disputes with the British government was a crucial legal argument in this effort to empower state elites and bureaucrats and thereby also build administrative structures that would limit British interference.

Travancore's claims of territorial sovereignty and its status as a 'progressive' state enabled the state's bureaucrats to negotiate a compromise with British colonial officials whereby Travancore judges could remain involved in the exercise of jurisdiction over European British subjects. Ultimately, however, it was the British idea of divisible sovereignty that won out in the dispute. The universalization of the decision into a generally applicable political precedent soon enabled the government of India to claim extensive criminal jurisdiction within the territory of the princely states more generally.

Baroda and Jurisdiction over Telegraphs

The telegraph-based communication system, established in South Asia in the second half of the nineteenth century,[149] facilitated increasing levels of state surveillance but also led to concerns about leaks of confidential information sent through the telegraph. Control over telegraph lines, therefore, was closely linked to the stability of British colonial rule.[150] These security concerns extended to lines

that the non-provision of 'good government' was a ground for states to be stripped of jurisdiction. See Copland, *The British Raj and the Princes*, (n 12) 108–112; and McLeod, *Sovereignty, Power, Control*, (n 49) 119, 247.

[147] For a description of these reforms, see Jeffrey, *The Decline of Nayar Dominance*, (n 145) 70–103.

[148] ibid 74.

[149] The first telegraph line in South Asia was laid in 1851 and the entire system was opened to the public in 1855. See Mel Gorman, 'Sir William O'Shaughnessy, Lord Dalhousie, and the Establishment of the Telegraph System in India', *Technology and Culture*, 12/4 (1971), 581–601.

[150] Deep Kanta Lahiri Choudhury, *Telegraphic Imperialism: Crisis and Panic in the Indian Empire, c. 1830–1920* (New York: Palgrave Macmillan, 2010), 7–8, 37–49.

in the princely states as they were closely interwoven with British Indian territory. As a result, there were numerous disputes over the construction of telegraph lines within and across the states.[151] A look at the development of the telegraph in Baroda can provide some insight.

In 1873, the government of India granted the Bombay, Baroda, and Central India Railway Company (BBCIR, a private British company) a licence to operate the telegraph line that ran alongside the railway line between the towns of Miyagam and Dabhoi in Baroda; BBCIR already operated the railway line in question. It is unclear under what authority the licence was issued and there was no discussion about the legal framework that would govern the operation of the telegraph line. Ten years later, the government of India sought Baroda's formal consent for the application of the Indian Telegraph Act 1876 (a British Indian legislation) to the line, stating that the measure was 'usual' and 'the necessity for it had escaped notice' earlier.[152]

In response, the *diwan* of Baroda, Kazi Shahabuddin,[153] argued that the Telegraph Act was not applicable to the line in question as it was 'constructed at the expense of the Baroda Government', was 'situated entirely in Baroda territory', and was 'under the jurisdiction of His Highness's Government'. After explicitly linking control over the telegraph line to its presence within Baroda territory, he went on to explain the role of the BBCIR. He asserted that the company was simply Baroda's agent, operating the line for and on behalf of the state, implying that Baroda continued to exercise ultimate authority over the telegraph line. Based on the claim that the princely states were separate legal entities from British India, he argued that as with any other statute passed by the British Indian legislature, the Telegraph Act did not apply to Baroda. Making the legislation applicable to the state would, he contended, be a 'detriment to the integrity of jurisdiction and other rights of His Highness's Government'.[154] Much like Madhava Rao and Sashiah Shastri had done

[151] Conflicts generated by struggles over the control of infrastructure and resources were common. See, for instance, the overview of a dispute over water and dams with Mysore in Sunil Amrith, *Unruly Waters: How Mountain Rivers and Monsoons Have Shaped South Asia's History* (London: Allen Lane, 2018), 129–131, 161–163; and the discussion of a dispute over railways with Mysore in Priyasha Saksena, 'Jousting Over Jurisdiction: Sovereignty and International Law in Colonial South Asia, c. 1858–1950', SJD dissertation, Harvard University, 2018, 107–122. These conflicts could have far-reaching consequences. In some instances, states managed to carve out relative autonomy to pursue their own development strategies. See Sunila S. Kale, 'Structures of Power: Electrification in Colonial India', *Comparative Studies of South Asia, Africa and the Middle East*, 34/3 (2014), 457–461. In others, private companies exploited ambiguities over the legal status of the states to gain access to mineral resources at minimal cost. See Mircea Rainau, '"A Mass of Anomalies": Land, Law, and Sovereignty in an Indian Company Town', *Comparative Studies in Society and History*, 60/2 (2018), 369–377.

[152] Letter from the Foreign Under-Secretary, Government of India to the Agent to the Governor-General at Baroda, 16 June 1883, Proceedings of the Government of India in the Foreign Department, Internal, Financial, Judicial, Military, July 1884, no. 63, IOR/P/2331.

[153] For a discussion of Shahabuddin's life, see 'Kazi Shahabuddin', in *Indian Statesmen*, (n 111) 225–232.

[154] Letter from the *diwan* of Baroda to the Agent to the Governor-General at Baroda, 14 January 1884, Proceedings of the Government of India in the Foreign Department, Internal, Financial, Judicial, Military, July 1884, no. 67, IOR/P/2331.

in the Liddell case, Kazi Shahabuddin defended the Baroda's right to control activities in its territory.

The government of India, however, disputed Shahabuddin's claim on finances, asserting that the telegraph line had been constructed and was maintained at its cost, and not at the cost of the Baroda state. More significantly, it relied on the precedent of the state of Hyderabad to note that the application of the Telegraph Act to the princely states was not 'an unusual measure' and simply provided the advantage of uniformity across India.[155] The government of India later clarified that would be satisfied if Baroda enacted its own law 'following the provisions' of the Telegraph Act and the rules thereunder.[156]

When the Baroda Telegraph Act was finally drafted,[157] the grant of the operation licence by the government of India became a point of contention. The *diwan* noted that there was no existing engagement between Baroda and the government of India requiring the viceroy's consent for the establishment of telegraph lines in Baroda territory. As a result, the draft Baroda Act required the state to issue a licence to the BBCIR in supersession of the licence that had been issued by the government of India. This was an indication that Baroda was attempting to retain as much control over the line as possible by claiming that it was the appropriate authority for the issue of licences in relation to telegraphs in state territory. The agent to the governor-general (AGG) at Baroda noted that the draft Act provided the state with the authority to make rules for the conduct of telegraph lines but did not take exception to this provision since it was framed more as an 'assertion of State prerogative than with any view of interfering with the working of the line'.[158]

The government of India was not as relaxed about the assertion as the AGG, stating that Baroda was required to pass a law 'in the spirit' of the Telegraph Act, the main principle of which was to vest in the governor-general 'complete control' over the telegraphic system in British India. It argued that a Baroda enactment framed along those lines would have vested control over state telegraph lines in the governor-general. Instead, the draft statute reserved that control to the state itself and would consequently defeat the British objective of securing control over the whole telegraphic system of the region. It therefore reverted to its demand for Baroda's consent to the application of the Telegraph Act to the line. It also objected to the 'assertion of State prerogative' by Baroda in retaining the power to frame

[155] Letter from the Officiating Foreign Under-Secretary, Government of India to the Agent to the Governor-General at Baroda, 19 March 1884, Proceedings of the Government of India in the Foreign Department, Internal, Financial, Judicial, Military, July 1884, no. 68, IOR/P/2331.

[156] Letter from the Foreign Secretary, Government of India to the Agent to the Governor-General at Baroda, 23 July 1884, Proceedings of the Government of India in the Foreign Department, Internal, Financial, Judicial, Military, July 1884, no. 71, IOR/P/2331.

[157] Draft Telegraph *nibandh*, Proceedings of the Government of India in the Foreign Department, Internal, May 1887, no. 274, IOR/P/3038.

[158] Letter from the Agent to the Governor-General at Baroda to the Foreign Secretary, Government of India, 15 February 1886, Proceedings of the Government of India in the Foreign Department, Internal, May 1887, no. 273, IOR/P/3038.

rules for telegraph lines as 'inappropriate'.[159] The government of India's arguments relied on the idea that sovereign powers were divided between the British and the princely states. Consequently, the British government could claim the exercise certain sovereign powers within the territory of the princely states; in this case, it happened to be the power to determine the law applicable to telegraph lines situated within state territory.

In the attempt to retain control over its telegraph lines, Baroda delayed granting consent for the application of the Telegraph Act to its territory for years. As a result, the construction of telegraph lines in the state ground to a halt. In 1890, the issue began to be pursued more vigorously since there were increased fears of an accident on railway lines that did not have parallel telegraph lines.[160] The government of India refused to permit construction until the state extended the Telegraph Act to Baroda territory.[161] To resolve the issue, the *diwan*, Manibhai Jashbhai, one of Kazi Shahabuddin's successors, suggested a compromise. First, he proposed that the telegraph lines in Baroda that were connected with the general telegraph system of British India (as distinguished from local lines that lay completely within Baroda territory) would be worked according to the spirit of the Telegraph Act, with control (including the power to issue licences) vesting with the government of India. Second, he argued that jurisdiction with respect to offences under the Telegraph Act on telegraph lines in Baroda continue to vest with Baroda courts. He argued that this arrangement would preserve Baroda's 'jurisdictional integrity', while ensuring that through telegraph lines were worked on a general and uniform system.[162]

The AGG found the *diwan*'s proposal satisfactory,[163] but the government of India refused to accept anything 'short of the complete and unconditional application of the Indian Telegraph Act by the Darbar to the lines in the Baroda State'. It also refused to accept a carve-out for local lines, demanding that the Telegraph Act be made applicable to all lines.[164] After another two years, the *diwan* finally conveyed

[159] Letter from the Foreign Secretary, Government of India to the Agent to the Governor-General at Baroda, 12 May 1887, Proceedings of the Government of India in the Foreign Department, Internal, May 1887, no. 276, IOR/P/3038.

[160] Letter from the Officiating Agent to the Governor-General at Baroda to the Foreign Secretary, Government of India, 6 May 1890, Proceedings of the Government of India in the Foreign Department, Internal, July 1890, no. 343, IOR/P/3742.

[161] Letter from the Public Works Secretary, Government of India to the Public Works Secretary, Government of Bombay, Railway Branch, 21 June 1890, Proceedings of the Government of India in the Foreign Department, Internal, July 1890, no. 348, IOR/P/3742.

[162] Letter from the *diwan* of Baroda to the Agent to the Governor-General at Baroda, 11 August 1891, Proceedings of the Government of India in the Foreign Department, Internal, October 1891, no. 319, IOR/P/3968.

[163] Letter from the Officiating Agent to the Governor-General at Baroda to the Foreign Secretary, Government of India, 15 August 1891, Proceedings of the Government of India in the Foreign Department, Internal, October 1891, no. 318, IOR/P/3968.

[164] Letter from the Foreign Under-Secretary, Government of India to the Agent to the Governor-General at Baroda, 13 October 1891, Proceedings of the Government of India in the Foreign Department, Internal, October 1891, no. 320, IOR/P/3968.

Baroda's consent to the application of the Telegraph Act 'to all present and future telegraph lines in the Baroda State, that may be connected to the Imperial system, or, being isolated, may be thrown open to the public whose messages are charged for'.[165] Jurisdiction over offences against the Telegraph Act, however, remained with Baroda courts, except in cases involving European British subjects.[166]

As with the Travancore dispute over criminal jurisdiction, Baroda's dispute over the laws to be applied to telegraph lines within its territory (a dispute over legislative jurisdiction) demonstrates the significance of the differing conceptions of sovereignty that the princely states and the British government favoured. Baroda officials relied on the idea of 'territorial sovereignty' to argue that the state was the exclusive and absolute sovereign over everything in its territory. Therefore, Baroda had the sole right to enact its own laws and to have its courts exercise jurisdiction with respect to telegraph lines within state territory even if the lines were part of a larger system connected with British India. Since the idea of territorial sovereignty implied that there was a single sovereign with respect to any piece of territory, Baroda officials argued that other entities such as the British government could not exercise any sovereign authority over Baroda territory, i.e. over telegraph lines that lay completely within state territory.

Much as Travancore bureaucrats had done, Baroda officials sought to establish a single point of legal authority within state territory. The similarity of arguments is, perhaps, unsurprising as Madhava Rao had been Kazi Shahabuddin's predecessor as *diwan* of Baroda, and had delivered a series of lectures to the minor ruler, Sayajirao Gaekwad III, emphasizing the importance of a well-run administration to minimize British interference in the state.[167] Shahabuddin had served as the head of the Finance Department during Madhava Rao's tenure as *diwan* and had been his close confidante.[168] He also carried on the extensive reforms that Madhava Rao had started in the state, including changes to the land revenue system, investment in education through the opening of a number of schools, the institution of competitive examinations for the civil service, and the establishment of an extensive public works system. These were analogous to the reforms carried out in Travancore, and among the varied reasons they were carried out was the need to impress colonial officials and conform to British ideals of responsible rule. More significantly, these reforms included the institution of a bureaucracy that concentrated power in the hands of the *diwan* and his subordinates at the expense of local

[165] Letter from the *diwan* of Baroda to the Agent to the Governor-General at Baroda, 1 February 1893, Proceedings of the Government of India in the Foreign Department, Internal, August 1893, no. 59, IOR/P/4401.

[166] Letter from the Foreign Under-Secretary, Government of India to the Agent to the Governor-General at Baroda, 18 July 1893, Proceedings of the Government of India in the Foreign Department, Internal, August 1893, no. 69, IOR/P/4401.

[167] See, in particular, Madhava Rao, *Minor Hints*, (n 144) 285–289.

[168] 'Kazi Shahabuddin', in *Indian Statesmen*, (n 111) 230–231.

nobles who had traditionally enjoyed enormous privileges.[169] Shahabuddin himself had been heavily involved in a similar effort of centralizing power during his tenure as the *diwan* of Kutch; there, he had pleaded the state's case against British interference in relation to the rights of the local *zamindars* (landholders).[170] The construction of sovereignty as 'absolute' and 'territorial' in the course of disputes with the British government fit with the princely states' general efforts to create strong, centralized governments in the late nineteenth century.

Baroda's claims of territorial sovereignty or even its reliance on the status as a 'model' state did not go very far. British officials defined sovereignty as divisible to argue that certain sovereign powers in relation to the princely states vested with the British government, with the remainder left to the Baroda state. As a result, the British government claimed the power to determine the laws applicable to telegraph lines even if they lay completely within Baroda territory. British officials also used the precedent of other princely states like Hyderabad to argue that Baroda was required to apply British Indian legislation to and cede partial jurisdiction over telegraph lines within its territory. Tupper's *Indian Political Practice* used the Baroda case itself as the basis of a generally applicable principle.[171] Soon, other princely states were also deprived of control over telegraph lines.[172] Relying on the twin principles of divisible sovereignty and precedent, therefore, enabled British officials to cement colonial control by integrating princely state infrastructure into the broader imperial system, but also claim that the states were 'sovereign' in the sense that they retained the exercise of jurisdiction over most offences committed along telegraph lines.

Conclusion

The Travancore and Baroda disputes are only two of several late nineteenth-century jurisdictional conflicts between the princely states and the British government. The vast colonial archives are brimming with debates over sovereignty that occurred in the everyday administration of the empire, including in disputes with states like Bhopal[173] and Hyderabad.[174] As the two case studies I have discussed in

[169] David Hardiman, 'Baroda: The Structure of a "Progressive" State', in *People, Princes and Paramount Power*, 107–135.

[170] 'Kazi Shahabuddin', in *Indian Statesmen*, (n 111) 228.

[171] Tupper, *Indian Political Practice*, (n 83) i, 194–195.

[172] For complaints by the princely states about the loss of such control, see Appendix 8 to Cabinet Paper RTC 31(2), Relations with Indian States, September 1931, IOR/L/PS/13/550.

[173] In 1863, Bhopal protested the exercise of jurisdiction by the British political agent over British subjects residing in the state. For a more detailed discussion, see D. K. Sen, *The Indian States, Their Status, Rights and Obligations* (London: Sweet and Maxwell, 1930), 99–101.

[174] Hyderabad attempted to shut down a court that settled civil cases among Europeans residing in the state. See Beverley, *Hyderabad, British India, and the World*, (n 7) 221–256.

this chapter demonstrate, the late nineteenth-century colonial encounter in South Asia generated two versions of sovereignty: absolute and divisible.

British jurists like Henry Maine insisted that sovereignty was 'divisible'; so entities like the princely states were sovereigns 'of a certain kind' to which international law applied 'in some sense'. Political officers in the government of India (such as Charles Aitchison, Charles Lewis Tupper, and William Lee-Warner) adopted this view of sovereignty and built on Maine's insights to develop a system of precedent as a mechanism to determine the specific division of sovereign powers between the states and the British government. Parsing through the post-1857 shift in British imperial ideology towards maintaining 'native' rule is critical to understand these two moves. The construction of the states as entities that only possessed some sovereign powers with the remainder being exercised by the British government was seen as both historical fact (since Maine argued that 'traditional' Asian societies were different from 'modern' centralized European nation-states) and a tremendously forceful legal argument that balanced the imperial push towards extensive British jurisdiction in the states and the political need to maintain the princes as allies. This latter assertion was also enabled by the system of precedent, in terms of which determinations made in a specific case were universalized into general principles and considered to be applicable to all states. The reliance on examples of the historical exercise of power soon enabled the British to reduce the princes' guarantees under individual treaties to mere 'scraps of paper'[175] and entrench their paramountcy in the region.

By simultaneously recognizing the states as sovereign and not so, colonial officials softened the divide between the imperial and the international and reinforced the significance of legal arguments made in the jurisdictional disputes that permeated British relations with the princely states. Law in general, and the concept of sovereignty in particular, became the language that the participants in these disputes used to articulate their differences.[176] And since sovereignty is polysemic, the princely states relied on a different set of arguments, claiming that sovereignty was absolute, unitary, and linked with the control of territory; they were, therefore, entitled to exercise all sovereign rights within their territory.

The 'sovereignty as territory' argument had two main aims. The first was to limit British interference in the internal affairs of the states, which was intensifying in the late nineteenth century. In this, the princes and their advisors can be situated within a broader tradition of protest against colonial authorities. Madhava Rao, for instance, relied on the international law treatise authored by Emer de Vattel that, tellingly, was also a source of inspiration to American colonists who had

[175] I borrow this term from A. P. Nicholson, *Scraps of Paper: India's Broken Treaties, Her Princes, and the Problem* (London: Ernest Benn Limited, 1930).

[176] John Fabian Witt, 'Anglo-American Empire and the Crisis of the Legal Frame (Will the Real British Empire Please Stand Up?)', *Harvard Law Review*, 120/3 (2007), 783–784.

rebelled against British authorities a century prior.[177] The 'territorial sovereignty' argument of the princely states is also similar to the 'absolute sovereignty' claim of nineteenth-century international lawyers from the 'semi-periphery' to argue for autonomy and equality.[178] In the case of the princely states, the idea of territorial sovereignty was not only externalized as a defence against British interference, but also had a second, inter-linked aim that was directed inwards. During the late nineteenth century, many states were engaged in the task of creating centralized, bureaucratic states. Although this effort met a variety of goals, it also helped to maintain the façade of well-administered states to minimize British intervention. It was frequently carried out at the expense of local nobles, who often exercised tremendous influence that had the potential to undercut monarchical authority within the state.[179] For instance, as a Marathi *brahmin* in Travancore, Madhava Rao was himself the beneficiary of a common move by ruling princes of importing western-educated administrators from outside the state to replace local nobles who had an independent power base within the state.[180] In addition to engaging in legislative and administrative activities to counter the power of the nobility and to intervene more extensively in the lives of their subjects, states also moulded an image of centralized control through the idea of territorial sovereignty.

These versions of sovereignty articulated by the British and the states in the latter half of the nineteenth century did not remain static during the entire period of colonial rule. As I argue in the next chapter, while legal language continued to provide a fertile means for debate, the strengthening of anticolonial nationalism at the turn of the century reconfigured relations between the British and the princes and led to new sets of arguments about sovereignty and political order.

Copyright Note

177 For a discussion of Vattel's influence on the American colonists, see David Armitage, *Foundations of Modern International Thought* (Cambridge: Cambridge University Press, 2013), 222–225.

178 For a discussion of this argument of semi-peripheral international lawyers, see Becker Lorca, *Mestizo International Law*, (n 102) 62–65.

179 For instance, the Kathiawar rulers relied on the 'rights of independent sovereignty' to limit the support provided by the British to *girassias* (local landholders) who often set up alternate power bases challenging sovereign authority. See Memo submitted by the *vakeels* of Junagadh, Nawanagar, Bhavnagar, and Dhrangadhra, 11 July 1871, IOR/L/PS/6/597; Letter from the *nawab* of Junagadh, the *jam* of Nawanagar, the *thakur* of Bhavnagar, the *thakur* of Dhrole, the *thakur* of Wadhawan, the *thakur* of Choora, the *khan* of Bantwa, and the *malik* of Banjana to the Governor and President in Council, Bombay, 1 January 1872, IOR/L/PS/6/597; and Letter from the Foreign Secretary, Government of India to the Political Secretary, Government of Bombay, no. 1451P, 2 July 1872, IOR/L/PS/6/597. See also, Copland, *The British Raj and the Indian Princes*, (n 12) 112–116.

180 Ramusack, *The Indian Princes and their States*, (n 12) 112, 182–186.

Chapter Four
The Controversy Over Divisible Sovereignty
The Princes and the Indian States Committee

Sovereignty in Flux

One evening in January 1925, four army officers stationed in the British Indian metropolis of Bombay finished a round of golf and decided to head to the Taj Mahal Palace hotel for drinks. While driving through the posh neighbourhood of Malabar Hill, they encountered a woman being assaulted and dragged into a car by a gang of men. They rescued the woman, Mumtaz Begum, from her alleged abductors, but this was only the beginning of a sordid tale of passion, revenge, and murder. Mumtaz revealed that she had been a palace dancer at the court of Tukojirao III Holkar XIII Bahadur, the *maharaja* of the princely state of Indore. She also alleged that she had been abused during her stay in the state and so had made her way to Bombay where she started living with a businessman named Abdul Kadir Bawla. Bawla, travelling with Mumtaz on that fateful evening, was shot by the assailants and died in hospital.[1] Nine men were tried for his murder; all but two were found guilty.[2]

In the meantime, rumours surrounding Tukojirao's connection with the incident began to swirl. Police investigations revealed that many of the assailants were employees of the state of Indore.[3] The Bombay press alleged that the Indore state treasury financed the defence of the accused, implying that Tukojirao himself had been involved in ordering the failed abduction.[4] On account of the extraordinarily public nature of the allegations against Tukojirao, the British were forced to act against a ruling prince, whose position they had sworn to uphold under treaty and political practice. They offered him a commission of inquiry to investigate his role in the affair and to save him the ignominy of a criminal trial.[5] Tukojirao was, however, furious at the turn of events, and vehemently argued that 'neither on the

[1] 'A Hold-Up by Desperadoes', *The Times of India* (13 January 1925).

[2] 'Three to be Hanged', *The Times of India* (25 May 1925). A snapshot of the case and the trial can be found in P. B. Vachha, *Famous Judges, Lawyers and Cases of Bombay: A Judicial History of Bombay During the British Period* (Bombay: N. M. Tripathi Private Ltd., 1962), 329–338.

[3] 'Indore Arrests', *The Times of India* (22 January 1925).

[4] 'Indore to Foot Heavy Bill', *The Times of India* (6 February 1926).

[5] 'Viceroy Decides', *The Times of India* (2 February 1926). Such commissions of inquiry were appointed in a situation when, in the view of the governor-general, there arose the question of depriving a ruling prince 'temporarily or permanently of any of the rights, dignities, powers or privileges, to which he as a Ruler is entitled'. The commission's role was to offer advice and it was only appointed if the prince who was the subject of the inquiry agreed to the appointment. The specific procedure was laid out in a

Sovereignty, International Law, and the Princely States of Colonial South Asia. Priyasha Saksena, Oxford University Press.
 DOI: 10.1093/oso/9780192866585.003.0004

analogy of international law, nor as a matter resting upon treaty, [was] a Prince of [his] position liable to be tried'.[6] Instead of accepting the commission, Tukojirao abdicated in favour of his son.[7]

As scholars like Angma Jhala have argued, the Malabar Hill murder (as it was branded in the local press) brought into focus the lives of the Indian princes and the position of colonized women in relation to elite men.[8] It also highlighted the complex relationship between the British colonial state and the princes, one that 'cannot be simplistically determined as one of either independence or dependency'.[9] Much like the late nineteenth-century jurisdictional disputes described in the previous chapter, this case raised questions about the nature and extent of the sovereign powers exercised by the British and the princes, including on the scope of British authority to try ruling princes, the legal basis of commissions of inquiry, and the significance of the treaties between the British government and the princely states.

The concept of sovereignty was in immense flux in the aftermath of the First World War. Scholars have chronicled the role played by interwar international institutions in state-making, the establishment of eclectic modes of international administration in central and eastern Europe, and the management of non-European territories that were considered to be unable to govern themselves.[10] Jurists redefined sovereignty to create new legal species, such as mandated territories or entities at the 'fringes' of the international system, which were outside the traditional subject of the state and often marked by their incompleteness in comparison with the state.[11] The invention of these novel legal personalities placed additional

government of India resolution passed in 1920, the text of which can be found in D. K. Sen, *The Indian States, Their Status, Rights and Obligations* (London: Sweet and Maxwell, 1930), 232–234.

6 The text of Tukojirao's letter to the Political Department was published in various newspapers. See 'Beneath His Dignity: Holkar's Reply', *The Times of India* (4 March 1926).

7 'Indore Abdication', *The Times of India* (1 March 1926).

8 Angma Dey Jhala, *Courtly Indian Women in Late Imperial India* (London: Pickering & Chatto, 2008), 125–159; and Angma D. Jhala, 'The Malabar Hill Murder Trial of 1925: Sovereignty, Law and Sexual Politics in Colonial Princely India', *The Indian Economic and Social History Review*, 46/3 (2009), 373–400. On the parallel way that elite Asian men relied on their economic and social capital to prevail in legal cases against white women, see Nurfadzilah Yahaya, 'Class, White Women, and Elite Asian Men in British Courts During the Late Nineteenth Century', *Journal of Women's History*, 31/2 (2019), 101–123.

9 Jhala, 'The Malabar Hill Murder Trial of 1925', (n 8) 398.

10 See Nathaniel Berman, '"But the Alternative is Despair": European Nationalism and the Modernist Renewal of International Law', *Harvard Law Review*, 106/8 (1993), 1792–1903; and Antony Anghie, 'Colonialism and the Birth of International Institutions: Sovereignty, Economy, and the Mandate System of the League of Nations', *New York University Journal of International Law and Politics*, 34/3 (2002), 513–634.

11 See Rose Parfitt, '*Empire des Nègres Blancs*: The Hybridity of International Personality and the Abyssinia Crisis of 1935–36', *Leiden Journal of International Law*, 24/4 (2011), 849–872; Natasha Wheatley, 'Spectral Legal Personality in Interwar International Law: On New Ways of Not Being a State', *Law and History Review*, 35/3 (2017), 753–787; and Megan Donaldson, 'The League of Nations, Ethiopia, and the Making of States', *Humanity: An International Journal of Human Rights, Humanitarianism, and Development*, 11/1 (2020), 6–31.

pressure on establishing the boundaries of the international. In the context of the British empire, the escalating controversy over the international status of the dominions also raised questions about the frontier between international, imperial, and national law, with the language of sovereignty playing a key role in attempts to draw these borders.[12]

While engaging in debates over the status of legal persons such as mandates and dominions, interwar jurists critiqued absolute state sovereignty and contended that sovereign powers could be and often were divided among different bodies. However, as I argue in this chapter, although they relied on the shared language of 'divisible' sovereignty, they used this vocabulary in contrasting ways. Some argued that parcelling out sovereign powers among distinct entities created the path for the establishment of international courts to compulsorily resolve inter-state disputes and limit the exercise of state power. Others resorted to the terminology of divisible sovereignty to lay the foundations of institutional mechanisms to intervene in the internal administration of societies that were considered to be unable to manage their own affairs, thereby bolstering already influential colonial powers that occupied dominant positions within interwar international organizations.[13]

The language of sovereignty was also reinterpreted in the colonial world, including in interwar South Asia. Given the states' existence within a broader imperial system in which the British government exercised control over their external affairs, the late nineteenth-century princely strategy of defining sovereignty as territorial had proved to be largely futile in the face of the colonial state's expansion of extraterritorial jurisdiction rooted in the idea of divisible sovereignty. Despite the entrenchment of British paramountcy, debates over the legal status of the states persisted in cases like the Malabar Hill murder. In fact, as Stephen Legg argues, the establishment of international institutions generated additional uncertainties because of conflicting views on the applicability of League of Nations conventions to the states.[14] The participation of princes such as Ganga Singh of Bikaner and Bhupinder Singh of Patiala in imperial and international conferences, including in sessions of organizations such as the League of Nations, brought them into contact with international debates on the varied political orders that could be constructed by relying on the vernacular of divisible sovereignty. Building on this experience, the princes and state administrators became, once again, significant players in

[12] For some recent evaluations of the debates over dominion status, see Thomas Mohr, 'The Statute of Westminster, 1931: An Irish Perspective', *Law and History Review*, 31/4 (2013), 749–791; Donal Coffey, '"The Right to Shoot Himself": Secession in the British Commonwealth of Nations', *The Journal of Legal History*, 39/2 (2018), 117–139; and Peter C. Oliver, '"Dominion Status": History, Framework and Context', *International Journal of Constitutional Law*, 17/4 (2019), 1173–1191.

[13] For more on this divide amongst interwar activists, see Mark Mazower, *Governing the World: The History of an Idea* (London: Allen Lane, 2012), 118–136; and Stephen Wertheim, 'The League of Nations: A Retreat from International Law?', *Journal of Global History*, 7/2 (2012), 210–232.

[14] Stephen Legg, 'An International Anomaly? Sovereignty, the League of Nations and India's Princely Geographies', *Journal of Historical Geography*, 43 (2014), 96–110.

interwar South Asian debates on the definition of sovereignty, alongside British politicians, colonial officials, and anticolonial nationalists.

In addition to global influences, changes in local context also had profound implications for the relationship between the British government and the princely states. As historians of the princely states have noted, the strengthening of anticolonial nationalism in the first two decades of the twentieth century forced the British to reach out to the states for support, increasing the space for the princes to claim wider sovereign powers and to argue for more robust limitations on British interference in their internal affairs.[15] On account of the heightened role for the princes in South Asian and imperial politics, earlier British policy of enforcing the political isolation of the states slowly deteriorated.[16] The princes took this opportunity to start acting jointly; while individual disputes between some states and the British government persisted,[17] collective action was crucial to shaping the relationship after the First World War.

This united front came to a head at the Indian States Committee, appointed in 1927 to report upon the nature of the relationship between the British government and the princely states. Although there is considerable scholarship on the changing nature of these ties in the interwar period, scholars have only briefly examined the legal arguments that were made by the princes and colonial officials in their attempts to resolve disputes and clarify the nature of their association.[18] As I have argued in this book though, the legal concept of sovereignty played a key role in defining the relationship between the British government and the princely states. By focusing on the hearings before the Indian States Committee, I illustrate the way most participants in debates over sovereignty in interwar South Asia critiqued

[15] See Ian Copland, *The Princes of India in the Endgame of Empire, 1917–1947* (Cambridge: Cambridge University Press, 1997), 27–32; and Barbara Ramusack, *The Indian Princes and their States* (Cambridge: Cambridge University Press, 2004), 128–129.

[16] In the nineteenth century, the British insisted that the states communicate with each other only through the medium of British political officers. At one stage, the government of Bombay even refused to accept joint petitions from the Kathiawar states, arguing that 'if by treaty and custom they are separate entities unable to enter into foreign negotiations, it seemed to this Government desirable that each State should look for redress on account of its own individual grievances to the Government of Bombay'. See Letter from the Political Secretary, Government of Bombay to the Foreign Secretary, Government of India, 12 March 1891, Proceedings of the Government of India in the Foreign Department, Internal, July 1891, no. 48, IOR/P/3967. The strict policy of isolation was loosened with imperial assemblages and coronation *durbars* and finally on account of princely participation in the war effort. See Ramusack, *The Indian Princes and their States*, (n 15) 126.

[17] For a fascinating discussion of Cochin's attempts to use the international law principle of 'prior occupancy' to exert control over the British port of Cochin in the interwar period, see Devika Shankar, 'A Slippery Sovereignty: International Law and the Development of British Cochin', *Comparative Studies in Society and History*, 64/3 (2022), 820–844.

[18] See Barbara Ramusack, *The Princes of India in the Twilight of Empire: Dissolution of a Patron-Client System, 1914–1939* (Columbus, OH: Ohio State University Press, 1978); S. R. Ashton, *British Policy Towards the Indian States, 1905–1939* (London: Curzon Press, 1982); Ian Copland, *The British Raj and the Indian Princes: Paramountcy in Western India, 1857–1930* (Bombay: Orient Longman, 1982), 241–296; Copland, *The Princes of India in the Endgame of Empire*, (n 15) 15–182; and Ramusack, *The Indian Princes and their States*, (n 15) 105–131, 245–274.

absolutist approaches to the doctrine, preferring instead to claim that sovereignty was 'divisible'. However, much like their international law counterparts, actors in the South Asian context also used this shared vocabulary of divisible sovereignty to pursue quite different political projects. The British government relied on a 'flexible' division of sovereign powers to expand its authority over the princely states, while the states claimed that the division of sovereign powers was based on 'consent' to limit the interventions of the British government in their internal affairs.

In this chapter, I explore both the international and South Asian debates on sovereignty in the interwar period. I first examine the definitions of sovereignty put forth by interwar international actors and review the contrasting visions of international order that they built relying on this vocabulary. Some international lawyers, such as Hersch Lauterpacht and James Brierly, took a relatively 'legalistic' approach to international relations and used the language of divisible sovereignty to envision a major role for international courts to 'discipline' politics. British politicians such as Alfred Zimmern and Robert Cecil, however, took a more 'political' approach and advocated divisible sovereignty as the basis for expanding the political power of international institutions to resolve international problems. I then examine the views of British colonial officials in South Asia, who adopted an approach similar to their counterparts in London and advocated the necessity of defining sovereignty in a 'flexible' manner that depended on political interests to be able to resolve colonial problems. This pragmatic approach to legal concepts enabled the British government to extend the scope and exercise of their powers in the states based on 'imperial interests'. I then turn to the response of the princely states, which developed their own definition of sovereignty, moving away from their previous emphasis on territoriality. To maintain the fiction that they were 'allies' of the Crown, they adopted the argument that sovereignty was 'divisible', which they had never overtly used in earlier decades. However, to limit British interference and carve out a space for themselves in the struggle for power, they focused on 'treaty rights' and 'state consent' rather than 'imperial interests' to determine the way sovereign powers were divided between the states and the British government. Both the British government and the princely states, therefore, used the language of 'divisible' sovereignty but in very different ways. They placed sophisticated versions of these arguments before the Indian States Committee, which I examine in the final part of this chapter.

Sovereignty in Interwar International Law

International lawyers, as Hilary Charlesworth notes, 'revel in a good crisis' since it 'provides a focus for the development of the discipline'.[19] The First World War was

[19] Hilary Charlesworth, 'International Law: A Discipline of Crisis', *Modern Law Review*, 65/3 (2002), 377.

precisely such a crisis, an event that is considered to mark a turning point in the history of international law. After the war, international lawyers started to argue that the nineteenth-century discipline had been unduly formalistic and focused relentlessly on an untrammelled version of sovereignty.[20] They considered such a definition of sovereignty to be ideologically dangerous as it appeared to condone even the most extreme actions taken by states, pushing the world into war.[21] The critique of absolutist state sovereignty constituted a key element of the self-conscious reimagination of the discipline of international law in the early twentieth century.

The 'move to institutions'[22] after the war, epitomized by the establishment of the League of Nations,[23] further complicated discussions around the character of sovereignty.[24] Within the context of the British empire, the legal status of the self-governing dominions posed additional vexing questions. After the dominions were admitted to the League as separate members, most jurists recognized that they had some international status; exactly what that was remained unclear.[25] The eminent imperial constitutional lawyer A. B. Keith concluded that the empire was a 'flexible and ingenious'[26] web of complex relationships that was bound together by the Crown as a formal expression of imperial unity.[27] This understanding of imperial structures could only be achieved with the recognition of sovereignty as capable of being divided and shared by various authorities.[28]

[20] David Kennedy, 'International Law and the Nineteenth Century: History of an Illusion', *Quinnipiac Law Review*, 17/1 (1997), 100–104.

[21] Richard Collins, 'Classical Legal Positivism in International Law Revisited', in Jörg Kammerhofer and Jean D'Aspremont, eds., *International Legal Positivism in a Post-Modern World* (Cambridge: Cambridge University Press, 2014), 25–28.

[22] I borrow this phrase from David Kennedy, 'The Move to Institutions', *Cardozo Law Review*, 8/5 (1987), 841–988.

[23] There is considerable scholarship on the League of Nations, both contemporaneous and modern. For a review of the historiography on the League, see Susan Pedersen, 'Back to the League of Nations', *American Historical Review*, 112/4 (2007), 1091–1117.

[24] See Geoffrey Butler, 'Sovereignty and the League of Nations', *British Year Book of International Law*, 1 (1920–1921), 35–44; and P. E. Corbett, 'What Is the League of Nations?', *British Year Book of International Law*, 5 (1924), 119–148.

[25] See Lassa Oppenheim, *International Law: A Treatise*, i: *Peace*, ed. Ronald F. Roxburgh (3rd edn, London: Longmans, Green and Co., 1920), 170; Malcolm M. Lewis, 'The International Status of the British Self-Governing Dominions', *British Year Book of International Law*, 21 (1922–1923): 21–41; Philip Noel-Baker, *The Present Juridical Status of British Dominions in International Law* (London: Longmans, 1929); and K. C. Wheare, *The Statute of Westminster, 1931* (Oxford: Clarendon Press, 1933).

[26] A. B. Keith, *The Constitution, Administration and Laws of the Empire* (New York: Henry Holt & Company, 1924), 4.

[27] A. B. Keith, *The Governments of the British Empire* (London: Macmillan and Co., 1935), 25–26.

[28] A. B. Keith, *The Sovereignty of the British Dominions* (London: Macmillan and Co., 1929), 1.

This was the fluid context in which the work of Hersch Lauterpacht[29] and James Brierly[30] gained pre-eminence.[31] Both advocated for the divisibility of sovereignty. Brierly argued that the doctrine of sovereignty placed states above the law and hampered the development of international institutions.[32] Instead, he claimed that sovereignty was 'merely a term that we find convenient when we wish to refer collectively a number of particular powers that states have traditionally claimed for themselves the right to exercise'.[33] Lauterpacht contended that absolute sovereignty placed limitations on the judicial resolution of international disputes by implying that states were only bound by law that they had accepted.[34] He preferred to define sovereignty as 'a delegated bundle of rights' and 'divisible, modifiable and elastic'.[35]

Brierly and Lauterpacht relied on the division of sovereign powers between states and supranational organizations to achieve the 'constitutionalization of politics'.[36] Brierly considered the League of Nations as 'the only hope of the eventual

[29] Lauterpacht was the Whewell Professor of International Law at Cambridge from 1938 to 1947. For further details, see Elihu Lauterpacht, *The Life of Sir Hersch Lauterpacht* (Cambridge: Cambridge University Press, 2010).

[30] Brierly was the Chichele Professor of Public International Law at Oxford from 1922 to 1947. See Humphrey Waldock, 'Brierly, James Leslie (1881–1955)', in David Cannadine, ed., *Oxford Dictionary of National Biography*, online edn (Oxford: Oxford University Press, 2004), https://doi.org/10.1093/ref:odnb/32069, accessed 29 September 2020.

[31] Given the significance of Lauterpacht and Brierly in the field, there is considerable scholarship on their work and influence. See Carl Landauer, 'J. L. Brierly and The Modernization of International Law', *Vanderbilt Journal of Transnational Law*, 25/5 (1993), 881–918; Martti Koskenniemi, *The Gentle Civilizer of Nations: The Rise and Fall of International Law, 1870–1960* (Cambridge: Cambridge University Press, 2001), 353–412; Martti Koskenniemi, 'Hersch Lauterpacht', in Jack Beatson and Reinhard Zimmermann, eds., *Jurists Uprooted: German-Speaking Émigré Lawyers in Twentieth-Century Britain* (Oxford: Oxford University Press, 2004), 601–662; James Crawford, 'Public International Law in Twentieth-Century England', in *Jurists Uprooted*, 681–708; Casper Sylvest, *British Liberal Internationalism, 1880–1930: Making Progress?* (Manchester: Manchester University Press, 2009), 205–206; Iain Scobbie, 'Hersch Lauterpacht', in Bardo Fassbender and Anne Peters, eds., *The Oxford Handbook of the History of International Law* (Oxford: Oxford University Press, 2012), 1179–1184; and Richard Collins, 'The Progressive Conception of International Law: Brierly and Lauterpacht in the *Interbellum* Period', in Robert McCorquodale and Jean-Pierre Gauci, eds., *British Influences on International Law, 1915–2015* (Leiden: Brill Nijhoff, 2016), 437–487.

[32] J. L. Brierly, *The Law of Nations: An Introduction to the International Law of Peace* (2nd edn, Oxford: Clarendon Press, 1936), 39, 62–65.

[33] J. L. Brierly, 'The Sovereign State Today', in Hersch Lauterpacht and C. H. M. Waldock, eds., *The Basis of Obligation in International Law and Other Papers* (Oxford: Clarendon Press, 1958), 350.

[34] Hersch Lauterpacht, *The Function of Law in the International Community* (Oxford: Clarendon Press, 1933), 3–4. The book expanded on claims that Lauterpacht initially made in earlier published articles, including Hersch Lauterpacht, 'The Doctrine of Non-Justiciable Disputes in International Law', *Economica*, 24 (1928), 277–317; and Hersch Lauterpacht, 'The Nature of International Law and General Jurisprudence', *Economica*, 37 (1932), 301–320.

[35] Hersch Lauterpacht, 'Sovereignty and Federation in International Law', in Elihu Lauterpacht, ed., *International Law: Being the Collected Papers of Hersch Lauterpacht*, iii: *The Law of Peace* (Cambridge: Cambridge University Press, 1977), 8.

[36] Koskenniemi, *The Gentle Civilizer of Nations*, (n 31) 382. See also Collins, 'The Progressive Conception of International Law', (n 31) 455. A considerable amount of contemporaneous scholarship portrayed the League as signifying a movement from chaos to order and from politics to law. For an overview of these moves in the literature, see Kennedy, 'The Move to Institutions'(n 22).

triumph of law and reason in international relations'.[37] Lauterpacht desired 'the subjection of the totality of international relations to the rule of law'.[38] The establishment of the League and the Permanent Court of International Justice was, in his view, a step towards 'an emerging "constitutional" architecture for international law'.[39] Lauterpacht and Brierly, therefore, deconstructed sovereignty to push for the establishment of a 'legalist' international institution, structured around a court that would mandatorily settle inter-state disputes to establish 'the reign of law over politics'.[40]

Other critics of absolute state sovereignty, however, privileged 'politicians' judgement above judicial settlement' in international institutions.[41] International lawyers were marginal players in the interwar American foreign policy establishment.[42] This scepticism of the role of lawyers in international institutions was more overt among British politicians involved in negotiations over the League's establishment.[43] Although initially envisaged as a 'guarantee of peace',[44] British proposals for the League started to encompass economic and colonial questions under the influence of Alfred Zimmern[45] and Jan Smuts.[46] These moves to expand the scope of the League were accompanied by increasing doubt about the effectiveness of the judicial settlement of disputes, as seen in the writings of Robert Cecil.[47] Cecil's position was echoed in a memorandum authored by Zimmern in which he

37 Brierly, *The Law of Nations*, (n 32) 222.

38 Hersch Lauterpacht, 'The Grotian Tradition in International Law', *British Year Book of International Law*, 23 (1946), 51.

39 Collins, 'The Progressive Conception of International Law', (n 31) 454.

40 I borrow this phrase from Wertheim, 'The League of Nations', (n 13) 212.

41 ibid 213. For a description of the divide over the appropriate structure of the League among interwar American international lawyers, see David Kennedy, 'When Renewal Repeats: Thinking Against the Box', *New York University Journal of International Law and Politics*, 32/2 (2000), 378–379.

42 Stephen Wertheim, 'The League That Wasn't: American Designs for a Legalist-Sanctionist League of Nations and the Intellectual Origins of International Organization, 1914–1920', *Diplomatic History*, 35/5 (2011), 797–836; and Benjamin Allen Coates, *Legalist Empire: International Law and American Foreign Relations in the Early Twentieth Century* (Oxford: Oxford University Press, 2016), 152–176. On the more general scepticism of legalist ideas of international law in interwar United States, see Samuel J. Astorino, 'The Impact of Sociological Jurisprudence on International Law in the Inter-War Period: The American Experience', *Duquesne Law Review*, 34/2 (1996), 277–298.

43 Mazower, *Governing the World*, (n 13) 129; and Wertheim, 'The League of Nations', (n 13) 223–227.

44 I borrow this term from Peter J. Yearwood, *Guarantee of Peace: The League of Nations in British Policy, 1914–1925* (Oxford: Oxford University Press, 2009).

45 Zimmern was trained as a classicist but became involved in the British government's proposals on interwar international institutions. See D. J. Markwell, 'Zimmern, Sir Alfred Eckhard (1879–1957)', in *Oxford Dictionary of National Biography*, https://doi.org/10.1093/ref:odnb/37088, accessed 5 October 2020; and Mark Mazower, *No Enchanted Palace: The End of Empire and the Ideological Origins of the United Nations* (Princeton, NJ: Princeton University Press, 2009), 66–103.

46 Smuts was prime minister of South Africa and was involved in the design of the Mandate System. See Shula Marks, 'Smuts, Jan Christiaan (1870–1950)', in *Oxford Dictionary of National Biography*, https://doi.org/10.1093/ref:odnb/36171, accessed 5 October 2020; and Mazower, *No Enchanted Palace*, (n 45) 28–65.

47 Cecil advised the British delegation to the Paris Peace Conference. See Martin Ceadel, 'Cecil, (Edgar Algernon) Robert Gascoyne- [known as Lord Robert Cecil], Viscount Cecil of Chelwood (1864–1958)', in *Oxford Dictionary of National Biography*, https://doi.org/10.1093/ref:odnb/32335, accessed 5 October 2020.

advocated a political rather than a juridical approach for dispute settlement; this draft became the basis for Britain's position at the Paris Peace Conference.[48]

In this 'political' incarnation, the divisibility of sovereignty epitomized by international institutions laid the groundwork for the development of techniques to expand the role of such institutions and enable colonial powers to manage the non-European world.[49] New states created in eastern Europe were subjected to minority protection regimes that had imperial roots.[50] Colonial problems were more explicitly internationalized outside Europe. Under the Mandate System, German colonies and Ottoman territories were placed under the management of mandatory powers (colonial states such as the United Kingdom and France or British dominions such as Australia and South Africa) that were overseen by the Permanent Mandates Commission of the League.[51] Since the territories were considered to be 'inhabited by peoples not yet able to stand by themselves', they were placed under the 'tutelage' of 'advanced nations' who were guided by the principle that 'the well-being and development of such peoples form a sacred trust of civilisation'.[52]

The Mandate System was based on the idea that sovereign powers could be parcelled out among several entities, including the League, the mandatory powers, and the people of the mandated territory, although it was never clear where sovereignty resided.[53] Despite the shared invocation of divisible sovereignty, the Mandate System, with its focus on administration and development, was a world away from the legalist ideal of using international dispute settlement to tame politics through

[48] Yearwood, *Guarantee of Peace*, (n 44) 1–58, 83–85.

[49] The idea of the League as a political and administrative rather than a judicial body can be most clearly seen in relation to colonial questions, an issue on which Lauterpacht had been curiously ambivalent. See Koskenniemi, *The Gentle Civilizer of Nations*, (n 31) 359. Lauterpacht's vast scholarship explicitly discusses colonial issues only on a few occasions. See Hersch Lauterpacht, 'International Law and Colonial Questions, 1870–1914', in Elihu Lauterpacht, ed., *International Law: Being the Collected Papers of Hersch Lauterpacht*, ii: *The Law of Peace* (Cambridge: Cambridge University Press, 1975), 95–144; and Hersch Lauterpacht, 'The Mandate Under International Law in the Covenant of the League of Nations', in *International Law*, iii: *The Law of Peace*, (n 35) 29–84.

[50] Laura Robson, 'Capitulations Redux: The Imperial Genealogy of the Post-World War I "Minority" Regimes', *American Historical Review*, 126/3 (2021): 978–1000.

[51] For contemporaneous literature on the Mandate System, see Quincy Wright, *Mandates Under the League of the Nations* (Chicago, IL: The University of Chicago Press, 1930); and Norman Bentwich, *The Mandates System* (London: Longmans, 1930). For recent historical assessments, see Michael D. Callahan, *Mandates and Empire: The League of Nations and Africa, 1914-1931* (Eastbourne: Sussex Academic Press, 1998); Simon Jackson, 'Diaspora Politics and Developmental Empire: The Syro-Lebanese at the League of Nations', *Arab Studies Journal*, 21/1 (2013), 166–190; Natasha Wheatley, 'Mandatory Interpretation: Legal Hermeneutics and the New International Order in Arab and Jewish Petitions to the League of Nations', *Past & Present*, 227 (2015), 205–248; Susan Pedersen, *The Guardians: The League of Nations and the Crisis of Empire* (Oxford: Oxford University Press, 2015); Natasha Wheatley, 'New Subjects in International Law and Order', in Glenda Sluga and Patricia Clavin, eds., *Internationalisms: A Twentieth-Century History* (Cambridge: Cambridge University Press, 2016), 265–286; and Sean Andrew Wempe, 'A League to Preserve Empires: Understanding the Mandates System and Avenues for Further Scholarly Inquiry', *American Historical Review*, 124/5 (2019), 1723–1731.

[52] Article 22, Covenant of the League of Nations, 1919.

[53] Leonard V. Smith, 'Sovereignty Under the League of Nations Mandates: The Jurists' Debates', *Journal of the History of International Law*, 21/4 (2019), 563–587.

law. As Antony Anghie contends, the malleability of sovereignty freed the League from restrictions imposed by assertions of sovereignty, enabling the Mandate System to create new techniques to obtain access to the interior of mandated territories and 'create the social and political infrastructure necessary to support a functioning sovereign state'. The structures of the Mandate System ultimately empowered the League and mandatory powers to integrate the mandated territories into the broader international economy based on claims of economic development, while subordinating the interests of the mandate peoples.[54] As Balakrishnan Rajagopal has demonstrated, these techniques had a long imperial history, being the basis of indirect rule in the British empire.[55]

This link between flexible ideas of sovereignty and imperial technologies was even more explicit in debates over the nature of sovereignty that were taking place in the colonies. The intellectual arguments of Alfred Zimmern, Jan Smuts, and Robert Cecil had been shaped by their long involvement in colonial politics, and specifically the Round Table movement that advocated closer relations between Britain and the self-governing dominions.[56] Their ideas on divisible sovereignty were reinterpreted in other colonial contexts, including interwar South Asia. In the rest of this chapter, I focus on the way the British government and the princely states developed their differing political projects relying on the shared vocabulary of divisible sovereignty. Akin to the British politicians in London, colonial officials in South Asia also claimed that sovereignty was divisible to expand the powers of the British government in their dealings with the princely states; it is to them that I now turn.

The Indian Political Department and the Move to Laissez-Faire

The First World War cast a long shadow over South Asia.[57] Nearly 1.7 million Indians served in various capacities during the war, after moderates in the Indian

[54] Antony Anghie, *Imperialism, Sovereignty and the Making of International Law* (Cambridge: Cambridge University Press, 2005), 135–136, 180.

[55] Balakrishnan Rajagopal, *International Law from Below: Development, Social Movements, and Third World Resistance* (Cambridge: Cambridge University Press, 2003), 57–58.

[56] On the Round Table movement, see John Kendle, *The Round Table Movement and Imperial Union* (Toronto: University of Toronto Press, 1975); Jeanne Morefield, '"An Education to Greece": The Round Table, Imperial Theory and the Uses of History', *History of Political Thought*, 28/2 (2007), 328–361; Duncan Bell, *The Idea of Greater Britain: Empire and the Future of World Order, 1860–1900* (Princeton, NJ: Princeton University Press, 2007), 269–270; and Andrea Bosco, *The Round Table Movement and the Fall of the 'Second' British Empire (1909–1919)* (Newcastle: Cambridge Scholars Publishing, 2017).

[57] For recent scholarship on India's role in the war, see Shrabani Basu, *For King and Another Country: Indian Soldiers on the Western Front, 1914–18* (New Delhi: Bloomsbury, 2015); Santanu Das, *India, Empire, and First World War Culture: Writings, Images, and Songs* (Cambridge: Cambridge University Press, 2018); George Morton-Jack, *The Indian Empire At War: From Jihad to Victory, The Untold Story of the Indian Army in the First World War* (London: Little, Brown, 2018); Roger D. Long and Ian Talbot, eds., *India and World War I: A Centennial Assessment* (London: Routledge, 2018); and Radhika Singha, *The Coolie's Great War: Indian Labour in a Global Conflict, 1914–1921* (London: Hurst, 2020).

National Congress, one of British India's main political parties, urged them to enlist in the hope of being rewarded with self-government for their 'loyalty' to the empire.[58] However, the war also stimulated transnational campaigns involving diaspora populations aiming to win independence through political violence, thereby strengthening the anticolonial movement that had been kickstarted in the last few decades of the nineteenth century.[59] Despite some tokenistic efforts at political reform to include Indians in government, anticolonial resistance was largely met with repression.[60] In the face of increasingly strident anticolonial nationalism and war, the British looked for support to maintain imperial stability, with the princely states emerging, once again, to the forefront of efforts to buttress the authority of the colonial state, in a move that Ian Copland has termed the 'politics of counterpoise'.[61]

As I described in the previous chapter, the British response to the 1857 revolt had focused on incorporating the princely states into the imperial hierarchy while consolidating colonial control through the twin principles of 'divisible sovereignty' and 'precedent'. By the turn of the twentieth century, colonial policy whittled away what the princes considered to be their sovereign rights, including jurisdiction over railways, posts, and telegraphs; the right to operate mints; and the right to import weapons.[62] The British also made a dramatic intervention in Manipur in 1891, claiming the authority to execute rebels in the state for waging war against the Crown.[63] Interventionist policy was cemented under the viceroyalty of Lord

[58] Gajendra Singh, 'India and the Great War: Colonial Fantasies, Anxieties and Discontent', *Studies in Ethnicity and Nationalism*, 14/2 (2014), 343–344.

[59] Ian Talbot, *A History of Modern South Asia: Politics, States, Diasporas* (New Haven, CT: Yale University Press, 2016), 117–118. These activists carried on the tradition of 'revolutionary terrorism' that had gained momentum after the colonial government's decision to partition the province of Bengal in 1905. See Sumit Sarkar, *Modern India, 1885–1947* (Delhi: Macmillan India, 1983), 144–149. For a study of the role of political violence in the Indian liberation movement, see Durba Ghosh, *Gentlemanly Terrorists: Political Violence and the Colonial State in India, 1919–1947* (Cambridge: Cambridge University Press, 2017).

[60] The Indian Councils Act 1892 increased the number of 'non-official' members of the executive council so that local bodies could be more involved in the nomination process. The Indian Councils Act 1909 increased the representative element of imperial and provincial legislative councils although their resolutions remained non-binding. See A. B. Keith, *A Constitutional History of India, 1600–1935* (2nd edn, London: Methuen & Co., 1937), 228–232; Sarkar, *Modern India*, (n 59) 138–140; Barbara D. Metcalf and Thomas R. Metcalf, *A Concise History of Modern India* (2nd edn, Cambridge: Cambridge University Press, 2006), 160–161; and Sumit Sarkar, *Modern Times: India, 1880s–1950s, Environment, Economy, Culture* (Ranikhet: Permanent Black, 2014), 14–15.

[61] Copland, *The Princes of India in the Endgame of Empire*, (n 15) 27.

[62] ibid 20.

[63] The British intervened on behalf of the ruler who had changed his mind about abdicating and precipitated a rebellion. The leaders of the revolt were tried and executed for waging war against the Crown. For details, see Caroline Keen, *An Imperial Crisis in British India: The Manipur Uprising of 1891* (London: I. B. Tauris, 2015). The government of India's proclamation justifying its authority to try rebels in a state that was not British territory can be found in 'Resolution and Proclamation by the Government of India, 21 August 1891', in Adrian Sever, ed., *Documents and Speeches on the Indian Princely States*, i (Delhi: B. R. Publishing, 1985), 335–336.

Curzon,[64] with several states being placed under temporary British administration and some rulers being deposed. Although most princes aided British efforts to clamp down on anticolonial protests and supported the war effort, the British realized that the support of the princes could not be taken for granted.[65]

These political changes precipitated a reworking of British policy towards the princely states, with colonial authorities professing a less interventionist attitude towards the states. The new approach relied on redefining sovereignty as a set of powers that were divided between the colonial government and the princely states based on the pragmatic notion of the 'interests of empire'. Despite the revamped strategy, the aim remained the same as that of the precedent-based theory of divisible sovereignty in the late nineteenth century: to ensure that the British could claim the princely states as somewhat sovereign allies but also maintain control over their actions for the larger imperial project. So although the new approach was supposed to be based on non-intervention, it, in fact, laid the foundation for a new push towards greater interference in the states in the 1920s.[66]

The new policy was termed '*laissez-faire*' and the first signs of the change could be seen in a 1909 speech delivered by Lord Minto,[67] who succeeded Curzon as viceroy. Minto repeated Britain's commitment to respecting princely state treaties and claimed that British policy was 'with rare exceptions one of non-interference in the internal affairs of Native States'. He also issued a mild rebuke to over-zealous British political officers who wished to introduce large-scale administrative changes in the states, claiming that it was 'easy to overestimate the value of administrative efficiency'. Instead, he insisted that 'reforms should emanate from Durbars themselves, and grow up in harmony with the traditions of the State'. Although political officers had a duty to correct any 'abuses and corruption' in the states, he also considered that the wisest course was 'to accept the general system of administration to which the Chief and his people have been accustomed' as they were 'well adapted to the needs and relations of the ruler and his people'. This assertion

[64] Curzon was appointed viceroy in 1898 and served till 1905. His time in India was overshadowed by famine, plague, and the decision to partition the province of Bengal. See David Gilmour, 'Curzon, George Nathaniel, Marquess Curzon of Kedleston (1859–1925)', in *Oxford Dictionary of National Biography*, https://doi.org/10.1093/ref:odnb/32680, accessed 8 October 2020.

[65] See Ramusack, *The Princes of India in the Twilight of Empire*, (n 18) 38–40, 96; Copland, *The Princes of India in the Endgame of Empire*, (n 15) 21, 30; Ramusack, *The Indian Princes and their States*, (n 15) 122–123; and Tony McClenaghan, *For the Honour of My House: The Contribution of the Indian Princely States to the First World War* (Warwick: Helion and Company, 2019).

[66] Ian Copland contends that the increased intervention in the affairs of the states in the 1920s can be linked to changes in personnel and British dismay at the increasingly assertive attitude of the princes. See Copland, *The Princes of India in the Endgame of Empire*, (n 15) 44–50. However, I would argue that the foundation of the broader interventionist movement of the 1920s was encoded within the move to laissez-faire itself.

[67] Minto was appointed viceroy in 1905 and worked with John Morley, the secretary of state for India, on the programme for constitutional reform. See Carman Miller and Philip Woods, 'Kynynmound, Gilbert John Elliot Murray, fourth earl of Minto (1845–1914)', in *Oxford Dictionary of National Biography*, https://doi.org/10.1093/ref:odnb/33001, accessed 13 October 2020.

of 'non-interference' was, however, a heavily qualified one. Since the British government guaranteed the internal independence of the states and had undertaken to protect them against external aggression, Minto argued that it had also 'assumed a certain degree of responsibility for the general soundness of their administration and would not consent to incur the reproach of being an indirect instrument of misrule'.[68] Intervention was, therefore, legitimate when it related to the maintenance of 'good government' in the states.

Although the claims of non-interference rang hollow, British policy towards the princely states in the early twentieth century did change in one key respect. As I discussed in the previous chapter, late nineteenth-century British political officers relied on historical precedent to determine how sovereign powers were divided between the states and the British government, claiming that principles generated from cases relating to one state were applicable to similar cases in all states. In his Udaipur speech, however, Minto assailed 'subservience to precedent' and instead asserted that fashioning a uniform policy with respect to all the states was a difficult task on account of the 'diversity of conditions'. Consequently, he claimed that he had 'made it a rule to avoid as far as possible the issue of general instructions' and instead 'endeavoured to deal with questions as they arose with reference to existing treaties, the merits of each case, local conditions, antecedent circumstances, and the particular stage of development, feudal and constitutional, of undivided principalities'. Despite abandoning precedent as an organizing principle of British policy, Minto claimed that the government of India still had the authority to intervene in the states; such interference would be to 'safeguard the interests of the community as a whole as well as those of the Paramount Power' in relation to matters such as 'railways, telegraphs, and other services of an Imperial character'.[69] By building on earlier British claims to jurisdiction over state infrastructure that attempted to weld British India and the princely states into a single economic unit, Minto opened the door for relying on 'imperial interests' to determine the division of sovereign powers between the princely states and the British government.

The new British policy relating to the states was fleshed out in a text compiled by the civil servant Charles Lennox Somerville Russell, with an introduction authored by Minto's powerful foreign secretary, Harcourt Butler.[70] The *Manual of*

[68] 'Speech delivered at the State Banquet at Udaipur, 3 November 1909', in *Speeches by the Earl of Minto, Viceroy and Governor General of India* (Calcutta: Superintendent Government Printing, India, 1911), 324–325. The references to non-intervention in Minto's speech generated enthusiastic reactions from the princes. Lady Minto claimed that they considered it equivalent to 'their Magna Charta'. See Mary Minto, *India, Minto and Morley, 1905–1910* (London: Macmillan and Co., 1934), 342.

[69] 'Speech delivered at the State Banquet at Udaipur', (n 68) 324.

[70] Butler was appointed foreign secretary in 1907 and was later the chairman of the Indian States Committee in 1928–1929. See F. H. Brown, 'Butler, Sir (Spencer) Harcourt (1869–1938)', rev. Francis Robinson, in *Oxford Dictionary of National Biography*, https://doi.org/10.1093/ref:odnb/32218, accessed 13 October 2020). Butler's appointment as foreign secretary generated a storm of protest from within the Political Department as he had no experience of state matters and did not possess the requisite seniority. See Ashton, *British Policy Towards the Indian States*, (n 18) 42–43.

Instructions to Officers of the Political Department of the Government of India[71] was issued confidentially to political officers in 1909.[72] A significant portion of the *Manual's* introduction echoed Minto's Udaipur speech. Butler emphasized that the government of India's policy was one of 'non-interference in the internal affairs of States'. Consequently, political officers were to 'ordinarily refrain from offering advice unless it is sought'; they were to 'not interfere between the Durbar and its subjects'; and finally, and perhaps most importantly, in a statement that summed up the document, they were to 'leave well alone'. Butler contended that the government of India was opposed to 'anything like pressure on Durbars to introduce British methods of administration', preferring instead that reforms 'emanate from the Durbar, and grow up in harmony with the traditions of the State'. Such an approach would ensure stability since '[t]he methods sanctioned by tradition in States are generally well adapted to the needs and relations of the ruler and people', while reforms that brought efficiency but were unsuited to local conditions had the potential to weaken the loyalty of the people to the rulers.[73]

Like Minto, however, Butler added a rider to this declaration of non-interference. He claimed that since the British guaranteed the internal independence of the states and pledged to protect them from external aggression, they had also assumed 'some responsibility for the maintenance of order and fairly efficient government in them, and cannot consent to incur the reproach of being an indirect instrument of oppression'. Consequently, the government of India had the right to interfere when there was misrule in the states although the degree of maladministration that merited such intervention was a question that had to be decided on the merits in each case. Generally, he advocated that no 'overt measures' be taken unless 'misrule reaches a pitch which violates the elementary laws of civilisation'.[74]

Butler expanded on this emphasis on treating political questions relating to each state according to their 'merits' by claiming that questions of British policy could not be 'reduced to terms of compendious generalisation' since the 'circumstances of States vary enormously as regards treaties, local conditions, economic and political, and the idiosyncracies [*sic*] of Ruling Chiefs'. Although he admitted that it was imperative for political officers to receive some general instructions for guidance,

[71] *Manual of Instructions to Officers of the Political Department of the Government of India* (1909), IOR/R/2/18/117. Despite its significance, the *Manual* was described as 'a singularly uninspiring publication' by the political officer Kenneth Fitze. See Kenneth Fitze, *Twilight of the Maharajas* (London: John Murray, 1956), 25. Perhaps on account of its dry nature, the *Manual* has only been briefly considered by scholars. See Copland, *The British Raj and the Indian Princes*, (n 18) 209; Ashton, *British Policy Towards the Indian States*, (n 18) 44; Copland, *The Princes of India in the Endgame of Empire*, (n 15) 31; and Ramusack, *The Indian Princes and their States*, (n 15) 97.

[72] Copland, *The Princes of India in the Endgame of Empire*, (n 15) 31.

[73] *Manual of Instructions to Officers of the Political Department of the Government of India* (1909), iii–v, IOR/R/2/18/117.

[74] *Manual of Instructions to Officers of the Political Department of the Government of India* (1909), iv, IOR/R/2/18/117.

he noted that the rules set out in the *Manual* were necessarily 'elastic' since uniformity was 'unattainable and undesirable'. He termed precedents to be 'valuable as a guide, but no more' since they could only be applied when all conditions were the same, which they rarely were among different states. Reliance on history and political practice, long a cornerstone of British colonial policy towards the princely states, was relegated to the past. Butler instead argued that the government of India would regulate matters based on 'imperial concern or because the States require some protection'. These issues included: the employment of Europeans, Americans, and Australians by the states; mining concessions; coinage and currency; military cooperation; posts, telephones, and telegraphs; railway management and jurisdiction; and opium.[75] The protection of imperial interests, therefore, became the primary basis for determining the circumstances in which the British would intervene in the affairs of the states and thereby also the grounds that governed the extent of sovereign powers exercised by the British in relation to the states.

With this change in policy, the precedent-based *Indian Political Practice* was soon supplanted by the coolly practical *Manual* with its relentless focus on imperial interests.[76] Like their counterparts in the Foreign Office in London who argued in favour of a 'political' League of Nations to manage colonial issues, political officers in early twentieth-century South Asia also advocated a functionalist approach that was focused on solving specific problems with the tools available to them. British colonial officials characterized the relationship between the princely states and the British government as 'political'; consequently, importance had to be given not only to purely legal instruments like treaties but also to 'imperial interests'. Since the scope of these imperial interests remained undefined,[77] this turn towards functionalism in British colonial thought provided an unrelenting means to expand the scope of British jurisdiction within the states and minimize authority of the states over their own internal affairs.[78]

[75] *Manual of Instructions to Officers of the Political Department of the Government of India* (1909), i–ii, iv, IOR/R/2/18/117.

[76] In 1929, the Indian States Committee noted that political officers were trained in administrative work in a British district and then passed 'examinations in Lyall's "Rise and expansion of the British Dominion in India", Lyall's "Asiatic studies", Tod's "Rajasthan", Malcolm's "Central India", Sleeman's "Ramblings and Recollections", the Introduction to Aitchison's Treaties, and the Political Department Manual'. See *Report of the Indian States Committee* (1929), para 75. *Indian Political Practice*, perhaps the most significant nineteenth-century text on relations between the British and the princely states, did not even feature in the study materials of new political officers.

[77] In 1929, the Political Department came up with an impressively long list of the various situations that would require British intervention to protect the interests of the empire but also qualified it as being a 'purely tentative and non-committal statement of the various factors' that might come under the heading of 'imperial necessity'. See Note by H. Wilberforce-Bell, 7 November 1929, IOR/R/1/1/4679(1).

[78] Barbara Ramusack argues that once the original policies and principles of late nineteenth-century British policy had been discarded, 'the British hierarchy seemed unable, or unwilling, to formulate any set of consistent principles to guide their relations with the princes'. See Ramusack, *The Princes of India in the Twilight of Empire*, (n 18) 61–62. Rather than inability, I would focus on unwillingness; by claiming that the 'interests of the empire' were the sole consideration for deciding disputed exercises of sovereign powers, the British were greatly able to expand their own authority.

The exploitation of the flexibility of 'imperial interests' is exemplified in one of the most notorious cases of British intervention in the states in the 1920s: the dispute between the government of India and the state of Hyderabad over the fertile, cotton-producing region of Berar. In 1853, Hyderabad had been persuaded to 'assign' Berar to the East India Company in lieu of payments for military protection; half a century later, Lord Curzon bullied the *nizam* (ruler) to permanently hand over the management of the region for a fixed annual payment.[79] In 1925, the *nizam*, Mir Osman Ali Khan,[80] decided to reclaim full sovereignty over Berar in a letter to the viceroy, Lord Reading.[81] Since the *nizams* of Hyderabad 'have been independent in the internal affairs of their State just as much as the British Government in British India' save for matters relating to foreign affairs, he argued that the dispute over Berar was 'a controversy between two Governments that stand on the same plane without any limits of subordination of one to the other'. Therefore, he proposed that 'the dispute should be investigated and reported upon by a Commission of impartial men'.[82]

Reading rejected this demand, noting that '[t]he sovereignty of the British Crown is supreme in India, and therefore no Ruler of an Indian State can justifiably claim to negotiate with the British Government on an equal footing'. Since the British government guaranteed the internal and external security of the princes, it also had the 'ultimate responsibility for taking remedial action' in cases 'where Imperial interests are concerned, or the general welfare of the people of a State is seriously and grievously affected by the action of its Government'. Reading noted that the 'varying degrees of internal sovereignty' that the states enjoyed were 'all subject to the due exercise by the Paramount Power of this responsibility'.[83] This conceptualization of sovereignty as 'divisible', with the precise allocation of sovereign powers between the states and the British government being determined by 'imperial interests', is the clearest statement of the approach taken by political officers to questions of sovereignty in the interwar period.

The Berar case exemplifies the distinction between the approaches taken by British international lawyers like Hersch Lauterpacht and James Brierly, who

[79] Ian Copland, 'The Hyderabad (Berar) Agreement of 1933: A Case Study in Anglo-Indian Diplomacy', *The Journal of Imperial and Commonwealth History*, 6/3 (1978), 285.

[80] As the last of the *nizams* of Hyderabad, the life of Osman Ali Khan has attracted significant scholarly attention. See Zubaida Yazdani and Mary Chrystal, *The Seventh Nizam: The Fallen Empire* (London: The Author, 1985); V. K. Bawa, *The Last Nizam: The Life and Times of Mir Osman Ali Khan* (New Delhi: Penguin, 1991); and Barbara Ramusack, 'Asaf Jah VII [Osman Ali Khan] (1886–1967)', in *Oxford Dictionary of National Biography*, https://doi.org/10.1093/ref:odnb/48824, accessed 19 October 2020.

[81] Reading was appointed viceroy in 1921. See A. Lentin, 'Isaacs, Rufus Daniel, first marquess of Reading (1860–1935)', in *Oxford Dictionary of National Biography*, https://doi.org/10.1093/ref:odnb/34119, accessed 19 October 2020.

[82] '*Nizam* to Viceroy, 20 September 1925', in *Documents and Speeches on the Indian Princely States*, ii, (n 63) 413–415.

[83] 'Viceroy to *nizam*, 27 March 1926', in *Documents and Speeches on the Indian Princely States*, ii, (n 63) 416–418.

argued in favour of the supremacy of law over politics, and British colonial officials in South Asia who, akin to politicians in London, pursued a relentlessly pragmatic policy on the question of the sovereignty of the princely states. Colonial administrators agreed that sovereignty was 'divisible' but argued that legal concepts had to be 'flexible' and 'imperial interests' rather than 'law' or even 'precedent' would determine the exercise of sovereign powers in the region. However, it was this very emphasis on the flexibility of legal concepts that both provoked and enabled a backlash from the princely states.

Divisible Sovereignty and the Princely States

The launch of mass, often violent, anticolonial agitations at the turn of the twentieth century provoked the colonial state 'to cultivate and politicise for imperial purposes the Indian princes'.[84] Ian Copland and Barbara Ramusack have documented how the princes emerged as key partners in British attempts to curb anticolonial nationalism by suppressing local organizations with nationalist links and extraditing British Indian political suspects who sought refuge within princely territory.[85] The First World War 'speeded up and initiated further changes in imperial attitudes and policies and in Indian society that provided new opportunities for the princes to demonstrate their value as allies to both British and Indian leaders'.[86] In addition to proving themselves as 'natural leaders' through military service, princes such as Ganga Singh of Bikaner,[87] Bhupinder Singh of Patiala,[88] and Ranjitsinhji of Nawanagar[89] became imperial and international players by participating in imperial war conferences and later by representing India at the League of Nations.[90]

[84] Copland, *The Princes of India in the Endgame of Empire*, (n 15) 28.

[85] Ramusack, *The Princes of India in the Twilight of Empire*, (n 18) 95–97; Copland, *The Princes of India in the Endgame of Empire*, (n 15) 30; and Ramusack, *The Indian Princes and their States*, (n 15) 129.

[86] Ramusack, *The Princes of India in the Twilight of Empire*, (n 18) 35.

[87] For details of Ganga Singh's life, see K. M. Panikkar, *His Highness the Maharaja of Bikaner: A Biography* (London: Oxford University Press, 1937); and Barbara Ramusack, 'Singh, Ganga (1880–1943)', in *Oxford Dictionary of National Biography*, https://doi.org/10.1093/ref:odnb/31885, accessed 18 October 2020.

[88] For details of Bhupinder Singh's life, see Barbara Ramusack, 'Singh, Sir Bhupinder (1891–1938)', in *Oxford Dictionary of National Biography*, https://doi.org/10.1093/ref:odnb/35408, accessed 18 October 2020. A collection of his speeches relating to state affairs can be found in Bhupinder Singh, *Public Pronouncements by His Highness the Maharaja Dhiraj of Patiala in connection with the Indian States Committee* (London: Spottiswoode, Ballantyne and Co., 1928).

[89] As a famous cricketer and someone who had more influence in relation to the small size of his state, Ranjitsinhji has attracted a significant amount of scholarly attention. See Simon Wilde, *Ranji: The Strange Genius of Ranjitsinhji* (London: Aurum Press, 1999); Ann Chambers, *Ranji: Maharaja of Connemara* (Dublin: Wolfhound Press, 2003); Mario Rodrigues, *Batting for the Empire: A Political Biography of Ranjitsinhji* (New Delhi: Penguin Books, 2003); Satadru Sen, *Migrant Races: Empire, Identity and K. S. Ranjitsinhji* (Manchester: Manchester University Press, 2004); and Simon Wilde, 'Ranjitsinhji Vibhaji, maharaja jam sahib of Navanagar (1872–1933)', in *Oxford Dictionary of National Biography*, https://doi.org/10.1093/ref:odnb/35190, accessed 14 May 2021.

[90] Ramusack, *The Princes of India in the Twilight of Empire*, (n 18) 43–44.

These stages provided opportunities for the princes and their advisors to carve out a higher profile for themselves and the states more broadly as well as to mingle with scholars, politicians, and activists who were in the process of redefining sovereignty to reimagine the world. Building on these experiences, the princes also relied on the language of sovereignty to challenge British paramountcy. Akin to interwar international lawyers such as Hersch Lauterpacht (who later became an advisor to the state of Hyderabad), and in contrast with British politicians and colonial officials, the princes favoured parcelling out sovereignty amongst different entities to place limits on the exercise of state—specifically colonial—power.

Princely participation (or lack thereof) in decision-making relating to 'all-India' matters such as maritime customs, excise policy, and railway jurisdiction emerged as a key arena of conflict. The construction of communications infrastructure in the late nineteenth century had increased trade links between British India and the states, with the states soon finding themselves at the mercy of decisions made by the government of India. For example, maritime states were forced to adopt British Indian tariff rates to prevent traders from circumventing duties by importing through the states while consumers in inland states effectively paid British Indian as well as state tariffs.[91] The princes proposed a range of solutions, including exempting goods imported by the states from British Indian customs duties, providing states with a share in British Indian customs revenue, and having state representation on rate-setting bodies like the tariff board. As Ian Copland notes, the princes increasingly traced most of their problems to their lack of influence in imperial decision-making.[92]

Once princely demands were strengthened by their service to the empire during the war, the British began to contemplate the creation of formal structures where the princes could discuss their views and offer opinions to the government of India. At two informal conferences convened in Delhi in 1916 and 1917, the participating princes overcame internal squabbling to present a scheme of reforms.[93] They

[91] A discussion of these two different implications of British Indian tariffs on the states can be found in George MacMunn, *The Indian States and Princes* (London: Jarrolds Publishers, 1936), 236–238. On the dispute over sea customs in the context of the states of the Western India States Agency, see John McLeod, *Sovereignty, Power, Control: Politics in the States of Western India, 1916–1947* (Leiden: Brill, 1999), 88–114.

[92] Copland, *The Princes of India in the Endgame of Empire*, (n 15) 56–58. Several states sent lengthy representations to the government of India protesting 'taxation without representation' and alleging that exaction of customs duties on goods imported through British Indian ports but meant for consumption in the states amounted to a transit duty, which the government had persuaded all states to abolish. See Letter from the Political Member, Government of Gwalior to the Resident at Gwalior, 21 March 1922, IOR/L/PS/10/1211/1; Letter from the *diwan* of Baroda to the Resident at Baroda, 3 April 1922, IOR/L/PS/10/1211/1; and Letter from the Chief Secretary, Government of Mysore to the Resident at Mysore, 3 March 1923, IOR/L/PS/10/1211/1. The full range of reform proposals can be found in the memo *The Position of Indian States in the Future Indian Polity*, 1926, NAI—Bhopal, Chamber Section, Bundle No. 4, File No. 7, Old File No. 1/26.

[93] For details on the splits among the princes as to the exact proposals of the scheme, see Copland, *The Princes of India in the Endgame of Empire*, (n 15) 38–40.

sought to establish two bodies: a Chamber of Ruling Princes through which the viceroy and the princes would jointly engage with proposals to maintain the states' internal autonomy and a Joint Committee of Reference comprised of representatives of the states and British India to advise on questions that were of 'common concern', such as tariffs, currency, and railway policy.[94] The demand for a joint committee was a non-starter but the Chamber of Princes was established within the broader constitutional reforms enacted after the war.[95] Given the large number of states, the size of the Chamber was a concern; ultimately, it consisted of 108 permanent members and 12 representatives of 'lesser' chiefs. Most of the Chamber's activities were conducted by the Standing Committee that was elected at each session and a chancellor who was its principal officer and liaison between the government of India and the princes.[96]

Although several major states (including Hyderabad, Mysore, and Indore) did not join the Chamber,[97] and its advisory and deliberative nature meant that it was largely unable to effect change,[98] it proved to be an important means through which the princes pursued their objectives, one of which was the (re)definition of the relationship between the states and the British as paramount power. The creation of the Chamber also had the effect of generalizing disputes between the princes and the British government. While individual disputes continued to exist, the creation of a collective forum expanded discussions between the princes and the British to broader issues of political reform from the individual jurisdictional disputes that had proliferated in the late nineteenth century.

For the princes, these closer economic and political links with British India came at a price, with the government of India intervening in their affairs based on 'imperial interests'. Attempts to minimize such interventions became more urgent in light of the stated British policy of 'the gradual development of self-governing institutions with a view to the progressive realisation of responsible Government

[94] Draft Memorandum on the Scheme for Establishing Improved Relations between the Government of India and the Indian States, NAI—Bhopal, Chamber Section, Bundle No. 4, File No. 7, Old File No. 1/26; and Draft Scheme, NAI—Bhopal, Chamber Section, Bundle No. 4, File No. 7, Old File No. 1/26.

[95] For details of the reforms and how they worked in practice, see Sarkar, *Modern India*, (n 59) 165–168; Metcalf and Metcalf, *A Concise History of Modern India*, (n 60) 167–168; Sugata Bose and Ayesha Jalal, *Modern South Asia: History, Culture, Political Economy* (4th edn, London: Routledge, 2018), 114–115; and Stephen Legg, 'Dyarchy: Democracy, Autocracy, and the Scalar Sovereignty of Interwar India', *Comparative Studies of South Asia, Africa and the Middle East*, 36/1 (2016), 44–65.

[96] Urmila Phadnis, *Towards the Integration of Indian States, 1919–1947* (Bombay: Asia Publishing House, 1968), 27, 30–31. For a discussion of the organization of the Chamber, its membership, and its powers and functions, see R. P. Bhargava, *The Chamber of Princes* (New Delhi: Northern Book Centre, 1991), 31–63.

[97] Ian Copland notes that the Chamber came to be dominated 'by a group of middle-sized, mainly Rajput states'. See Copland, *The Princes of India in the Endgame of Empire*, (n 15) 47. Attitudes among the rulers towards the Chamber did not remain static. For instance, although Sultan Jahan, the *begum* of Bhopal, kept aloof from the Chamber, her son, Hamidullah Khan was elected chancellor on two occasions. See Siobhan Lambert-Hurley, *Muslim Women, Reform and Princely Patronage: Nawab Sultan Jahan Begam of Bhopal* (London: Routledge, 2007), 64.

[98] Phadnis, *Towards the Integration of Indian States*, (n 96) 28–29.

in India as an integral part of the British Empire'.[99] Although the promise of self-government was vague and accompanied by the repression of anticolonial movements,[100] it unnerved the princes, who feared interference by a government that was responsible to the British Indian electorate. This trepidation was exacerbated by the often-antagonistic relationship they had with Indian anticolonial nationalists.[101] The princes also faced increasing criticism in the nationalist press, which portrayed them as irresponsible and pleasure-loving autocrats completely under the thumb of their British masters.[102] In such a situation, many princes believed that they faced a fight for their sheer existence.

To benefit from close economic ties with British India but simultaneously maintain their political distinctiveness, the princely states adopted a new strategy in the interwar period. They moved away from their late nineteenth-century assertions of exclusive, territorial sovereignty to explicitly adopt the language of divisible sovereignty, which hitherto had been the refuge of the British government. For the princes, however, the division of sovereign powers was not based on precedent or imperial interests but on state consent and the terms of treaties or engagements between the states and the British government. By arguing that sovereign powers were divisible, the princes imagined that they could participate in forums to discuss matters of common concern. Simultaneously, the focus on consent as the basis for the division of sovereign powers would, in their view, limit the interference of British officials to a specific list of issues, rather than being based on the nebulous idea of 'imperial interests'. By relying on the divisibility of sovereignty instead of their earlier insistence on territoriality, the princes hoped to both gain a voice in

99 'Speech of Edwin Montagu, House of Commons, 20 August 1917', in A. B. Keith, ed., *Speeches and Documents on Indian Policy, 1750–1921*, ii (London: Oxford University Press, 1922), 133.

100 The government preserved wartime powers of detention and trial without a jury; protests against such legislation were met with violence, as seen in the Amritsar massacre in 1919. See Metcalf and Metcalf, *A Concise History of Modern India*, (n 60) 168–169; Bose and Jalal, *Modern South Asia*, (n 95)120–121; and Kim A. Wagner, *Amritsar 1919: An Empire of Fear and the Making of a Massacre* (New Haven, CT: Yale University Press, 2019).

101 Although some British Indian politicians, such as Tej Bahadur Sapru, were close confidantes of the princely states, others considered them a hindrance to Indian independence. Jawaharlal Nehru, for instance, referred to the states as 'sinks of reaction and incompetence and unrestrained autocratic power, sometimes exercised by vicious and degraded individuals' that were 'propped up and artificially maintained by British Imperialism'. See 'Presidential address of Jawaharlal Nehru, Annual session of the All-India States' Peoples' Conference, 15 February 1939', in Maurice Gwyer and A. Appadorai, eds., *Speeches and Documents on the Indian Constitution, 1921–47*, ii (Bombay: Oxford University Press, 1957), 759. Taraknath Das was equally trenchant, calling on the princes to give up 'the retrograde tendency to autocratic government' and 'their special pretensions' since the idea of the princes 'having sovereign rights as rulers, is really a myth and a fiction'. See Taraknath Das, *Sovereign Rights of the Indian Princes* (Madras: Ganesh & Co., 1924), 16–18.

102 The princes were so concerned with what they considered to be unwanted propaganda and blackmail that they lobbied the government of India to enact legislation for special protection against press attacks, resulting in a storm of protest by anticolonial nationalists. See Ramusack, *The Princes of India in the Twilight of Empire*, (n 18) 122–128. An overview of the special legislation can be found in K. N. Chopra, *Law Relating to the Protection of the Administration of States in India* (Lahore: Universal Book Agency, 1939), 25–82.

all-India affairs and to restrict British interference into the internal affairs of the states. As was the case with proposals for the structure of interwar international institutions, the princes and the British government used the common language of divisible sovereignty to construct very different political structures.

Initial indications of this strategy can be seen in the reports prepared by a special committee of princes and their ministers in 1926 and 1927.[103] For the princes, the key to determining the relative powers of the states and the British government was state consent, which could be derived from treaties, engagements, or other types of formal relations. This emphasis on state consent could be broken down into several sub-arguments. First, the princes amplified their emphasis on treaties to argue that the states were 'in direct relations' with the British Crown with whom their treaties were 'originally contracted'.[104] Consequently, they claimed that the states were 'semi-international' in status since they were 'in alliance' with the Crown rather than being under the authority of the government of India.[105] As a result, they contended that these relations could not be transferred to a future responsible government of India without state consent.[106] Second, the princes argued that the relationship between the states and the Crown was 'legal' and governed by the original treaties and engagements. Hence, they sought the elimination of 'political practice' that was in 'fundamental opposition' to the treaties, maintaining that such usage had often been the result of states yielding under pressure. On account of this focus on 'law' over 'political practice', the princes argued that disputes between the states and the government of India ought to be referred to a judicial tribunal and called for the creation of a 'Supreme Court of Justice'.[107] Finally, by focusing on state consent, the princes also attempted to demarcate the 'internal affairs' of the states from matters that were of 'common concern' with British India (such as tariffs, railways,

[103] See Report of the Ministers' Meeting held at Bikaner, 1926, NAI—Bhopal, Chamber Section, Bundle No. 5, File No. 14, Old File No. 11; and Report of the Committee of Ministers appointed to consider the future position of the Indian states and other allied questions, 1927, NAI—Bhopal, Chamber Section, Bundle No. 4, File No. 7, Old File No. 1/26. For other discussions of the results of these meetings, see Ramusack, *The Princes of India in the Twilight of Empire*, (n 18) 140–142; and Copland, *The Princes of India in the Endgame of Empire*, (n 15) 62–64.

[104] Report of the Ministers' Meeting held at Bikaner, 1926, NAI—Bhopal, Chamber Section, Bundle No. 5, File No. 14, Old File No. 11.

[105] To emphasize the 'semi-international' status of the states, the princes also pushed for Political Department reforms to claim a diplomatic rather than a constitutional relationship. They sought a departmental head who was a 'comparative senior member of the *corps Diplomatique*' since such an officer would be 'well-accustomed' in the interpretation of treaties and his training would have equipped him 'to deal with the affairs of semi-international bodies such as are the Indian States today'. See Report of the Sub-Committee appointed to investigate the question of the present and future organization of the Political Department, Appendix C, Report of the Ministers' Meeting held at Bikaner, 1926, NAI—Bhopal, Chamber Section, Bundle No. 5, File No. 14, Old File No. 11.

[106] This argument tracks one made by the British constitutional lawyer A. B. Keith, in Keith, *The Constitution, Administration and Laws of the Empire*, (n 26) 260–261.

[107] Report of the Committee of Ministers appointed to consider the future position of the Indian states and other allied questions, 1927, NAI—Bhopal, Chamber Section, Bundle No. 4, File No. 7, Old File No. 1/26; and Chancellor's Office, Patiala, Note on the Future Position of Indian States, 1927, NAI—Bhopal, Chamber Section, Bundle No. 4, File No. 7, Old File No. 1/26.

posts, telegraphs, and currency) advocating that '[t]here would be no attempt to cross the border-land'. On matters of common concern, the princes proposed a range of structures, including the representation of the states in the houses of the British Indian legislature, joint consultation between the Chamber of Princes and the Council of State of the British Indian legislature on issues of common concern, and a separate All-India Committee of Joint Deliberation consisting of representatives of the states as well as British India.[108]

Although there were serious differences among the princes on the extent of political reform that was necessary within the states,[109] the chancellor, Bhupinder Singh, managed to unite the delegation that met the viceroy, Lord Irwin,[110] in May 1927.[111] They urged the appointment of a special committee to investigate the relationship of the states with the British Crown and suggest means for 'securing effective consultation and cooperation on an equitable basis between British India and Indian States on all matters of common interest'.[112] Irwin put the case for such an independent inquiry to the secretary of state for India,[113] Lord Birkenhead,[114] who was sceptical, but ultimately conceded.[115]

On 16 December 1927, Birkenhead appointed the Indian States Committee, whose terms of reference were

> (1) to report upon the relationship between the Paramount Power and the States with particular reference to the rights and obligations arising from:- (a) treaties, engagements and sanads, and (b) usage, sufferance and other causes; (2) to enquire into the financial and economic relations between British India and the States and to make any recommendations that the Committee may consider desirable or necessary for their more satisfactory adjustment.[116]

[108] Report of the Ministers' Meeting held at Bikaner, 1926, NAI—Bhopal, Chamber Section, Bundle No. 5, File No. 14, Old File No. 11.

[109] On these differences, see Ramusack, *The Princes of India in the Twilight of Empire*, (n 18) 141–142; and Copland, *The Princes of India in the Endgame of Empire*, (n 15) 62–63.

[110] Irwin was appointed viceroy in 1926. See D. J. Dutton, 'Wood, Edward Frederick Lindley, first earl of Halifax (1881–1959)', in *Oxford Dictionary of National Biography*, https://doi.org/10.1093/ref:odnb/36998, accessed 19 October 2020.

[111] On the discussions at this meeting, see Ashton, *British Policy Towards the Indian States*, (n 18) 118–119; Ramusack, *The Princes of India in the Twilight of Empire*, (n 18) 142–143; and Copland, *The Princes of India in the Endgame of Empire*, (n 15) 64–65.

[112] *Aide-Mémoire*, May 1927, IOR/R/1/1/1682(1). The princes claimed that the interests of the states would be best served by the nomination of a committee different from the one that was to be appointed to discuss constitutional development in British India. See Informal Conference held at Viceregal Lodge on 6 May 1927 to consider questions relating to Indian States, IOR/R/1/1/1653.

[113] Letter from the Government of India, Foreign and Political Department to the Secretary of State for India, 15 September 1927, IOR/R/1/1/1682(1).

[114] Birkenhead had been a successful barrister and author of legal texts before he entered Parliament. See John Campbell, *F. E. Smith, First Earl of Birkenhead* (London: Jonathan Cape, 1983); and John Campbell, 'Smith, Frederick Edwin, first earl of Birkenhead (1872–1930)', in *Oxford Dictionary of National Biography*, https://doi.org/10.1093/ref:odnb/36137, accessed 19 October 2020.

[115] Letter from the Secretary of State for India to the Viceroy, 8 December 1927, IOR/L/PS/10/1211/1.

[116] Questionnaire issued by the Indian States Committee, Appendix I, *Report of the Indian States Committee*, (n 76).

The Committee was chaired by Harcourt Butler, the former Indian foreign secretary and architect of the laissez-faire policy that had enabled British interference in princely state affairs based on 'imperial interests'. The other two members of the Committee were Sidney Peel, a former financial advisor to the British government,[117] and William Holdsworth, the Vinerian Professor of English Law at the University of Oxford and a pre-eminent legal historian whose works included a multi-volume history of English law.[118] The submissions of the states to the Committee together with the report that the Committee members produced form the most sophisticated versions of the sovereignty arguments that the princes and the British put forward during the 1920s.

Sovereignty Before the Indian States Committee

The Indian States Committee kicked off proceedings in early 1928 when its members toured individual states and held discussions with princes, state officials, and British political officers. The Committee also sent a questionnaire to all states, inviting written responses.[119] Some months later, the Committee held oral hearings in London. While states like Mysore and Hyderabad submitted individual replies to the questionnaire, a large number were represented by the Chamber of Princes.[120]

The Chamber's Standing Committee established a body termed the Special Organization to work on the issue. In addition to Bhupinder Singh of Patiala, the chancellor of the Chamber at the time, a number of princely state advisors were influential in developing the princes' legal case: K. N. Haksar, the political member of the state of Gwalior;[121] Lawrence Rushbrook Williams, the foreign minister

[117] See Pat Thane, 'Peel, Sir Sidney Cornwallis, baronet (1870–1938)', in *Oxford Dictionary of National Biography*, https://doi.org/10.1093/ref:odnb/47815, accessed 19 October 2020.

[118] Holdsworth was a close friend of Birkenhead from their time together at Oxford; he even dedicated several volumes of his history of English law to Birkenhead. See H. G. Hanbury, 'Holdsworth, Sir William Searle (1871–1944)', rev. David Ibbetson, in *Oxford Dictionary of National Biography*, https://doi.org/10.1093/ref:odnb/33933, accessed 19 October 2020.

[119] A copy of the questionnaire issued by the Committee can be found in Appendix I, *Report of the Indian States Committee*, (n 76). Replies to the questionnaire are collected in a single volume, *Replies Received to the Questionnaire Issued by the Committee*, IOR/V/26/272/3.

[120] Historians of South Asia have focused on the politics surrounding the Committee but have only briefly dwelt on the legal arguments made by the princes. For discussions of the Committee's proceedings, see R. J. Moore, *The Crisis of Indian Unity, 1917–1940* (Oxford: Clarendon Press, 1974), 32–33; Ramusack, *The Princes of India in the Twilight of Empire*, (n 18) 144–152; Ashton, *British Policy Towards the Indian States*, (n 18) 120–124; Copland, *The British Raj and the Indian Princes*, (n 18) 277–280; Ramusack, *The Indian Princes and their States*, (n 15) 128; and Copland, *The Princes of India in the Endgame of Empire*, (n 15) 65–72. Legal historians have traced the legal arguments made by the princes primarily within a broader discussion of Indian constitutional structures. See Rohit De, 'Between Midnight and Republic: Theory and Practice of India's Dominion Status', *International Journal of Constitutional Law*, 17/4 (2019), 1227–1228.

[121] The Haksar family had a long tradition of service in the states of Gwalior and Indore. For a brief snapshot, see Henny Sender, *The Kashmiri Pandits: A Study of Cultural Choice in North India* (Delhi: Oxford University Press, 1988), 97–104.

of Patiala;[122] K. M. Panikkar, a lawyer and political advisor to the *maharaja* of Kashmir;[123] and Leslie Scott, a Conservative privy councillor who was politically close to Lord Birkenhead and had a flourishing private legal practice.[124] Together, these aides developed a comprehensive case for the Committee's consideration through several different works: a book written by Panikkar on the relationship between the states and the British government;[125] a tract titled *The British Crown and the Indian States*, which comprised the Standing Committee's written submissions to the Committee;[126] Scott's written legal opinion,[127] and Scott's oral arguments before the Committee.[128]

An emphasis on state consent formed the lynchpin of the case put forth by the princes before the Committee, with treaties and other formal engagements being the key sources of such consent. The princes and their advisors repeatedly emphasized the importance of treaty rights, with Bhupinder Singh arguing that 'political practice' threatened to undermine the states' rights and privileges that had 'hitherto believed to be inviolably safeguarded by their treaties and engagements'.[129] This focus on treaties also enabled the states to argue that their relationship was with the British Crown rather than the government of British India.[130] Such a claim ensured that any move towards representative government in British India would not affect the states. Although the states claimed to be in alliance with the Crown, they admitted having given up some sovereign rights such as control over external affairs. Given this unusual position of the states, Panikkar advocated for the application

[122] Rushbrook Williams was a historian who taught at the University of Allahabad before he became involved as an advisor to the states. See Percival Spear, 'Obituaries: Professor L. F. Rushbrook Williams', *Asian Affairs*, 10/1 (1979), 113–114.

[123] K. M. Panikkar, *An Autobiography*, trans. K. Krishnamurthy (Madras: Oxford University Press, 1977), 33–38, 48–54, 67–79. On account of his nationalist leanings, the government of India included Panikkar's name in a list of political suspects, terming him as one who was prone to 'seditious talk', and concluding that he was 'anti-British' and 'thoroughly disloyal and anti-Government'. See Note on Antecedents of K. M. Panikkar, IOR/R/1/1/1714. For discussions of Panikkar's views on anticolonial nationalism, see Rita Paolini, 'An Indian Student in Oxford During World War I: Kavalam M. Panikkar Between Nationalism and Princely States', *Monde(s)*, 9 (2016), 59–74.

[124] P. A. Landon, 'Scott, Sir Leslie Frederic (1869–1950)', rev. Marc Brodie, in *Oxford Dictionary of National Biography*, https://doi.org/10.1093/ref:odnb/35992, accessed 22 October 2020.

[125] K. M. Panikkar, *An Introduction to the Study of the Relations of Indian States with the Government of India* (London: Martin Hopkinson, 1927).

[126] *The British Crown and the Indian States: An Outline Sketch Presented to the Indian States Committee on Behalf of the Standing Committee of the Chamber of Princes* (1928), IOR/L/PS/20/248. Panikkar claimed he wrote the first part of this study. See Panikkar, *An Autobiography*, (n 123) 79.

[127] Scott issued a joint opinion along with several other highly qualified jurists. See Joint Opinion of the Right Honourable Leslie F. Scott, KC, MP, Mr. Stuart Bevan, KC, MP, Mr. Wilfrid A. Greene, KC, Mr. Valentine Holmes, and Mr. Donald Somervell, Appendix III, *Report of the Indian States Committee*, (n 76). An earlier version of the opinion was published as 'The Crown and Indian States: English Counsels' Opinion', *Indian States Review* (27 October 1928), IOR/R/1/1/4673(2).

[128] The oral evidence submitted to the committee can be found in *Oral Evidence Recorded Before the Committee*, IOR/V/26//272/3.

[129] 'Speech delivered by the *maharaja* of Patiala on the occasion of the visit of the Indian States Committee to Patiala, February 1928', in *Public Pronouncements*, (n 88) 12–13.

[130] Joint Opinion, (n 127) para 7.

of 'a kind of semi-international law'.[131] On issues such as treaty interpretation, the princes argued that the principles of international law would be useful; Scott specifically argued that international law continued to govern the terms of the transfer of sovereign rights from the states to the Crown.[132]

The princes also aimed to reconcile their subordinate position with claims of being British allies, realizing that the language of territorial sovereignty was unsatisfactory for their purposes. Although they had previously admitted the possibility of ceding specific sovereign powers (such as control over external affairs) to the colonial state, they now moved to explicitly adopt the vocabulary of divisible sovereignty by asserting that sovereign powers were divided between the states and the British government. Panikkar turned to Henry Maine to contend that that the *sui generis* nature of the states amounted to a 'repudiation of the Austinian principle of sovereignty'. He termed '[t]he undivided sovereign of the Austinian school' to be 'a meaningless metaphysical conception'. He claimed that the principle of unitary sovereignty was the very reason that the states were declared to be 'non-sovereign communities'. Sovereignty, instead, was 'the complex of public powers', whose division was 'constantly undertaken in the relation between states'.[133] Leslie Scott agreed, noting that 'the complete sovereignty of the state is divided between the state and the Crown'.[134]

Despite sharing the view that sovereignty was divisible, the princes differed from colonial officials on the basis for splitting sovereign powers. Rather than focusing on historical precedent or pragmatic considerations of imperial interest, they advocated a 'contractual' view of sovereignty. They argued that the division of sovereign powers was set out in treaties, engagements, or other means by which the consent of the states could be determined. By focusing on consent, the princes aimed to limit the extensive jurisdiction that the British government claimed to exercise within the states. Since the states retained all powers of sovereignty that were not expressly conceded to the Crown, 'residuary jurisdiction' remained with the states.[135] In his legal opinion, Leslie Scott argued that '[t]he Crown has no sovereignty over any state by virtue of the Prerogative or any source other than cession

[131] Panikkar, *Relations of Indian States with the Government of India*, (n 125) xxi. In a later text, Panikkar pointed out that the states were foreign territory in relation to British India, states' subjects were not British subjects, and treaties made by the Crown were not *ipso jure* binding on the states; the states, therefore, had a 'subordinate international position'. See K. M. Panikkar, *Inter-Statal Law: The Law Affecting the Relations of the Indian States with the British Crown* (Madras: University of Madras, 1934), 25.

[132] Joint Opinion, (n 127) para 1.

[133] Panikkar, *Relations of Indian States with the Government of India*, (n 125) xix, 121, 125. This develops on an article written by Panikkar while he was a student at Oxford, in which he relied on Maine to argue '[t]he right of sovereignty is thus divided, but the proportion of that division depends upon the individual state and on the treaty by which it is bound'. See K. M. Panikkar, 'The Native States and Indian Nationalism', *The Modern Review*, 25/1 (1919), 37.

[134] Joint Opinion, (n 127) para 2.

[135] *The British Crown and the Indian States*, (n 126) 82.

from the ruler of the state', while 'all sovereign rights, privileges and dignities not so transferred remain vested in the ruler of the state'.[136]

The modification of obligations in the original treaties also depended on state consent. Panikkar claimed that 'the rights, jurisdictions and authorities of the sovereign princes of India are based on treaties and political practice arising out of mutual agreement, to alter which the consent of both the parties is required'.[137] Scott dismissed the attempts of British administrators to change the mutual rights and obligations by relying on precedent, arguing that 'usage' could only be considered a source of obligation if it was backed by agreement. He also noted that agreement could be inferred only under limited conditions when it could be proved that the contracting parties intended to enter into an agreement.[138]

By emphasizing treaty rights and consent, the states underlined the legal nature of their relationship with the Crown. The Standing Committee's sketch asserted that the states had 'absolute rights' that were 'based on contract with the Crown' and were ascertainable by 'the application of well-known legal principles'.[139] Scott built on this logic to argue that the relationship between the Crown and the states was a legal rather than a political one. Consequently, both sides had definite rights and obligations that could only be ascertained by reference to legal principles.[140]

Since the relationship was a legal one, the princes argued that the term 'paramountcy', and thereby the scope of the powers of the British government in relation to the states, was capable of being defined and limited, instead of being dependent on 'imperial interests'. Rather than challenging the entire edifice of paramountcy, the states chose to rely on the divisibility of sovereignty to limit it. Bhupinder Singh reiterated that the princes conceded the paramountcy of the British government but believed that 'paramountcy had in its origin a definitely circumscribed ambit, and should be equally defined in its operation'.[141] By adopting this conciliatory

[136] Joint Opinion, (n 127) para 2.

[137] Panikkar, *Relations of Indian States with the Government of India*, (n 125) 143–144.

[138] Joint Opinion, (n 127) paras 3(c) and 5(d).

[139] *The British Crown and the Indian States*, (n 126) 98.

[140] Joint Opinion, (n 127) para 1. Despite this claim of a legal relationship, there was some dissent among the princes over the creation of an independent judicial mechanism for settling disputes between the states and the Crown. The Standing Committee's official submission demanded the establishment of a tribunal to settle disputes so that the government of India shall 'no longer be a judge in their own cause'. See *The British Crown and the Indian States*, (n 126) 98. Mirza Ismail, the *diwan* of Mysore, which had submitted a separate response, told members of the Committee than an arbitration mechanism was required in the case of 'justiciable' questions between the states and the government of India although he conceded that 'purely political' questions ought to be left to the discretion of the viceroy. See Minutes of a Discussion at Government House, Mysore, between the Indian States Committee and representatives of the Mysore Government, 19 March 1928, 51–54, *Oral Evidence Recorded Before the Committee*, IOR/V/26//272/3. However, Mahdi Yar Jung, Hyderabad's political secretary, was concerned by the proposal for the judicial settlement of disputes, preferring instead to advocate for a political relationship. See Letter from the Political Secretary to the *nizam* to the Secretary to the Indian States Committee, 24 April 1928, NAI, Government of India, Foreign and Political Department, 1928, Reforms, File No. 12-R.

[141] 'Speech delivered by the *maharaja* of Patiala on the occasion of the visit of the Indian States Committee to Patiala, February 1928', in *Public Pronouncements*, (n 88) 15.

strategy, the princes aimed to minimize British interference in the internal affairs of the states but simultaneously retain a link with the British government as a defence against political attacks by anticolonial nationalists.

In his written opinion and oral arguments, Scott attempted to provide a definition of paramountcy that would satisfy these princely aspirations. He argued that paramountcy was 'the sum total of specific rights and obligations' that resulted from an '[a]greement between the Crown and a State by which the State cedes to the Crown certain rights in consideration of its accepting certain liabilities in connection with the foreign relations and security of the State'. The terms of the paramountcy agreement had to be ascertained 'by a consideration of what is essential to the constitution of the relationship, to the mutual acknowledgement of that minimum of rights and obligations without which Paramountcy would not be Paramountcy' and also 'by the rejection of every term, however reasonable, however convenient, which is not absolutely essential and necessary'.[142] Although specific instances such as misgovernment that imperilled the security of a state could justify British interference in internal state affairs, there was no 'general discretionary right' of the Crown to interfere with the internal sovereignty of the states. Instead, the rights and obligations possessed by the Crown on account of paramountcy were limited to 'foreign relations and external and internal security'. There was 'no justification for saying that the rights of the Crown in its capacity as Paramount Power extend beyond these matters'.[143]

Scott's arguments reflected the princes' desire for a clear definition of the scope of paramountcy and the recognition of the internal sovereignty of the states. To achieve these aims, the princes argued for a split between external affairs, authority over which had been ceded to the British, and internal affairs, over which the states claimed to retain full control.[144] On matters of 'common concern' such as railways or customs tariffs, the states contended that they retained sovereign rights to formulate policy while remaining open to the need to collaborate with the government of India. Various types of formal machinery could regulate such cooperation and allow for the 'border' between internal affairs and common matters to be maintained.[145] In sum, the princes relied on the idea of sovereign powers being divided based on consent to advocate a parcelling out of sovereign powers that would permit them to both retain their close and valued relationship with the British Crown in light of pressures from British Indian nationalists and limit British interference into their internal affairs to maximize the internal autonomy of the states.

142 Minutes of Evidence given before the Indian States Committee at Montagu House, Whitehall, 26 November 1928, 648, 650, *Oral Evidence Recorded Before the Committee*, IOR/V/26//272/3.

143 Joint Opinion, (n 127) paras 6(b) and 6(c).

144 Panikkar, *Relations of Indian States with the Government of India*, (n 125) 127.

145 *The British Crown and the Indian States*, (n 126) 98–99.

The British response to the princes' case, in the form of the political secretary's written opinion[146] and the report published by the Indian States Committee,[147] proved an unwelcome surprise to the princes, who considered their legal case to be comprehensive.[148] Although the Committee members were supposed to be independent, they had been briefed by British officials on the possible consequences of the report's conclusions. After being advised by Birkenhead,[149] Irwin wrote to Harcourt Butler to warn him that the terms of reference were limited to reporting on the 'actual position' of the states and did not extend to recommendations to revise the relationship between the states and the British government; he also suggested that Butler 'hint' to Scott that the Committee would not accept proposals for such changes.[150] Given the close relationship between the Committee members and the British government, and the fact that the Committee was chaired by Butler, who had been the principal author of the turn towards 'imperial interests' in the early decades of the twentieth century, it is productive to consider the Committee's report as part of the British reaction to the princes' arguments.

In their report, the members of the Committee conceded that 'the relationship of the states to the Paramount Power is a relationship to the Crown, that the treaties made with them are treaties made with the Crown, and that those treaties are of continuous and binding force as between the states which made them and the Crown'.[151] But instead of accepting the princes' argument in favour of 'semi-international' status with the possibility of international law applying in some instances, the Committee was somewhat more circumspect in its conclusions. It noted that the relationship between the states and the Crown was *sui generis* since the states had no parallel to their position in history and were governed by a 'body of convention and usage not quite like anything in the world'. Rather than being subject to international law or municipal law, the states were governed 'by rules

[146] Précis of Political Secretary's Opinion placed before the Indian States Committee, IOR/R/1/1/4673(1).

[147] *Report of the Indian States Committee*, (n 76).

[148] In letter to Bhupinder Singh, Leslie Scott claimed that he was 'absolutely convinced both of the justice and of the strength' of the case of the states, and boasted that the states were bound to both 'win recognition of the rights to which they are entitled in law' and 'get a sound, workable machinery which will be calculated to prevent infringements of their rights in the future' if they followed his advice. See Letter from Leslie Scott to the *maharaja* of Patiala, 18 December 1928, NAI—Bhopal, Chamber Section, Bundle No. 5, File No. 1, Old File No. 2/2.

[149] Ian Copland notes that Birkenhead was concerned about Butler's reputation as the architect of laissez-faire. See Copland, *The Princes of India in the Endgame of Empire*, (n 15) 70. However, as I have argued earlier, the laissez-faire policy itself laid the foundation for increasing intervention into the states through its focus on imperial interests.

[150] Letter from the Viceroy to Harcourt Butler, 19 February 1928, NAI, Government of India, Foreign and Political Department, 1928, Reforms, File No. 91-R.

[151] *Report of the Indian States Committee*, (n 76) para 38. Members of states peoples' movements that lobbied for political reform claimed that the Committee had not confirmed that direct relations with the Crown were distinct from relations with the government of India as an agent of the Crown; consequently, the Committee's conclusion was not nearly as favourable to the princes as they made out. See P. L. Chudgar, *Indian Princes under British Protection: A Study of their Personal Rule, their Constitutional Position and their Future* (London: Williams & Norgate Ltd., 1929), 149–155.

which form a very special part of the constitutional law of the Empire'. However, by accepting the claim that the relationship of the states was with the Crown and not the government of India, the Committee also recognized the concern of the states when it came to responsible government in British India. It opined that 'in view of the historical nature of the relationship between the Paramount Power and the Princes, the latter should not be transferred without their own agreement to a relationship with a new government in British India responsible to an Indian legislature'.[152]

The recognition of a direct relationship with the Crown turned out to be the lone bright spot for the princes in the Committee's report. Relying on Henry Maine, the Committee agreed that 'sovereignty has always been regarded as divisible'. But unlike the princes, whose advisors had argued in favour of a 'contractual approach', the Committee relied on a more flexible idea of the division of sovereign powers. The relationship between the states and the Crown, the Committee concluded, was not merely contractual but was a 'living, growing relationship shaped by circumstances and policy, resting … on a mixture of history, theory and modern fact'.[153] This conceptualization reframed Butler's original focus on 'imperial interests' in the Political Department's *Manual* to an emphasis on 'history, theory and modern fact' along with 'policy' considerations. The result, however, was the same: a pragmatic view for determining the way sovereign rights were divided between the princely states and the British government.

The Committee's conclusions matched the submissions made by British political officers. In one internal memo, political officials denounced Leslie Scott's arguments as 'somewhat preposterous'.[154] The deputy political secretary Charles Watson took issue with Scott's focus on treaties and consent. Since many of the treaties had been drawn up before the British became the paramount power, Watson claimed that they did not accurately reflect and 'define completely in all cases the relations which now exist between the Crown or Government and the Indian States'. Many treaties, he admitted, contained nothing on the right of interference; however, he claimed that 'it cannot be denied that such interference is not only the right but the duty of the Paramount Power'. He refused to accept that the relation between the Crown and the states was 'purely contractual', instead arguing that paramountcy was 'a source of rights' and, therefore, 'the only limit to interference with the sovereignty of the Protected States is the discretion of the Paramount Power itself'. In particular, changing circumstances required a readjustment in the division of sovereign powers since the 'Paramount Power has not only the interests

[152] *Report of the Indian States Committee*, (n 76) paras 43, 58. Members of peoples' movements in the states were dismayed at this portion of the report and argued that a responsible government would not be a 'new Government' but only 'a development of the existing Government'. See Chudgar, *Indian Princes under British Protection*, (n 151) 182–186.

[153] *Report of the Indian States Committee*, (n 76) paras 44, 39.

[154] Note by [AKK?], 1 November 1928, IOR/R/1/1/4673(1).

of one individual State to consider but also the welfare of neighbouring territory whether of British India or of other States'.[155]

The Committee built on these ideas, asserting that 'the Paramount Power has had of necessity to make decisions and exercise the functions of paramountcy beyond the terms of the treaties in accordance with changing political, social and economic conditions'. It was necessary and justifiable for the Crown to extend its jurisdiction within the states—for instance, over cantonment areas, European British subjects, or servants of the Crown—despite specific clauses in treaties against such extension.[156] By taking this view, the Committee confirmed that the extension of British sovereign powers was based on the idea of 'imperial interests', which had underlined Butler's laissez-faire policy, rather than the consent of states.

State consent was also unnecessary to modify the treaty relations between the states and the Crown. Unlike the princes, who had rejected the significance of 'usage' that was not backed by agreement, Charles Watson argued that 'the explicit provisions of the Treaties may be found to have been modified by practice and usage when accepted without protest by the parties to the Treaties'.[157] The Committee expanded this sentiment to conclude that usage had 'shaped and developed the relationship between the Paramount Power and the states from the earliest times, almost ... from the date of the treaties themselves'. Usage had supplied material when treaties, engagements, and *sanads* did not exist, and also operated 'to determine questions on which the treaties, engagements and sanads are silent'; therefore, usage was a 'constant factor in the interpretation of these treaties engagements and sanads'. In the words of the Committee, '[u]sage, in fact, lights up the dark places of the treaties'.[158]

By emphasizing usage, policy, and circumstances, the British rejected the idea that the relationship between the states and the British as paramount power was a legal one, focusing instead on the significance of political discretion. Proposals relating to the resolution of disputes between the states and the government of India provide an example. The Committee was circumspect about judicial resolution. Instead, the members suggested that the viceroy rely on his political knowledge to appoint a representative committee that would provide advisory opinions, with the final decision being left to the secretary of state for India.[159]

Interpreting the relationship between the states and the British government as a 'political' one also enabled colonial officials to claim that their powers in relation to the states were incapable of being defined or limited. Bertrand Glancy, the political secretary, maintained that any attempt to define or codify paramountcy

[155] Note by C. C. Watson, 9 November 1928, IOR/R/1/1/4673(1).
[156] *Report of the Indian States Committee*, (n 76) paras 21, 56.
[157] Note by C. C. Watson, 9 November 1928, IOR/R/1/1/4673(1).
[158] *Report of the Indian States Committee*, (n 76) paras 40, 52.
[159] *Report of the Indian States Committee*, (n 76) para 70.

was objectionable 'both because a complete list of the practical restraints on their powers would be unpalatable to the Princes and because new conditions may give rise to new occasions and new ways of the Paramount Power exerting its authority'.[160] The Committee's report followed suit, insisting that it was 'impossible' to define paramountcy owing to the rapidly changing conditions of the world and 'imperial necessity'. Paramountcy had to 'remain paramount', the Committee noted rather unhelpfully, and had to 'fulfil its obligations, defining or adapting itself according to the shifting necessities of the time and the progressive development of the states'. Since the Committee had a broad interpretation of paramountcy, it concluded that it would be historically inaccurate to suggest that paramountcy only vested definite rights and imposed definite duties on the Crown with respect to a specific set of matters, i.e. foreign affairs and internal and external security. Instead, it concluded that the Crown had the power and the duty to do all acts that were considered 'necessary for imperial purposes, for the good government of India as a whole, the good government of individual states, the suppression of barbarous practices, the saving of human life, and for dealing with cases in which rulers have proved unfit for their position'.[161] Imperial interests, therefore, could justify almost any action taken by the British in relation to the states.

The flexibility of sovereign power also blurred the lines between the internal and the external, at least in the case of the princely states. Since the paramount power had the duty 'to protect the states against rebellion or insurrection', the Committee noted that it also possessed 'correlative obligations in cases where its intervention is asked for or has become necessary'. Intervention was, in the eyes of the Committee, both the right and the obligation of the British as paramount power and could take place 'for the benefit of the Prince, of the state, of India as a whole'. Rather than affirming the internal autonomy of the states, the Committee listed several situations in which the British government would be required to intervene into internal state affairs to preserve peace within and outside the state as well as for the economic benefit of India as a whole. Even in relation to areas of common concern, the Committee was lukewarm about the possibility of establishing formal machinery to ensure state participation in decision-making, proposing instead that the viceroy have the discretion to appoint committees that could advise him on questions that affected the states and British India.[162] This final suggestion encapsulates the British approach to their relationship with the princely states: they viewed it as a political one that was defined primarily by imperial interests, a conviction that ultimately empowered the British government in their relations with the states.

[160] Précis of Political Secretary's Opinion placed before the Indian States Committee, IOR/R/1/1/4673(1).
[161] *Report of the Indian States Committee*, (n 76) paras 57, 42.
[162] *Report of the Indian States Committee*, (n 76) paras 49, 51–55, 63–66, 69.

To further buttress the Committee's approach, one of its members, William Holdsworth published a piece accusing the princes of 'unduly' magnifying the importance of treaties and minimizing the importance of usage, which, in his view, was contrary to historical fact.[163] The Committee also obtained the support of the London barrister Julian Palmer, who claimed that Leslie Scott's 'contractual' approach was a 'specious attempt to gain the advantages (without assuming the liabilities) of international status' and suffered from 'radical unsoundness'.[164]

The Committee's emphasis on imperial necessity as the basis for extensive British powers drew vociferous responses from the states. Although the princes claimed to accept 'wholly and without qualification, the Paramountcy of the British Crown', they also feared that they 'would have no rights' if the 'extreme view of Paramountcy' adopted by the Committee prevailed.[165] Their advisors spelled out these concerns in greater detail. Donald Somervell, one of the co-signatories of Scott's legal opinion, pointed out that the Committee's view of the British-princely relationship as a 'living growing relationship shaped by circumstances and policy' conflicted with 'the many solemn undertakings by the Crown to the states to "maintain unimpaired their privileges, rights, and dignities"'.[166] Others were more trenchant. Bhupinder Singh's legal advisor, D. K. Sen, claimed that the Committee had 'translated the doctrine of paramountcy into a theory of divine rights of the Paramount Power'.[167] The prime minister of Bikaner, Manubhai Mehta,[168] warned of the consequences of 'uncontrolled' paramountcy, claiming that it would result

[163] W. S. Holdsworth, 'The Indian States and India', *Law Quarterly Review*, 46/3 (1930), 407–446. However, Holdsworth admitted that Britain's suzerainty over the states had 'elements of consent' because of 'the quasi-international element in the relationship between the Paramount Power and the States'. As a result, usage could not 'be altered at the will and pleasure of the Paramount Power, because the usage defines the distribution between the Paramount Power and the States of the various powers involved in sovereignty, and thus sets limits to the powers which it confers upon both parties to the relationship'. See ibid 427–428. This reference to consent led Manubhai Mehta to claim that Holdsworth had conceded the princes' argument. See Note on Paramountcy, NAI—Bhopal, Chamber Section, Bundle No. 15, File No. 51, Old File No. P/56.

[164] Julian Palmer, *Sovereignty and Paramountcy in India* (London: Stevens and Sons, 1930), 17.

[165] Note communicated to the Viceroy by the Standing Committee of the Chamber of Princes on the occasion of their conference with His Excellency before his visit to England, upon the Report of the Indian States' Committee, 28 June 1929, NAI—Bhopal, Chamber Section, Bundle No. 7, File No. 2, Old File No. 2/5. See also the concerns expressed by Bhupinder Singh in a letter to his fellow princes in Circular letter from the *maharaja* of Patiala, 29 April 1929, NAI—Bhopal, Chamber Section, Bundle No. 7, File No. 2, Old File No. 2/5 and the views expressed in an informal meeting of the princes in *Proceedings of the Meetings of the Chamber of Princes (Narendra Mandal)* (1930), 50–51.

[166] D. B. Somervell, 'The Indian States', *British Year Book of International Law*, 11 (1930), 57. In fact, K. N. Haksar accused the Committee members of deliberately misunderstanding the sources on which they based their arguments. See K. N. Haksar, An Analysis of the Butler Committee's Report with Comments, NAI—Bhopal, Chamber Section, Bundle No. 7, File No. 2, Old File No. 2/5.

[167] Sen, *The Indian States, Their Status, Rights and Obligations*, (n 5) 205. A. P. Nicholson, a British journalist who was sympathetic to the princes, also used the language of the 'divine right of paramountcy' in his denunciation of the Committee's report. See A. P. Nicholson, *Scraps of Paper: India's Broken Treaties, Her Princes, and the Problem* (London: Ernest Benn Limited, 1930), 62.

[168] Mehta had been the *diwan* of Baroda between 1916 and 1927, after which he moved to Bikaner as the prime minister. See R. Venkoba Rao, 'Sir Manubhai N. Mehta', in *Ministers in Indian States* (Trichinopoly: Wednesday Review Press, 1928), 13–14.

in 'a steady decline of [states'] internal autonomy and an ever-growing erosion of their Sovereignty under the crushing inroads of imperialistic necessity'.[169]

As these debates demonstrate, the British government and the princes continued to articulate very different visions of the nature of their relationship. While the princes admitted the paramountcy of the Crown, they also claimed 'to be members of the British Empire in their own right exercising their own sovereignty within their own territories and subject only to the necessary limitations upon their powers which result from the division of sovereignty between them and the Paramount Power'. This 'division of Indian sovereignty' was, in their view, 'definite and not indefinite, and the rights and obligations of both High Contracting parties must be capable of determination'.[170] In contrast to this legalistic view of the relationship, British colonial officials put forth a more flexible representation of the division of sovereign powers, claiming that 'imperial interests' determined the extent to which the British could intervene in the affairs of the states.

British colonial officials and princely state representatives, therefore, relied on the common language of divisible sovereignty but defined it in different ways to support their own interests. Specifically, they relied on the vernacular of divisible sovereignty to support their alternative visions of the nature of the relationship between the British government and the princely states as well as the broader imperial order. These arguments paralleled those made by international lawyers and activists during debates over the establishment of international institutions such as the League of Nations. The exchange of ideas between imperial and international locations was enabled by the participation of princes like Ganga Singh and Bhupinder Singh and their advisors such as Rushbrook Williams in international conferences, including meetings of the League.[171] The arguments before the Indian States Committee, therefore, also exemplify the ways in which international legal language was reinterpreted by actors across colonial networks in South Asia.

Conclusion

The Indian States Committee proceedings provide a snapshot of the approaches taken by the princely states and the British government to defining sovereignty

[169] Note on the Report of the Indian States Committee, 1928–29, NAI—Bhopal, Chamber Section, Bundle No. 7, File No. 2, Old File No. 2/5.

[170] Note communicated to the Viceroy by the Standing Committee of the Chamber of Princes on the occasion of their conference with His Excellency before his visit to England, upon the Report of the Indian States' Committee, 28 June 1929, NAI—Bhopal, Chamber Section, Bundle No. 7, File No. 2, Old File No. 2/5.

[171] For the argument on how the League provided a model for later discussions of Indian constitutional reform in which the princes were involved, see Stephen Legg, 'Imperial Internationalism: The Round Table Conference and the Making of India in London, 1930–1932', *Humanity: An International Journal of Human Rights, Humanitarianism, and Development*, 11/1 (2020), 32–53.

in the early decades of the twentieth century. Although many states continued to pursue individual jurisdictional disputes with the government of India, the establishment of the Chamber of Princes provided the states with the infrastructure to build coalitions and collectively present their arguments to the British government. Examining these shared assertions of the princes, therefore, provides a good overview of their legal arguments on interpreting the doctrine of sovereignty.

While the princes and the British government adopted the diametrically opposed language of absolute and divisible sovereignty in jurisdictional disputes in the late nineteenth century, the contrasts between them in the interwar period were a bit more nuanced. During this time, both the princes and the British claimed that sovereignty was divisible. This broad conceptualization was in line with the post-First World War global trend in which international lawyers and politicians sharply criticized absolutist state sovereignty. But this superficial consensus on the divisibility of sovereignty masked deeper differences between the two sides on the specific ways in which divisible sovereignty can and was interpreted and utilized.

The gathering strength of the anticolonial movement at the turn of the twentieth century provides the necessary backdrop within which to examine the differing politics, aims, and interests of the princely states and the British government; all these played a critical role in shaping their legal arguments relating to the doctrine of sovereignty. Colonial officials aspired to expand British control over state affairs but also had to ensure that the states could be maintained as allies in the face of the threat that anticolonial nationalism presented for the stability of the empire. To balance these two aims, and much as they had done in the late nineteenth century after the 1857 revolt, British political officers claimed that sovereignty was divisible. However, instead of relying on precedent, they argued that the division of sovereign powers between the British government and the princely states was determined by 'imperial interests'. This argument recognized that the states exercised some sovereign powers but also safeguarded and extended the exercise of British power by leaving the bulk of decision-making to colonial discretion. Despite the move to laissez-faire, which was supposed to increase state autonomy, the flexibility of the idea of divisible sovereignty entrenched British authority to interfere in state affairs.

The princes also relied on the porous border between the national, imperial, and international spheres but with the rather different aims of preserving their autonomy and increasing their ability to engage with other parties on the international stage. The polysemic idea of sovereignty, once again, provided them with the vernacular to press for these ambitions. Like the British, the princes were wary of the growing vigour of anticolonial movements since many nationalists did not limit their activities to British India but also allied with peoples' movements that demanded political reform in the states. With the monarchical positions of the princes under increasing pressure, their advisors decided that the states needed to preserve their relationship with the British government. A link with the Crown, they determined, would provide them with enough support to buttress their own sovereign power, at least over their people. Consequently, they decided to drop the nineteenth-century contention of territorial sovereignty, which was the basis of the claim of a separate political existence for the states, in favour of the argument that sovereign powers were divided between the states and the Crown. This explicit acknowledgement of the divisibility of sovereign powers differentiated interwar princely strategy from earlier decades. However, by recognizing that sovereignty was divisible, the princes also opened internal state affairs to British interference. Although admitting British paramountcy was a political necessity, the princes wanted to limit the exercise of British authority within their states as far as possible. Therefore, they argued that the division of sovereign powers was based not on imperial interests but rather on state consent, thereby claiming a greater role for the states themselves in determining the extent of the exercise of British sovereign power.

Although the princes managed to obtain a confirmation that their relationship was directly with the Crown, thereby handing them with a formidable argument against anticolonial activists, the legal case before the Indian States Committee was largely a failure for them, with the British government renewing its interference in state affairs with extra vigour.[172] However, the constant flow and exchange of ideas encapsulated in their arguments before the Committee made it logical for the princes and their advisors to choose as their next strategy yet another idea with a long imperial and international history—federation, which is the focus of the following chapter.

[172] Even after the disappointing results before the Committee, some princes considered seeking further legal resolution of the question, either through the appointment of a special judicial tribunal or by approaching the Privy Council, a move that the British government was keen to avoid. See Note communicated to the Viceroy by the Standing Committee of the Chamber of Princes on the occasion of their conference with His Excellency before his visit to England, upon the Report of the Indian States' Committee, 28 June 1929, NAI—Bhopal, Chamber Section, Bundle No. 7, File No. 2, Old File No. 2/5; Letter from the Secretary of State for India to the Viceroy, 6 June 1929, IOR/R/1/1/1841; and Note by C. C. Watson, 10 June 1929, IOR/R/1/1/1841.

Chapter Five
Political Negotiations
The Princes in the Federation Debates

Sovereignty and Federation

'Purdah is being strictly observed in the heart of London', observed an October 1930 piece in *The Daily Telegraph* on the *maharanis* of Alwar and Patiala,[1] referring to the complex system of veiling and restricted social contact followed by many elite South Asian women.[2] The *maharanis* of Baroda and Kashmir and the *begum* of Bhopal, on the other hand, were 'among the more modern wives who are going about seeing London'.[3] The 'turbaned figures'[4] of the princes were subjected to similarly breathless reportage; they were described as wearing 'their native costumes of gorgeous coloured silks, ornamented with jewels' at a Buckingham Palace dinner.[5] The princes were in London to attend the first session of the Round Table Conference (RTC), convened to discuss proposals for Indian constitutional reform. Despite the invitation, the princes were not expected to make a significant contribution to the deliberations. One correspondent claimed that they held 'a watching brief' and would intervene only if the agreed settlement threatened their position.[6] Much of the reporting on their attendance revolved around 'the glamour of the east',[7] focusing, for instance, on 'the vivid green of the Maharajah of Alwar's turban'.[8]

Despite being reduced to caricatures in the London press, the princes had come with plans to be considered as serious players in the debates on political reform. At the first plenary session, Tej Bahadur Sapru,[9] a lawyer and member of the National

[1] 'Purdah in the Heart of London', *The Daily Telegraph* (29 October 1930).

[2] Although the veil is usually associated with Islam, scholars have described how the practice of *pardah* (which literally translates to 'curtain') is common among high-caste Hindu women as well. See Hanna Papanek, 'Purdah: Separate Worlds and Symbolic Shelter', *Comparative Studies in Society and History*, 15/3 (1973), 289–325.

[3] 'Purdah in the Heart of London', *The Daily Telegraph* (29 October 1930).

[4] 'Today's Social Gossip', *Daily Mail* (23 October 1930).

[5] 'Royal Dinner Party to Indian Princes', *The Daily Telegraph* (4 November 1930).

[6] Ellis Ashmead-Bartlett, 'Round Table Conference: Prospect of an Agreed Report Almost Impossible', *The Daily Telegraph* (27 October 1930).

[7] 'A Gorgeous Scene', *The Daily Telegraph* (13 November 1930).

[8] 'The Round Table', *The Times* (13 November 1930).

[9] See S. K. Bose, *Tej Bahadur Sapru* (New Delhi: Government of India, Ministry of Information and Broadcasting, Publications Division, 1978); Mohan Kumar, *Sir Tej Bahadur Sapru: A Political Biography* (Gwalior: Vipul Prakashan, 1981); Rima Hooja, *Crusader for Self-Rule: Tej Bahadur Sapru & the Indian National Movement* (Jaipur: Rawat Publications, 1999); and D. A. Low, 'Sapru, Sir Tej

Sovereignty, International Law, and the Princely States of Colonial South Asia. Priyasha Saksena, Oxford University Press.
 DOI: 10.1093/oso/9780192866585.003.0005

Liberal Federation, a moderate British Indian political party, made the case for a federation to unite the 'arbitrarily divided' British India and princely states. He appealed to the princes 'as Indians first and Indian Princes next' to 'come forth on this occasion and say whether they are prepared to join an all-India federation'.[10] To the astonishment of those present, the princes 'one after another, declared their newly-found belief in All-India Federation'.[11] Ganga Singh of Bikaner was first, declaring that federation was 'the only satisfactory solution of India's problem'.[12] He was followed by Sayajirao Gaekwad of Baroda, Hari Singh of Kashmir, Akbar Hydari (on behalf of Hyderabad),[13] and Mirza Ismail (on behalf of Mysore),[14] all of whom announced that they were willing to join a federation of British India and the princely states.[15]

The princes' performance at the RTC came 'like a bolt from the blue' and 'made them instant celebrities',[16] but it also raised several questions. How had the princes, whose primary interest till this point had been the preservation of their own sovereignty, agreed to become part of a larger union with British Indian provinces? What would such a federation look like and what would be the implications of federation on the relations between the states and the Crown? How would sovereign powers be demarcated among the federal government, the provinces, and the states?

This move towards federalism in 1930s South Asia wasn't unusual. In recent years, there has been an explosion in scholarly literature on the global 'federal moment'[17] in the middle of the twentieth century. Scholars have traced how federation was a mechanism to restructure empires at a time when they were under increasing

Bahadur (1875–1949)', in David Cannadine, ed., *Oxford Dictionary of National Biography*, online edn (Oxford: Oxford University Press, 2004), https://doi.org/10.1093/ref:odnb/47758, accessed 14 April 2021.

[10] 'The Round Table: Speeches at Plenary Session', *The Times* (18 November 1930).

[11] Viscount Templewood, *Nine Troubled Years* (London: Collins, 1954), 50.

[12] 'Speech by His Highness the Maharaja of Bikaner, 17 November 1930', in Maurice Gwyer and A. Appadorai, eds., *Speeches and Documents on the Indian Constitution, 1921–47*, ii (Bombay: Oxford University Press, 1957), 746. Sapru's speech and Ganga Singh's response were suspiciously synchronized, leading to allegations of collusion. See Francis Wylie, 'Federal Negotiations in India 1935–9, and After', in C. H. Philips and Mary Doreen Wainwright, eds., *The Partition of India: Policies and Perspectives, 1935–47* (Cambridge, MA: M. I. T. Press, 1970), 520. Mirza Ismail claimed that Ganga Singh agreed to make the offer of federation only after he offered to do so first. See Mirza Ismail, *My Public Life: Recollections and Reflections* (London: George Allen & Unwin, 1954), 63.

[13] Hydari served in the government of India before he moved to Hyderabad where he held several posts, including finance minister and prime minister. See 'M.A.N. Hydari', in *Eminent Mussalmans* (Madras: G.A. Natesan & Co., 1926), 491–507.

[14] Mirza was *diwan* of Mysore between 1926 and 1941 before moving to occupy the same position in Jaipur and Hyderabad. See H. G. Balakrishna, 'Inaugural Address', in Suryanath U. Kamath, ed., *Studies on Dewan Sir Mirza Ismail* (Bangalore: The Mythic Society, 1998), 1–5.

[15] < Ian Copland, *The Princes of India in the Endgame of Empire, 1917–1947* (Cambridge: Cambridge University Press, 1997), 89.

[16] ibid.

[17] I borrow this term from Michael Collins, 'Decolonisation and the "Federal Moment"', *Diplomacy & Statecraft*, 24/1 (2013), 21–40.

stress.[18] The concept of sovereignty was key to understanding and articulating federal ideas. Proponents contended that federal structures were made possible through the division of sovereign powers across different political entities.[19] Federalist language, however, was used for contrasting political purposes. As Adom Getachew has demonstrated in her nuanced study of Black Atlantic federalists such as Kwame Nkrumah and Eric Williams, the creation of federations in Africa and the Caribbean split up sovereign powers among different levels of government but also strengthened state sovereignty at the federal level.[20] The plasticity of federalism, as Merve Fejzula argues, made it the ideal language for advancing imperial interests as well as for overcoming them.[21] So instead of being alternatives to the nation-state,[22] mid-century African federations highlight how the federal framework provided a common language for developing competing ideas of political order.[23]

An equally rich tapestry of federal ideas made their way into the political discourse of 1930s South Asia as an offshoot of the language of divisible sovereignty that pervaded the region, gaining traction during a time of intense political turmoil. The princes were disappointed with the outcome of the proceedings before the Indian States Committee, while anticolonial nationalists were furious with the lack of political reform in British India. As I describe later in the chapter, federation offered a way forward for many officials and activists, albeit for different reasons. A considerable proportion of the British establishment considered federation to be the best means of 'holding India to the Empire',[24] although some feared that it would lead to the gradual establishment of representative institutions in India. Anticolonial nationalists were also split on federation; while some moderates were

[18] See Holly Case, 'The Strange Politics of Federative Ideas in East-Central Europe', *The Journal of Modern History*, 85/4 (2013), 833–866; Talbot C. Imlay, 'International Socialism and Decolonization during the 1950s: Competing Rights and the Postcolonial Order', *American Historical Review*, 118/4 (2013), 1105–1132; Jennifer Foray, 'A Unified Empire of Equal Parts: The Dutch Commonwealth Schemes of the 1920s–40s', *The Journal of Imperial and Commonwealth History*, 41/2 (2013), 259–284; Frederick Cooper, *Citizenship between Empire and Nation: Remaking France and French Africa, 1945–1960* (Princeton, NJ: Princeton University Press, 2014); Gary Wilder, *Freedom Time: Negritude, Decolonization and the Future of the World* (Durham, NC: Duke University Press, 2015); and Gil Rubin, 'From Federalism to Binationalism: Hannah Arendt's Shifting Zionism', *Contemporary European History*, 24/3 (2015), 393–414.

[19] For discussions on divisible sovereignty in American federalism, see Alison LaCroix, *The Ideological Origins of American Federalism* (Cambridge, MA: Harvard University Press, 2010); and Don Herzog, *Sovereignty RIP* (New Haven, CT: Yale University Press, 2020), 93–163.

[20] Adom Getachew, *Worldmaking After Empire: The Rise and Fall of Self-Determination* (Princeton, NJ: Princeton University Press, 2019), 107–141.

[21] Merve Fejzula, 'The Cosmopolitan Historiography of Twentieth-Century Federalism', *The Historical Journal*, 64/2 (2021), 477–500.

[22] Samuel Moyn, 'Fantasies of Federalism', *Dissent* (Winter 2015), https://www.dissentmagazine.org/article/fantasies-of-federalism, accessed 15 February 2022.

[23] Chris Vaughan, 'The Politics of Regionalism and Federation in East Africa, 1958–1964', *The Historical Journal*, 62/2 (2019), 519–540.

[24] I borrow this phrase from Carl Bridge, *Holding India to the Empire: The British Conservative Party and the 1935 Constitution* (New Delhi: Sterling Publishers, 1986).

in favour, most considered it a means to delay the institution of responsible government in British India. Despite their show of unity at the RTC, the princes and their advisors also emerged divided. Although many of them relied on federal language to construct a political order in which state autonomy and the monarchical system of government could be protected within a broader framework that enabled co-operation with British India and the Crown, some believed that federation would destroy the states and proposed the alternative of confederation.

The concept of sovereignty played a key role in the imagination of all these federal and confederal structures. While federation has received the express attention of historians of the princely states,[25] scholars have parsed through meanings of sovereignty in the federal debates primarily to trace the history of Indian constitutionalism.[26] Although a vital part of the history of domestic constitutional structures, federal proposals also generated arguments about the relationship of the princely states with other parts of the empire and with other states and international institutions. Many states relied on their 'semi-international' status to insist on retaining direct relations with the British Crown, thereby engaging in the broader debate of the appropriate boundaries between the domestic, imperial, and international spheres. Since the national and the international are entangled ways of thinking about modernity,[27] exploring the federal debates in South Asia is also critical to understanding the ways in which these players conceptualized the international.

In this chapter, I explore both the international and South Asian debates on federalism. I first examine the different political orders that interwar international actors imagined by relying on federal ideas. International lawyers such as Hersch Lauterpacht and James Brierly hoped that world federation would be a means to discipline the sovereign nation-state. For others, such as the politician Philip Kerr and the socialist activist Barbara Wootton, federation was a mechanism to strengthen state sovereignty. The ability of federation to buttress state authority was also a theme in the work of imperial federationists such as James Bryce and Lionel Curtis. Since these imperial federal ideas bled into colonial landscapes,

[25] See Barbara Ramusack, *The Princes of India in the Twilight of Empire: Dissolution of a Patron-Client System, 1914–1939* (Columbus, OH: Ohio State University Press, 1978), 185–228; S. R. Ashton, *British Policy Towards the Indian States, 1905–1939* (London: Curzon Press, 1982), 128–192; Copland, *The Princes of India in the Endgame of Empire*, (n 15) 73–182; and Barbara Ramusack, *The Indian Princes and their States* (Cambridge: Cambridge University Press, 2004), 245–274.

[26] See Andrew Muldoon, *Empire, Politics and the Creation of the 1935 India Act* (Farnham: Ashgate, 2009); Sarath Pillai, 'Fragmenting the Nation: Divisible Sovereignty and Travancore's Quest for Federal Independence', *Law and History Review*, 34/3 (2016), 743–782; Rama Sundari Mantena, 'Anticolonialism and Federation in Colonial India', *Ab Imperio*, 3 (2018), 36–62; Kavita Saraswathi Datla, 'Sovereignty and the End of Empire: The Transition to Independence in Colonial Hyderabad', *Ab Imperio*, 3 (2018), 63–88; Sunil Purushotham, 'Federating the Raj: Hyderabad, Sovereign Kingship, and Partition', *Modern Asian Studies*, 54/1 (2020), 157–198; and Sunil Purushotham, 'Sovereignty, Federation, and Constituent Power in Interwar India, ca. 1917–39', *Comparative Studies of South Asia, Africa and the Middle East*, 40/3 (2020), 421–433.

[27] Glenda Sluga, *Internationalism in the Age of Nationalism* (Philadelphia, PA: University of Pennsylvania Press, 2013), 3.

I then examine the political context of federation in interwar South Asia, focusing on the aims and interests of the British government and the princely states in developing federal ideas. Although they used the shared language of federation, both sides were also much more internally divided than before. Some British officials considered federation to be a means to extend their authority in South Asia, while others feared the reverse. The princes emerged more clearly split into opposing camps. While all princes agreed on the importance of dividing sovereign powers among different entities to maintain state autonomy in the face of political rivals and to build relationships with the Crown and British India, they disagreed about the impact of federation on state sovereignty. The 'federationists' preferred close relations with British India and legal restrictions on the Crown's authority to intervene in state affairs, while the 'confederationists' or 'anti-federationists' preferred to rely on the protection of the Crown against interference by elected British Indian politicians. I examine three moments in the federal debates when this divide most clearly affected the legal arguments made by the princes and their advisors: the birth of federation, the wrangling over federation or confederation as a political structure, and the final federal offer. By examining the views of a variety of federalism's interwar supporters (and detractors), I build on the previous chapter's discussion of how the divisibility of sovereignty could be advocated by those who wished to subject politics to 'the rule of law' as well as those who wished to increase the power of political entities to act in the international arena. The malleability of federalism in 1930s South Asia demonstrates how arguments for splitting up sovereignty can serve, and have served, a variety of political impulses and projects.

Federalism in Interwar International Law

Although the term 'federalism' is surprisingly difficult to define,[28] at the most basic level, it relies on the delineation of authority among different levels of government with the boundary between national and subnational governments remaining subject to change.[29] On account of this division of sovereign powers, federalism has always been a puzzle for international law. In recent years, the federal structures of the United States have come under scrutiny because of their apparent impact on the country's compliance with international legal obligations.[30] There is also

[28] For an overview of the debates over the meaning of federalism, see Daniel Halberstam, 'Federalism: Theory, Policy, Law', in Michael Rosenfeld and András Sajó, eds., *The Oxford Handbook of Comparative Constitutional Law* (Oxford: Oxford University Press, 2012), 578–580.

[29] Jenna Bednar, 'The Political Science of Federalism', *Annual Review of Law and Social Science*, 7 (2011), 270–271.

[30] See Bruno Simma and Carsten Hoppe, 'From *LaGrand* and *Avena* to *Medellín*—A Rocky Road Toward Implementation', *Tulane Journal of International and Comparative Law*, 14/1 (2005), 7–60; Margaret E. McGuinness, 'Three Narratives of *Medellín v. Texas*', *Suffolk Transnational Law Review*, 31/2 (2008), 227–246; and Benjamin Beiter, 'Beyond *Medellín*: Reconsidering Federalism Limits on the Treaty Power', *Notre Dame Law Review*, 85/3 (2010), 1163–1196.

considerable scholarship on whether and to what extent federal subunits can enter into relations with foreign states,[31] raising questions about the types of entities that can become subjects of international law and the scope of the international sphere more broadly. These questions aren't new; nineteenth-century international lawyers struggled to reconcile the theory of absolute sovereignty with the existence of partly sovereign subunits of a federal state.[32]

The increasing acceptance of the divisibility of sovereignty after the First World War bolstered proposals for a world federation that would discipline the sovereign state.[33] James Brierly claimed that federation was the only conceivable basis for world government since loose organizations such as the League of Nations were weakened by their dependence on the willingness of member states.[34] His contemporary Hersch Lauterpacht contended that world federation would eliminate 'the deification of the state'[35] and hoped that it would 'secure the freedom and the dignity of human personality' by requiring the 'direct participation of the individual in the creation of the central deliberative and legislative organs of the association of States'.[36] Federation, in their view, was a mechanism to limit state sovereignty.

Other interwar actors recognized that federal structures simply shifted the exercise of sovereign powers to a different level of government. The British politician and journalist Philip Kerr[37] argued that federation would be created when peoples of the world 'pool[ed] their sovereignty … in that sphere which lies beyond national rights, and create[d] an organism, responsible to themselves, through which

[31] See Jack Goldsmith, 'Federal Courts, Foreign Affairs, and Federalism', *Virginia Law Review*, 83/8 (1997), 1617–1716; Judith Resnik, 'Law's Migration: American Exceptionalism, Silent Dialogues, and Federalism's Multiple Ports of Entry', *Yale Law Journal*, 115/7 (2006), 1564–1671; and Michael J. Glennon and Robert D. Sloane, *Foreign Affairs Federalism: The Myth of National Exclusivity* (Oxford: Oxford University Press, 2016).

[32] See William Edward Hall, *International Law* (Oxford: Clarendon Press, 1880), 22; John Westlake, *Chapters on the Principles of International Law* (Cambridge: Cambridge University Press, 1894), 87–89; and T. J. Lawrence, *The Principles of International Law* (Boston, MA: D. C. Heath & Co., 1895), 73–75.

[33] Richard Collins argues that interwar international lawyers like Hersch Lauterpacht and James Brierly favoured world federation because they tended to minimize the distinctions between domestic and international law. See Richard Collins, 'The Progressive Conception of International Law: Brierly and Lauterpacht in the *Interbellum* Period', in Robert McCorquodale and Jean-Pierre Gauci, eds., *British Influences on International Law, 1915–2015* (Leiden: Brill Nijhoff, 2016), 451–453.

[34] J. L. Brierly, 'The Sovereign State Today', in Hersch Lauterpacht and C. H. M. Waldock, eds., *The Basis of Obligation in International Law and Other Papers* (Oxford: Clarendon Press, 1958), 354. The essay was originally published in 1949.

[35] Hersch Lauterpacht, 'Westlake and Present Day International Law', *Economica*, 15 (1925), 324.

[36] Hersch Lauterpacht, 'Sovereignty and Federation in International Law', in Elihu Lauterpacht, ed., *International Law: Being the Collected Papers of Hersch Lauterpacht*, iii: *The Law of Peace* (Cambridge: Cambridge University Press, 1977), 20. The essay remained unpublished, but in an editor's note, Lauterpacht's son, Elihu Lauterpacht, estimates that it was written in the early spring of 1940.

[37] Kerr played a significant role in the unification of South Africa and participated in the Round Table Conferences on Indian political reform. See J. R. M. Butler, *Lord Lothian, 1882–1940* (London: Macmillan and Co., 1960); Alex May, 'Kerr, Philip Henry, eleventh marquess of Lothian (1882–1940)', in *Oxford Dictionary of National Biography*, https://doi.org/10.1093/ref:odnb/34303, accessed 1 April 2021; and Alex May, 'Milner's Kindergarten (*act.* 1902–1910)', in *Oxford Dictionary of National Biography*, https://doi.org/10.1093/ref:odnb/93711, accessed 1 April 2021.

they can control world issues by law, instead of by the savage and often meaningless means of war'.[38] This ability of federalism to strengthen state authority through an amalgamation of sovereign powers is even more explicit in the work of the socialist Barbara Wootton,[39] Kerr's fellow member in the Federal Union.[40] Wootton considered efforts to address inequality within national borders to be insufficient and advocated the establishment of a world federation that could engage in large-scale economic planning.[41]

This malleability of the federal project also engendered its fraught relationship with empire. Holly Case has argued that some interwar schemes for regional federations in eastern and central Europe were meant 'to reorganize and thus lend new legitimacy to empires' while others were 'either implicitly or explicitly anti-imperial'.[42] The numerous proposals to reorganize the British empire along federal lines occupied similarly complex positions. British constitutional thought is generally focused on the unitary nature of the state because of the long shadow cast by the jurist A. V. Dicey who castigated federal government as 'weak government'.[43] Despite Dicey's dismissal of federalism,[44] there was a robust federal tradition in British political thought. Dicey's close friend, the jurist and parliamentarian James Bryce,[45] relied on the divisibility of sovereignty to become the foremost

38 Philip Kerr, 'The Only Road to International Peace', in Philip Kerr and Lionel Curtis, *The Prevention of War* (New Haven, CT: Yale University Press, 1923), 67. For a broader discussion of Kerr's federal ideas, see John Pinder, 'Prophet Not Without Honour: Lothian and the Federal Idea', *The Round Table*, 72/286 (1983), 207–220.

39 Wootton was trained in the classics and economics; her later scholarship focused on criminology and social work. See A. H. Halsey, 'Wootton [*née* Adam], Barbara Frances, Baroness Wootton of Abinger (1897–1988)', in *Oxford Dictionary of National Biography*, https://doi.org/10.1093/ref:odnb/39876, accessed 19 March 2021; Ann Oakley, *A Critical Woman: Barbara Wootton, Social Science and Public Policy in the Twentieth Century* (London: Bloomsbury Academic, 2011); and Pat Thane, 'Barbara Wootton (1897–1988): Pioneering Social Scientist, Feminist and Policymaker', *Women's History Review*, 23/5 (2014), 793–798.

40 For a history of the Federal Union, see Richard Mayne, John Pinder, and John C. de V. Roberts, *Federal Union: The Pioneers: A History of the Federal Union* (Basingstoke: Macmillan, 1990).

41 Barbara Wootton, *Socialism and Federation* (1941), https://federalunion.org.uk/socialism-and-federation/, accessed 17 March 2021. Wootton opposed proposals by neoliberal economists to use federations to weaken the state. See Ellen Jacobs, '"An Organizing Female with a Briefcase": Barbara Wootton, Political Economy and Social Justice, 1920–1950', *Women's History Review*, 16/3 (2007), 439–441; Oakley, *A Critical Woman*, (n 39) 159–162; and Or Rosenboim, 'Barbara Wootton, Friedrich Hayek and the Debate on Democratic Federalism in the 1940s', *The International History Review*, 36/5 (2014), 894–918. For more on neoliberal ideas of federation during this period, see Quinn Slobodian, *Globalists: The End of Empire and the Birth of Neoliberalism* (Cambridge, MA: Harvard University Press, 2018), 91–120.

42 Case, 'The Strange Politics of Federative Ideas in East-Central Europe', (n 18) 842–843.

43 A. V. Dicey, 'Federal Government', *Law Quarterly Review*, 1/1 (1885), 95.

44 A. V. Dicey, *Introduction to the Study of the Law of the Constitution* (8th edn, London: Macmillan and Co. 1915), xc.

45 Bryce was appointed Regius Professor of Civil Law at Oxford in 1870 and was a Liberal member of parliament between 1880 and 1907. See H. A. L. Fisher, *James Bryce: Viscount Bryce of Dechmont, O. M.*, 2 vols (London: Macmillan and Co., 1927); Christopher Harvie, 'Bryce, James, Viscount Bryce (1838–1922)', in *Oxford Dictionary of National Biography*, https://doi.org/10.1093/ref:odnb/32141, accessed 23 March 2021; and John T. Seaman Jr., *Citizen of the World: The Life of James Bryce* (London: I. B. Tauris, 2006).

late nineteenth-century advocate of federalism.[46] Bryce admired the ability of American federalism to foster a 'double patriotism' in which the allegiances of citizens to two governments produced strength and stability.[47] In the British context, Bryce advocated a 'soft' federalism that rested on moral constraints on parliamentary sovereignty rather than enforcement by courts.[48] By emphasizing federalism's flexibility and its ability to provide stability, Bryce claimed that it could present a model to advance British power while resolving questions such as Ireland's place in the empire.[49] Bryce was a key member of the Imperial Federation League, a prominent *fin de siècle* actor in debates over establishing 'Greater Britain' that would unite Britain with the settler colonies,[50] with the 'elusiveness of the federalist agenda' enabling accord among a diverse group of thinkers.[51]

By the early twentieth century, imperial federalist schemes had to contend with demands for autonomy by the self-governing dominions, resulting in debates on the relationship between federation and state sovereignty akin to those carried out over world federation. Opponents argued that imperial federation would dilute dominion sovereignty by making matters such as tariffs and immigration subject to the imperial parliament. Proponents viewed the debate through a different lens, claiming that imperial federation would institutionalize the role of the dominions in imperial decision-making.[52] The interwar imperial federation advocate Lionel Curtis,[53] for instance, proposed the creation of a separate parliament and government for imperial affairs, relegating the British parliament and government to the

[46] James Bryce, *The American Commonwealth*, i (London: Macmillan and Co., 1888), 342.

[47] Casper Sylvest, 'James Bryce and the Two Faces of Nationalism', in Ian Hall and Lisa Hill, eds., *British International Thinkers from Hobbes to Namier* (New York, NY: Palgrave Macmillan, 2009), 169. The argument that federalism provided stability also aligned with Bryce's interpretation of the American constitution as a conservative document. See H. A. Tulluch, 'Changing British Attitudes Towards the United States in the 1880s', *The Historical Journal*, 20/4 (1977), 825–840.

[48] Jordan de Campos-Rudinsky, 'James Bryce and Parliamentary Sovereignty', *Modern Intellectual History*, 19/3 (2022), 734–756.

[49] Sylvest, 'James Bryce and the Two Faces of Nationalism', (n 47) 169. See also Christopher Harvie, 'Ideology and Home Rule: James Bryce, A. V. Dicey and Ireland, 1880–1887', *English Historical Review*, 91/359 (1976), 298–314; and George Boyce, 'Federalism and the Irish Question', in Andrea Bosco, ed., *The Federal Idea: The History of Federalism from Enlightenment to 1945*, i (London: Lothian Foundation Press, 1991), 128–129.

[50] Michael Burgess, 'The Federal Plan of the Imperial Federation League 1892: Milestone or Tombstone', in *The Federal Idea*, (n 49) i, 140.

[51] Duncan Bell, *The Idea of Greater Britain: Empire and the Future of World Order, 1860–1900* (Princeton, NJ: Princeton University Press, 2007), 15.

[52] Carolyn Holbrook, 'Anzac, Empire and War: Australian Nationalism and the Campaign for Imperial Federation', *Australian Historical Studies*, 52/1 (2021), 47.

[53] Curtis played a role in the unification of South Africa and became part of the Round Table. See Deborah Lavin, *From Empire to International Commonwealth: A Biography of Lionel Curtis* (Oxford: Oxford University Press, 1995); and Alex May, 'Curtis, Lionel George (1872–1955)', in *Oxford Dictionary of National Biography*, https://doi.org/10.1093/ref:odnb/32678, accessed 2 April 2021. For discussions of Curtis's relationship with the earlier tradition of imperial federation, see Daniel Gorman, 'Lionel Curtis, Imperial Citizenship, and the Quest for Unity', *The Historian*, 66/1 (2004), 81; and Jeanne Morefield, '"An Education to Greece": The Round Table, Imperial Theory and the Uses of History', *History of Political Thought*, 28/2 (2007), 338–339.

same status as those of the dominions.[54] Since imperial affairs would be conducted by the imperial rather than the British government,[55] imperial federation (or in Curtis's words, a commonwealth) would enable the dominions to achieve their full measure of sovereignty.[56] Although the interwar federal project was ultimately derailed by questions over the relationship between the imperial polity and India,[57] Curtis played a key role in the introduction of a particular strain of federal ideas into the political landscape of South Asia. The flexibility of federation, which provided a means to both strip away the powers of a sovereign state and to empower the state by buttressing sovereignty, made it an attractive proposition for actors across the political spectrum in South Asia.

The Stakes of Federalism in Interwar South Asia

The interwar period was a particularly volatile time in South Asia, with Mohandas Gandhi's strategy of non-violent non-cooperation marking the turn of anticolonial nationalism to mass politics. These large-scale movements responded to the increasing repression that accompanied the minimal political reforms enacted by the colonial state.[58] The framework for such reform was laid in an official 1917 statement that British policy would favour 'the gradual development of self-governing institutions with a view to the progressive realisation of responsible Government in India as an integral part of the British Empire'.[59] The main legal device to manage this slow and controlled grant of self-government was 'dyarchy', which split the exercise of sovereign powers among different levels of government.[60] Governmental functions such as education, health, agriculture, and local self-government were transferred to Indian ministers who were responsible to elected provincial

[54] Lionel Curtis, *The Problem of the Commonwealth* (Toronto: The Macmillan Company of Canada Ltd., 1916), 130, 154–155.

[55] Andrea Bosco, 'Lothian, Curtis, Kimber and the Federal Union Movement (1938–1940)', *Journal of Contemporary History*, 23/3 (1988), 467.

[56] Holbrook, 'Anzac, Empire and War', (n 52) 56.

[57] S. R. Mehrotra, 'Imperial Federation and India, 1868–1917', *Journal of Commonwealth and Comparative Politics*, 1/1 (1961), 29–40; Dewitt Clinton Ellinwood Jr., 'The Round Table Movement and India, 1909–1920', *Journal of Commonwealth Political Studies*, 9/3 (1971), 183–209; and Bell, *The Idea of Greater Britain*, (n 51) 269.

[58] See Sumit Sarkar, *Modern India, 1885–1947* (Delhi: Macmillan India, 1983), 178–187; Barbara D. Metcalf and Thomas R. Metcalf, *A Concise History of Modern India* (2nd edn, Cambridge: Cambridge University Press, 2006), 167–175; and Sugata Bose and Ayesha Jalal, *Modern South Asia: History, Culture, Political Economy* (4th edn, London: Routledge, 2018), 119–130.

[59] 'Speech of Edwin Montagu, House of Commons, 20 August 1917', in A. B. Keith, ed., *Speeches and Documents on Indian Policy, 1750–1921*, ii (London: Oxford University Press, 1922), 133.

[60] For contemporaneous scholarship on dyarchy and its working, see Lionel Curtis, *Dyarchy* (Oxford: Clarendon Press, 1920); Sachidananda Sinha, *Dyarchy in Indian Provinces in Theory and Practice* (London: East India Association, 1926); Kerala Putra, *The Working of Dyarchy in India, 1919–1928* (Bombay: D. B. Taraporevala Sons and Co., 1928); and A. Appadorai, *Dyarchy in Practice* (London: Longmans, Green and Co., 1937).

legislative assemblies. However, colonial officials retained control over crucial provincial functions such as police, justice, and land revenue, while the central government remained wholly under British authority.[61]

The origins of dyarchy can be traced to the relentless campaigning of Lionel Curtis, who recognized the need to establish a mechanism to incorporate India into an imperial federation, although he conceded that India could not be granted 'full responsible government'.[62] The solution that he presented was 'specific devolution', later known as dyarchy.[63] By splitting up sovereign powers between the central and provincial governments, and entrusting only specific provincial functions to elected ministers, dyarchy ensured that self-government was only permitted with respect to matters in which Indian political leaders 'could not damage "the well-being of the whole community" '.[64] Curtis's proposal faced criticism from colonial civil servants but ultimately formed the basis of the Government of India Act 1919. Debates over world and imperial federation, therefore, are key to understanding Indian political reforms as well, since it was Curtis's familiarity with the division of sovereign powers in those federal structures that enabled him to envisage dyarchy.[65]

This reluctant acceptance of dyarchy was limited to reform in British India. Colonial officials were even more sceptical of the prospect of dividing sovereign powers between British India and the princely states, claiming that federal proposals would 'gravely alarm not only the Princes but also certain important sections of British Indian opinion'.[66] The political secretary, John Thompson,[67] noted that British Indian nationalists would consider a federal relationship with the states as 'a device of the British Government to retard the pace of British India's constitutional development'.[68] British political officers themselves also resisted federation, partly on account of their generally conservative disposition to political

[61] See Sarkar, *Modern India*, (n 58) 165–168; Metcalf and Metcalf, *A Concise History of Modern India*, (n 58) 167–168; and Bose and Jalal, *Modern South Asia*, (n 58) 115. For a full list of reserved and transferred powers, see Stephen Legg, 'Dyarchy: Democracy, Autocracy, and the Scalar Sovereignty of Interwar India', *Comparative Studies of South Asia, Africa and the Middle East*, 36/1 (2016), 45.

[62] Curtis, *Dyarchy*, (n 60) xxii.

[63] Mehrotra, 'Imperial Federation and India', (n 57) 37; Ellinwood Jr., 'The Round Table Movement and India', (n 57) 195; Deborah Lavin, 'Lionel Curtis and Indian Dyarchy', in *The Federal Idea*, (n 49) i, 197; and Legg, 'Dyarchy', (n 61) 49–50.

[64] Ellinwood Jr., 'The Round Table Movement and India', (n 57) 195.

[65] Lavin, 'Lionel Curtis and Indian Dyarchy', (n 63) 197; and Legg, 'Dyarchy', (n 61) 48–52.

[66] Letter from the Government of India, Foreign and Political Department to the Secretary of State for India, 15 September 1927, IOR/R/1/1/1682(1).

[67] Thompson was made political secretary despite lacking experience in the states in order to protect him from nationalist attacks in response to his role in the repression in Punjab in the aftermath of the Amritsar massacre. See Copland, *The Princes of India in the Endgame of Empire*, (n 15) 45.

[68] Note by J. P. Thompson, 28 August 1926, IOR/R/1/1/1620(1); and Minutes of the proceedings of the sub-committee appointed to discuss future relations between British India and the Indian states, 19 November 1926, IOR/R/1/1/1620(1).

reform in India. Bertrand Glancy,[69] for instance, envisaged the establishment of a structure that barred British India and the states from interfering in each other's affairs to maintain the distinctiveness of both 'democratic' British India and the monarchical states.[70] He was also scathing of proposals that would require formal committees to be appointed in the case of disputes with the states, thereby reducing the powers of the Political Department.[71] There was, therefore, an element of self-preservation in the attitude of political officials who feared for their own future in the event there were more direct relations between British India and the states or if the states started to take part in decision-making, eliminating the need for political officers to act as mediators.

In the face of such opposition, the political project of federalism in interwar South Asia gained ground only once the princely states decided to endorse it with the broad aim of shoring up their own authority.[72] The federal proposal at the first RTC marked a major change in the states' own strategy since earlier moves along the same lines had failed. During hectic parleys among the princes towards the end of the war (in which Lionel Curtis also participated), Sayajirao Gaekwad of Baroda had proposed the establishment of a council of states 'on the pattern of the German Bundesrath' to enable the states to participate in discussions on issues that affected them.[73] After the more 'conservative' princes expressed reluctance at participating in a federal parliament, the princes abandoned those proposals and instead focused their demands on the establishment of a Chamber of Princes, which was included within the 1919 constitutional reforms.[74] Princely opposition to federation continued as late as July 1930.[75] British officials understood this stance to be linked to the states' scepticism of the surrender of sovereignty that would be necessitated by the creation of a federal legislature and executive.[76]

The political context of the late 1920s provides an indication of the reasons for the change in the princes' hearts. By this time the princes were under increasing political pressure. In determining that sovereignty was divided based on 'imperial interests', the *Report of the Indian States Committee*, discussed in the previous

[69] Glancy was appointed political secretary in 1934 and played a major role in the negotiations over federation. See Ian Talbot, 'Glancy, Sir Bertrand James (1882–1953)', in *Oxford Dictionary of National Biography*, https://doi.org/10.1093/ref:odnb/51173, accessed 8 April 2021.

[70] Note by B. J. Glancy, 27 April 1927, IOR/R/1/1/1668(1).

[71] Note by B. J. Glancy, 29 May 1929, IOR/R/1/1/4679(1).

[72] The political officer Arthur Lothian claimed that the princes' support of the federal idea 'brought federation from being a mere aspiration into the realm of practical politics'. See Arthur Lothian, *Kingdoms of Yesterday* (London: John Murray, 1951), 143.

[73] Stanley Rice, *Life of Sayaji Rao III Maharaja of Baroda*, ii (London: Oxford University Press, 1931), 161.

[74] Copland, *The Princes of India in the Endgame of Empire*, (n 15) 39–41.

[75] K. M. Panikkar, *An Autobiography*, trans. K. Krishnamurthy (Madras: Oxford University Press, 1977), 83.

[76] Minutes of the proceedings of the sub-committee appointed to discuss future relations between British India and the Indian states, 17 September 1926, IOR/R/1/1/1620(1); and Note by C. C. Watson on item 1 of the agenda for the political officers' conference, IOR/R/1/1/1668(1).

chapter, provided ammunition for the government of India to intervene in the internal affairs of the states. The princes were even more concerned about the exercise of paramountcy by a government of India that would be responsible to the British Indian electorate. Although anticolonial leaders such as Gandhi advocated a policy of non-interference in state affairs until British India itself had attained *swaraj* (self-rule),[77] some British Indian activists banded together with disaffected state subjects to form states' peoples' movements that aimed to secure a share in state power.[78] These associations usually met in British Indian territory because of the proscription of political activity in the states and soon developed ties with each other. The All India States' Peoples' Conference (AISPC) was founded in Bombay in 1927 to call for political reform in the states and made a series of moves to attack the ruling princes.[79] It released a pamphlet on the alleged excesses of Bhupinder Singh of Patiala, accusing him of torture, arbitrary arrests, the misuse of public funds, and the abduction and trafficking of young women.[80] Members of the AISPC petitioned the League of Nations, seeking an inquiry into forced labour practices in the states.[81] P. L. Chudgar and G. R. Abhyankar, both highly regarded in the states' peoples' movements, published works that were highly critical of the administration of the princely states.[82]

The Standing Committee's two principal advisors, K. N. Haksar and K. M. Panikkar, proposed a federal solution to combat this progressively insurgent situation, with federation defined to extend the princes' legalistic arguments before the Indian States Committee. Although the states would have to give up control over certain sovereign functions to the federal government, they argued that this would simply formalize existing British paramountcy over the states.[83] Since the division of sovereign powers between the federal government and the states would be clearly set out in a federal constitution to which the states consented, federation would enable the princes to circumscribe the scope of British authority by limiting it to specific issues of 'common concern' to British India and the states. A common federal executive and legislature would also enable the princes to participate in decision-making from which they had previously been excluded. However, the focus on state consent to constitutional provisions would ensure that the influence

[77] M. K. Gandhi, *The Indian States' Problem* (Ahmedabad: Navajivan Press, 1941), 7–28.

[78] John McLeod, *Sovereignty, Power, Control: Politics in the States of Western India, 1916–1947* (Leiden: Brill, 1999), 37.

[79] Ramusack, *The Princes of India in the Twilight of Empire*, (n 25) 161–162.

[80] Bhupinder Singh was later exonerated of these allegations in an official inquiry. See Ramusack, *The Princes of India in the Twilight of Empire*, (n 25) 194; and Copland, *The Princes of India in the Endgame of Empire*, (n 15) 81. A copy of the report can be found in *Indian Annual Register*, i (1930), 506–520.

[81] Joseph McQuade, 'Beyond an Imperial Foreign Policy?: India at the League of Nations, 1919–1946', *The Journal of Imperial and Commonwealth History*, 48/2 (2020), 284.

[82] G. R. Abhyankar, *Problem of Indian States* (Poona: Aryabhushan Press, 1928); and P. L. Chudgar, *Indian Princes under British Protection: A Study of their Personal Rule, their Constitutional Position and their Future* (London: Williams & Norgate Ltd., 1929).

[83] K. N. Haksar and K. M. Panikkar, *Federal India* (London: Martin Hopkinson Ltd., 1930), 41.

of British officials and Indian nationalists in state affairs would remain limited. The establishment of a federal court would also limit encroachments by the federal centre into the internal autonomy of the states.[84] In addition, federation would also preserve the monarchical structures of the states and enable the princes to maintain direct links with the Crown,[85] thereby eliminating activists from the states' peoples' movements as political alternatives within the states. As was the case in other parts of the world, federalism in the South Asian context provided a model to both divide sovereign powers between the federal and state governments, and to centralize power within the states in the hands of the princes.[86]

The language of federalism was also co-opted by British officials who viewed a federation of British India and the princely states as the best mechanism of retaining control over South Asia. Much like the princes, the British were also facing new political pressures in the late 1920s. A 1927 commission to review the working of the Indian constitution was boycotted by anticolonial nationalists. The country also faced labour strikes, student demonstrations, peasant rebellions, and a wide-ranging revolutionary movement.[87] After the viceroy, Lord Irwin, declared that British policy in relation to India contemplated 'the attainment of Dominion Status',[88] politicians opposed to Indian independence relied on federation as a way forward. A federal constitution could be drafted to retain enormous sovereign power in the hands of unelected British viceroys and governors. Federation would also provide stability by bringing in the princely states to act as a conservative bulwark against the radicalism of anticolonial nationalists.[89] Once again, federalism provided the language for the division of sovereign powers among different levels of government but also for the centralization of authority in the hands of specific state actors.

The position of federation amongst British Indians was mixed. Some intellectuals viewed it as a mechanism to establish direct democracy by empowering local citizens' assemblies.[90] Most sections of the organized anticolonial political

[84] Ramusack, *The Princes of India in the Twilight of Empire*, (n 25) 201; and Copland, *The Princes of India in the Endgame of Empire*, (n 15) 80.

[85] On the states' quest to preserve their monarchical form of government, see Pillai, 'Fragmenting the Nation' (n 26); and Purushotham, 'Federating the Raj', (n 26) 174–179.

[86] This parallels the argument that American federalism demonstrated 'a shift from a world of diffuse sovereignty to one where authority was increasingly imagined as concentrated in the hands of only two legitimate sovereigns', i.e. the federal and state governments. See Gregory Ablavsky, 'Empire States: The Coming of Dual Federalism', *Yale Law Journal*, 128/7 (2019), 1792.

[87] Sarkar, *Modern India*, (n 58) 261–279; Metcalf and Metcalf, *A Concise History of Modern India*, (n 58) 190; and Bose and Jalal, *Modern South Asia*, (n 58) 128.

[88] 'Statement by His Excellency the Viceroy, Lord Irwin, on "Dominion Status as the Goal of the Indian Political Evolution" and "Decision to hold a Round Table Conference", 31 October 1929', in *Speeches and Documents on the Indian Constitution, 1921–47*, (n 12) i, 225.

[89] Some princes agreed with this interpretation, attempting to build their own significance by claiming to be conservative counterweights to radical nationalists. See Mantena, 'Anticolonialism and Federation in Colonial India', (n 26) 47–51; and Datla, 'Sovereignty and the End of Empire', (n 26) 67–71.

[90] Tejas Parasher, 'Federalism, Representation, and Direct Democracy in 1920s India', *Modern Intellectual History*, 19/2 (2022), 444–472.

movement opposed it, although moderates in the Liberal party were in favour. Many moderates were also close confidantes of the princes; Chimanlal Setalvad had persuaded several princes to invest in a struggling nationalist newspaper,[91] while Tej Bahadur Sapru was a legal advisor to a number of them.[92] Since sections of the British establishment opposed dominion status, Sapru argued that responsible government could only be achieved in British India if the princes were present as a 'stabilizing force' in a federation.[93] He also believed that federation would hasten democratic reforms within the states.[94] Although their arguments were superficially similar to many British politicians, these anticolonial nationalists favoured federation as a mechanism to achieve dominion status rather than impede it.

Despite the emergence of this unlikely coalition of interests, the princes, British officials, and anticolonial nationalists were all much more internally divided than before. Not all princely states favoured federation; some changed their views over time. British officials also exhibited a variety of positions when it came to federation. And despite the support of the Liberals, most anticolonial nationalists remained firmly opposed to federation. Just as with world and imperial federal proposals, the malleability of federation in interwar South Asia enabled it to be a common language for many different political interests, with groups agreeing that sovereignty was divisible, but on little else. It was a mechanism for the states to pursue relationships with British India and the Crown as well as to maintain political autonomy. It was also a means for British officials and anticolonial nationalists to both impede and hasten political reform. The vernacular of divisible sovereignty that was the basis of federation was equally plastic. It was used to justify limitations on the exercise of authority by the colonial government in state affairs, to buttress the supremacy of the princes as autocratic monarchs within their states, to bring about political reform within the states, and to enable the exercise of discretionary power by unelected colonial officials. The co-option of the federal structure for these varied uses was highlighted throughout the course of the federation debates, but at three moments in particular: the birth of federation, the wrangling over federation or confederation as a political structure, and the final negotiations over the states' instruments of accession to federation.

[91] Ramusack, *The Princes of India in the Twilight of Empire*, (n 25) 168.

[92] Sapru wrote legal opinions for the states of Gwalior, Bikaner, Bhopal, and Kashmir. See Tej Bahadur Sapru, *Responsa: Selected Legal Opinions*, ed., K. N. Raina (Bombay: N. M. Tripathi Private Limited, 1976). He also appeared as defence counsel in inquiries against the rulers of Patiala, Nabha, and Rewa. See Kumar, *Sir Tej Bahadur Sapru*, (n 9) 5.

[93] D. A. Low, 'Sir Tej Bahadur Sapru and the First Round Table Conference', in D. A. Low, ed., *Soundings in Modern South Asian History* (Canberra: Australian National University Press, 1968), 294–329. See also R. J. Moore, *The Crisis of Indian Unity, 1917–1940* (Oxford: Clarendon Press, 1974), 145–147; Ashton, *British Policy Towards the Indian States*, (n 25) 135; and Ramusack, *The Princes of India in the Twilight of Empire*, (n 25) 201–202.

[94] Hooja, *Crusader for Self-Rule*, (n 9) 69.

The Genesis of the Federal Idea

Federation, as a viable albeit incoherent political project, was born in the frenetic discussions during the 1930 RTC over proposals for Indian constitutional reform. Unhappy with the Indian States Committee's refusal to define paramountcy,[95] the princes saw the RTC as a space to 'deal with the whole field of political supremacy exercised either as direct sovereignty or as paramountcy by Great Britain in India'.[96] The viceroy, Lord Irwin, feared that the princes would come to the RTC with 'a case prepared somewhat on the lines of that put up by Leslie Scott before the Butler Committee'.[97] After the secretary of state for India, William Wedgwood Benn,[98] concluded that the princes could not use the RTC as a forum to reargue their case on paramountcy,[99] Irwin shot down princely attempts to reiterate 'the legal theory of paramountcy' and instead convinced them to concentrate on 'all-India matters'.[100]

British resistance to discussing paramountcy at the RTC pushed some princely state advisors to cobble together a plan for federation. K. N. Haksar and K. M. Panikkar, who had been instrumental in developing the princes' case before the Indian States Committee, believed that federation was the perfect mechanism for the princes to achieve their diverse aims: it would enable the princes to participate in all-India decision-making while also limiting the ability of British officials to intervene in princely affairs by defining matters on which the states would be internally autonomous.[101] To build a coalition of support, they produced a book titled *Federal India*,[102] which presented a flattering vision of federation.[103] Haksar then relied on his personal relationship with Tej Bahadur Sapru to bring him

[95] 'Speeches by the *maharajas* of Patiala, Kashmir, and Bikaner, and the *nawab* of Bhopal, 27 February 1930', *Indian Annual Register*, i (1930), 488–492.

[96] 'Speech by the *maharaja* of Patiala, 27 February 1930', *Indian Annual Register*, i (1930), 486–487.

[97] Letter from the Viceroy to the Secretary of State for India, 15 March 1930, NAI, Government of India, Foreign and Political Department, 1930, Special, File No. 22-S.

[98] Benn was a former Liberal who joined the Labour party in 1927. See Leslie Hale, 'Benn, William Wedgwood, first Viscount Stansgate (1877–1960)', rev. Mark Pottle, in *Oxford Dictionary of National Biography*, https://doi.org/10.1093/ref:odnb/30705, accessed 14 April 2021.

[99] Letter from the Secretary of State of India to the Viceroy, 26 March 1930, NAI, Government of India, Foreign and Political Department, 1930, Special, File No. 22-S.

[100] Minutes of a conference at Viceregal Lodge, 14 and 15 July 1930, IOR/L/PS/13/557; Letter from Irwin to Wedgwood Benn, 18 July 1930, IOR/L/PS/13/557; and Letter from the Viceroy to the Secretary of State of India, 2 August 1930, IOR/L/PS/13/557.

[101] Letter from Haksar to the Editor of the *Manchester Guardian*, 6 November 1930, IOR/L/PS/13/547. British officials also connected princely support for federation with the achievement of the twin aims of attaining equality with British India on decision-making in matters of common concern and limiting the discretionary powers of intervention. See Letter from the Secretary of State of India to the Viceroy, 19 November 1930, IOR/L/PS/13/547.

[102] Panikkar later claimed that he wrote the entire draft, with Haksar's name being added before publication to ensure greater credibility. See Panikkar, *An Autobiography*, (n 75) 83–84.

[103] British officials alleged that Haksar hoped that the book would help to convince the princes to support federation. See Note by P. J. Patrick, 31 October 1930, IOR/L/PS/13/547.

into the federal fold.[104] On board the SS Narkunda to London for the RTC, Sapru reached an agreement with Akbar Hydari, the finance minister of Hyderabad, and Mirza Ismail, the *diwan* of Mysore, on a federal plan;[105] this unity was cemented with additional discussions in London.[106] After the princes dramatically agreed to a federal solution in the RTC's first plenary session, conference delegates were divided into subcommittees 'to devise concrete formulas for a federation'.[107] It soon became clear that the princely consensus was a superficial one. The states' advisors came up with at least three different schemes for federation although they shared some common factors: one each proposed by the team of Haksar and Panikkar, Akbar Hydari, and Mirza Ismail.[108]

To some extent, the princes and their advisors recycled the arguments that they had made before the Indian States Committee, with divisible sovereignty remaining key. All three federal schemes aimed to demarcate the state, federal, imperial, and international spheres by dividing the exercise of sovereign powers among the Crown, the federal centre, and provincial and state governments. Haksar and Panikkar advocated a federal constitution that would enable '[t]he distribution and delimitation of public powers', and define 'the respective spheres of authority of the central and local governments'.[109] Hydari agreed on the need for a constitutional structure in which '[t]he whole field of administration of Greater India, meaning thereby British India and Indian States India, may be divided into three circles',[110] i.e. the Crown, the federal government, and the provincial or state governments. Mirza Ismail argued that a federal constitution was key to uniting polities as disparate as the British Indian provinces and the states since it could create institutions with properly defined functions.[111]

The mechanism of this division of sovereign powers was also significant. Federations appealed to the states since they were structured around written constitutions that divided sovereign powers among the different levels of government

[104] Haksar's daughter was married to one of Sapru's sons. See K. N. Haksar, 'Intimate Glimpses', in K. N. Raina and K. V. Gopala Ratnam, eds., *Tej Bahadur Sapru: Profiles and Tributes* (Chandigarh: Tej Bahadur Sapru Commemoration Volume Committee, 1971), 109–115.

[105] Copland, *The Princes of India in the Endgame of Empire*, (n 15) 86; and Ramusack, *The Indian Princes and their States*, (n 25) 252. George Schuster, the finance minister of the government of India, who was also on board the ship, provides an account of Hydari's plans for federation in his memoir. See George Schuster, *Private Work and Public Causes: A Personal Record, 1881–1978* (Cowbridge: D. Brown and Sons, 1979), 105. For a general discussion of the informal conferencing that took place aboard such ships taking delegates to and from the RTCs, see Stephen Legg, 'Political Lives at Sea: Working and Socialising To and From the India Round Table Conference in London, 1930–1932', *Journal of Historical Geography*, 68 (2020), 21–32.

[106] Letter from the Secretary of State of India to the Government of India, Reforms Department, 13 November 1930, IOR/L/PS/13/547.

[107] Ramusack, *The Indian Princes and their States*, (n 25) 252.

[108] Copland, *The Princes of India in the Endgame of Empire*, (n 15) 87.

[109] Haksar and Panikkar, *Federal India*, (n 83) 23.

[110] Note by Akbar Hydari, 2 October 1930, IOR/L/PS/13/548.

[111] 'Speech on the Round Table Conference in Bangalore, 19 August 1930', in *Speeches by Amin-ul-Malik Sir Mirza M. Ismail*, i (Bangalore: Superintendent at the Government Press, 1930), 556–557.

based on the consent of the parties involved.[112] Advocates of federation argued that the federal government would only exercise the powers that were granted to it.[113] A federal structure, therefore, had the potential to deal with princely concerns around the arbitrary exercise of British paramountcy. This element of state consent was given particular prominence in Haksar and Panikkar's scheme. They proposed the establishment of a constitutional structure that included states 'by their consent' and created machinery 'which shall guarantee their rights' while 'reserv[ing] necessary powers to a common central government'. Since the states were 'not parts of British India' and possessed 'inherent rights' that were 'guaranteed to them by treaties with the British Crown', a federal constitution required 'a full reservation of their rights' as 'the territories administered by the rulers have full freedom to remain outside a national Indian State unless they can be persuaded to come in voluntarily'.[114]

By relying on state consent as the determining factor in the division of sovereign powers, federation could simultaneously preserve state autonomy and enable state participation in policy-making on issues of common concern. It was federalism's ability to perform this balancing act that made it so attractive to the princes. Haksar and Panikkar aimed for a structure in which the federal government had 'sufficient power to hold together the subordinate administrations' while ensuring that 'the required autonomy of the subordinate administrations is not infringed in local matters'. Federation, therefore, could preserve the separate sovereign status of the states, at least in all matters on which authority was not specifically ceded to the federal government.[115] Hydari's scheme also relied on a classification of sovereign authority into three categories—Crown, federal, and provincial/state—in accordance with 'their nature'. The Crown would be responsible for defence and external relations; the federal government would have control over communications, ports, posts, telegraphs, and telephones; and the provinces and states would have authority over '[a]ll matters not specifically included among Crown or Federal subjects'. Hydari's scheme, therefore, envisaged 'the largest measure of provincial autonomy' possible,[116] thereby ensuring the continued existence of the states as semi-sovereign units. Mirza Ismail also threw his support behind a constitution that provided 'full autonomy in the Provinces' along with 'responsibility at the Centre' and 'a close association between British India and the States in matters of common concern'.[117] He proposed that the Crown only retain control over defence

[112] Sunil Purushotham has noted the significance of a written constitution in shifting away from the 'vague and indeterminate system of paramountcy' to a rigid delineation of powers. See Purushotham, 'Sovereignty, Federation, and Constituent Power in Interwar India', (n 26) 425.

[113] Memorandum enclosed in circular letter from Bhopal, 12 May 1931, IOR/L/PS/13/547.

[114] Haksar and Panikkar, *Federal India*, (n 83) 13, 17–18.

[115] ibid 5, 33.

[116] Note by Akbar Hydari, 2 October 1930, IOR/L/PS/13/548. See also Moore, *The Crisis of Indian Unity*, (n 93) 139.

[117] 'Speech at the First Round Table Conference, 20 November 1930', in *Speeches by Amin-ul-Malik Sir Mirza M. Ismail*, ii (Bangalore: Superintendent at the Government Press, 1936), 9.

and foreign affairs, while other issues of common concern be transferred to the federal centre.[118]

This emphasis on state autonomy in the federal proposals also aimed to ensure that the states could maintain a monarchical form of government after British India moved towards representative democracy. Hydari proposed that British Indian provinces be governed by a Crown-appointed governor while the states continue to 'be ruled by a hereditary Ruler recognised by the Crown'.[119] Haksar and Panikkar took inspiration from the German empire, a union of states ruled by different royal families, to construct their federal proposal. Since the German constitution 'recognised local sovereignties by leaving the member-states intact with their own institutions, councils and governments, and only certain defined powers were transferred to the central government', they argued that it was a suitable model to ensure the independent existence of the princes without weakening central authority.[120] Mirza also acknowledged that the states were keen 'to retain their individuality' and 'to safeguard their internal autonomy'.[121]

Along with the preservation of monarchy, a federal structure also had the ability to institutionalize respect for the states' treaty rights. Haksar and Panikkar argued that federation could 'guarantee ... the sovereign rights of the states' that the Crown was bound to uphold 'by its treaties and engagements with Indian rulers to protect and maintain their sovereignty'. Since the states were 'entitled to insist upon adequate guarantees for the preservation of all their rights except those that must be assigned to the national government to make it effective', the federal court would have jurisdiction 'to declare illegal and *ultra vires* any executive or legislative measure which goes against the clauses of a treaty'.[122] Hydari was instructed to argue that Hyderabad's treaties were with the Crown and could not be transferred to a dominion government of India without state consent.[123] In Hydari's scheme therefore, the Crown retained the authority to conduct relations with the states instead of being transferred to the federal government of India.[124]

In all three schemes, federation became a forum for the princes to champion an interpretation of sovereignty that was conducive to their efforts of maintaining their sovereign autonomy and a link with the Crown while building a higher profile in South Asia and the broader empire, thereby laying claim to a semi-international status. By asserting that sovereignty was divisible, the states attempted to strike an

[118] Moore, *The Crisis of Indian Unity*, (n 93) 139–140; and Bridge, *Holding India to the Empire*, (n 24) 54.

[119] Note by Akbar Hydari, 2 October 1930, IOR/L/PS/13/548.

[120] Haksar and Panikkar, *Federal India*, (n 83) 16–17, 56–62.

[121] 'Speech on the Round Table Conference in Bangalore, 19 August 1930', in *Speeches by Amin-ul-Malik Sir Mirza M. Ismail*, (n 117) i, 558.

[122] Haksar and Panikkar, *Federal India*, (n 83) ix, 18, 20.

[123] Instructions to the Hyderabad delegation to the RTC, enclosed in Letter from Terence Keyes to C. C. Watson, 29 September 1930, IOR/L/PS/13/548.

[124] Note by Akbar Hydari, 2 October 1930, IOR/L/PS/13/548.

appropriate balance between beneficial relations with the Crown and British India and independence in internal affairs. By focusing on state consent, much as they had done before the Indian States Committee, princely advisors tried to preserve as much autonomy for the states as possible. Dividing sovereign powers among the various units in a federation was also a mechanism to ensure the continued existence of the states as monarchical units within a political space that was swarming with demands for democracy.

Despite broad agreement on these aims, the three plans for federation outlined above also differed in significant ways. Questions soon arose on how the states would participate in the federation.[125] All three schemes struggled to come up with a suitable structure for the federal legislature since a representative body would result in British Indian provinces dominating the states because of their larger population. Haksar and Panikkar therefore proposed that matters of common concern 'be decided by a Federal Council in which British India and the states are proportionately represented', with executive authority being shared by the federal council and the viceroy's executive council.[126] Hydari was also concerned by the states being overwhelmed by British India and proposed the establishment of a new all-India council, which would be 'very small and aristocratic', with thirty six members from the provinces, twenty four from the states, and twelve nominated by the Crown.[127] Mirza proposed the most complicated structure for the states' participation. He advocated that the states 'immediately' join the existing upper house of the British Indian legislature on an 'in and out footing', participating in decisions on all-India questions while abstaining on 'purely British Indian legislation'.[128]

Disagreements over the mechanism of federation were linked to more serious conflicts over the overlapping questions of the extent to which the states would federate with British India and the nature of the relationship between the states and the Crown.[129] Haksar and Panikkar outlined the need for a federal court to adjudicate on disputes between the states and other parts of the federation, arguing that the existing system in which the government of India made decisions claiming to be the 'paramount power' was flawed since it acted as 'both party and judge'. Disputes instead ought to be 'decided according to the principles of law and evidence', with the states having 'the right of argument through counsel' and 'the opportunity to

[125] Minutes of the informal meeting in the Prime Minister's Room at the House of Commons, 3, 8, and 9 December 1930, IOR/L/PS/13/545.

[126] Haksar and Panikkar, *Federal India*, (n 83) 102.

[127] Note by Akbar Hydari, 2 October 1930, IOR/L/PS/13/548; and Bridge, *Holding India to the Empire*, (n 24) 53. See also Moore, *The Crisis of Indian Unity*, (n 93) 138; and Ashton, *British Policy Towards the Indian States*, (n 25) 134.

[128] Note by P. J. Patrick, 31 October 1930, IOR/L/PS/13/547. See also 'Speech on the Round Table Conference in Bangalore, 19 August 1930', in *Speeches by Amin-ul-Malik Sir Mirza M. Ismail*, i, (n 117) 557–558.

[129] As Barbara Ramusack notes, the princes considered 'the two goals of a definition of paramountcy and a rationalization of their constitutional position' to be equally important. See Ramusack, *The Princes of India in the Twilight of Empire*, (n 25) 199.

weigh the evidence produced against their claims'.[130] Haksar and Panikkar were, therefore, concerned with limiting the powers exercised by the British government in relation to the states. Hydari, on the other hand, favoured strong reserve powers for the Crown, envisaging that the Crown would provide a 'binding force' since it 'would be sovereign over British India and paramount over Indian States India'.[131] Mirza's scheme attempted to have it both ways. He admitted the necessity for a federal court 'that shall have powers to decide justiciable matters at issue between themselves and the Government of India and the Provinces, or even between the different States themselves'.[132] However, his scheme retained the viceroy's power to intervene in the states subject to discussions with a board of advisors from the states.[133]

These differences in the federal schemes can be traced to the states' balancing act in pushing for federation. The key purpose of federation for the princes was to shore up state authority in the face of internal and external challenges while retaining the flexibility to cooperate with Britain and British India on a limited set of concerns. But this was a general ambition and attempts to draw up specific proposals led to varying conclusions based on the kind of balance that the drafters attempted to draw. Princes and advisors concerned about British interventions into state affairs favoured schemes that limited the exercise of sovereign power by unelected colonial officials, while those who treated British Indian politicians and states' peoples movements as the main threat to state authority preferred to create structures that would enable British support for the states. The language of divisible sovereignty enabled the creation of federal structures that espoused both these aims.

The terms of the three schemes reflected these varied goals. Building on their relationships with moderate nationalists such as Sapru, Haksar and Panikkar emphasized the states' participation in all-India institutions and the mandatory judicial resolution of disputes between British India and the states. Through their scheme, they aimed to curtail the 'political' nature of the relationship between British India and the states, which they considered to be arbitrary. The reform-minded Mirza was also concerned with the states obtaining a voice in the determination of policy on all-India matters but was willing to admit that the discretionary powers of the viceroy could not be eliminated altogether.[134] Both schemes focused on the limitation of paramountcy through the establishment of a legalistic relationship between the states and the Crown that was subject to adjudication through a federal court or discussion by an advisory board.

130 Haksar and Panikkar, *Federal India*, (n 83) 125–127.

131 Note by Akbar Hydari, 2 October 1930, IOR/L/PS/13/548.

132 'Speech on the Round Table Conference in Bangalore, 19 August 1930', in *Speeches by Amin-ul-Malik Sir Mirza M. Ismail*, (n 117) i, 558.

133 Note by P. J. Patrick, 31 October 1930, IOR/L/PS/13/547.

134 S. R. Ashton has argued that Mirza's plan was influenced by demands for representative government by the local states' peoples movement. See Ashton, *British Policy Towards the Indian States*, (n 25) 134.

Haksar, Panikkar, and Mirza also advocated the creation of stronger links between British India and the states through the equal participation of the states in all-India affairs, laying emphasis on the idea of the states becoming a 'co-equal partner' with British India in the future constitution.[135] This placed them firmly within the 'political reform' camp of the princely states although they did not advocate for parliamentary democracy within the states or a truly representative federal government. Instead, they aimed to restructure the relationships among the states, British India, and the Crown to entrench the princely monarchies within the larger frame of multiple sovereignties in the region.

This advocacy of closer relations between British India and the states was not, however, welcomed by everyone. As the Liberal politician Chimanlal Setalvad later noted, '[t]he real reason behind the willingness of the Princes to enter the Federation was their desire to throw off the yoke of Political Department ... [and] the irritating meddlesomeness of paramountcy in their affairs' rather than being 'prepared to have their political relations transferred to the Federal Government with a majority of British Indians in the legislatures and in the ministry'.[136] Hydari's proposal reflects this sentiment; it relied on strengthening the Crown's guarantees of protecting the states from the menace of Indian anticolonial nationalists and states' peoples movements. Unlike the other two schemes, Hydari's plan envisioned only a loose relationship between the states and British India on a very narrow list of issues. His primary motivation for advocating the division of sovereign powers was to enable the states to claim a direct relationship with the Crown.

Divisible sovereignty in a federation then was capable of being co-opted for advocating political reform and closer relations between the states and British India as well as for strengthening autocratic princely power and the influence of the Crown in state affairs. The future relationship between the princely states and British India became one of the main fault lines within the princely community during the 1930s.

Much like the princely states, anticolonial nationalists also emerged divided over the federal idea. The Congress leadership had boycotted the RTC and instead passed a resolution demanding *purna swaraj* (complete independence).[137] Although other anticolonial parties attended, differences arose among them over the issues of separate electorates for Dalits and Muslim representation in the legislatures.[138] Some Liberals, who broadly supported federation, were also dismayed at a federal scheme that entrenched autocracy within the states, sharing this view

[135] In advocating close links with British India, Robin Moore claims that Mirza was influenced by the arguments of Haksar and Panikkar. See Moore, *The Crisis of Indian Unity*, (n 93) 140.

[136] Chimanlal Setalvad, *Recollections and Reflections: An Autobiography* (Bombay: Padma Publications, 1946), 361.

[137] See 'Resolution on Complete Independence and the Round Table Conference passed by the Lahore Session of the Indian National Congress, 31 December 1929', in *Speeches and Documents on the Indian Constitution, 1921–47*, (n 12) i, 227.

[138] Moore, *The Crisis of Indian Unity*, (n 93) 158–164.

with states' peoples groups.[139] In British India, therefore, the division of sovereign powers in a federation was seen both as a means to impede independence and as a mechanism to progress, perhaps slowly, to self-government.

British politicians and officials also had an equally diverse range of opinions on federation. The Labour party, which formed the minority government in Britain at the time, was in favour of federation in principle, seeing it as a 'speedy and consensual solution of the Indian problem'.[140] The Liberals came on board when they were assured of princely participation.[141] Several in the Conservative party considered federation to be a useful tool for the maintenance of colonial control over South Asia; prominent among these supporters was Samuel Hoare, the party's delegate to the RTC and soon to become secretary of state for India.[142] Hoare considered federation 'as an opportunity of avoiding democracy in the central government', thereby providing a means to 'retain in our hands the realities and verities of British control'.[143] To support this view, Hoare relied on a legal opinion by two German international lawyers, Viktor Bruns and Carl Bilfinger.[144] The opinion, which had been commissioned by the princes, argued that a federation could only be established if the states entered into fresh treaties with the Crown since the states retained their independent international legal personality despite conceding specific rights to the British as paramount power.[145] Hoare was more interested in the precedent of the German empire that the two jurists discussed in their memo. He noted that the German states' house, composed of members appointed by the federating units, had veto powers over legislation passed by a representative assembly.[146] The presence of the princely states within the federation, therefore, would be a matter of comfort for the colonial state as they could act as a bulwark against the more radical anticolonial nationalists. In Hoare's vision, the division of sovereign powers

[139] Ramusack, *The Princes of India in the Twilight of Empire*, (n 25) 204–205, 208.

[140] Nicholas Owen, *The British Left and India: Metropolitan Anti-Imperialism, 1885–1947* (Oxford: Oxford University Press, 2007), 180.

[141] Moore, *The Crisis of Indian Unity*, (n 93) 149–153.

[142] Hoare, later Lord Templewood, was involved in the federal negotiations during his time as secretary of state for India. See R. J. Q. Adams, 'Hoare, Samuel John Gurney, Viscount Templewood (1880–1959)', in *Oxford Dictionary of National Biography*, https://doi.org/10.1093/ref:odnb/33898, accessed 7 May 2021.

[143] Moore, *The Crisis of Indian Unity*, (n 93) 155.

[144] Bruns was the director of the Kaiser Wilhelm Institute for International Law and was succeeded by Bilfinger. After the rise of the Nazis, Bruns attempted to pursue a normal career without overtly identifying himself as a Nazi while Bilfinger appears to have been more collaborationist as he was a party member. See Detlev F. Vagts, 'International Law in the Third Reich', *American Journal of International Law*, 84/3 (1990), 673, 680.

[145] Viktor Bruns and Carl Bilfinger, *Memorandum Relating to the Proposed Constitution of a Federal Union of All-India* (1930), Templewood Collection, Mss Eur E/240/52(b). For further discussion of the memo, see N. D. Varadachariar, *Indian States in the Federation* (Humphrey Milford: Oxford University Press, 1936), 29.

[146] Bridge, *Holding India to the Empire*, (n 24) 56.

afforded by federation was a means to centralize and retain a large portion of control within British hands. With the establishment of a national government dominated by the Conservative party in 1931, this soon became the official policy of the British government in London.

Political officers in South Asia, however, had a very different view of federation. Many were annoyed because Whitehall had committed to all-India federation despite being informed of Delhi's preference for more limited reforms.[147] They were keen to nip in the bud any changes that would reduce their authority over the states and thereby place their jobs at risk. They also claimed that federation would result 'in a loss of sovereignty for the princes'.[148] As Ian Copland remarks, most political officers were of the view that the states would be unable to survive in a democratic environment where they would be subject to the onslaught of the nationalists.[149] Given this pressure to reform, political officers such as Ronald Wingate argued that the states would not be able to act as the desired 'conservative and moderating influence' in a self-governing India.[150] In this view, the divided sovereignty of a federal government would strengthen anticolonial nationalists by expanding functions in which Indians could govern themselves.

Within a few short months of the birth of the federal project, all its initial backers faced internal wrangling over their support. The princes disagreed over the extent to which they ought to associate with British India; anticolonial nationalists remained unable to agree on specific constitutional structures; British officials were unsure of whether federation would strengthen or hinder the empire. The fear that federation would lay the foundation of Britain's loss of control over South Asia was most visible in the views of a minority of the Conservative party. This faction, led by Winston Churchill and Lord Salisbury, opposed any suggestion of a responsible central government as a part of the package for Indian political reform.[151] Churchill earned the backing of about eighty members of parliament and a substantial section of the press; his position also commanded enormous grassroots popularity. The 'diehards', as the group came to be known, started a relentless campaign against Indian self-government by resolving to wreck federation.[152] The princes, already split over their support for federation, played a key role in this strategy.

[147] Copland, *The Princes of India in the Endgame of Empire*, (n 15) 97.
[148] Ashton, *British Policy Towards the Indian States*, (n 25) 148.
[149] Copland, *The Princes of India in the Endgame of Empire*, (n 15) 97.
[150] Ronald Wingate, *Not in the Limelight* (London: Hutchinson, 1959), 140.
[151] Templewood, *Nine Troubled Years*, (n 11) 48.
[152] Copland, *The Princes of India in the Endgame of Empire*, (n 15) 114; and Ramusack, *The Indian Princes and their States*, (n 25) 260. Andrew Muldoon discusses the pro- and anti-federation propaganda carried on by the India Office and the diehards in Muldoon, *Empire, Politics and the Creation of the 1935 India Act*, (n 26) 187–199.

Federation or Confederation?

The princes, as significant as they were for the birth of federation, became even more important in attempts to destroy it, with British officials opposed to the federal project exploiting their internal disagreements. Much of the British support for federation depended on the princely states acting as a counterbalance to anticolonial nationalists: Conservative diehards therefore calculated that the British government would refuse to grant self-government to British India without the presence of the states as a safeguard.[153] British political officers began to emphasize 'the difficulties that would result from federation' in their conversations with the princes,[154] drawing the ire of federation supporters who considered these cautionary statements to be part of a deliberate plan to sabotage the federal project.[155]

Even without such external influences, several princes and advisors began to have second thoughts about federation. After initial support, Osman Ali Khan of Hyderabad, and his finance minister, Akbar Hydari, both cooled to the federal idea.[156] Rulers of small states were particularly concerned, fearing that they would not 'survive as independent polities' unless the federal chambers were large enough to include all states, a difficult proposition given that there were over five hundred of them.[157] This argument was taken up with increasing vigour by Bhupinder Singh of Patiala with the backing of Gulab Singh of Rewa, Udaibhan Singh of Dholpur, Sadiq Muhammad Khan of Bahawalpur, and Raza Ali Khan of Rampur. They all believed that an association with British India would ultimately lead to the extinction of the states.[158] In June 1931, Bhupinder Singh circulated a memorandum highlighting his concerns with federation to his fellow princes; he also released it to the press.[159]

Bhupinder Singh's memo took issue with the federationists' claim that the division of sovereign powers in a federal structure would empower the states by balancing their twin desires to remain autonomous polities and participate in policy-making on all-India concerns. For instance, Ganga Singh of Bikaner argued that '[t]he inherent Sovereignty and autonomy and the Treaties and other

[153] Copland, *The Princes of India in the Endgame of Empire*, (n 15) 114; and Ramusack, *The Indian Princes and their States*, (n 25) 260.

[154] Ramusack, *The Princes of India in the Twilight of Empire*, (n 25) 209. In general, there were very few political officers who supported federation, and those who did, for instance, Terence Keyes, the resident at Hyderabad, were actively disliked by more senior officials. See Ashton, *British Policy Towards the Indian States*, (n 25) 133.

[155] Haksar even complained that political officers who exercised their influence to keep the states out of federation were being rewarded. See Letter from K. N. Haksar to Tej Bahadur Sapru, 18 February 1933, Sapru Papers, Version II, 2nd series, Reel 8, IOR Neg 5004.

[156] Ramusack, *The Princes of India in the Twilight of Empire*, (n 25) 209.

[157] ibid 255. See also Copland, *The Princes of India in the Endgame of Empire*, (n 15) 91–93.

[158] 'Revolt Against Federal Plan', *Morning Post* (10 June 1931); and 'Anti-Federalists Supported', *The Statesman* (12 June 1931). See also Ramusack, *The Princes of India in the Twilight of Empire*, (n 25) 212.

[159] 'Maharaja of Patiala's Warning to Ruling Princes', *The Times of India* (17 June 1931). See also Copland, *The Princes of India in the Endgame of Empire*, (n 15) 98.

rights of the States and their subjects have been duly safeguarded and will be maintained intact . . . except only to the extent to which we may be prepared voluntarily to delegate them to the Federal Executive and the Federal Legislature, in which the States rightly claim an equal voice, and in which such portion of their Sovereignty as they delegate will be equally shared by the States in Common with British India'.[160] His prime minister, Manubhai Mehta, was even more forthright; federation, he claimed, 'pricks the bubble of undefined paramountcy'.[161] The Chamber's new chancellor, Hamidullah Khan of Bhopal, also reassured his fellow princes that the federal scheme would secure the states' sovereign rights 'except in so far as the states themselves voluntarily and of their own free will and consent assign to the federal government' and would guarantee that 'British India and the States will be co-equal partners and the present position in which the States are placed in practical subordination to the present Government of India would cease'.[162] In the federationists' view, divisible sovereignty would enable the states to preserve their sovereign status and monarchical form of government, limit the arbitrariness of British intervention based on paramountcy, and effectively participate, along with their British Indian counterparts, in decision-making on crucial issues of all-India importance. Bhupinder Singh, however, argued otherwise.

Sovereignty formed the nub of the differences between the federationists and anti-federationists. Bhupinder Singh admitted that 'in a federal constitution the ordinary powers of sovereignty are elaborately divided between the Federal Government and the component States'. But Bhupinder Singh challenged the federationists' claim that the princes would be able to maintain their sovereign status by citing the German jurist Georg Jellinek to contend that federation would destroy the plurality of the constituent states since it was 'a legal union which creates a paramount power over the federated States which are not necessarily sovereign but in place of sovereignty enjoy a definitely limited share of statal power and authority'. Far from maintaining the states' sovereign autonomy and monarchical form of government, a federal state would extinguish 'the international personality of the component States'.[163]

Bhupinder Singh also refuted the assertion that federation would limit British interference in the states' affairs while permitting the states to participate in decision-making on issues of common concern. The federal scheme, he contended, was 'fraught with the greatest dangers' since 'these powers of paramountcy will lie outside the scope of the Federal Constitution' and would 'continue to be exercised

[160] Speech by the *maharaja* of Bikaner in reply to the address of welcome on his return from Europe presented by the Municipal Board, Bikaner, 9 February 1931, IOR/L/PS/13/603.

[161] Note by P. J. Patrick, 21 May 1931, IOR/L/PS/13/603.

[162] Note on the implications of federation enclosed in circular letter from Bhopal, 12 May 1931, IOR/L/PS/13/547.

[163] Note on Federation and the Indian States, [13] June 1931, NAI, Government of India, Foreign and Political Department, 1931, Special, File No. 31-S.

by the representatives of the Crown in the same arbitrary and unreasonable manner as before'. In fact, the future of the states was 'dark, uncertain and gloomy under the federal constitution' since it vested powers of interference in the Crown's representatives and in the federal government. He relied on the precedents of the extension of federal powers in the 'colonial federations' of Australia and Canada to argue that the states' representation in the federal legislature and the adjudication of disputes by a federal court would not effectively protect the states' sovereignty. Even if a suitable federal constitution could be devised, it would 'be impossible to secure adequate representation of all the States which is absolutely necessary in order to safeguard their existence and interest'. Instead of providing a lifeline to the states, Bhupinder Singh claimed that federation was 'a radical innovation; it subverts the very basis of the well-tried and time honoured political institutions of the States; it attempts to destroy their individuality and political culture ... is a revolution as far-reaching as the absorption of the States in British India'.[164]

In a separate memo, Bhupinder Singh elaborated on the alternative of a 'confederation', in which the states would first enter into a union with each other 'before their entering into a convention with British India for matters of common concern so that it will be a case of two interests seeking a relationship for the settlement of questions of joint interest and simultaneously preserving their internal sovereignty'. Although vague about the specifics, Bhupinder Singh envisaged the ultimate structure to be a fairly loose union of two equal entities—British India and the union of states—with both polities being equally represented in any confederal institutions.[165] In his view, such a constitutional structure would ensure the largest measure of autonomy for the states, thereby going a long way to preserve their separate sovereign status.

Bhupinder Singh's confederation scheme ostensibly shared the same aims as the three federal schemes drafted by Haksar/Panikkar, Mirza, and Hydari. All of them agreed that sovereign powers had to be appropriately divided to achieve the necessary balance among the states' varied desires: to maintain their relationship with the Crown through treaties, to participate in all-India affairs, and to preserve their separate sovereign status by defending their internal autonomy against British interference and the demands of states' peoples' movements. But they disagreed sharply on the best mechanism to achieve this balance, largely on account of their drastically differing views on the relationship with British India. Like Akbar Hydari, Bhupinder Singh also feared being overwhelmed by British Indian nationalists in the event of the states joining a representative federal legislature. Therefore, his scheme of confederation sought to limit the subjects that would be considered to be matters of common concern and to redefine the institutional

[164] ibid.

[165] Statement Explanatory of Memorandum on Federation and the Indian States, undated, IOR/L/PS/13/603.

relationship of the British Indian and states' representatives as a discussion council rather than a federal legislature. In making this proposal, Bhupinder Singh seemed to draw inspiration from the League of Nations, whose meetings he had attended as an Indian representative, and which he saw as a forum that could be replicated in the South Asian context. The more tightly integrated model of federation, according to him, would not preserve state sovereignty as pro-federationists argued, but would destroy it instead.

Although India Office officials dismissed Bhupinder Singh's memorandum as 'half-baked',[166] it caused a crisis within princely ranks, with Haksar accusing him of being 'a tool of ... the Political Department'[167] and wrecking federation because of his personal animosity against Ganga Singh and Hamidullah, both known supporters of the project.[168] Haksar denounced the confederation scheme as 'idiotic'[169] and 'manifestly absurd',[170] but it soon gathered support from the rulers of Rampur, Bahawalpur, Kutch, Sachin, Limbdi, and Sangli, and ministers including S. M. Bapna of Indore and Prabhashankar Pattani of Bhavnagar.[171] Although Bhupinder Singh's plan was outvoted at a conference of the princes in Bombay in June 1931,[172] he continued to claim the support of at least thirty states.[173]

At the second RTC in 1931, Patiala's prime minister, Liaquat Hyat Khan—together with Prabhashankar Pattani, Yeshwantrao Holkar of Indore, and Udaibhan Singh of Dholpur—presented a detailed version of Bhupinder Singh's confederation proposal as means to provide 'adequate and substantial safeguards for the maintenance and preservation of the internal sovereignty of the States'.[174] The scheme proposed that the states first constitute themselves into a single unit, which would then collectively federate with British India 'for purposes of specified matters of common interest only'; this was a relatively short list of federal subjects. The confederationists also went further than the federationists on the division of sovereign powers among different levels of government. Not being content with a

[166] Note by P. J. Patrick, 21 August 1931, IOR/L/PS/13/603.

[167] Letter from K. N. Haksar to Tej Bahadur Sapru, 22 July 1931, Sapru Papers, 1st series, Reel 1, IOR Neg 4987.

[168] Letter from K. N. Haksar to Tej Bahadur Sapru, 12 June 1931, Sapru Papers, 1st series, Reel 1, IOR Neg 4987.

[169] Letter from K. N. Haksar to Tej Bahadur Sapru, 13 July 1931, Sapru Papers, 1st series, Reel 1, IOR Neg 4987.

[170] Letter from K. N. Haksar to Tej Bahadur Sapru, 16 June 1931, Sapru Papers, 1st series, Reel 1, IOR Neg 4987.

[171] Letter from K. N. Haksar to Tej Bahadur Sapru, 11 June 1931, Sapru Papers, 1st series, Reel 1, IOR Neg 4987; Copland, *The Princes of India in the Endgame of Empire*, (n 15) 99; and Ramusack, *The Indian Princes and their States*, (n 25) 256.

[172] Letter from K. N. Haksar to Tej Bahadur Sapru, 13 July 1931, Sapru Papers, 1st series, Reel 1, IOR Neg 4987.

[173] Letter from the *maharaja* of Patiala to Lord Willingdon, 17 August 1931, NAI, Government of India, Foreign and Political Department, 1931, Special, File No. 31-S.

[174] 'Speech by Liaquat Hyat Khan at the Second Indian Round Table Conference, 30 November 1931', in Adrian Sever, ed., *Documents and Speeches on the Indian Princely States*, ii (Delhi: B. R. Publishing, 1985), 494–497.

division between federal and state subjects, they also advocated splitting jurisdiction over 'policy and legislation' and 'administration'. Under this proposal, certain matters would be under federal control for both purposes, while others (for instance, railway lines that were within state territory) would be under federal authority only for the purposes of policy and legislation, with administration being left to the states.[175] By restricting the functions of the federal government, the confederationists also hoped that it would have limited expenditure that could be met by modest indirect taxes.[176] The combination of limited federal jurisdiction and funding would, the confederationists' hoped, preserve the separate, autonomous existence of the states.

The confederationists also pushed for a constitution that provided for 'the maintenance and preservation of the traditional and time-honoured relations between the States and the British Crown'.[177] To maintain the states' monarchical structures, they demurred from proposals for direct elections to the federal legislature by the states' peoples. Instead, they proposed that the confederation of states would serve as the electoral college for the election of representatives to the federal legislature. The jurisdiction of the federal court was also to be restricted to constitutional questions, with disputes between the Crown and the states, or between the states and the central or provincial governments of British India, or between the states *inter se* being referred to an 'impartial Court of Arbitration, distinctly separate from the Federal Court'.[178] Instead of establishing closer relations between the states and British India in which disputes would be resolved through a judicial process, confederationists sought greater protections for the states in the form of a stronger relationship with the Crown, limited powers of the federal government, and more informal means of dispute settlement such as arbitration. Unlike the federationists, who harnessed divisible sovereignty to ensure greater legal protections for the states in a written constitution, the confederationists used the same language to entrench a closer political relationship between the states and the Crown.

The confederal proposal obtained the backing of smaller states but important states such as Hyderabad, Mysore, Baroda, and Gwalior remained ambivalent, splitting the princely order down the middle.[179] An informal meeting before the start of the March 1932 Chamber session was the start of a rapprochement. The major players—Bhupinder Singh, Hamidullah, and Ganga Singh—agreed to set

[175] 'Memorandum by His Highness the Maharaja of Indore, His Highness the Maharaja Rana of Dholpur, Nawab Liaquat Hyat Khan and Sir Prabhashankar Pattani', in *Speeches and Documents on the Indian Constitution, 1921–47*, (n 12) ii, 747.

[176] Copland, *The Princes of India in the Endgame of Empire*, (n 15) 107; and Ramusack, *The Indian Princes and their States*, (n 25) 256.

[177] 'Speech by Liaquat Hyat Khan at the Second Indian Round Table Conference, 30 November 1931', in *Documents and Speeches on the Indian Princely States*, (n 174) ii, 494–497.

[178] 'Memorandum by His Highness the Maharaja of Indore, His Highness the Maharaja Rana of Dholpur, Nawab Liaquat Hyat Khan and Sir Prabhashankar Pattani', in *Speeches and Documents on the Indian Constitution, 1921–47*, (n 12) ii, 747.

[179] Copland, *The Princes of India in the Endgame of Empire*, (n 15) 105–106.

up a committee under the chairmanship of C. P. Ramaswamy Aiyar,[180] the constitutional advisor to Travancore, to report on the feasibility of the confederation scheme and the safeguards needed to protect the states in a federation.[181] After the 'Delhi Pact',[182] the Chamber of Princes resolved that the states would join an all-India federation subject to certain conditions: the adoption of 'necessary safeguards', the assurance that states' treaty rights would be 'inviolate and inviolable', and the commitment that the 'sovereignty and internal independence' of the states would remain intact.[183]

Although federationists like Haksar exulted in the Chamber's resolution,[184] the Delhi Pact proved to be fragile. The Aiyar committee only provided a qualified endorsement of federation, clarifying that the states' accession was subject to sufficient representation in the federal legislature, a bar on the revision of treaty rights without state consent, a limited federal government with authority confined to subjects specifically assigned to it by the states, and a guaranteed right of secession.[185] The committee also listed several 'fundamental principles' for inclusion in the federal constitution. These encompassed safeguards from intervention by the federal government in the internal affairs of a state, a guarantee that residuary sovereign powers would reside with the states, and a continued connection between federal India and Britain.[186] Although Sapru termed the Aiyar committee proposals consistent with the federal scheme,[187] they seemed to be an awkward mix of the aims of the federation and confederation factions: closer relations with British India and greater participation in all-India matters, but also greater autonomy for the states and limited federal jurisdiction, united only by a broad commitment to the maintenance of princely sovereignty and monarchical form of government. While the princes were united by the cause of protecting their sovereignty, they continued to differ on the best mechanism to protect their autonomy. For many princes, a close relationship with the Crown was necessary 'to prevent

[180] Aiyar was an able lawyer and had spent many years in the service of the government of India. He was first appointed the legal and constitutional advisor to the *maharaja* of Travancore before being appointed *diwan* in 1936, a post he retained till Travancore's accession to the dominion of India in 1947. See Saroja Sundararajan, *Sir C. P. Ramaswamy Aiyar* (New Delhi: Allied Publishers, 2002).

[181] Copland, *The Princes of India in the Endgame of Empire*, (n 15) 108. Panikkar claimed that he was responsible, along with Aiyar, for drafting the terms of the report. See Panikkar, *An Autobiography*, (n 75) 88.

[182] K. M. Panikkar, *The Indian Princes in Council: A Record of the Chancellorship of His Highness the Maharaja of Patiala* (Humphrey Milford: Oxford University Press, 1936), 105.

[183] 'Resolution passed by the Chamber of Princes, 1 April 1932', *Indian Annual Register*, i (1932), 380.

[184] Letter from K. N. Haksar to Tej Bahadur Sapru, 3 April 1932, Sapru Papers, Version II, 2nd series, Reel 8, IOR Neg 5004.

[185] Urmila Phadnis, *Towards the Integration of Indian States, 1919–1947* (Bombay: Asia Publishing House, 1968), 66; Copland, *The Princes of India in the Endgame of Empire*, (n 15) 110; Ramusack, *The Indian Princes and their States*, (n 25) 259.

[186] Phadnis, *Towards the Integration of Indian States*, (n 185) 66–67; Copland, *The Princes of India in the Endgame of Empire*, (n 15) 110–111; Ramusack, *The Indian Princes and their States*, (n 25) 259.

[187] Letter from Tej Bahadur Sapru to K. N. Haksar, 9 April 1932, Sapru Papers, Version II, 2nd series, Reel 8, IOR Neg 5004.

that State from being swallowed up not by Russia or Afghanistan, but by the monster of British India'.[188] Others, however, claimed that such a relationship would strengthen the Crown's claims of unfettered powers of paramountcy.

Things came to a head at an informal conference called by the viceroy, Lord Willingdon,[189] in September 1932, in which he warned the princes that 'too rigid a definition' of paramountcy would significantly 'weaken the Crown's ability to protect the States, and make the relationship less human'. Over the determined attempts of Hamidullah to challenge this statement, Akbar Hydari announced that he did not consider 'any limitation or definition of the functions and claims of Paramountcy to be desirable' and Gulab Singh professed that 'all the safeguards of the States for the future lay in the undefined powers of paramountcy'.[190] Willingdon egged them on, reiterating that the 'the personal discretion of the Viceroy ... in a Federated India would probably be their greatest safeguard'.[191] Hamidullah and Ganga Singh then tried to push through a proposal for the mandatory judicial settlement of disputes between the states and the Crown to prevent the British from acting as both party and judge to a dispute.[192] In this, they faced resistance from the political secretary, Charles Watson, who pointed to the danger of fettering the discretion of the viceroy in favour of the rulings of a 'cast-iron tribunal, restricted to legal issues and devoid of that elasticity and understanding of political values which appear essential for the protection of the Indian States'.[193] Gulab Singh and Hydari also added to these objections, arguing that the mandatory acceptance of tribunal decisions would prevent the states from appealing to the Crown on 'personal' grounds.[194] In his report on the conference, Willingdon expressed his satisfaction at the cleavages between the 'Bikaner Bhopal group' and other states, noting that the latter were unwilling to fetter the discretion of the Crown's representative and had expressed 'pronounced' opposition to the proposals for mandatory arbitration.[195]

With the rejection of proposals for defining paramountcy and the mandatory judicial settlement of disputes, the anti-federationists appeared to be succeeding in

[188] Letter from K. N. Haksar to Tej Bahadur Sapru, 5 October 1932, Sapru Papers, Version II, 2nd series, Reel 8, IOR Neg 5004.

[189] Willingdon had served as governor of Bombay and Madras before being appointed viceroy in 1931. See D. A. Low, 'Thomas, Freeman Freeman-, first marquess of Willingdon (1866–1941)', in *Oxford Dictionary of National Biography*, https://doi.org/10.1093/ref:odnb/33266, accessed 14 May 2021.

[190] Report by K. M. Panikkar on the conference between the Viceroy and the princes in September 1932, 24 October 1932, NAI—Bhopal, Chamber Section, Bundle No. 20, File No. 17, Old File No. P/115.

[191] Minutes of a meeting held at Viceregal Lodge, Simla, 20 September 1932, IOR/R/1/1/4688(1).

[192] Minutes of a meeting between the Viceroy and the Standing Committee, 20 September 1932, IOR/R/1/1/4688(1); and Minutes of a meeting held at Viceregal Lodge, Simla, 22 September 1932, IOR/R/1/1/4688(1).

[193] Appendix I to Minutes of a meeting between the Viceroy and the Standing Committee, 20 September 1932, IOR/R/1/1/4688(1).

[194] Report by K. M. Panikkar on the conference between the Viceroy and the princes in September 1932, 24 October 1932, NAI—Bhopal, Chamber Section, Bundle No. 20, File No. 17, Old File No. P/115.

[195] See Letter from Lord Willingdon to Samuel Hoare, 28 September 1932, IOR/R/1/1/4688(1); and Letter from the Government of India, Foreign and Political Department to the Secretary of State for India, 25 October 1932, IOR/L/PS/13/550.

their attempts to establish a loose confederation accompanied by strong imperial guarantees to protect the states. They were also steadily gaining allies, including Ranjitsinhji of Nawanagar, who was elected chancellor of the Chamber in March 1932. Although initially enthusiastic about federation as a means to amplify the role that he could play in the empire, Ranjitsinhji soon realized that a closer relationship with British India might threaten the existence of the states because of the demands for democratic governance.[196] His concerns appear to have been reinforced by his foreign minister, Lawrence Rushbrook Williams, who had been contacted by the diehards to support their cause.[197] At a Chamber session in 1933, Ranjitsinhji warned that federation 'will inevitably work as to destroy at least in its effective form the very principle of Indian kingship and both economically and politically the monarchical principles will suffer'.[198] The British government made fresh proposals to clarifiy that each state could define the extent of its participation in federation through a negotiated 'instrument of accession' listing the subjects on which the state proposed to accede; on all other matters, the autonomy of the state would remain unaffected.[199] This explanation provided some comfort to the princes, with a committee of ministers under the chairmanship of Akbar Hydari recommending that the structure ought to be 'recognised as acceptable' subject to the fulfilment of certain demands.[200]

This guarded approval did not last long; when the draft Government of India Bill was published in January 1935, princely advisors discovered that certain provisions differed from the position that had been agreed during meetings between the states' legal representatives and the India Office.[201] One of the primary concerns was clause 6 of the Bill, which made the entire Act applicable to an acceding state. This provision was unacceptable to the ministers 'for thereby everything in the Act becomes *ipso facto* binding upon the States' rather than permitting rulers to accept specific provisions of the Act through an instrument of accession.[202] The princes were equally scathing. Hamidullah observed that the scheme 'falls far short of many of our vital demands'. Ganga Singh described the Bill as 'a profound surprise and disappointment'. Bhupinder Singh denounced the Bill as a 'counterfeit' scheme

[196] Satadru Sen, *Migrant Races: Empire, Identity and K. S. Ranjitsinhji* (Manchester: Manchester University Press, 2004), 160–162.

[197] Panikkar, *An Autobiography*, (n 75) 88–89. Haksar claimed that Ranjitsinhji had fallen under the influence of the 'unscrupulous' Rushbrook Williams and the 'money-grabbing' Leslie Scott. See Letter from K. N. Haksar to Tej Bahadur Sapru, 5 October 1932, Sapru Papers, Version II, 2nd series, Reel 8, IOR Neg 5004.

[198] 'Speech by the *jam saheb* of Nawanagar, 24 March 1933', *Indian Annual Register*, i (1933), 478–479.

[199] *Proceedings of the Joint Committee on Indian Constitutional Reform, Vol. I (Part I): Report* (1934).

[200] Report of the proceedings of the Committee of States' Ministers in Bombay, 12, 13, and 14 December 1934, IOR/L/PS/13/603.

[201] This charge was repeated by Haksar although he was not present at the conference. See Letter from K. N. Haksar to Tej Bahadur Sapru, 27 March 1935, Sapru Papers, Version II, 2nd series, Reel 8, IOR Neg 5004.

[202] Letter from Hydari to Glancy, 21 February 1935, IOR/L/PS/13/607.

that had 'nothing in common, except in name, to the scheme which in its general outline we accepted at the first Round Table Conference'. Gulab Singh called the scheme 'a dangerous experiment'.[203]

A joint letter drafted by Bhupinder Singh, Ganga Singh, and Hamidullah encapsulated the princely response to the federal model in the draft Bill. To ensure that the states would be able to retain as much autonomy as possible, they sought clear constitutional provisions that required only specific sovereign powers to be transferred to the federal government, with residuary jurisdiction vested with the states. They also pushed for the states to have the power of passing concurrent legislation on federal subjects, provided there was no repugnancy between state and federal laws, and sought to limit federal executive authority within the states. They raised concerns about the 'special responsibility' powers of the governor-general, under which he could act 'to prevent any grave menace to peace or tranquillity of India'. Such extensive authority, the states feared, could empower the governor-general to intervene in the internal affairs of the states; paramountcy, therefore, remained indeterminate. The princes instead sought to refocus on treaties, demanding that the constitution explicitly recognize the sanctity of the states' treaties with the Crown. By insisting on entering the federation through bilateral 'treaties' that imposed reciprocal obligations on the states and the Crown, rather than unilateral 'instruments of accession', which did not have any indication of the extent of the Crown's obligations to protect the states, they also sought a confirmation of the semi-international status of the states.[204] All these were concerns that had been raised by the princes before the Indian States Committee and repeatedly on other occasions in the interwar period.

The federation/confederation debate revealed the key cleavages among the princes on the best mechanism to protect state autonomy and of the differing uses of the language of divisible sovereignty. The divisibility of sovereignty became the basis to pursue conflicting goals: some used it to establish a close relationship with British India in which the states would have a bigger voice while others believed it was useful to draw the states nearer to the Crown that would use discretionary powers to protect the princes. Although separate camps among the princes favoured differing political structures, their broad aims remained analogous: the preservation of the states as separate, sovereign, and monarchical political units within a federal framework that could provide linkages with British India and the Crown, thereby enabling them to redraw the boundaries between the domestic and international spheres by achieving a semi-international status. These demands were reflected in the joint letter that led to further negotiations between the British

[203] Report of the speeches at the conference of Indian princes in Bombay, 25 February 1935, IOR/L/PS/13/682.

[204] Letter from the rulers of Patiala, Bhopal, and Bikaner to Lord Willingdon, 27 February 1935, IOR/L/PS/13/607.

government and princely representatives.[205] After receiving assurances on the nature of federation, the Hydari committee gave its approval.[206] The Government of India Act (GoI Act), which set out the constitutional structure for federation, became law after receiving royal assent on 2 August 1935.[207]

The Negotiations Over the Instruments of Accession

The princes remained centre stage in the federal debates even after the passage of the GoI Act because of a major caveat: the provisions on federation would only come into force with the accession of a significant proportion of the princely states.[208] The British government, therefore, had one final task: convincing the states to sign instruments of accession (IoAs) that would bring federation into place. Since the IoAs would manage the relationship between the princely states and the federal government, their terms became subject to heated negotiations in which the preservation of state sovereignty became, once again, a key site of debate.

In these deliberations, the usual princely advisors—K. N. Haksar, K. M. Panikkar, C. P. Ramaswamy Aiyar, Akbar Hydari, and Manubhai Mehta—were joined by a battery of foreign lawyers. Osman Ali Khan of Hyderabad appointed the British constitutional lawyer Walter Monckton[209] as his advisor in 1933.[210] Bhupinder Singh of Patiala recruited a retired American judge, William Wadhams,[211] who he met on a trip to Paris, and attempted to persuade the Standing Committee to

[205] Letter from the Secretary of State for India to the Government of India, 14 March 1935, IOR/L/PS/13/607; and Letter from the Secretary of State for India to the Viceroy, 23 March 1935, IOR/L/PS/13/607.

[206] Letter from the Viceroy to the Secretary of State for India, 25 March 1935, IOR/L/PS/13/607.

[207] This was despite the best efforts of Winston Churchill to obstruct the passage of the law. See Richard Austen Butler, *The Art of the Possible* (London: Hamish Hamilton, 1971), 45–58.

[208] GoI Act, s 5 provided that federation would come into force on accession by the rulers of at least half the states to be represented in the upper house of the federal legislature and constituting at least half the population of the states.

[209] Monckton advised Edward VIII during the abdication crisis. See Lord Birkenhead, *Walter Monckton: The Life of Viscount Monckton of Brenchley* (London: Weidenfeld and Nicolson, 1969); H. Montgomery-Hyde, *Walter Monckton* (London: Sinclair-Stevenson, 1991); and Martin Pugh, 'Monckton, Walter Turner, first Viscount Monckton of Brenchley (1891–1965)', in *Oxford Dictionary of National Biography*, https://doi.org/10.1093/ref:odnb/35061, accessed 17 May 2021.

[210] The appointment was made on the recommendation of Donald Somervell, who had advised the princes during the hearings before the Indian States Committee. See Montgomery-Hyde, *Walter Monckton*, (n 209) 36–37. Francis Wylie, however, claimed that the *nizam* hired Monckton because he thought that Monckton had influence over the Conservative party. See Wylie, 'Federal Negotiations in India 1935–9, and After', (n 12) 521. Monckton was briefed by the London firm, Coward, Chance & Co. (now better known as the multinational law firm, Clifford Chance), which also advised the Chamber of Princes. For details on Coward Chance's dealings with the princes, see Judy Slinn, *Clifford Chance: Its Origins and Development* (Cambridge: Granta Editions, 1993), 87.

[211] Wadhams was appointed a judge of the City Court of the City of New York in 1907 and elected a judge at the Court of General Sessions in 1914. Later, he was a delegate to the Paris Peace Conference. See William Henderson Wadhams, *The Reminiscences* (1950), 2, Columbia University Oral History Collection, Lamont Library Microforms, Harvard University.

let him represent the Chamber.[212] Udaibhan Singh of Dholpur, a leading anti-federationist, favoured John Hartman Morgan,[213] a brash English lawyer who advised the diehard mouthpiece, the *Morning Post*.[214] The princes were unsure of hiring an American, but Panikkar was horrified at the idea of a diehard lawyer representing the states.[215] He managed to convince the Standing Committee to hire both Wadhams and Morgan, but Wadhams was dismissed when Udaibhan Singh was elected chancellor in February 1936. Wadhams blamed Morgan for his ouster but maintained his association with the princes since Bhupinder Singh continued to brief him.[216]

The internal politics of the princes' legal team also had broader ramifications for the negotiations over the IoAs. Although the passage of the GoI Act had temporarily papered over dissensions among the princes, old debates over the appropriate relationship among the states, the federal government, and the Crown soon resurfaced. While maintaining that sovereign powers were divided among the Crown, the federal government, and the provinces and states, the princes were keen to retain a large measure of sovereign autonomy. The princes hoped to limit the powers of the federal government by acceding only on a narrow list of federal subjects; they also continued to emphasize the importance of their treaty rights. Treaties epitomized state consent and the princes argued that treaty rights had to be respected even after states acceded to the federation.[217]

With the shared goal of maintaining state sovereignty while establishing profitable relationships with British India and the Crown in mind, the princes and their advisors carved out different paths for achieving their aim. Federationists argued that the division of sovereign powers in the GoI Act would enable the princes to achieve an appropriate balance between state autonomy and co-operation with other political entities. Anti-federationists, on the other hand, argued that the GoI Act would lead to the destruction of the states. To resolve the situation, the princes set up committees to examine the constitutional and financial aspects of the GoI Act in October 1936. Although Udaibhan Singh hoped that Morgan's appointment would help to convince the princes to reject federation, he met with considerable opposition.[218] The constitutional committee was stacked with federationists, including Bhupinder Singh, Ganga Singh, Manubhai Mehta, Panikkar,

212 Wadhams later claimed that he had been hired specifically because he was an American since the princes did not want a British lawyer and 'preferred to have independent advice'. See ibid 112.

213 Morgan was a professor of constitutional law at University College, London, and combined it with advisory work. See G. W. Keeton, 'Morgan, John Hartman (1876–1955)', in *Oxford Dictionary of National Biography*, https://doi.org/10.1093/ref:odnb/35105, accessed 17 May 2021.

214 Ramusack, *The Indian Princes and their States*, (n 25) 266–267.

215 Copland, *The Princes of India in the Endgame of Empire*, (n 15) 147.

216 Note by P. J. Patrick, 5 June 1936, IOR/L/PS/13/608.

217 For a discussion of how the treaty relationship was seen as a personal one between the state's monarch and the Crown, see Pillai, 'Fragmenting the Nation', (n 26) 758–765.

218 Copland, *The Princes of India in the Endgame of Empire*, (n 15) 149–150.

and Haksar.[219] The pro- and anti-federation factions clashed at meetings held in the early months of 1937, with the advisors submitting rival legal opinions to support their views.

In his memo, Morgan claimed that the GoI Act would result in the sovereignty of the states being 'very considerably impaired and wholly transformed'. Pointing to the Act's provision that permitted the federal legislature to directly legislate for the states, he argued that the allegiance of the states' subjects would be 'divided between the ruler and the Federation'. He referred to precedents from Australia and Canada where, in his view, the judiciary had permitted a creeping overreach of the federal government at the expense of the states' powers. He also took issue with the use of the term 'instrument of accession', claiming that the British government had deliberately refused to use the term 'treaty' to exclude the application of principles of treaty interpretation such as 'no treaty can be taken to restrict by implication the exercise of rights of sovereignty'.[220]

Much like the confederationists had argued in years before, Morgan believed that despite dividing sovereign powers, the close-knit structure of a federation would empower the federal government over the states rather than enabling the states to maintain their monarchical status and expand their autonomy. This wasn't an altogether partisan view. In his work detailing the working of the GoI Act, Shafa'at Ahmad Khan, a former delegate to the RTCs, noted that 'to anyone who has followed the trend of federations all over the world, it is clear that a ruler will find it extremely difficult if not impossible to maintain a vital distinction between Federal and non-Federal subjects in his domain'. He went on to claim that '[n]ational solidarity and unity, the irresistible pressure and march of the Centre, the growth of representative systems in States and the gradual abolition of economic barriers, will make serious inroads on their sovereignty'.[221]

Morgan's case against federation, however, went beyond legal advice to include personal insults against Wadhams, the main pro-federation legal advisor. Although Morgan did not name Wadhams, he ridiculed the 'foreign lawyer imported for the occasion' as someone who was unfamiliar with the constitutional practices and law of the British empire and instead relied on 'rhetoric' and 'loud arguments', which he claimed were 'common practices' in American lower courts.[222] These unsolicited attacks did not endear Morgan to the other princely advisors. Haksar called him 'positively abusive' and 'intolerably aggressive', noting that he had 'not yet met any one who had a good word to say for him'.[223] Christopher Brunyate, advisor to the state of Hyderabad, termed his remarks on Wadhams as 'really quite intolerable'

219 Phadnis, *Towards the Integration of the Indian States*, (n 185) 105.
220 Opinion of J. H. Morgan, 17 February 1937, Federal Papers, Vol. II, NMML.
221 Shafa'at Ahmad Khan, *The Indian Federation: An Exposition and Critical Review* (London: Macmillan and Co., 1937), 36, 110–111.
222 Opinion of J. H. Morgan, 17 February 1937, Federal Papers, Vol. II, NMML.
223 Letter from K. N. Haksar to K. M. Panikkar, 23 March 1937, Federal Papers, Vol. II, NMML.

and thought that Morgan had 'lost his head'.[224] Even Paul Patrick at the India Office termed Morgan as a man who was 'clearly not reliable as regards courtesy'.[225]

Apart from personal dislike, Morgan also faced a spirited challenge to his legal interpretation of the GoI Act. Panikkar countered him by pointing to the opinions of other well-respected lawyers, notably the princes' long-time counsel, Tej Bahadur Sapru, who differed sharply from Morgan on the implications of the Act. Sapru did not consider that 'the sovereignty of the States is affected at all by this Act except so far as the States voluntarily concede certain powers'; instead, the draft IoA 'reinforces the sovereignty' of the states. The applicability of federal legislation to states' subjects was 'implicit and inherent in the idea of federation' and did not constitute any further concession of state sovereignty other than the specific functions ceded by the execution of the IoA. He also dismissed Morgan's concerns that the doctrine of 'implied powers' as applied in Canada and Australia would serve to expand the powers of the Indian federation at the expense of the states. In his view, the GoI Act was unique since it envisaged that the Indian states would enter federation through the means of IoAs that could not be overridden by the Act; this, he claimed, was not the case in the colonial federations.[226]

Sapru's views were a continuation of the long pro-federation sentiment within the princely camp that envisioned divisible sovereignty as the basis of close relations between the states and British India in a structure in which the princes could play a pivotal political role. Much like Haksar and Panikkar had argued in their initial federal propaganda, Sapru considered state consent to cede sovereign authority in the IoAs to be an effective limit on the unlimited expansion of British power within the states. Comforted by Sapru's opinion, the states' constitutional committee dismissed Morgan's concerns, concluding, 'the safeguards have been substantially met'.[227] The princes' move in favour of federation was cemented by Bhupinder Singh's election as chancellor in February 1937; he fired Morgan and reappointed Wadhams as the sole legal advisor to the Chamber.[228]

Although pro-federationists appeared to have won the internal legal debate, with some advisors claiming that federation would soon be in place,[229] the mood within the broader princely camp soon shifted. Provincial elections were held in

[224] Letter from Christopher Brunyate to Mirza Ali Yar Khan, 12 March 1937, Federal Papers, Vol. II, NMML.

[225] Note by P. J. Patrick, undated, IOR/L/PS/13/664.

[226] Opinion of Tej Bahadur Sapru, 22 February 1937, Federal Papers, Vol. II, NMML. Sapru's views on federation were shared by several British lawyers, including Walter Monckton, Wilfrid Greene, William Jowitt, and Gavin Simonds. See 'Hydari Committee Members' Statement', *Indian Annual Register*, i (1937), 347.

[227] Report of the Constitutional Committee of the Chamber of Princes, [?] February 1937, Federal Papers, Vol. II, NMML. The report of joint session of the Constitutional Committee and the Federal Finance Committee reached the same conclusion. See Joint Report of the Constitutional and the Federal Finance Committees on the Opinion of J. H. Morgan, Federal Papers, Vol. II, NMML.

[228] Letter from the Secretary of State for India to the Viceroy, 8 March 1937, IOR/L/PS/13/610.

[229] K. N. Haksar, *Indian States and the Federation* (Bombay: D. B. Taraporelava Sons & Co., 1937), 6.

British India in 1937; against all expectations, the Congress party won almost half the seats, with absolute majorities in five out of eleven provinces.[230] During the election campaign, Congress leaders like Jawaharlal Nehru had demanded the establishment of a popular constituent assembly rather than a federation that would be hamstrung by the presence of 'backward' elements like the princely states.[231] A resolution passed at the annual Congress session in February 1938 called for 'full responsible government and the guarantee of civil liberty' in the states although the party remained organizationally aloof from the states' peoples' movements, offering only 'moral support and sympathy'.[232] Still, the resolution served to legitimate the participation of individual Congress members in popular protests in the states, unsettling the princes.[233] The apparent links between British Indian and state protesters cemented the anti-federationists' view that a close federal relationship would ultimately spell disaster for the states. Shaken by this experience, the princes' support for federation started to wane, not only among sceptics such as Akbar Hydari but even among earlier enthusiasts like Ganga Singh and Mirza Ismail.[234]

British officials mailed the 'final offer' on accession to federation amidst this febrile atmosphere in January 1939; the states were given six months to respond.[235] Given the focus on state consent in the federationist camp, the princes had been relying on their ability to insert specific limitations in the IoAs to protect their

[230] Sarkar, *Modern India*, (n 58) 349.

[231] Purushotham, 'Sovereignty, Federation, and Constituent Power in Interwar India', (n 26) 428.

[232] 'Resolution of the Indian National Congress, 21 February 1938', *Indian Annual Register*, i (1938), 299–300. For overviews of the development of Congress policy towards the states, see S. H. Patil, *The Congress Party and Princely States* (Bombay: Himalaya Publishing House, 1981); and Barbara Ramusack, 'Congress and the People's Movement in Princely India: Ambivalence in Strategy and Organization', in Richard Sisson and Stanley Wolpert, eds., *Congress and Indian Nationalism: The Pre-Independence Phase* (Berkeley, CA: University of California Press, 1988), 377–403. For discussions of Congress activities in specific states, see John R. Wood, 'Indian Nationalism in the Princely Context: the Rajkot Satyagraha of 1938–9', in Robin Jeffrey, ed., *People, Princes and Paramount Power: Society and Politics in the Indian Princely States* (Delhi: Oxford University Press, 1978), 240–274; James Manor, 'Gandhian Politics and the Challenge to Princely Authority in Mysore, 1936–47', in D. A. Low, ed., *Congress and the Raj: Facets of the Indian Struggle, 1917–47* (2nd edn, New Delhi: Oxford University Press, 2004), 405–434; and Robin Jeffrey, 'A Sanctified Label—"Congress" in Travancore Politics, 1938–48', in *Congress and the Raj: Facets of the Indian Struggle*, 435–472.

[233] Wood, 'Indian Nationalism in the Princely Context: the Rajkot Satyagraha of 1938–9', (n 232) 255. For a princely view of the protests, see Narendra Singh Sarila, *Once a Prince of Sarila: Of Palaces and Tiger Hunts, of Nehrus and Mountbattens* (London: I. B. Tauris, 2008), 137–142. Most British officials thought that Congress support of such political protests was aimed at forcing the states to concede that their federal representatives would be elected rather than appointed, enabling the Congress to command a majority in the federal legislature when it came into being. See Dharmjit Singh, *Lord Linlithgow in India, 1936–1943* (Jalandhar: ABD Publications, 2005), 115.

[234] Letter from the Crown Representative to the Secretary of State for India, 6 October 1938, IOR/L/PS/13/616; Letter from the *maharaja* of Bikaner to Lord Linlithgow, 17 June 1939, IOR/L/PS/13/621; and Letter from Lord Zetland to Lord Linlithgow, 5 July 1939, IOR/L/PS/13/621. British political officers shared the view that the hostile nature of the Congress provincial governments was dimming earlier princely enthusiasm for federation. See Kenneth Fitze, *Twilight of the Maharajas* (London: John Murray, 1956), 83.

[235] Note by P. J. Patrick, 3 March 1939, IOR/L/PS/13/618.

treaty rights. However, an explanatory note that accompanied the draft IoA in the offer clarified that the states would be unable to do so. Instead, states would have to rely on representation in the federal legislature to prevent the passage on any legislation inimical to their interests or the special responsibility powers of the governor-general that were discretionary in nature.[236] The states were, however, deeply sceptical of the ability of either of the provisions to provide sufficient protection for their autonomy. Even voting together as a bloc, the states would form only a minority of representatives in the federal legislature; British Indian representatives would, if they so wished, easily be able to outvote their state counterparts on any issue. The states had also experienced British unwillingness to offer protection during the political protests that had erupted after the provincial elections and doubted whether the position would be different in later years.[237] This discomfort was buttressed by a legal opinion from Tej Bahadur Sapru who confirmed that there was no legal reason for the British refusal to include specific clauses in the IoA to protect treaty rights. Sapru also expressed concern at the possibility of an elected government exerting pressure on the governor-general to avoid using his special responsibility powers to protect the states.[238]

The princes' reaction to the final offer was, therefore, uniformly critical. Although the Hydari-headed committee of ministers concluded that an all-India federation was the only viable mechanism for the states to maintain their separate sovereign status, it also considered the circulated drafts to be 'fundamentally unsatisfactory' for the protection of the states' sovereign rights and sought significant amendments before they could be accepted.[239] Another group of ministers, meeting under the chairmanship of C. S. Angre, the *diwan* of Gwalior, also found the offer to be disappointing.[240] At a princes' conference in June 1939, Ganga Singh, the erstwhile champion of federation, denounced the federal scheme of the GoI Act and beseeched his fellow princes to have 'the courage and the foresight to save the States from untold harm and terrible disaster'.[241] Although the conference did not 'close the door on an All-India Federation', the princes called the terms of the offer 'unacceptable'.[242] In this final analysis, federation had moved quite far from the princes' original proposal of a mechanism to impose legal limits on the exercise of British and British Indian authority in the states and to strengthen the ability of the

[236] Note on States' Rights, [undated], IOR/L/PS/13/618.

[237] On the British ambivalence to act during earlier protests, see R. J. Moore, 'British Policy and the Indian Problem, 1936–40', in *The Partition of India*, (n 12) 82–83; and Copland, *The Princes of India in the Endgame of Empire*, (n 15) 170–171.

[238] Opinion of Sir Tej Bahadur Sapru, In Re: the Baroda State, 10 May 1939, IOR/L/PS/13/644.

[239] Report of Proceedings of the Committee of States' Ministers, 12, 13, and 14 April, 1939, Bombay, IOR/L/PS/13/621.

[240] 'Speech by the *jam saheb* of Nawanagar, 10 June 1939', *Indian Annual Register*, i (1939), 430–431.

[241] Speech delivered by the *maharaja* of Bikaner at the Conference of Princes and Ministers held at Bombay, 10 June 1939, IOR/L/PS/13/621.

[242] Resolution passed at the General Conference of Princes and Representatives of States at Bombay, 12 June 1939, IOR/L/PS/13/621.

states to participate in decision-making on matters of common concern. Instead, the princes preferred to create a political structure that would cement additional protections for their treaty rights and maintain a direct, personal relationship with the Crown. Both these visions, however, relied on the flexible language of divisible sovereignty to entrench the semi-international position of the states.

Conclusion

The federal debates of the 1930s were an extension of the princely states' prolonged attempts to define sovereignty in manner that would protect their interests. Although the states had rarely presented a united front, their differences were much more visible during these long negotiations, with the princes and their advisors falling into rival pro- and anti-federation camps. While advisors such as K. N. Haksar and K. M. Panikkar remained firm federationists throughout the decade, many princes, such as Udaibhan Singh, were either staunch detractors of federation or, as the examples of Ganga Singh and Bhupinder Singh demonstrate, rather prone to changing their views on the feasibility of the federal project itself.

As before the Indian States Committee, the concept of sovereignty played a pivotal role during the federal negotiations. By this time, the princes had settled into the view that sovereignty was divisible, and more specifically that sovereign powers were divided among the states, the government of India, and the Crown. Given this broad agreement over the divisibility of sovereignty, a federal constitutional structure appeared to be the obvious choice for the states. But as was the case with contemporaneous attempts by international lawyers and political activists to establish world, imperial, and regional federations, the proposal for a federation of British India and the princely states encompassed multiple, often conflicting aims.

The princes and their advisors united around the broad aims of protecting the autonomy of the states—specifically the rights that were guaranteed to the states under their treaties with the British government—and redrawing the boundaries between the imperial and the international by redefining the states as 'semi-international' entities that had direct relations with the Crown. Beyond these shared goals, however, they splintered into pro- and anti-federation factions depending on what they considered to be the greatest threat to state sovereignty. The federationists aimed to limit British interference in the internal affairs of the states through clear, written constitutional provisions and the judicial settlement of disputes. They also sought to establish closer political and economic relations with British India and constitutional structures that would enable the states to participate fully in decision-making. All these mechanisms, they believed, would work towards expanding state autonomy to the greatest possible extent. The anti-federationists, on the other hand, had a diametrically opposed view of the political situation in South Asia. In their view, the real danger to the monarchical structures of the states came not from British interference but from radical anticolonial nationalists in British India who had allied with political protestors within the states. Therefore, they wished to create only a loose, confederal relationship between the states and British India that would be limited to cooperation on a narrow set of common issues. Instead of demanding the judicial settlement of disputes, they believed that the viceroy's discretionary powers would be the best means for the states to protect their rights and to maintain a close relationship with the Crown.

At the three key junctures in the federal debates—the birth of federation, the federation/confederation divide, and the negotiations over the IoAs—the flexibility of divisible sovereignty enabled both princely blocs to rely on the same language to pursue vastly different aims. At all three points, the princes recapitulated the same arguments over the ways in which divisible sovereignty in a federation could be used to bolster state autonomy as well as to strip the states of their monarchical rights. Despite the untiring efforts of the federationist advisors, the princes refused to accede to the federal structure that was established by the GoI Act, perhaps alarmed by the strength of nationalist performance in the provincial elections in British India and by the increasing demands for political reform within the states. Panikkar considered the rejection of the federal offer to be 'a personal defeat' and quit the Chamber's committee of ministers.[243]

The viceroy, Lord Linlithgow,[244] continued to work towards persuading the states to accede, noting that the princes' reaction had been much more divided than initial accounts of the Bombay conference made it appear.[245] A report by Madhav Rau, a member of the Mysore council, claimed that several rulers and ministers had viewed federation positively but 'this attitude found no open expression at the Conference' because of the partisanship displayed by the chancellor, Digvijaysinhji of Nawanagar.[246] Despite Linlithgow's efforts, the secretary of state for India, Lord Zetland,[247] stood firm, refusing to offer any substantial concessions to meet the princes' concerns.[248] After a hostile meeting with the princes in August

[243] Panikkar, *An Autobiography*, (n 75) 119–120.

[244] Linlithgow had earlier been appointed to the joint select committee on Indian constitutional reform. See Robin J. Moore, 'Hope, Victor Alexander John, second marquess of Linlithgow (1887–1952)', in *Oxford Dictionary of National Biography*, https://doi.org/10.1093/ref:odnb/33974, accessed 18 May 2021.

[245] Letter from Lord Linlithgow to Lord Zetland, 7 July 1939, IOR/L/PS/13/621; Letter from the Crown Representative to the Secretary of State for India, 12 August 1939, IOR/L/PS/13/621; Letter from the Secretary of State for India to the Crown Representative, 18 August 1939, IOR/L/PS/13/621; and Letter from the Secretary of State for India to the Crown Representative, 22 August 1939, IOR/L/PS/13/621.

[246] Note by N. Madhava Rau, undated, enclosed in Letter from Mirza Ismail to P. J. Patrick, 17 June 1939, IOR/L/PS/13/621.

[247] Zetland was known to be cool to federation, a trait that has been attributed to an old-fashioned view to India cultivated while he was an aide-de-camp to Lord Curzon when he was viceroy. See Philip Woods, 'Dundas, Lawrence John Lumley, second marquess of Zetland (1876–1961)', in *Oxford Dictionary of National Biography*, https://doi.org/10.1093/ref:odnb/32932, accessed 18 May 2021.

[248] Letter from Lord Zetland to Lord Linlithgow, 17 July 1939, IOR/L/PS/13/621; Letter from Lord Zetland to Lord Linlithgow, 17 August 1939, IOR/L/PS/13/621; Letter from the Secretary of State for

1939, Linlithgow concluded that offering further concessions would not be of any advantage in persuading them to accede, and so told the princes that the federal offer was 'final and as exhaustive'.[249] The princes' reactions soon became irrelevant. By the time Linlithgow's letter informing Zetland of these developments reached London, Germany had invaded Poland, and Britain had declared war.[250] In his handwritten comments on Linlithgow's letter, Zetland remarked, 'the Federal offer is now in cold storage'.[251] Federation was never revived, and as the next chapter shows, the states disappeared from the landscape of South Asia a decade later.

India to the Crown Representative, 17 August 1939, IOR/L/PS/13/621; and Letter from the Secretary of State for India to the Viceroy, 18 August 1939, IOR/L/PS/13/621.

[249] Letter from Lord Linlithgow to Lord Zetland, 24 August 1939, IOR/L/PS/13/621.
[250] Copland, *The Princes of India in the Endgame of Empire*, (n 15) 181.
[251] Note by Lord Zetland, undated, on Letter from Lord Linlithgow to Lord Zetland, 24 August 1939, IOR/L/PS/13/621.

Chapter Six
Building the Nation
The Princely States in the Age of Decolonization

Independence and the Princely States

On 9 August 1947, Hanwant Singh, the newly installed *maharaja* of Jodhpur, met the viceroy, Lord Mountbatten,[1] and the secretary of the States' Department, V. P. Menon,[2] at the lavish Imperial hotel in New Delhi. Jodhpur was a border state; it was geographically contiguous with what would become the dominions of India and Pakistan on 15 August. In theory, the states could choose to accede to either of the two dominions, but Jodhpur's overwhelmingly Hindu population appeared hostile to throwing their lot in with Muslim-majority Pakistan, or so Menon suggests in his authoritative account of the 'integration' of the states into India.[3] There is evidence, however, of popular demonstrations in support of Pakistan in the state at the time, not unusual for a place that had close economic ties with Sind and western Punjab, which would form part of Pakistan.[4]

Although Jodhpur had sent representatives to the Indian constituent assembly during the reign of Hanwant Singh's father, he found himself wavering on the issue of accession. He met with Muhammad Ali Jinnah, leader of the Muslim League, who allegedly signed a blank sheet of paper and handed him a fountain pen to fill out the conditions under which the state would accede to Pakistan. The *maharaja*'s secretary, Kesari Singh, persuaded him to consult his family before deciding and leaked news of the meeting to the *diwan*, C. S. Venkatachar, who sent word of the possible pact to Mountbatten, resulting in the summons to Delhi.[5]

[1] Mountbatten was supreme commander of the allied forces in south-east Asia during the Second World War, after which he was appointed viceroy of India. See Philip Ziegler, 'Mountbatten, Louis Francis Albert Victor Nicholas, first Earl Mountbatten of Burma (1900–1979)', in David Cannadine, ed., *Oxford Dictionary of National Biography*, online edn (Oxford: Oxford University Press, 2004), https://doi.org/10.1093/ref:odnb/31480, accessed 27 August 2021.

[2] Menon rose through the civil service ranks to become reforms commissioner and constitutional advisor to the viceroy of India before being appointed secretary to the States' Department in 1947. See Narayani Basu, *V. P. Menon: The Unsung Architect of Modern India* (London: Simon & Schuster, 2020).

[3] V. P. Menon, *The Story of the Integration of the Indian States* (New York: Macmillan, 1956), 117; and 'Viceroy's Personal Report no. 17, 16 August 1947', in Nicholas Mansergh, ed., *The Transfer of Power 1942–7*, xii (London: Her Majesty's Stationery Office, 1970–83), 767.

[4] Ian Copland, 'The Princely States, the Muslim League, and the Partition of India in 1947', *The International History Review*, 13/1 (1991), 43.

[5] Menon, *The Integration of the Indian States*, (n 3) 116; and K. M. Panikkar, *An Autobiography*, trans. K. Krishnamurthy (Madras: Oxford University Press, 1977), 164.

Sovereignty, International Law, and the Princely States of Colonial South Asia. Priyasha Saksena, Oxford University Press.
 DOI: 10.1093/oso/9780192866585.003.0006

Menon later claimed that Hanwant Singh used Jinnah's offer to demand 'impossible concessions' from the Indian side although he was told 'not to be swayed by false promises'.[6] He also realized that Jodhpur's accession to Pakistan could trigger a tide of Rajputana border states joining the other dominion. With the concurrence of the states' minister, Vallabhbhai Patel, Menon offered Hanwant Singh a slew of privileges, including arms imports, famine relief, and a new railway line, in exchange for accession to India. Mountbatten, for his part, warned the *maharaja* of communal trouble in his state if he disregarded the apparent wishes of a majority of his people.[7] Hanwant Singh succumbed to this mixture of bribery and coercion and signed the instrument of accession but not before making a one final stand: he held a revolver to Menon's head and told him that 'he would shoot him down like a dog if he betrayed the starving people of Jodhpur'.[8] In Menon's telling, the *maharaja* was simply told that his 'juvenile theatricals' would not abrogate the state's accession to India.[9]

Jodhpur was not alone in its capitulation; over five hundred states ultimately acceded to India,[10] while nine acceded to Pakistan.[11] This spectacular—and apparently sudden—change in the princes' fortunes raises several questions. How had the states, which had refused to sign similar instruments of accession just a few years prior during the federal debates, come to this point? Why, after years of arguing about their sovereign status, did they agree to accede to the Indian dominion? Under what conditions were these accessions made possible and what was the role played by legal arguments in the negotiations over accession? How was the patchwork of sovereignties that constituted colonial South Asia ultimately transformed into the two nation-states of India and Pakistan in 1947?

Despite the centrality of the state in international law, scholars have long challenged the idea that it is the 'natural' or 'fundamental' building block of the modern world order.[12] Recent historical scholarship has also questioned narratives of the inexorable move from empire to nation-state in the mid-twentieth century by tracing how political actors instead envisaged 'an open-ended constellation of contending political futures'[13] in their struggles to transform

[6] Menon, *The Integration of the Indian States*, (n 3) 117.

[7] Menon, *The Integration of the Indian States*, (n 3) 117; and 'Viceroy's Personal Report no. 17, 16 August 1947', in *The Transfer of Power*, (n 3) xii, 767.

[8] 'Viceroy's Personal Report no. 17, 16 August 1947', in *The Transfer of Power*, (n 3) xii, 767.

[9] Menon, *The Integration of the Indian States*, (n 3) 117.

[10] *White Paper on Indian States* (1950), 1.

[11] For an account of the accession of these states to Pakistan, see Yaqoob Khan Bangash, *A Princely Affair: The Accession and Integration of the Princely States of Pakistan, 1947–1955* (Karachi: Oxford University Press, 2015).

[12] John Ruggie, 'Territoriality and Beyond: Problematizing Modernity in International Relations', *International Organization*, 47/1 (1993), 139–174; and John Agnew, 'The Territorial Trap: The Geographical Assumptions of International Relations Theory', *Review of International Political Economy*, 1/1 (1994), 53–80.

[13] Manu Goswami, 'Imaginary Futures and Colonial Internationalisms', *American Historical Review*, 117/5 (2012), 1462.

empire.[14] Such political ferment also engulfed the British empire, with activists working towards creating independent nation-states, articulating anti-imperial internationalisms,[15] espousing federations as a political form to balance competing interests, and advocating the Commonwealth of Nations as a mechanism for refashioning the empire.[16] Numerous motivations undergirded these political proposals: the maintenance of British influence in parts of the empire, the empowerment of local elites, the protection of interests of white settlers, the continuation of existing modes of indigenous governance, and the preservation of the autonomy of newly decolonized states.[17]

In most cases, these alternative structures did not last. Federations split up into nation-states[18] and resistance from several newly-independent states transformed the Commonwealth into a looser, more informal organization.[19] As Antony Anghie notes, the mid-twentieth century saw a specific vision of sovereignty and the nation-state win out.[20] Historians have considered the role of socio-economic practices, ideas of economic development, cultural identities, and technological advancements in the imagination and construction of nations.[21] Law also plays a critical role in state-making;[22] in the provocative framing of Luis Eslava and

[14] On empires as a persistent political form, see Jane Burbank and Frederick Cooper, *Empires in World History: Power and the Politics of Difference* (Princeton, NJ: Princeton University Press, 2011).

[15] Goswami, 'Imaginary Futures and Colonial Internationalisms', (n 13).

[16] Wm. Roger Louis and Ronald Robinson, 'The Imperialism of Decolonization', *The Journal of Imperial and Commonwealth History*, 22/3 (1994), 462–511; John Darwin, *The Empire Project: The Rise and Fall of the British World-System, 1830–1970* (Cambridge: Cambridge University Press, 2011), 514–565; and Daniel Haines, 'A "Commonwealth Moment" in South Asian Decolonization', in Leslie James and Elisabeth Leake, eds., *Decolonization and the Cold War: Negotiating Independence* (London: Bloomsbury, 2015), 185–202.

[17] For instance, Ghana's Kwame Nkrumah sought to use the idea of a pan-African federation 'to secure rather than transcend national independence'. See Adom Getachew, 'Securing Postcolonial Independence: Kwame Nkrumah and the Federal Idea in the Age of Decolonization', *Ab Imperio*, 3 (2018), 93.

[18] For an overview of the rise and fall of regional federations in Africa and the Caribbean, see Michael Collins, 'Decolonisation and the "Federal Moment"', *Diplomacy and Statecraft*, 24/1 (2013), 21–40; and Adom Getachew, *Worldmaking After Empire: The Rise and Fall of Self-Determination* (Princeton, NJ: Princeton University Press, 2019), 107–141.

[19] For an overview of the transformation of the Commonwealth because of the challenges posed by Indian and Pakistani independence, see R. J. Moore, *Making the New Commonwealth* (Oxford: Clarendon Press, 1987).

[20] Antony Anghie, 'Bandung and the Origins of Third World Sovereignty', in Luis Eslava, Michael Fakhri, and Vasuki Nesiah, eds., *Bandung, Global History, and International Law: Critical Pasts and Pending Futures* (Cambridge: Cambridge University Press, 2017), 542.

[21] See Benedict Anderson, *Imagined Communities: Reflections on the Origins and Spread of Nationalism* (London: Verso Books, 1983); Eric Hobsbawm, *Nations and Nationalism since 1790* (Cambridge: Cambridge University Press, 1990); Partha Chatterjee, *The Nation and its Fragments: Colonial and Postcolonial Histories* (Princeton, NJ: Princeton University Press, 1993); and Manu Goswami, *Producing India: From Colonial Economy to National Space* (Chicago, IL: University of Chicago Press, 2004).

[22] On the role of law in creating a national identity in Biafra, see Samuel Fury Childs Daly, 'A Nation on Paper: Making a State in the Republic of Biafra', *Comparative Studies in Society and History*, 62/4 (2020), 868–894.

Sundhya Pahuja, 'making and remaking the state is a project of international law'.[23] Scholarly literature has focused on the drafting of independence constitutions,[24] the emphasis placed by international organizations on territory for state sovereignty,[25] and the significance of the international law requirement of recognition for making the nation-state the desired endgame of decolonization.[26]

In the South Asian context, there are additional factors that need to be considered to understand the acceptance of the nation-state as the default form of postcolonial political organization since independent India had a slightly easier time being recognized than most former colonies. Unlike other non-self-governing colonial territories, India—which referred to British India together with the princely states[27]—had been a member of several international organizations prior to independence. Scholars such as Lanka Sundaram had long claimed that India's membership of the League of Nations signified that international law did not recognize any cleavage between British India and the princely states, resulting in 'the juridical unity of India' being 'definitely established and tacitly recognised'.[28] Therefore, anticolonial nationalists such as Jawaharlal Nehru were relatively confident that the new state would, despite contestations over the exact scope of its territory, succeed to the international legal personality of the colonial entity of India, including its membership of the United Nations (UN). Muhammad Ali Jinnah, on the other hand, maintained that the colonial entity of India would cease to exist on 15 August 1947, after which the two succeeding dominions would have equal international status and be eligible to continue with existing rights and obligations. When the question was referred to the UN, Ivan Kerno, the Assistant Secretary-General for Legal Affairs, opined that the partition of British India constituted the secession of part of an existing state to create a new state (Pakistan); the part that remained (India), therefore, would continue with existing treaty rights and obligations.[29] As

[23] Luis Eslava and Sundhya Pahuja, 'The State and International Law: A Reading from the Global South', *Humanity: An International Journal of Human Rights, Humanitarianism, and Development*, 11/1 (2020), 118.

[24] Harshan Kumarasingham, ed., *Constitution-Making in Asia: Decolonisation and State-Building in the Aftermath of the British Empire* (London: Routledge, 2016).

[25] Stuart Elden, 'Contingent Sovereignty, Territorial Integrity and the Sanctity of Borders', *SAIS Review of International Affairs*, 26/1 (2006), 11–24.

[26] Prasenjit Duara, 'The Cold War and the Imperialism of Nation-States', in Richard H. Immerman and Petra Goedde, eds., *The Oxford Handbook of the Cold War* (Oxford: Oxford University Press, 2013), 86–101; and Itty Abraham, *How India Became Territorial: Foreign Policy, Diaspora, Geopolitics* (Stanford, CA: Stanford University Press, 2014).

[27] United Kingdom, Interpretation Act 1889, s 18(5).

[28] Lanka Sundaram, 'The International Status of India', *Journal of the Royal Institute of International Affairs*, 9/4 (1930), 452.

[29] V. P. Menon, *The Transfer of Power in India* (Princeton, NJ: Princeton University Press, 1957), 404–407; and Rosalyn Higgins, *The Development of International Law Through the Political Organs of the United Nations* (London: Oxford University Press, 1963), 321–322. A copy of Kerno's legal opinion can be found in a later International Law Commission memorandum on the succession of states in international law. See International Law Commission, The Succession of States in relation to Membership in the United Nations, A/CN.4/149, 3 December 1962, http://legal.un.org/ilc/documentation/english/a_cn4_149.pdf, accessed 15 February 2022.

a result, India retained UN membership, while Pakistan had to apply for membership; it was ultimately admitted on 30 September 1947.[30]

Instead of recognition, Indian officials were concerned with what they saw as the messy political map of South Asia. The territory of what would become the dominion of India was interspersed with princely state territory that would be foreign to the new nation, posing a problem for its political 'unity and economic viability'; this difficulty was also more acute for India than it was for Pakistan.[31] As I argue in this chapter, for many of independent India's new leaders, centralized control and a consolidation of the nation-state's territories were obvious necessities for the planned economy and the nationalist development model that they considered to be the basis for building the new nation. This unified national space for development was created through the articulation of the specific legal idea of territorial sovereignty by elite Indian politicians and bureaucrats. The princes, on the other hand, continued to push for political frameworks akin to those they had favoured since the early twentieth century: loose federal or confederal frameworks structured by layered conceptions of sovereignty that would enable them to maintain their political autonomy while retaining the beneficial aspects of their relationships with the new dominions and the Crown. By paying attention to the South Asian context, it is possible to trace the way a particular conception of sovereignty—that of exclusive, absolute territoriality, focused on the creation of centralized economic units—became dominant in the years of decolonization, while drowning out visions of alternative political orders based on the idea of divisible sovereignty.

In this chapter, I explore the significance of the language of sovereignty during the political crucial period of the 1940s. I start by examining the major international law debates that emerged from the shadows of the Second World War. While international law scholarship was focused on the prosecution of international crimes and the establishment of international organizations, debates in 1940s South Asia were firmly focused on sovereignty and the role of law in the creation of new states. I review the different visions for postcolonial South Asia that numerous actors—anticolonial political parties in British India, princes, and their bureaucrats—advocated for in the decades leading up to independence. I also analyse the legal basis of these political configurations; while those who favoured centralized states relied on the language of territorial sovereignty, others who preferred a more open political map depended on the vocabulary of divisible sovereignty. I then focus on the influence of 'developmentalism' on the structure of the new postcolonial political order to trace how alternative political possibilities were

[30] United Nations, Security Council, Resolution 29, Admission of New Members to the UN, S/RES/29, 12 August 1947, https://undocs.org/S/RES/29(1947), accessed 15 February 2022; and United Nations, General Assembly, Resolution 108(II), Admission of Yemen and Pakistan to membership in the United Nations, A/RES/108(II), 30 September 1947, https://documents-dds-ny.un.org/doc/RESOLUTION/GEN/NR0/038/15/pdf/NR003815.pdf?OpenElement, accessed 15 February 2022.

[31] Copland, 'The Princely States, the Muslim League, and the Partition of India in 1947', (n 4) 56.

abandoned in favour of a centralized state and the 'integration' of the states into postcolonial India. This process was exemplified by the legal dispute over the state of Hyderabad, which forms the final part of the chapter, and underscores how a unified Indian state space was constructed through the articulation of a specific vision of territorial sovereignty.

International Law in the 1940s

The Second World War cast a long shadow over international law. The failure of the League of Nations in preventing the use of armed force caused international lawyers to, once again, re-examine their conceptions of the nature and purpose of international law. Some, such as Hersch Lauterpacht, turned their focus to the individual in international law. Lauterpacht's text on human rights was published in 1950[32] and carried forward his concern for the protection of the individual in his writings during the war.[33] He also dismissed arguments that individuals could not be held responsible for war crimes under international law since it only regulated states.[34] With this emphasis on individual rights and criminal responsibility, it is clear that Lauterpacht's postwar scholarship was shaped by the horrors of the Holocaust, even if the Nuremberg trials themselves were largely about the prosecution of Nazi aggression and conduct during war.[35]

Other international lawyers preferred a more pragmatic approach. Wolfgang Friedmann,[36] for instance, argued that much of prevailing international law had ceased to exist in the face of war and advocated that international lawyers focus on analysing trends that would shape the law of the future.[37] Others, such as Arnold McNair,[38] did not lose faith in international law but admitted that mainstreaming it

[32] Hersch Lauterpacht, *International Law and Human Rights* (London: Stevens & Sons, Ltd., 1950).

[33] Hersch Lauterpacht, 'The Law of Nations, the Law of Nature and the Rights of Man', *Transactions of the Grotius Society*, 29 (1943), 1–33.

[34] Hersch Lauterpacht, 'The Law of Nations and the Punishment of War Crimes', *British Year Book of International Law*, 21 (1944), 58.

[35] Samuel Moyn, 'From Aggression to Atrocity: Rethinking the History of International Criminal Law', in Kevin Jon Heller et al., eds., *The Oxford Handbook of International Criminal Law* (Oxford: Oxford University Press, 2020), 341–360.

[36] Friedmann was dismissed from judicial service on account of his Jewish faith when the Nazis came to power. He spent several years in Britain, Australia, and Canada, before finally moving to the United States. See John N. Hazard, Louis Henkin, and Oliver J. Lissitzyn, 'In Memoriam: Wolfgang Gaston Friedmann, 1907–1972', *American Journal of International Law*, 67/1 (1973), 102–103; and John Bell, 'Wolfgang Friedmann (1907–1972), with an Excursus on Gustav Radbruch (1878–1949)', in Jack Beatson and Reinhard Zimmermann, eds., *Jurists Uprooted: German-Speaking Émigré Lawyers in Twentieth Century Britain* (Oxford: Oxford University Press, 2004), 517–534.

[37] Wolfgang Friedmann, 'International Law and the Present War', *Transactions of the Grotius Society*, 26 (1940), 211–233.

[38] McNair was elected to the International Court of Justice in 1946 and served as its president between 1952 and 1955. See R. Y. Jennings, 'McNair, Arnold Duncan, first Baron McNair (1885–1975)', in *Oxford Dictionary of National Biography*, https://doi.org/10.1093/ref:odnb/31397, accessed 17 August 2021.

would not have prevented the war.[39] This realistic attitude towards the possibilities of international law fit with McNair's emphasis on legal practice.[40] He shared this approach to international law with Georg Schwarzenberger,[41] whose text, *Power Politics*,[42] was published in 1941, along with an article using the lens of the law of neutrality to make the case for a 'functional approach' to international law.[43]

With the privileging of eclectic and situational readings of the law,[44] restructured and newly established international institutions played a central role in the postwar period. The replacement of the League of Nations with the new United Nations system provided the background for the emergence of international institutional law as a sub-discipline of international law. One of the principal protagonists in this drama was the British international lawyer, C. Wilfred Jenks,[45] who used his experience at the International Labour Organization (ILO) to become a central figure in the development of the law relating to international organizations.[46] For Jenks, the war made the task of rethinking the structure of international organizations more urgent,[47] with the ILO serving as a template.[48] International organizations were key to the development of a redesigned international order after the Second World War, raising familiar questions about the potential friction between state sovereignty and international cooperation.[49]

[39] Arnold McNair, 'The Need for the Wider Teaching of International Law', *Transactions of the Grotius Society*, 29 (1943), 85–98.

[40] See Arnold McNair, 'Aspects of State Sovereignty', *British Year Book of International Law*, 26 (1949), 6–47; and Arnold McNair, 'International Law in Practice', *Transactions of the Grotius Society*, 32 (1946), 154–165.

[41] Schwarzenberger emigrated to Britain after the Nazis came to power and taught at University College London. See L. C. Green, 'Georg Schwarzenberger (1908–1991)', *American Journal of International Law*, 86/2 (1992), 341–342; and Stephanie Steinle, 'Georg Schwarzenberger (1908–1991)', in *Jurists Uprooted*, (n 36) 663–680.

[42] Georg Schwarzenberger, *Power Politics* (London: Jonathan Cape, 1941).

[43] Georg Schwarzenberger, 'The "Aid Britain" Bill and the Law of Neutrality: Some Reflections on the Scope of the Functional Approach to International Law', *Transactions of the Grotius Society*, 27 (1941), 1–29.

[44] For a discussion of pragmatic visions of international law in the American context, see Afroditi Giovanopoulou, 'Pragmatic Legalism: Revisiting America's Order After World War II', *Harvard International Law Journal*, 62/2 (2021), 325–374.

[45] Jenks spent his entire working like in the secretariat of the International Labour Organization, ultimately rising to the post of director-general. See Elihu Lauterpacht, 'Jenks, Clarence Wilfred (1909–1973)', in *Oxford Dictionary of National Biography*, https://doi.org/10.1093/ref:odnb/37599, accessed 17 August 2021.

[46] Guy Fiti Sinclair, 'C. Wilfred Jenks and the Futures of International Organizations Law', *European Journal of International Law*, 31/2 (2020), 525–542. In a piece written towards the end of the war, Jenks argued that 'international lawyers must now be prepared to recognize as one of the major divisions of their subject the comparative law of the constitutions of international organizations'. See C. Wilfred Jenks, 'Some Constitutional Problems of International Organizations', *British Year Book of International Law*, 22 (1945), 11.

[47] C. Wilfred Jenks, 'The Significance Today of Lorimer's "Ultimate Problem of International Jurisprudence"', *Transactions of the Grotius Society*, 26 (1940), 35–65.

[48] C. Wilfred Jenks, 'The International Labour Organisation as a Subject of Study for International Lawyers', *Journal of Comparative Legislation and International Law*, 22/1 (1940), 36–56.

[49] P. E. Corbett, 'World Order—An Agenda for Lawyers', *American Journal of International Law*, 37/2 (1943), 207–221.

New international institutions such as the United Nations also played a role in the management of decolonization but ended up replicating the structures of nineteenth-century colonial international law[50] since their roots lay in debates on the management of British imperial internationalism.[51] International law's critical role in the process of decolonization, however, remained on the fringes of the legal scholarship of the period. Discussions around colonies were often confined to the nature of trusteeship under the proposed UN system.[52] The creation of new states in Asia attracted little comment in international law journals of the time, except in connection with state succession to treaties.[53] International law scholarship, therefore, focused on the consequences of decolonization for international law rather than the role played by international law in the processes of decolonization and state creation. However, iterations of the legal concept of sovereignty were central to these undertakings in 1940s South Asia.

The Many Visions of Postcolonial South Asia

The final years of the British in South Asia were marked by war, famine, military mutiny, and explosive violence. Unlike the First World War, which had attracted broad-based support from Indian anticolonial nationalists, the Second World War split nationalist opinion. Members of the Congress resigned their posts in provincial governments after the viceroy, Lord Linlithgow, made a declaration of war against Germany without consulting Indian representatives and refused to consider forming a responsible government. The Muslim League and the communists (after the Nazis invaded the Soviet Union), on the other hand, supported the war effort.[54] The princes also contributed men, money, and material, and benefitted from the British decision to impose wartime emergency measures, which clamped down on domestic political agitations in the states.[55] The draconian regulations also weakened the anticolonial movement, particularly after much of the Congress leadership was jailed in August 1942.[56] The government of India's wartime policies

[50] Antony Anghie, *Imperialism, Sovereignty and the Making of International Law* (Cambridge: Cambridge University Press, 2005), 196, 199.

[51] Mark Mazower, *No Enchanted Palace: The End of Empire and the Ideological Origins of the United Nations* (Princeton, NJ: Princeton University Press, 2009), 1–27.

[52] Norman Bentwich, 'Colonial Mandates and Trusteeships', *Transactions of the Grotius Society*, 32 (1946), 121–134; and Clive Parry, 'The Legal Nature of the Trusteeship Agreements', *British Year Book of International Law*, 27 (1950), 164–185.

[53] J. Mervyn Jones, 'State Succession in the Matter of Treaties', *British Year Book of International Law*, 24 (1947), 360–375.

[54] Sumit Sarkar, *Modern India, 1885–1947* (Delhi: Macmillan India, 1983), 375–385.

[55] Barbara Ramusack, *The Princes of India in the Twilight of Empire: Dissolution of a Patron-Client System, 1914-1939* (Columbus, OH: Ohio State University Press, 1978), 232; and Ian Copland, *The Princes of India in the Endgame of Empire, 1917–1947* (Cambridge: Cambridge University Press, 1997), 183–187.

[56] Sarkar, *Modern India*, (n 54) 388–396.

fuelled inflation, leaving millions dead in a devastating famine caused by soaring food prices.[57] A series of protest movements sprang up by the end of the war. Indian naval ratings mutinied in Bombay in early 1946; student activism increased; there were incessant labour strikes; and both British India and the princely states combated peasant rebellions.[58]

Although the newly-elected Labour government in Britain did not have a general plan to retreat from empire, anticolonial struggle and the increasing economic costs of imperial administration led to the decision to kickstart negotiations over Indian independence, which were complicated by the political deadlock over the call for a separate homeland for South Asian Muslims.[59] Historians have differed over the specific nature of this demand, but there is broad agreement about the lack of territorial attachment in visions of what would ultimately become the state of Pakistan.[60] So while the Muslim League's Muhammad Ali Jinnah argued that Hindus and Muslims in South Asia constituted two separate 'nations', he remained 'extraordinarily vague in his calls for Pakistan as a clearly demarcated territorial state'.[61] A significant amount of historical scholarship has noted that it was likely that he was arguing for treating the Hindus and the Muslims at par as two equal nations to obtain safeguards for the Muslim minority within a united, confederal India, rather than seeking 'a separate, sovereign territorial state'.[62]

Given this lack of congruity between 'nation' and 'territory', activists put forth innumerable schemes for what a Muslim homeland in South Asia ought to look like, including the reorganization of Muslim-majority areas into an autonomous unit within a broader Indian federation and a new confederation of Muslim-majority provinces.[63] The Muslim League's 1940 resolution only demanded that 'geographically contiguous units are demarcated into regions which should be so constituted, with such territorial readjustments as may be necessary, that the areas

[57] Sugata Bose and Ayesha Jalal, *Modern South Asia: History, Culture, Political Economy* (4th edn, London: Routledge, 2018), 141.

[58] Yasmin Khan, *The Great Partition: The Making of India and Pakistan* (New Haven, CT: Yale University Press, 2007), 26–29; and Sarkar, *Modern India*, (n 54) 418–425.

[59] Barbara D. Metcalf and Thomas R. Metcalf, *A Concise History of Modern India* (2nd edn, Cambridge: Cambridge University Press, 2006), 209–212; and Ian Talbot, *A History of Modern South Asia: Politics, States, Diasporas* (New Haven, CT: Yale University Press, 2016), 131–137.

[60] For contrasting approaches on the formation of Pakistan, see Ayesha Jalal, *The Sole Spokesman: Jinnah, The Muslim League and the Demand for Pakistan* (Cambridge: Cambridge University Press, 1985); David Gilmartin, *Empire and Islam: Punjab and the Making of Pakistan* (Berkeley, CA: University of California Press, 1988); and Faisal Devji, *Muslim Zion: Pakistan as a Political Idea* (Cambridge, MA: Harvard University Press, 2013).

[61] David Gilmartin, 'Partition, Pakistan, and South Asian History: In Search of a Narrative', *Journal of Asian History*, 57/4 (1998), 1081.

[62] Ishita Banerjee-Dube, *A History of Modern India* (New Delhi: Cambridge University Press, 2015), 411; Sunil Khilnani, *The Idea of India* (New Delhi: Penguin, 1997), 162–163; and Jalal, *The Sole Spokesman* (n 60).

[63] R. J. Moore, *Escape from Empire: The Attlee Government and the Indian Problem* (Oxford: Clarendon Press, 1983), 51–52; Sarkar, *Modern India*, (n 54) 377–378; and Bose and Jalal, *Modern South Asia*, (n 57) 154–155.

in which the Muslims are numerically in a majority as in the north-western and eastern zones of India, should be grouped to constitute 'Independent States' in which the constituent units shall be autonomous and sovereign'.[64] As Ayesha Jalal notes, the resolution did not mention either 'partition' or 'Pakistan' and the League made little attempt to make this vague statement more complete or coherent.[65] Other Muslims opposed partition altogether; in Punjab, the Unionist party preferred to defend regional rather than religious interests.[66]

British Indian politics also faced a reckoning with questions over the position of other communities. The Akali Dal, claiming to represent the Sikhs in Punjab, demanded the 'redistribution' of the province into two divisions within a broader Indian federation—the Muslim-majority western one and the more communally plural eastern part that they named 'Azad Punjab'.[67] The religious categories that took centre-stage in these political negotiations were themselves contested. B. R. Ambedkar, for instance, sought to separate Dalits from caste Hindus in a bid to obtain Dalit political autonomy.[68] The princely states posed additional hurdles in the negotiations over the transfer of power since many princes continued to regard Indian independence as an existential threat to the states and sought mechanisms to conserve their autonomy. They aspired to create political structures that would help them to balance relationships with the Crown and independent India (and Pakistan) with state autonomy.

With these numerous claims to political power forming the backdrop of the negotiations, the various plans of devolution drafted during the 1940s advanced frameworks with multiple layers of authority. Permitting a wide variety of political entities at different levels of government to exercise sovereign power appeared to be the key to establishing political structures that would satisfy all the parties in the mix. Sovereignty, once again, became key to negotiations over the political future of South Asia; it was the concept that enabled the princes—as well as other political groups—to envisage appropriate constitutional structures most suitable for their aspirations. The princely reaction to two proposals in particular—the Cripps offer

[64] 'Resolution of the All-India Muslim League, 23 March 1940', in Syed Sharifuddin Pirzada, ed., *Foundations of Pakistan: All-India Muslim League Documents, 1906–1947*, ii (Karachi: National Publishing House, 1970), 341.

[65] Jalal, *The Sole Spokesman*, (n 60) 58–59.

[66] Metcalf and Metcalf, *A Concise History of Modern India*, (n 59) 208.

[67] Amar Sohal, 'Ideas of Parity: Muslims, Sikhs and the 1946 Cabinet Mission Plan', *South Asia: Journal of South Asian Studies*, 40/4 (2017), 716.

[68] Sekhar Bandopadhyay, 'Transfer of Power and the Crisis of Dalit Politics in India, 1945–47', *Modern Asian Studies*, 34/4 (2000), 893–942. These efforts were hampered by Dalit political fragmentation and the Congress's use of electoral rules to marginalize the Scheduled Castes Federation from political power. See Dwaipayan Sen, '"No matter how, Jogendranath had to be defeated": The Scheduled Castes Federation and the Making of Partition in Bengal, 1945–1947', *The Indian Economic and Social History Review*, 49/3 (2012), 321–364. For an overview of Ambedkar's shifting views on partition, see Jesús Francisco Cháirez-Garza, '"Bound hand and foot and handed over to the caste Hindus": Ambedkar, Untouchability and the Politics of Partition', *The Indian Economic and Social History Review*, 55/1 (2018), 1–28.

and the Cabinet mission plan—provides a sense of what they considered to be their political future.

In 1942, Stafford Cripps[69] drafted a proposal that provided for dominion status for India after the war and the election of a constitution making body, which the provinces and states had the option to not join.[70] Instead of the single territorial unit of independent India, the Cripps proposal envisioned several different political successors to the British colonial state in South Asia, including the princely states and some provinces, all of which would continue to exist as relatively autonomous entities. Congress leaders were sceptical of the provision that effectively enabled provinces to secede from the union. Initial discussions were still positive since Cripps implied that Indian politicians would be allowed to participate in wartime decision-making. But talks failed when Cripps backtracked from his position because of pressure from Conservatives in Britain.[71]

Despite the debacle with British Indian politicians, the princes favoured the plan as it provided the possibility for the states to remain relatively aloof of any new constitutional structure, thereby preserving their autonomy. The princes were particularly upbeat about assurances that the states would continue to enjoy British support after Indian independence. At a meeting with a delegation from the Chamber of Princes in March 1942, Cripps told the princes:

> [s]o far as the paramountcy treaties were concerned, these would remain unaltered unless any State desired to get rid of the paramountcy in order to be able to accommodate itself the better to the new conditions.... in our treaty with the Union [of India] we should have to make any necessary arrangements for the passage of troops, etc. which might be required for the carrying out of our treaties with the States. So far as the undertaking of our obligations of defence of the States was concerned ... there was no insuperable difficulty from the naval point of view so long as we held Ceylon, or from the Air point of view so long as we had the aerodromes which were necessary in one or other of the States ... [S]umming it all up, we should stand by our treaties with the States unless they asked us to revoke them.[72]

[69] Cripps was expelled from the Labour party in 1939 but was appointed leader of the House of Commons by Winston Churchill. He returned to Labour after the war and was appointed chancellor of the exchequer. See Peter Clarke and Richard Toye, 'Cripps, Sir (Richard) Stafford (1889–1952)', in *Oxford Dictionary of National Biography*, https://doi.org/10.1093/ref:odnb/32630, accessed 24 August 2021.

[70] Metcalf and Metcalf, *A Concise History of Modern India*, (n 59) 205; Banerjee-Dube, *A History of Modern India*, (n 62) 392; and Bose and Jalal, *Modern South Asia*, (n 57) 159.

[71] Moore, *Escape from Empire*, 11–12 (n 63); and Sarkar, *Modern India*, (n 54) 386–388.

[72] 'Note by Cripps on interview with the delegation of the Chamber of Princes, 28 March 1942', in *The Transfer of Power*, (n 3) i, 510–511. Cripps repeated these views in a press conference a few days later. See 'Proceedings of a press conference held by Cripps on 29 March 1942', in *The Transfer of Power*, (n 3) i, 541–544. Cripps had earlier assured the rulers of Nawanagar and Bikaner, in a separate interview, that the British policy was that 'the Treaties with the Crown would remain unaffected'. See 'Note

Indian independence, Cripps indicated, would not lead to any change in the princes' relationship with the Crown, which intended to fulfil all treaty commitments to the states, including defence obligations; this assurance was reiterated by the government of India's political secretary, Kenneth Fitze.[73] Ever since the federal negotiations, the princes had considered treaty rights in general and their relationship with the Crown in particular as mechanisms to limit the ability of Indian anticolonial nationalists to demand political and economic reform within the states. British support, in their view, would bolster their position in negotiations with the politicians of independent India over the future relationship between the dominion and the states. The combination of a constitutional framework that divided sovereign powers amongst several different levels of government (centre, province, and state) and provided the options of retaining an independent relationship with the Crown and seceding from the Indian union provided ample means of maintaining state autonomy. Relying on the language of divisible sovereignty, the Cripps proposal appeared to furnish an appropriate political compromise to fulfil princely aspirations.

The princes were also invigorated by the efforts of Hamidullah Khan of Bhopal, who was elected chancellor of the Chamber of Princes in 1944. He obtained a verbal assurance from the political secretary Conrad Corfield that the British government acknowledged 'the right of States on the lapse of Paramountcy, to enter into negotiations with foreign powers'.[74] Although vague, the statement reinforced the position taken in the *Report of the Indian States Committee* that British rights under paramountcy would not be transferred to the independent government of India; the states, therefore, would be free to continue their relationship with the Crown, if they so desired, or pursue other alliances. Once again, the states attempted to balance their relationships with the Crown, with soon-to-be independent India, and with foreign powers, alongside state autonomy, thereby attempting to redraw relationships among the domestic, regional, imperial, and international spheres. Alliances with the British government would, in Hamidullah's view, enable the continuation of monarchies in some form in a decolonized South Asia.

Despite Hamidullah's optimism about a future princely-British alliance, officials in London questioned its viability. They conceded the possibility of maintaining a diplomatic link with the states after Indian independence; the defence obligations under the treaties were, however, an entirely different matter, particularly after the withdrawal of the British army from South Asia. Despite the specific language of 'protection' in many princely treaties, and in sharp contrast to the British

by Cripps on interview with the Jam Saheb and Maharaja of Bikaner, 26 March 1942', in *The Transfer of Power*, (n 3) i, 487.

[73] 'Linlithgow to Amery, 14 December 1942', in *The Transfer of Power*, (n 3) iii, 370–372; and 'Amery to Linlithgow, 12 January 1943', in *The Transfer of Power*, (n 3) iii, 493–496.

[74] Copland, *The Princes of India in the Endgame of Empire*, (n 55) 216.

government's earlier public pronouncements affirming its commitment to those treaties, Clement Attlee concluded that Britain's ties to the princes would have to be repudiated. Since the princes had not breached any treaty provisions, the British government relied on the international law doctrine of *rebus sic stantibus* to unilaterally terminate the treaties, claiming that the end of British supremacy in South Asia constituted such a fundamental change in circumstances that treaty obligations could no longer be fulfilled.[75]

The British instead looked for alternative means to secure the status of the states after their departure. In March 1946, Stafford Cripps returned to India as part of the so-called Cabinet mission; he was joined by the secretary of state for India, Lord Pethick-Lawrence,[76] and a fellow cabinet member, A. V. Alexander.[77] In relation to British India, their plan proposed a three-tiered structure in which the federal centre would have control over defence, external affairs, and communications, with residual powers residing in the provinces that would be grouped together to handle most other functions of government through common legislatures. Muslim-majority provinces in the east and west would constitute two of the groups while the Hindu-majority provinces of the centre and south would constitute the third group.[78] The mission also recommended that the recently elected provincial legislatures form the electoral colleges for the constituent assembly, which was to be established to draft the constitution for independent India.[79] Akin to the earlier Cripps proposal, the Cabinet mission plan also depended on dividing the exercise of sovereign powers among various levels of government to satisfy the varied claims to political power. Both the Muslim League and the Congress accepted the plan but had radically different understandings of it. The League considered the groupings of the provinces to be permanent and thereby forming the basis of future secession while the Congress argued that compulsory groupings violated provincial autonomy.[80] After Nehru questioned the viability of the groupings, Jinnah called for 'direct action'. Relations among Hindus, Muslims, and Sikhs deteriorated sharply, with violence engulfing Bengal, Bihar, and Punjab.[81]

75 ibid 219–221, 273–275. The denunciation attracted strong criticism from those sympathetic to the princes. See R. K. Ranadive, *The Legal Rights of the Indian States and of their Subjects, or The Truth About the Indian States* (Baroda: The Good Companions, 1950), 59–60.

76 Pethick-Lawrence was appointed secretary of state for India in 1945. See Brian Harrison, 'Lawrence, Frederick William Pethick-, Baron Pethick-Lawrence (1871–1961)', in *Oxford Dictionary of National Biography*, https://doi.org/10.1093/ref:odnb/35491, accessed 25 August 2021.

77 Alexander had little knowledge of Indian affairs and was unhappy about the British decision to withdraw from India. See David Howell, 'Alexander, Albert Victor, Earl Alexander of Hillsborough (1885–1965)', in *Oxford Dictionary of National Biography*, https://doi.org/10.1093/ref:odnb/30368, accessed 25 August 2021.

78 Metcalf and Metcalf, *A Concise History of Modern India*, (n 59) 215; Banerjee-Dube, *A History of Modern India*, (n 62) 417–418; Talbot, *A History of Modern South Asia*, (n 59) 134; and Bose and Jalal, *Modern South Asia*, (n 57) 162.

79 Menon, *The Transfer of Power in India*, (n 29) 265–266.

80 Sarkar, *Modern India*, (n 54) 430.

81 Talbot, *A History of Modern South Asia*, (n 59) 134–135; and Bose and Jalal, *Modern South Asia*, (n 57) 162–163.

In the face of this upheaval, the princes' concerns became subservient to the broader British goal of reaching a settlement with the British Indian political parties. Still, the Cabinet mission did have to deal with question of the effect of Indian independence on paramountcy.[82] On 16 May, the mission issued a document summarizing its recommendations, where the only reference to the states was in the following assertion:

> Paramountcy can neither be retained by the British Crown nor transferred to the new Government.... the States are ready and willing to cooperate in the new development of India. The precise form which their cooperation will take must be a matter for negotiation during the building up of the new constitutional structure, and it by no means follows that it will be identical for all the States.[83]

In a more detailed memorandum published on 22 May, the mission observed:

> ... the British Government could not and will not in any circumstances transfer paramountcy to an Indian Government.... When a new fully self-governing or independent Government or Governments come into being in British India, His Majesty's Government's influence with these Governments will not be such as to enable them to carry out the obligations of paramountcy. Moreover, they cannot contemplate that British troops would be retained in India for this purpose. Thus, as a logical sequence and in view of the desires expressed to them on behalf of the Indian States, His Majesty's Government will cease to exercise the powers of paramountcy. This means that the rights of the States which flow from their relationship to the Crown will no longer exist and that all rights surrendered by the States to the paramount power will return to the States. Political arrangements between the States on the one side and the British Crown and British India on the other will thus be brought to an end. The void will have to be filled either by the States entering into a federal relationship with the successor Government or Governments in British India, or, failing this, entering into particular political arrangements with it or them.[84]

Although both these statements envisaged that the states would enter into some sort of political relationship with independent India, Stafford Cripps verbally

[82] The members of the Cabinet mission were, apparently, largely unaware of the extent of the territorial possessions of the states, having only been briefed on British India. See Edward Wakefield, *Past Imperative: My Life in India, 1927–1947* (London: Chatto & Windus, 1966), 210–211.

[83] 'Statement by Cabinet Delegation, 16 May 1946', in *The Transfer of Power*, (n 3) vii, 585.

[84] 'Memorandum on States' Treaties and Paramountcy, 22 May 1946', in *The Transfer of Power*, (n 3) vii, 522–523. Philip Mason considered the statement that the states would have to make their own arrangements with India rather 'like telling a rabbit to make its own arrangements with a tiger', made worse since '[t]he rabbit had lived so long in so secure a hutch that it did not know it was a rabbit'. See Philip Mason, *A Shaft of Sunlight: Memories of a Varied Life* (London: André Deutsch, 1978), 212.

acknowledged that the logical implication of the mission's proposals was that the states would 'become wholly independent'.[85] The consequences of this 'independence', however, remained unclear. Neither of the mission's official statements confirmed whether the British would be willing to enter into fresh treaties with the states although Pethick-Lawrence orally observed that 'there seemed to him no reason why Great Britain should not continue to have treaty relations with the States ... but that clearly the treaties would have to be very greatly modified to fit the new circumstances'.[86]

Despite the studied lack of clarity from British officials,[87] the princes welcomed the Cabinet mission's declaration on paramountcy.[88] Although not wholly enamoured of the British withdrawal from South Asia, the dilution of British defence obligations, or the unilateral termination of their treaties, they were encouraged by the apparent acceptance of the states' independence simultaneously with Indian independence.[89] In Hamidullah's view, the mission's endorsement of the princes' longstanding demands for greater autonomy implied that 'if the States fail to secure reasonable and acceptable terms in regard to their adherence to the all-India Constitution, they would be free inter alia to negotiate the terms of future relationship with any foreign power and that foreign power may be England'.[90]

Since the Cabinet mission had recommended that the new Indian constituent assembly also include representatives of the states,[91] the princes were left to directly negotiate their political future with British Indian politicians. Relying on the belief that the states would become 'independent' and continue to enjoy British support, the princes' strategy relied on hammering out an agreement that would ensure the continued existence of multiple sovereignties in the subcontinent even if bound together in a loose alliance. The princes, therefore, persisted in pushing for the same confederal framework that many of them had sought during the long federal negotiations. In their view, sovereign functions would largely be exercised at the state and provincial level with some powers (such as defence) being ceded to a federal centre. Like in earlier decades, the princes relied on the language of divisible sovereignty to establish a political structure that would provide maximum state autonomy while providing the means for the states to maintain crucial economic ties with British Indian provinces. Many princes also aimed to pursue independent foreign relations with each other and with other nations, relying on the

[85] 'Text of Cripps' press conference, 16 May 1946', in *The Transfer of Power*, (n 3) vii, 597.

[86] 'Note of a meeting of Cabinet Delegation and Wavell with representatives of the Standing Committee of the Chamber of Princes, 2 April 1946', in *The Transfer of Power*, (n 3) vii, 98.

[87] See, for instance, 'Wavell to Bhopal, 19 August 1946', in *The Transfer of Power*, (n 3) viii, 260.

[88] See, for instance, 'Bhopal to Wavell, 19 June 1946', *The Transfer of Power*, (n 3) vii, 978–981.

[89] Barbara Ramusack, *The Indian Princes and their States* (Cambridge: Cambridge University Press, 2004), 271–272.

[90] 'Bhopal to Wavell, 29 July 1946', in *The Transfer of Power*, (n 3) viii, 133.

[91] Menon, *The Transfer of Power in India*, (n 29) 265–266.

divisibility of sovereignty to redraw the boundaries among the domestic, regional, imperial, and international spheres.

The success of the princely plan depended on their ability to maintain a united front to parlay with Indian political leaders on an equal basis. Hamidullah, therefore, tried to rally the states into forming a confederation named 'Rajasthan', with himself as the chief negotiator on behalf of all the princes, but this plan fell apart after Panikkar and Ramaswamy Aiyar refused to back it. Princely ties were further eroded by linguistic and religious communalism, with Hamidullah facing the antagonism of Hindu princes and ministers because of his faith and perceived closeness with the Muslim League.[92] The divide was also ideological. Some princes were willing to embrace democracy to ally with India, their biggest economic partner, but more conservative princes wanted nothing to do with the newly established constituent assembly. Keen to secure the future of their states within an independent India, Sadul Singh of Bikaner and Yadavindra Singh of Patiala became the principal leaders of the group opposing Hamidullah. Under their influence, the states of Cochin, Baroda, Jaipur, Rewa, Jodhpur, Bikaner, and Patiala sent delegates to the constituent assembly.[93]

While the princes failed to adopt a uniform position on their future, British India slid into further chaos. Peasant rebellions and labour strikes gathered force and communal violence spiralled across several provinces after the failure of the Cabinet mission.[94] Rather than agree to a political framework that spread sovereign powers across different levels of government, many within the Congress and on the Hindu right started to see the partition of British India as a mechanism to 'cut out the troublesome Muslim-majority districts in the North West and East, and allow them to inherit the rest of British India, with a union centre uncompromised by having to share power with the Muslim League'.[95]

In the midst of escalating violence, the new viceroy, Louis Mountbatten, developed a plan that involved three elements: the mixed provinces of Punjab and Bengal would be partitioned along religious lines; Hindu-majority provinces would remain in the existing constituent assembly of India; and Muslim-majority provinces would be given a choice to join the existing assembly or a new one for Pakistan.[96] Alternative plans for a united, sovereign

[92] Panikkar claimed that Hamidullah's plan of 'Rajasthan' would be 'a vivisection of Hindu power'. See Panikkar, *An Autobiography*, (n 5) 147–150. Later assessments of Panikkar's work have argued that he had a distinctively pro-Hindu bias in his history writing. See Tarashankar Banerjee, *Sardar K. M. Panikkar: The Profile of a Historian* (Calcutta: Ratna Prakashan, 1977), 93–102. Penderel Moon, a British civil servant deputed to the state of Bahawalpur in the run-up to partition, claimed that the idea of the states constituting a third dominion had the backing of the Political Department. See Penderel Moon, *Divide and Quit* (London: Chatto & Windus, 1961), 106.

[93] Copland, *The Princes of India in the Endgame of Empire*, (n 55) 237–239, 242–245.

[94] Sarkar, *Modern India*, (n 54) 432–437.

[95] Joya Chatterji, 'Decolonization in South Asia: The Long View', in Martin Thomas and Andrew Thompson, eds., *The Oxford Handbook of the Ends of Empire* (Oxford: Oxford University Press, 2018), 264–265.

[96] Banerjee-Dube, *A History of Modern India*, (n 62) 425.

Bengal;[97] an independent state of Khalistan for the Sikhs in Punjab; and independence or autonomy for the Pashtuns of the North-West Frontier province and the Baluchs of the province of Baluchistan were all abandoned. Although earlier plans had imagined a patchwork of South Asian sovereignties, by June 1947, the creation of India and Pakistan as a two separate, territorially sovereign nation-states became an accepted fact.[98]

The partition plan did not include the princely states, which attempted to carve out alternate futures. In the minds of the princes, accession to India or Pakistan was only one of the available options in the negotiations. Some pursued independence, while others sought loose association agreements with the new dominions.[99] Several rulers thought that India and Pakistan would be too weak to survive for long and made plans to fill the power vacuum by fusing neighbouring states into a union or extending their own domains by annexing surrounding territory.[100] Many princes engaged with foreign powers and tried to delineate their future relationship with the new dominions. In June 1947, Ramaswamy Aiyar announced that Travancore intended to declare independence. The state chose representatives to be sent to India and Pakistan after independence and negotiated with the United States to obtain diplomatic recognition. Hamidullah developed a scheme involving a confederation of Bhopal and other states in the northwest with Pakistan. When it did not come to fruition, he decided that Bhopal would sit out of the constituent assembly and instead pursue diplomatic relations with India and Pakistan. The *nizam* of Hyderabad appointed a trade commissioner in London, had discussions with France about establishing a diplomatic mission, and negotiated with Portugal about the use of the port at Goa.[101] Some of the state's advisors also considered a possible link with Pakistan but this proposal collapsed after Jinnah managed to offend the *nizam* during a personal meeting.[102] In July 1947, after failing to convince the *nizam* to accede to India, Mirza Ismail resigned from his position as the prime

[97] Bidyut Chakrabarty, 'An Alternative to Partition: The United Bengal Scheme', *South Asia: Journal of South Asian Studies*, 26/2 (2003), 193–212.

[98] Banerjee-Dube, *A History of Modern India*, (n 62) 425–426. See also, Pankaj Mishra, 'Exit Wounds', *New Yorker* (13 August 2007), https://www.newyorker.com/magazine/2007/08/13/exit-wounds, accessed 15 February 2022. Even after partition was agreed, there was debate over the exact nature of the division. At various points, Pakistan was imagined as encompassing not just the eastern and western wings as it came to be, but also as possibly including a land corridor joining the two wings or including the Andaman and Nicobar Islands (in the Bay of Bengal) as 'maritime connecting points between these wings, or including the princely states of Hyderabad and Junagadh, situated within the body politic of India'. See Faisal Devji, 'The Minority as Political Form', in Dipesh Chakrabarty, Rochona Majumdar, and Andrew Sartori, eds., *From the Colonial to the Postcolonial: India and Pakistan in Transition* (New Delhi: Oxford University Press, 2007), 92.

[99] Ramusack, *The Indian Princes and their States*, (n 89) 273.

[100] Ian Copland, *State, Community and Neighbourhood in Princely North India, c. 1900–1950* (Basingstoke: Palgrave Macmillan, 2005), 135–138.

[101] Copland, *The Princes of India in the Endgame of Empire*, (n 55) 250–251, 253.

[102] Mason, *A Shaft of Sunlight*, (n 84) 207.

minister of Hyderabad, following which the executive council issued a statement declaring that the state had no intention of acceding to either India or Pakistan.[103]

As these debates demonstrate, the future map of South Asia was being continually redrawn even after Indian independence and partition. Although the partition plan had been announced in June, the final award of territory to the dominions of India and Pakistan was only published on 17 August, two days after independence.[104] The position of the princely states also remained unclear. The numerous actors involved in the negotiations over decolonization all advocated multiple, competing, jostling constructs for the political future of the region. Many preferred confederal structures in which different types of political entities (such as states, provinces, and the federal centre) could exercise sovereign powers. The Cripps mission proposal, the Cabinet mission plan, and the innumerable schemes devised by various princes and their ministers were all structured around the idea that sovereignty was divisible. These configurations followed from the federal discussions of the 1930s, where similar constitutional structures had been tabled. After decades of negotiations involving loose frameworks of provinces and states, it was far from inevitable that colonial South Asia would be transformed into two independent nation-states in 1947. However, the rise of the developmental state—and its links with territorial sovereignty in the South Asian context—submerged these alternative proposals and the language of divisible sovereignty altogether.

Territorial Sovereignty and the Developmental State

Concerns around 'development' permeated colonial South Asia, with anticolonial nationalism being predicated on the vision of a better economic future once independence was achieved.[105] Economic factors, therefore, played a significant role in the articulation of specific kinds of political structures. Political leaders like Jawaharlal Nehru and B. R. Ambedkar favoured 'a strong centre that could ensure proper formulation and implementation of policies on education, economy and development at a national level'.[106] Although Ambedkar aimed to establish a centralized state to enact radical social reform and legal protections for marginalized

[103] Copland, *The Princes of India in the Endgame of Empire*, (n 55) 253.

[104] Khan, *The Great Partition*, (n 58) 1–3. For discussions of the drawing of the border, see Lucy Chester, *Borders and Conflict in South Asia: The Radcliffe Boundary Commission and the Partition of Punjab* (Manchester: Manchester University Press, 2009); and Joya Chatterji, 'The Fashioning of a Frontier: The Radcliffe Line and Bengal's Border Landscape, 1947–52', *Modern Asian Studies*, 33/1 (1999), 185–242.

[105] On the reliance on 'development' as a means of legitimacy for anticolonial nationalism, see Chatterjee, *The Nation and its Fragments*, (n 21) 202–205; and Goswami, *Producing India*, (n 21) 276.

[106] Banerjee-Dube, *A History of Modern India*, (n 62) 456.

groups,[107] the general discourse of development in mid-twentieth-century India was more circumspect and almost universally associated with economic planning and industrialization.[108] In this, anticolonial nationalists were part of a broader transnational mode of economic thought that favoured a strong role for the state in the economy. This national developmentalist framework can be traced to the influence of late nineteenth-century political economists like Friedrich List,[109] with additional international examples by the 1930s, including Soviet planning, New Deal interventions in the United States, Nazi and Fascist economics, and Japanese policies.[110]

Support for planning crossed a range of political divides. Leading advocates included technocrats in the Indian Civil Service and princely state officials such as the Mysore *diwan*, M. Visvesvaraya, whose influential text, *Planned Economy for India*,[111] argued that planning was a means for national discipline and regeneration.[112] The Congress Socialist Party, a socialist caucus within the Indian National Congress, also pushed for industrial modernity alongside redistributive commitments. Perhaps the most consequential endorsement came from Nehru himself, who argued that planning was 'inevitable' to efficiently utilize the country's limited resources.[113] Planning also had the approval of Indian industrialists, eight of whom authored the 1944 publication, *A Plan of Economic Development for India*.[114] These varied voices on the necessity of economic planning coalesced in the activities of

[107] Rowena Robinson, 'Planning and Economic Development: Ambedkar versus Gandhi', in Biswamoy Pati, ed., *Invoking Ambedkar: Contributions, Receptions, Legacies* (Delhi: Primus Books, 2014), 59–71.

[108] An exception was Gandhi, who advocated decentralized village-based production in a confederal framework loosely binding together states and provinces. See Subrata Ghatak, 'Gandhian Economic Thought and the Economic Policy of the Indian National Congress', in Mike Shepperdson and Colin Simmons, eds., *The Indian National Congress and the Political Economy of India 1885–1985* (Aldershot: Avebury, 1988), 282–290; Benjamin Zachariah, *Developing India: An Intellectual and Social History, c. 1930–50* (Delhi: Oxford University Press, 2005), 158; and Karuna Mantena, 'Popular Sovereignty and Anti-Colonialism', in Richard Bourke and Quentin Skinner, eds., *Popular Sovereignty in Historical Perspective* (Cambridge: Cambridge University Press, 2016), 309–313. On Gandhi's critique of a centralized state more generally, see Karuna Mantena, 'On Gandhi's Critique of the State: Sources, Contexts, Conjectures', *Modern Intellectual History*, 9/3 (2012), 535–563.

[109] On List's influence on anticolonial nationalists in South Asia, see Goswami, *Producing India*, (n 21) 209–241.

[110] Zachariah, *Developing India*, (n 108) 43.

[111] M. Visvesvaraya, *Planned Economy for India* (Bangalore: Bangalore Press, 1934).

[112] Khilnani, *The Idea of India*, (n 62) 70–71; and Zachariah, *Developing India*, (n 108) 245.

[113] Nehru included descriptions of an economic model for India in his many letters to the chief ministers after he became prime minister of independent India. See 'From a letter dated 3 March 1953', in Madhav Khosla, ed., *Letters for a Nation: From Jawaharlal Nehru to his Chief Ministers, 1947–1963* (New Delhi: Penguin, 2014), 170–173; 'From a letter dated 28 September 1953', in ibid 173–176; 'From a letter dated 15 September 1954', in ibid 179–181; 'From a letter dated 24 December 1954', in ibid 181–183; 'From a letter dated 13 July 1958', in ibid 189–192.

[114] Purushottamdas Thakurdas, et al., *Memorandum Outlining a Plan of Economic Development for India* (Harmondsworth: Penguin, 1945). See also Medha Kudaisya, '"The Promise of Partnership": Indian Business, the State, and the Bombay Plan of 1944', *Business History Review*, 88/1 (2014), 97–131.

the Congress's National Planning Committee, which was set up in 1938 and included industrialists, scientists, politicians, and academics.[115]

Conversations around political structures for independent India were also framed in terms of their conduciveness for planning. In a 1939 piece, Nehru argued that an essential prerequisite for planning was 'complete freedom and independence' such that the national planning authority had 'full power to give effect to its planning'.[116] Although this argument linked planning with the struggle for independence, it also implied a particular structure for the independent Indian government. A 'weak central authority', in Nehru's view, 'would be incapable of ensuring peace or co-ordinating vital matters of common concern and of speaking effectively for the whole country in the international sphere'.[117] This aspiration to extend the state's command over economic policy and resources had haunted earlier debates over fiscal control during the negotiations over federation. At that time, Congress leaders had sought extensive powers of taxation for the federal centre, while the states preferred a model in which they would retain those powers, with the centre being limited to raising indirect taxes.[118] After independence, Nehru was even more explicit in his linkage of political structures with economic measures. In a 1959 press conference, he defended his rejection of a weak federal government during the partition negotiations by arguing that such a political structure would have been unable to enact the economic measures that were necessary for the effective planning needed 'to make good after Independence'.[119]

In the minds of its advocates, the fulfilment of the aims of centralized planning also required the territorialization of the nation. British India had already been organized as a geographical space through the colonial technological networks of irrigation canals, roads, and railways.[120] Late nineteenth-century nationalist discourse built upon this order to envision a territorially bound national entity of

[115] Bidyut Chakrabarty, 'Jawaharlal Nehru and Planning, 1938–41: India at the Crossroads', *Modern Asian Studies*, 26/2 (1992), 276–281; Gyan Prakash, *Another Reason: Science and the Imagination of Modern India* (Princeton, NJ: Princeton University Press, 1999), 194–198; and Zachariah, *Developing India*, (n 108) 217. The Muslim League also set up an Economic Planning Committee in 1943. See Ian Talbot, 'Planning for Pakistan: The Planning Committee of the All-India Muslim League 1943–46', *Modern Asian Studies*, 28/4 (1994), 875–889.

[116] 'The Need for Planning for Free India, 4 June 1939', in S. Gopal, ed., *Selected Works of Jawaharlal Nehru*, ix (New Delhi: Jawaharlal Nehru Memorial Fund, 1976), 376–377.

[117] 'Letter from Jawaharlal Nehru to Rajendra Prasad, 5 July 1947', in S. Gopal, ed., *Selected Works of Jawaharlal Nehru*, 2nd series, iii (New Delhi: Jawaharlal Nehru Memorial Fund, 1985), 54.

[118] See the references to taxation in documents relating to the federal negotiations, including Comparison of the federal scheme affecting the States proposed by (1) the Federal Structure Committee, (2) His Highness of Dholpur, and (3) His Highness of Indore, 1931, IOR/L/PS/13/603; Letter from K. N. Haksar to Tej Bahadur Sapru, 3 March 1934, Sapru Papers, Version II, 2nd series, Reel 8, IOR Neg 5004; Note on a Memorandum Describing Federation as Dangerous to the States, 1936, IOR/L/PS/13/613; and Report of the Constitutional Committee of the Chamber of Princes, February 1937, Federal Papers, Volume II, NMML.

[119] 'Text of Nehru's press conference, 7 February 1959', in Madhavan K. Palat, ed., *Selected Works of Jawaharlal Nehru*, 2nd series, xlvi (New Delhi: Jawaharlal Nehru Memorial Fund, 2012), 152.

[120] Prakash, *Another Reason*, (n 115) 159–170.

India.[121] However, the colonial project of territory-making was a fractured process that was particularly unsettled in frontier regions.[122] And as previous chapters have shown, the landscape of colonial South Asia was riven by legal distinctions between British India and the princely states, which were exploited by Indian capitalists to their advantage. The Tata Iron and Steel Company, for instance, successfully played authorities in British India and the princely states off each other to gain access to valuable mineral resources in eastern India at minimal cost.[123] Advocates of planning, therefore, bemoaned 'the confusion created by the myriads of political units . . . perhaps without any parallel in the world'.[124]

For many anticolonial nationalists, the continued existence of the princely states, which created spaces for political and legal manoeuvring, was an obstacle for the achievement of economic sovereignty. They had long viewed the people of the states as being divided from their racial and religious brethren in British India by 'an imaginary line'. A 1928 report drafted by a committee chaired by Motilal Nehru viewed attempts to keep the states constitutionally separate from British India as a tool 'to convert the Indian States into an Indian Ulster'.[125] Motilal's son, Jawaharlal, castigated the states as 'Britain's fifth column in India'.[126] He considered the states to be a British mechanism to deliberately 'breed conflicts and impede planned development' by splitting up the region into 'anachronistic shells of power'.[127]

The ability to compete in an increasingly international economic order instead required centralized control, planning, co-ordination, and the consolidation of the state's territories. Although some scholars consider Nehru's focus on the creation of a modern Indian nation-state to be a stepping-stone towards the greater goal of erasing boundaries to create 'One World' united by justiciable, universal human rights,[128] his commitment to international organizations did not preclude carving out a 'domestic' sphere that was outside the jurisdiction of those institutions.[129] As

[121] For a discussion of the creation of an imagined conception of 'Bharat' as a spatially bound national entity amongst late nineteenth-century upper caste, middle class Hindus, see Goswami, *Producing India* (n 21).

[122] Thomas Simpson, 'Bordering and Frontier-Making in Nineteenth-Century British India', *The Historical Journal*, 58/2 (2015), 513–542; Mark Condos and Gavin Rand, 'Coercion and Conciliation at the Edge of Empire: State-Building and its Limits in Waziristan, 1849–1914', *The Historical Journal*, 61/3 (2018), 695–718; and Abhilash Medhi, 'Infrastructural Contingencies and Contingent Sovereignties on the Indo-Afghan Frontier', *Modern Asian Studies*, 54/6 (2020), 1949–1986.

[123] Mircea Raianu, '"A Mass of Anomalies": Land, Law, and Sovereignty in an Indian Company Town', *Comparative Studies in Society and History*, 60/2 (2018), 369–377.

[124] Tulsi Ram Sharma, *The Location of Industries in India* (Bombay: Hind Kitabs Limited, 1946), 3–4, quoted in Raianu, 'A Mass of Anomalies', (n 123) 369.

[125] *Report of the All-Parties Conference* (1928), 72.

[126] Jawaharlal Nehru, *The Discovery of India* (Calcutta: The Signet Press, 1944; New Delhi: Oxford University Press, 1989), 312. Citations refer to the OUP edition.

[127] Prakash, *Another Reason*, (n 115) 208.

[128] Manu Bhagavan, 'Princely States and the Making of Modern India: Internationalism, Constitutionalism and the Postcolonial Moment', *The Indian Economic and Social History Review*, 46/3 (2009), 427–456; and Manu Bhagavan, 'A New Hope: India, the United Nations and the Making of the Universal Declaration of Human Rights', *Modern Asian Studies*, 44/2 (2010), 311–347.

[129] Kavita Saraswathi Datla, 'Sovereignty and the End of Empire: The Transition to Independence in Colonial Hyderabad', *Ab Imperio*, 3 (2018), 80.

was the case across the world, the dominant vision of internationalism in the minds of most Congress anticolonial nationalists 'focused on the international system as a source of strength and support for state-directed programmes of national development'.[130] In the Indian case, this unified national space for development had to be created and it was done through the articulation of a version of sovereignty that privileged exclusive and absolute control over defined territory. This idea of territorial sovereignty informed the vision of Congress politicians during the long independence negotiations in which they rejected constitutional schemes that proposed layering sovereign powers among several political entities in favour of a unified central government in a partitioned country.

The future of the princely states posed equally grave questions for a leadership that was intent upon consolidating territory to create a national economic space. The issue became particularly urgent after British officials implied that the states would become independent, leaving the possibility of independent Indian territory being punctuated by 'foreign' enclaves. To combat this eventuality, Congress politicians claimed that there was no legal obstacle to the powers of paramountcy being exercised by the government of India after its transition to dominion status.[131] This assertion built on the long-established claim of British Indian jurists that the Crown had entered into the treaties with the states in its capacity as the sovereign over British India rather than in its own right; the treaties would, therefore, continue to exist even after India achieved dominion status.[132] Extending this argument, the government of independent India could claim the right to exercise political and economic control over the states through pre-existing paramountcy powers. Congress leaders obtained support from B. R. Ambedkar, who defined paramountcy as a royal prerogative that was exercised on the advice of the cabinet, which after India achieved dominion status would be 'the advice of the Indian Cabinet'.[133] By maintaining paramountcy over the states, the government of independent India could exercise control over a consolidated mass of territory.

With the vision of creating a territorial unit, the language used by some anticolonial nationalists became increasingly confrontational. In April 1947, Nehru declared that states which did 'not join the Constituent Assembly now would be regarded as hostile States' and would 'have to bear the consequences of being so regarded'.[134] The situation unravelled further when the rulers of Bhopal,

[130] Sunil Amrith, 'Asian Internationalism: Bandung's Echo in a Colonial Metropolis', *Inter-Asia Cultural Studies*, 6/4 (2005), 558.

[131] Menon, *The Integration of the Indian States*, (n 3) 25.

[132] See P. S. Sivaswamy Aiyer, *Indian Constitutional Problems* (Bombay: D. B. Taraporevala Sons & Co., 1928), 211; Gurmukh Nihal Singh, *Indian States and British India: Their Future Relations* (Benaras: Nand Kishore & Bros., 1930), 96; and N. D. Varadachariar, *Indian States in the Federation* (Humphrey Milford: Oxford University Press, 1936), 13–17.

[133] 'Statement by Dr Ambedkar, 17 June 1947', in Adrian Sever, ed., *Documents and Speeches on the Indian Princely States*, ii (Delhi: B. R. Publishing, 1985), 630, 633.

[134] 'Pandit Nehru's Address, 18 April 1947', *Indian Annual Register*, i (1947), 212.

Travancore, and Hyderabad indicated that they would declare independence. At a meeting on June 13, Jinnah suggested that the states were sovereign except to the extent that they had entered into treaties with the Crown and were, therefore, free to either accede to either of the dominions or remain independent.[135] Although he provided a constitutional argument, it is likely that the League supported the independence of the states as a mechanism to 'seriously impair the unity and economic viability of the Indian Union', whose territory was largely interspersed with those of the states.[136] Nehru objected, contending that the states lacked sovereignty since they did not have the capacity to enter into international relations or to declare war. Although he admitted that the states did not necessarily have to join the constituent assembly of either dominion, he contended that they had to come to some arrangement about future relations; a declaration of independence was not one of the available options.[137]

Nehru reiterated this position in a combative speech two days later, insisting that the states must either join one of the two dominions or reach another arrangement with them. There was 'no third way out of the situation, third way meaning independence or special relation with a foreign power'. He also declared that 'we will not recognize any independence of any State in India; further, that any recognition of any such independence by any foreign power, which ever it may be and wherever it may be, will be considered an unfriendly act'.[138] The Congress working committee's resolution also declared that '[t]he relationship between the Government of India and the State would not be exhausted by lapse of paramountcy' and that '[t]he lapse does not lead to the independence of the State'.[139] Ambedkar published his own statement backing this position and advising the princes to give up 'the mirage of independence'. He also argued that the admission of 'an Indian State which declares itself as sovereign independent state' as a UN member would be 'a violation of the sovereign rights of the Union of India'.[140]

To cement the ability of the government of independent India to exercise authority over the states, Nehru persuaded Mountbatten to permit the soon-to-be created dominions to manage their relations with the states through a States' Department, which was, in effect, a renamed Political Department.[141] Mountbatten

[135] 'Minutes of Viceroy's eighteenth miscellaneous meeting, 13 June 1947', in *The Transfer of Power*, (n 3) xi, 322–323.

[136] Copland, 'The Princely States, the Muslim League, and the Partition of India in 1947', (n 4) 56.

[137] 'Minutes of Viceroy's eighteenth miscellaneous meeting, 13 June 1947', in *The Transfer of Power*, (n 3) xi, 323.

[138] 'Speech by Pandit Nehru to the All-India Congress Committee, 15 June 1947', in *Documents and Speeches on the Indian Princely States*, (n 133) ii, 624–625.

[139] 'Resolution of the All-India Congress Committee, 15 June 1947', in *Documents and Speeches on the Indian Princely States*, (n 133) ii, 626.

[140] 'Statement by Dr Ambedkar, 17 June 1947', in *Documents and Speeches on the Indian Princely States*, (n 133) ii, 633–634.

[141] 'Minutes of Viceroy's eighteenth miscellaneous meeting, 13 June 1947', in *The Transfer of Power*, (n 3) xi, 322–325. In doing so, Mountbatten overruled his political advisor Conrad Corfield's protests that establishing such departments prior to independence would imply that paramountcy was being

also realized that the Congress leadership would be more amenable to partition if he persuaded the states to accede.[142] He therefore started a campaign to dissuade the princes from declaring independence by declaring that the states would only be able to stay in the Commonwealth—which at the time consisted solely of countries that had the Crown as the head of state—if they acceded to either India or Pakistan.[143] Till then, British officials had been content to make ambiguous statements about whether Britain would maintain relations with the states after Indian and Pakistani independence. Mountbatten, however, explicitly stated that the states could only retain their relationship with the Crown if they entered into an arrangement with either dominion.[144] This was a crucial change in policy since the states had been banking on preserving a link with the Crown to fend off attempts by the new dominions to absorb them into their own territories. Instead, they faced the loss of British support, leaving them in a vulnerable position in the political negotiations.

The States' Department, headed by Vallabhbhai Patel on the Indian side, with V. P. Menon as its secretary, sought to define the states' relationships with the dominion of India under the shadow of economic concerns. Menon and Patel concluded that the lapse of paramountcy would hinder the continued functioning of the central government which 'rested on two pillars, one with foundations in the provinces and the other in the States'. Menon fretted that '[i]mportant cantonments and military installations' as well as railway lines were located within princely territory. Further, the execution of policy on crucial matters affecting 'all-India security and welfare' such as 'posts and telegraphs, control of arms and ammunition, extradition and surrender of fugitives, control of opium and other narcotics, ... overall food policy' all required co-ordination with the states through the residencies.[145]

This emphasis on the economic interdependence of British India and the states was even stronger in the government of India's post facto justification of its princely policy. In a 1950 white paper, the Ministry of States admitted that the lapse of paramountcy led to 'a serious vacuum not only with regard to the political relationship between the Central Government and the States but also in respect of the co-ordination of all-India policies in the economic and other fields'. Partition had

transferred despite the British government's numerous statements to the contrary. See Conrad Corfield, *The Princely India I Knew: From Reading to Mountbatten* (Madras: Indo-British Historical Society, 1975), 156.

142 Moore, *Escape from Empire*, (n 63) 297–298; and Copland, *The Princes of India in the Endgame of Empire*, (n 55) 253–254.

143 See 'Record of interview between Mountbatten and C. P. Ramawamy Aiyar, 2 May 1947', in *The Transfer of Power*, (n 3) x, 565–566; 'Note on relations between His Majesty's Government and the Indian States after the transfer of power, 24 May 1947', in *The Transfer of Power*, (n 3) x, 981–982; 'Minutes of Viceroy's Thirty Sixth Staff Meeting, 1 June 1947', in *The Transfer of Power*, (n 3) xi, 32; and 'Proceedings of Mountbatten's press conference, 4 June 1947', in *The Transfer of Power*, (n 3) xi, 115–116.

144 Copland, *The Princes of India in the Endgame of Empire*, (n 55) 255.

145 Menon, *The Integration of the Indian States*, (n 3) 94.

dealt 'a violent blow to the political, economic and geographical integrity of India'. Coping with the aftermath and ensuring 'the political strength, full economic development and cultural expression of the Indian people' necessitated '[t]he unity of what remained as India'.[146]

Menon understood that a territorial vision of Indian sovereignty was necessary to create a unified nation that could pursue its developmental policies while coping with the loss of territory to partition. He also realized that the princes possessed a 'keen desire … to safeguard their sovereignty' and concluded that 'some sort of organic bond should be forged between the Government of India and the States if the integrity of the country was to be preserved'. He revived an earlier proposal requiring the states to accede only on matters relating to defence, external affairs, and communications, three functions that were already exercised by the British as paramount power. Through this framework, 'the basic unity of India would be achieved', while the states would not lose any rights that they enjoyed. Alongside the instruments of accession, the princes were also asked to sign standstill agreements to extend the application of existing arrangements on 'railways, customs, harbours, irrigation, and the like' since any abrupt abrogation would result in 'administrative chaos of the gravest kind'.[147]

As a mark of the strategy's success, 114 states acceded to India in the first two weeks of August 1947 alone. Many princes were seduced by Indian guarantees of 'a privy purse in perpetuity' and 'privileges such as exemption from customs duties, the use of their titles, the right to fly their state flags on their cars, and to have police protection'.[148] Others seemed resigned to their fates, with the *maharaja* of Travancore acceding soon after his prime minister, C. P. Ramaswamy Aiyar, narrowly escaped an assassination attempt in July 1947.[149] The three-subject accession plan was accompanied by assurances that the independent Indian government 'would scrupulously respect [the states'] autonomous existence' on all other matters,[150] which dispelled some of the princes' fears.[151] Others had little joy at the lapse of paramountcy; some princes, in Kenneth Fitze's dramatic words, 'wept as they signed their own death warrants'.[152]

[146] *White Paper on Indian States*, (n 10) 32.

[147] Menon, *The Integration of the Indian States*, (n 3) 96–97, 104.

[148] Ramusack, *The Indian Princes and their States*, (n 89) 273.

[149] Copland, *The Princes of India in the Endgame of Empire*, (n 55) 258. See also 'Travancore to Mountbatten, 30 July 1947', in *The Transfer of Power*, (n 3) xii, 414. For an overview of the tumultuous events between Travancore's declaration of independence and its accession to India, see A. Sreedhara Menon, *Triumph and Tragedy in Travancore: Annals of Sir CP's Sixteen Years* (Kottayam: Current Books, 2001), 223–261. Aiyar's granddaughter claims that the decision to accede was made before the assassination attempt. See Shakunthala Jagannathan, *Sir C. P. Remembered: A Granddaughter's Reminiscences* (Mumbai: Vakils, Feffer & Simons Ltd., 1999), 112–113.

[150] 'Statement by Sardar Patel, 5 July 1947', in *Documents and Speeches on the Indian Princely States*, (n 133) ii, 635.

[151] Copland, *The Princes of India in the Endgame of Empire*, (n 55) 256.

[152] Kenneth Fitze, *Twilight of the Maharajas* (London: John Murray, 1956), 162. Arthur Lothian also noted that one of the princes 'even broke into tears and would not be comforted'. See Arthur Lothian, *Kingdoms of Yesterday* (London: John Murray, 1951), 192.

Britain's abandonment of its 'junior allies' played a key role in the capitulation of the states. Although Mountbatten successfully created the 'impression that he was a friend who was trying to help the princes',[153] his relentless pressure tactics in his meetings with the princes, likened to 'bullying' by M. A. Sreenivasan, the *diwan* of Gwalior,[154] accelerated the accessions. Mountbatten's actions were taken over the strenuous objections of his political advisor, Conrad Corfield, who considered the campaign to be 'a breach of promise' that filled him with 'nausea' and left him with the feeling that he 'had deserted [his] friends'.[155] Once Mountbatten rejected the idea of the states maintaining independent relations with the Crown, their scheme of layered sovereignty in a federal framework lay in tatters.

Without British support against British Indian nationalists and reformist protesters, the states' alternate imagination for postcolonial South Asia was soon overwhelmed by the territorial vision of the independent Indian government. The language of divisible sovereignty, so long a mainstay of princely discourse and envisaged as a mechanism for maintaining the states' distinctiveness and ability to preserve a 'semi-international' status, appeared to offer very little in the face of the demands of a nation-building project. Within two years of the accessions, and at odds with their previous assurances of a limited accession that would leave most sovereign powers with the states, Patel and Menon persuaded the princes to merge their states into larger units or neighbouring provinces, take steps to establish responsible government, and ultimately sign new instruments of accession to cede effectively all sovereign power to the new federal centre.[156] Menon later claimed that the original plan had never been to 'extinguish the States' but conceded that the States' Department had 'departed from this policy and started on their integration'.[157] Given the territorial vision of independent India, however, it would be naïve to think that the three-subject accession plan would ever have been sufficient to fulfil the demands of the developmental state.

There were, however, hiccups along the way to the smooth 'integration' of the states into the rest of India. Junagadh signed an instrument of accession with Pakistan although the decision was reversed after a hastily conducted plebiscite following the state's occupation by Indian troops.[158] Several states, such as Indore and Piploda, delayed signing the instruments of accession till after Indian independence.[159] And although the most conspicuous example of the legacy of the debates over the sovereignty of the princely states is the current contested status of

[153] Narendra Singh Sarila, *The Shadow of the Great Game: The Untold Story of India's Partition* (London: Constable, 2006), 316–317.

[154] M. A. Sreenivasan, *Of the Raj, Maharajas and Me* (New Delhi: Ravi Dayal Publisher, 1991), 216.

[155] Corfield, *The Princely India I Knew*, (n 141) 158–159.

[156] Copland, *The Princes of India in the Endgame of Empire*, (n 55) 262–265.

[157] Letter from V. P. Menon to Mirza Ismail, 2 May 1957, Mirza Ismail Papers, NMML.

[158] Rakesh Ankit, 'The Accession of Junagadh, 1947–48: Colonial Sovereignty, State Violence and Post-Independence India', *The Indian Economic and Social History Review*, 53/3 (2016), 371–404.

[159] Copland, *The Princes of India in the Endgame of Empire*, (n 55) 260.

Jammu and Kashmir, one of the most interesting illustrations of the afterlives of the princes comes from Hyderabad, the richest, most populous, and the most distinguished of all the states.

Hyderabad and India at the United Nations

Originally a governor in the Mughal empire, Mir Qamaruddin Khan established the Asaf Jahi dynasty as the relatively independent rulers of Hyderabad by his death in 1748.[160] Throughout the tumultuous eighteenth century, Hyderabad played a significant role in battles among the Marathas, Mysore, and the English and French East India Companies for supremacy in South Asia; by 1800, however, the state was firmly under British paramountcy.[161] By the middle of twentieth century, Hyderabad had an estimated population of seventeen million[162] and revenue that 'rivalled Belgium's and exceeded that of twenty member states of the United Nations'.[163] The seventh *nizam*, Mir Osman Ali Khan, was considered to be a symbol of Muslim kingship although Muslims were a minority of the state's population.[164] Given Hyderabad's position as the premier princely state, it has been the subject of considerable recent scholarly interest, which has traced its possible alternative political futures as well as the role of violence in its final 'integration' into India.[165] Proposals for Hyderabad's position after the British departure from South Asia included placing it within a Deccan states federation,[166] incorporating it within a united India to maintain Muslim parity at the federal centre, or carving it out as an independent state linked to the British Crown through a special treaty.[167] Hyderabad's significance in the princely order also meant that it had the potential to be a bellwether for the fate of the states more generally and thereby have

[160] A. G. Noorani, *The Destruction of Hyderabad* (London: Hurst & Company, 2014), 18; and Munis D. Faruqui, 'At Empire's End: The Nizam, Hyderabad and Eighteenth-Century India', *Modern Asian Studies*, 43/1 (2009), 5–43.

[161] Noorani, *The Destruction of Hyderabad*, (n 160) 18–20.

[162] *The Complaint of Hyderabad against the Dominion of India under Article 35(2) of the Charter of the United Nations*, 5, Dep. Monckton Trustees 48, Walter Monckton Papers, Balliol College Archives, Oxford.

[163] Copland, *The Princes of India in the Endgame of Empire*, (n 55) 8.

[164] Eric Lewis Beverley, *Hyderabad, British India and the World: Muslim Networks and Minor Sovereignty, c. 1850–1950* (Cambridge: Cambridge University Press, 2015). The political category of 'Muslim' was constructed under colonial conditions. See Ian Copland, '"Communalism" in Princely India: The Case of Hyderabad, 1930–1940', *Modern Asian Studies*, 22/4 (1988), 783–814; and Gyanendra Pandey, *The Construction of Communalism in Colonial North India* (Delhi: Oxford University Press, 1990).

[165] See, for instance, Datla, 'Sovereignty and the End of Empire' (n 129); Sunil Purushotham, 'Federating the Raj: Hyderabad, Sovereign Kingship, and Partition', *Modern Asian Studies*, 54/1 (2020), 157–198; and Sunil Purushotham, 'Internal Violence: The "Police Action" in Hyderabad', *Comparative Studies in Society and History*, 57/2 (2015), 435–466.

[166] Purushotham, 'Federating the Raj', (n 165) 184–185.

[167] Datla, 'Sovereignty and the End of Empire', (n 129) 71–72, 75.

considerable impact on the unified territorial vision of independent India advocated by Congress politicians. To underline the importance of the princely states in the creation of the postcolonial political structure of India, I focus on the key role played by legal arguments over sovereignty in determining Hyderabad's fate.

Feeling betrayed by the British denunciation of princely treaties,[168] the *nizam* made a bid for independence that gathered support from across Hyderabad's political and social spectrum: Muslim subjects, the landed elite, administrative officials, and two large Dalit organizations provided their backing.[169] Opposition came from the Hyderabad State Congress, which had been banned in the state till 1946, as well as the Arya Samaj and Hindu Mahasabha, both explicitly communalist Hindu organizations.[170] The state's Communist Party first backed accession to India but reversed its position in late 1947 and continued its armed rebellion for years.[171] Hyderabad's pursuit of independence was complicated by its position as a landlocked state that was surrounded by British Indian territory on all sides. The state sought to negotiate a route to the sea either by obtaining the return of the port of Masulipatnam (located in British India) or by securing the use of the port in Goa (part of Portugal's overseas territories) but was rebuffed on both counts.[172]

In the months before Indian independence, there were hectic negotiations over Hyderabad's future, with the state being offered accession on the three subjects of defence, external affairs, and communications. Walter Monckton, the *nizam*'s legal advisor, managed to wrangle an additional clause that would permit Hyderabad to remain neutral in case of a war between India and Pakistan. He believed that the deal preserved as much of Hyderabad's sovereignty as was possible under the circumstances but was unable to convince the *nizam*.[173] The fervent political atmosphere in the state forced the resignation of the prime minister, Mirza Ismail, after the influential Majlis-i-Ittehad-ul-Muslimeen (popularly known as the Ittehad) attacked him as a Congress agent.[174] Monckton soldiered on and was able to obtain a two-month extension from the informal 15 August deadline for Hyderabad to negotiate a new agreement with India.[175]

In November 1947, Hyderabad and the government of India executed a standstill agreement that retained pre-independence arrangements on matters of common concern (defence, external affairs, and communications), precluded India from

[168] 'Hyderabad to Mountbatten, 9 July 1947', in *The Transfer of Power*, (n 3) xii, 31–32.

[169] Purushotham, 'Internal Violence', (n 165) 439.

[170] Wilfred Cantwell Smith, 'Hyderabad: Muslim Tragedy', *Middle East Journal*, 4/1 (1950), 31–32.

[171] Srinath Raghavan, *War and Peace in Modern India* (Basingstoke: Palgrave Macmillan, 2010), 95; and Datla, 'Sovereignty and the End of Empire', (n 129) 81–82.

[172] Lord Birkenhead, *Walter Monckton: The Life of Viscount Monckton of Brenchley* (London: Weidenfeld and Nicolson, 1969), 116; and Noorani, *The Destruction of Hyderabad*, (n 160) 269–282.

[173] Birkenhead, *Walter Monckton*, (n 172) 230–231.

[174] Mirza Ismail, *My Public Life* (London: George Allen & Unwin Ltd., 1954), 105–108.

[175] Birkenhead, *Walter Monckton*, (n 172) 233.

sending troops to the state, and provided for arbitration in the case of disputes.[176] However, negotiations over the future relationship soon broke down. The Indian government contended that Hyderabad had banned the circulation of Indian currency in the state, granted a large loan to Pakistan, and illegally imported arms from Pakistan.[177] Hyderabad maintained that India had started an unofficial economic blockade leading to a shortage of essential supplies in the state. Indian officials demanded Hyderabad disband the Razakars, the volunteer-based paramilitary force of the Ittehad, claiming that they were responsible for attacks on Hindus in the state and across the border in Indian territory.[178] Press reports on these alleged atrocities, however, appear to have been greatly exaggerated and were often based on selective leaks from the rabidly anti-Muslim K. M. Munshi who Vallabhbhai Patel had handpicked to be India's agent-general in the state.[179] Hyderabad representatives made counter-accusations, insisting that militias trained by Indian provincial governments were responsible for violence against state residents.[180] After initially rejecting military intervention, Nehru came under domestic pressure and hinted that conflict might be a necessary evil.[181]

Despite the increasing tension, in June 1948, Hyderabad's prime minister, Mir Laik Ali, and Walter Monckton managed to negotiate heads of agreement with the Indian government.[182] Under the terms, Hyderabad agreed to pass legislation similar to India's on defence, external affairs, and communications; the state was allowed to retain a separate army of upto 20,000 soldiers that would be supplied by the Indian government and be subject to 'inspection'; the Indian government would only be permitted to send its troops in the case of a declared emergency; unlike other princely states, Hyderabad would also be able to maintain trade agencies in foreign countries although external relations more generally would be handled by the government of India.[183] These heads of government would govern relations

176 Noorani, *The Destruction of Hyderabad*, (n 160) 173.

177 Raghavan, *War and Peace in Modern India*, (n 171) 94–95; and Noorani, *The Destruction of Hyderabad*, (n 160) 180. See also the list of violations set out in 'Letter from V. P. Menon to Mir Laik Ali, 23 March 1948', in Z. H. Zaidi, ed., *Quaid-i-Azam Mohammad Ali Jinnah Papers*, ix (Islamabad: Quaid-i-Azam Papers Project, Culture Division, Government of Pakistan, 2003), 112–114. An Australian aviator, Sidney Cotton, who had come to Hyderabad to deal in groundnuts, ended up becoming the gunrunner in the arms imports. See John Zubrzycki, *The Last Nizam: An Indian Prince in the Australian Outback* (Sydney: Macmillan, 2006), 190–192.

178 Noorani, *The Destruction of Hyderabad*, (n 160) 187, 194–198.

179 Manu Bhagavan, 'The Hindutva Underground: Hindu Nationalism and the Indian National Congress in Late Colonial and Early Post-Colonial India', *Economic and Political Weekly*, 43/37 (2008), 46. Others are more sympathetic to Indian claims that the Razakars were responsible for atrocities across the border. See Manjiri N. Kamat, 'Border Incidents, Internal Disorder and the *Nizam*'s Claim for an Independent Hyderabad', in Waltraud Ernst and Biswamoy Pati, eds., *India's Princely States: People, Princes and Colonialism* (London: Routledge, 2007), 212–223.

180 Purushotham, 'Internal Violence', (n 165) 443–446.

181 Raghavan, *War and Peace in Modern India*, (n 171) 96; and Noorani, *The Destruction of Hyderabad*, (n 160) 195.

182 One view of the dramatic negotiations can be found in Alan Campbell-Johnson, *Mission with Mountbatten* (New York: E. P. Dutton & Co., 1953), 343–350.

183 Appendix III: Heads of Agreement, *White Paper on Hyderabad* (1948), 48–49.

between Hyderabad and India until a plebiscite was conducted to determine the wishes of the people on the state's future.[184] References to internal political reform and the demand for a constituent assembly for the state were dropped.[185] The clause permitting Hyderabad to maintain relatively independent trade relations with other countries also appeared to be a major victory and was in line with the state's previously unsuccessful attempts to create frameworks of layered sovereignty that would enable it to maintain different types of political relations with a variety of entities including the dominions of India and Pakistan, the Crown, and other foreign states.

Monckton's herculean efforts to persuade the *nizam* to agree to the heads of agreement failed.[186] Instead, the *nizam* wrote to the British prime minister, Clement Attlee, and the American president, Harry Truman, for assistance in resolving the dispute but was rebuffed. When India refused to agree to refer the dispute to arbitration per a clause in the standstill agreement, the *nizam* decided to approach the United Nations.[187] In this legal effort, Walter Monckton, Christopher Brunyate, and John Brunyate, who had advised the state since the federal negotiations, were joined by the high-powered international lawyers Hersch Lauterpacht, Clyde Eagleton, and John Foster.[188] Hyderabadi officials—Mir Nawaz Jung, the agent-general in London; Moin Nawaz Jung, the external affairs minister; and Zahir Ahmed, the secretary to the External Affairs Department—also played significant roles in the process.

The legal team struggled with the mechanics of approaching the UN. Hersch Lauterpacht initially raised doubts about Hyderabad's status as a 'state' and consequently its ability to appeal to the UN; he proposed that Pakistan, an already existing member-state raise the issue as a matter that 'endangers the maintenance of international peace or which may lead to international friction'.[189] Although initially receptive of this plan, state officials reconsidered their position a few weeks later and decided to approach the UN themselves.[190] Lauterpacht then gave written advice that Hyderabad was a state under international law since it possessed 'an independent government exercising normal governmental activities within a

184 Noorani, *The Destruction of Hyderabad*, (n 160) 192.

185 Birkenhead, *Walter Monckton*, (n 172) 249–250.

186 ibid 250–251.

187 Raghavan, *War and Peace in Modern India*, (n 171) 96–97.

188 There were tensions within the legal team, with Christopher Brunyate being sceptical of Lauterpacht's academic outlook towards practical problems. See Letter from Christopher Brunyate to Walter Monckton, 30 August 1948, Dep. Monckton Trustees 33, Monckton Papers; Memo by Christopher Brunyate, 30 August 1948, Dep. Monckton Trustees 33, Monckton Papers; and Elihu Lauterpacht, *The Life of Sir Hersch Lauterpacht* (Cambridge: Cambridge University Press, 2010), 319.

189 Letter from Christopher Brunyate to Walter Monckton, 2 June 1948, Dep. Monckton Trustees 33, Monckton Papers. Lauterpacht also suggested that both Pakistan and Hyderabad approach the UN simultaneously. See Letter from Christopher Brunyate to Walter Monckton, 21 June 1948, Dep. Monckton Trustees 33, Monckton Papers.

190 Letter from Christopher Brunyate to Hersch Lauterpacht, 28 June 1948, Dep. Monckton Trustees 33, Monckton Papers.

defined territory'. Specifically, he argued that Hyderabad had possessed a degree of international personality under British paramountcy since 'original basis of that relationship' was found 'in an international treaty'. On the lapse of the Crown's paramountcy, the state had gained 'complete international sovereignty' because of 'the absence of any legal claim or right on the part of a foreign Power to sovereignty' over it. In such circumstances, 'other states would be under a legal duty to grant . . . recognition' if Hyderabad sought it. Even if recognition was not obtained, Hyderabad still had 'the right to defend its integrity and independence' as recognition was 'purely declaratory of the existing fact of statehood and . . . a community which possesses the requisite condition of statehood is a state regardless of recognition'.[191] After much internal wrangling over which UN organ to approach,[192] the *nizam* telegrammed the president of the Security Council on 21 August 1948 to request that the dispute between Hyderabad and India be brought to the attention of the Council as it was 'likely to endanger the maintenance of international peace and security'.[193]

A detailed memorandum set out the legal basis of Hyderabad's claim to be 'an independent sovereign State'. The state was ruled by the *nizam*, who was advised by a council of ministers, a majority of whom were appointed from elected members of the legislature; the administration controlled a significant amount of territory and exercised 'normal governmental activities' over a large population. The state had 'an independent Judiciary' and 'its own army, police, currency, post and telephones, State-owned railways, and its own State bank'. The memo admitted that Hyderabad had been under British 'suzerainty' till 15 August 1947 but claimed that the relationship was 'in principle those of sovereign States' except for 'the exclusive right of the British Crown to represent Hyderabad in the field of foreign affairs' and 'the wide and overriding powers derived from so-called Paramountcy, the extent of which was a matter of dispute'. Relying on Henry Maine, the memo asserted that Hyderabad possessed 'a certain international status'. It also cited Frederick Pollock to argue that 'the analogy of international law might be found useful and persuasive' for interpreting relations between Britain and the states in 'doubtful' cases. Paramountcy, the memo insisted, only provided a 'residuary power of intervention' that was exercised 'in exceptional cases' and so was not 'a serious derogation from statehood'. In any case, paramountcy had ended on 15 August 1947 since the British government had repeatedly stated that paramountcy would not be transferred

[191] Lauterpacht's summary argument, 13 July 1948, Dep. Monckton Trustees 33, Monckton Papers.

[192] See Letter from Christopher Brunyate to Walter Monckton, 2 June 1948, Dep. Monckton Trustees 33, Monckton Papers; Letter from Christopher Brunyate to Walter Monckton, 21 June 1948, Dep. Monckton Trustees 33, Monckton Papers; Letter from Christopher Brunyate to Hersch Lauterpacht, 28 June 1948, Dep. Monckton Trustees 33, Monckton Papers; Note by Hersch Lauterpacht, 14 August 1948, Dep. Monckton Trustees 33, Monckton Papers; and Letter from Christopher Brunyate to Zahir Ahmed, 21 August 1948, Dep. Monckton Trustees 33, Monckton Papers.

[193] Cablegram from the Hyderabad Government to the President of the Security Council, 21 August 1948, S/986, https://digitallibrary.un.org/record/470967?ln=en, accessed 15 February 2022.

to a successor government of independent India. Consequently, Hyderabad had 'assumed—or resumed—the position of an independent sovereign State'.[194]

The dominion of India, the memo alleged, aimed 'to deny to Hyderabad that independence of status and of choice to which it is entitled by international law, and to coerce it into becoming part of the Dominion of India by way of accession'. Hyderabad's constructive proposals for creating a relationship with India 'short of accession and of renunciation of its independence' had been repeatedly rebuffed. Instead, India had 'violated the Standstill Agreement both by disregarding its essential clauses and by pursuing a general policy of unfriendliness, intimidation and overt aggression contrary to the spirit and the purpose of the Agreement'. Hyderabad's repeated requests to refer disputes to arbitration had been rejected by the Indian government, which was instead 'determined to pursue a policy, planned and systematic, of dictation and coercion in order to bring to an end the independence of Hyderabad'. India's actions included 'threatening statements of leading Indian politicians and an assiduously fostered propaganda in the press and on the wireless; ... encouragement, by connivance or active participation, of border incidents and actual invasions of Hyderabad territory ... and ... a ruthless economic blockade'. All these actions, the memo argued, constituted a violation of Article 2(4) of the UN Charter that prohibited the use of force or of threats of the use of force against the territorial integrity and political independence of any state.[195]

On 13 September, before the complaint was put on the Security Council's agenda, Indian troops invaded Hyderabad.[196] A press communiqué justified military action to restore 'law and order in the State' after Hyderabad's refusal to disband the Razakars.[197] The Security Council started discussion of the situation on 16 September. Moin Nawaz Jung, Hyderabad's representative, accused India of committing 'an act of aggression by invading the independent State of Hyderabad' in order 'to coerce the Government of Hyderabad to renounce the independence of its country and make it, politically and internationally, part of India'. India's justification of the invasion, he noted, was implausible since the standstill agreement prohibited India from sending troops into Hyderabad to maintain internal order. He also dismissed the assertion that the matter was within India's domestic jurisdiction; that claim could only be sustained if 'India has already annexed Hyderabad and that the territory of Hyderabad has become part of India'. He contended that Hyderabad met all international law requirements of statehood and buttressed his claim by relying on British government statements that 'we have regained complete sovereignty and that technically and legally we are independent'. He also

[194] *The Complaint of Hyderabad*, (n 162) 5–7.
[195] ibid 7–11, 13, 17.
[196] Official Indian histories have duplicitously referred to the invasion as a 'police action'. See the official Ministry of Defence publication, S. N. Prasad, *Operation Polo: The Police Action Against Hyderabad, 1948* (Delhi: Historical Section, Ministry of Defence, Government of India, 1972).
[197] Noorani, *The Destruction of Hyderabad*, (n 160) 199–200.

maintained that Hyderabad was 'ready to put forward constructive proposals for a general settlement' if hostilities were ended. However, 'the continued maintenance of the independence of Hyderabad, within the framework of the most integrated co-operation with India' was 'not only its legal right but its absolute moral duty to the people of Hyderabad'.[198] Despite claiming 'independence' then, the state of Hyderabad continued to envisage a close political relationship with the dominion of India, with each entity exercising different types of sovereign powers. Hyderabad's vision for the political future, therefore, was articulated through the language of divisible sovereignty that would enable it to have a profitable association with India alongside state autonomy to pursue other external relationships.

The Indian representative Ramaswami Mudaliar responded to Moin Nawaz Jung by stating that in India's view, 'Hyderabad is not competent to bring any question before the Security Council; that it is not a State; that it is not independent'. Any allegations relating to the Indian invasion were, in his view, completely irrelevant to Hyderabad's legal status on 21 August, the date that it had made the application to the Security Council. After Mudaliar sought time to publish documents supporting his argument, the matter was adjourned till 20 September.[199] Since the invasion had already begun, the Hyderabad delegation pressed for immediate action, with Mir Laik Ali later claiming that Alexander Cadogan, the British diplomat serving as the president of the Security Council, agreed to convene a special session on 18 September.[200]

Faced with a massacre of the local Muslim population,[201] the *nizam* announced a ceasefire on 17 September, with his troops surrendering to the Indian army.[202] When the Security Council reconvened on 20 September, Zahir Ahmed insisted that the delegation had not received any official instructions from the *nizam*. Mudaliar, on the other hand, claimed that he had received a telegram from the

[198] United Nations, Security Council, Official Records, 3rd year, 357th Meeting, S/PV.357, 16 September 1948, 12, 14–15, 17–18, https://undocs.org/en/S/PV.357, accessed 15 February 2022.

[199] ibid 18–19, 21–22.

[200] Mir Laik Ali, *Tragedy of Hyderabad* (Karachi: Pakistan Co-operative Book Society Ltd., 1962), 300.

[201] Indian troops either engaged in or at least permitted atrocities to be carried out against local Muslims during and after the invasion. Estimates of the number of Muslims who died range from 50,000 to 200,000. There were also allegations of Hindu mobs engaging in the widespread looting of Muslim households and businesses, the abduction and rape of Muslim women, and forced conversions. See Smith, 'Hyderabad: Muslim Tragedy', (n 170) 27–51; Noorani, *The Destruction of Hyderabad*, (n 160) 221–246; and Purushotham, 'Internal Violence', (n 165) 450–463. A goodwill mission sent to Hyderabad at Nehru's instance confirmed accounts of the massacre of Muslims, but Patel disavowed the contents of its report, which was never published. Omar Khalidi, a Hyderabadi scholar, obtained what he claimed were fragments of the report and published them as part of a collection of essays. See Pandit Sundarlal and Qazi Muhammad Abdulghaffar, 'A Report on the Post-Operation Polo Massacres, Rape and Destruction or Seizure of Property in Hyderabad State', in Omar Khalidi, ed., *Hyderabad: After the Fall* (Wichita, KN: Hyderabad Historical Society, 1988), 95–115. A. G. Noorani, however, has argued that these fragments are inaccurate. See A. G. Noorani, 'Of a Massacre Untold', *Frontline* (3 March 2001), https://frontline.thehindu.com/other/article30159646.ece, accessed 22 June 2022. A full copy of the report and some confidential notes attached to it are included as appendices 14 and 15 of Noorani, *The Destruction of Hyderabad* (n 160).

[202] Noorani, *The Destruction of Hyderabad*, (n 160) 211.

Indian agent-general at Hyderabad who sought to pass on a message from the *nizam* asking the Hyderabad delegation to withdraw the case from the Security Council. Mudaliar maintained that the withdrawal had been done before the Indian army reached Hyderabad's capital rather than under any pressure from India, an assertion that the Argentinian and Colombian delegates found hard to believe.[203]

The *nizam*'s alleged missive caused unrest within the Hyderabad legal team. Christopher Brunyate, John Foster, and Walter Monckton considered the *nizam* to be their client and wanted to follow his directions to withdraw the appeal. Hersch Lauterpacht wanted to continue advising Zahir Ahmed and Moin Nawaz Jung.[204] These internal rivalries did not have much longer to play out. On 22 September, the *nizam* notified the Security Council that the delegation had ceased to have any authority to represent either him or the state of Hyderabad before the UN.[205] At the next Security Council session, the Syrian, Colombian, and Argentinian delegates questioned the genuineness of the *nizam*'s communication and sought to send representatives to Hyderabad to ascertain the truth; this proposal never came to fruition.[206] Hyderabad's representatives were never heard on the matter again, but on 6 October, Pakistan requested permission to participate in the discussion,[207] which was granted on 15 December.[208]

The matter was finally discussed at a Security Council session in May 1949 where India was represented by B. N. Rau and Pakistan by Mohammed Zafrullah Khan. Rau defended India's military action in Hyderabad as a necessity in the face of the lawlessness of the Razakars, which he described as 'a fascist clique which had usurped power and was misusing it in a manner that threatened the tranquility of India as well as Hyderabad itself'. The *nizam*, he claimed, had withdrawn the UN petition as soon as the Razakars had lost power and the future relationship of Hyderabad and India was being decided by the people of the state. Rau also maintained that Hyderabad had 'never been a State in the international sense' and so could not be considered 'competent to appeal to the Security Council'. Hyderabad had never been recognized as an independent state; even the United Kingdom, per a July 1947 statement by Hartley Shawcross, the British delegate to the United

[203] United Nations, Security Council, Official Records, 3rd year, 359th Meeting, S/PV.359, 20 September 1948, 2–3, 7–10, https://undocs.org/en/S/PV.359, accessed 15 February 2022. Mir Laik Ali claimed that the radio address in which the *nizam* referred to the withdrawal of the petition from the Security Council had been drafted by K. M. Munshi. See Laik Ali, *Tragedy of Hyderabad*, (n 200) 306.

[204] Lauterpacht, *The Life of Sir Hersch Lauterpacht*, (n 188) 320–322.

[205] Cablegram from the *nizam* of Hyderabad to the United Nations, 22 September 1948, S/1011, https://digitallibrary.un.org/record/470279?ln=en, accessed 15 February 2022.

[206] United Nations, Security Council, Official Records, 3rd year, 360th Meeting, S/PV.360, 28 September 1948, 3–29, https://undocs.org/en/S/PV.360, accessed 15 February 2022.

[207] Letter from the Minister of Foreign Affairs of Pakistan to the President of the Security Council, 6 October 1948, S/1027, https://digitallibrary.un.org/record/648116?ln=en, accessed 15 February 2022.

[208] United Nations, Security Council, Official Records, 3rd year, 384th Meeting, S/PV.384, 15 December 1948, 41–42, https://undocs.org/en/S/PV.384, accessed 15 February 2022.

Nations, had refused to recognize the princely states 'as separate international entities'. Starting November 1947, there had also been a standstill agreement under which India had exclusive charge of Hyderabad's foreign affairs.[209]

Rau then invoked a territorially unified vision of India to bolster his case, pointing out that Hyderabad was 'in the heart of India' and so 'India cannot possibly recognize any of these Indian States lying within its borders as independent, any more than the United States of America can allow the independence of its southern states'. India, he repeated, 'cannot possibly agree to be dismembered or disintegrated by allowing any of these Indian States to claim international statehood'. Hyderabad, he asserted, 'was not a State in the international sense before the Indian Independence Act; it is not one now by virtue of the standstill agreement and the arrangements that followed it; and it cannot be one at any time in the future if India is to live. We cannot defy or ignore geography'. Based on this territorial conceptualization of the nation-state of India, Rau argued that it was obvious 'that any dispute with Hyderabad is not an international dispute. All matters relating to Hyderabad are now dealt with regularly by the Government of India as matters of domestic concern'. Since the issue was 'wholly within the domestic jurisdiction of India' rather than being of 'an international character', there was little useful purpose in it remaining before the Security Council.[210]

In response, Zafrullah Khan described India's military action as 'entirely unjustified', a 'breach of international peace', and 'a continuation of aggression which calls for redress'. Although he conceded that Hyderabad's foreign relations had been conducted by the British, he maintained that paramountcy ended when princely treaties were terminated. He referred to statements by several British officials to underline the claim that although the United Kingdom had hoped for the states to accede to either India or Pakistan, those states that did not do so, i.e., states like Hyderabad, were free to be independent. He also rejected the argument that the Hyderabad case was a domestic matter since 'the mere fact that its independence has been destroyed does not make the dispute a domestic matter for India'. Indian military action constituted, in his view, an act of aggression against an independent state and was a breach of international peace.[211] He described allegations of violence against Muslims after the invasion and urged the Council to take action to stop such persecution and organize a plebiscite to determine Hyderabad's future. In response to this impassioned submission, the Council's president simply thanked Zafrullah Khan and stated that he was 'sure that the members of the Council will keep this information in mind'.[212] Even the Argentinian and Egyptian

[209] United Nations, Security Council, Official Records, 4th year, 425th Meeting, S/PV.425, 19 May 1949, 2, 5–6, https://undocs.org/en/S/PV.425, accessed 15 February 2022.

[210] ibid 6–7. See also Letter from the Representative of India to the President of the Security Council, 18 May 1949, S/1324, https://digitallibrary.un.org/record/471674?ln=en, accessed 15 February 2022.

[211] ibid 8–10, 14–15.

[212] United Nations, Security Council, Official Records, 4th year, 426th Meeting, S/PV.426, 24 May 1949, 12–19, 28–31, https://undocs.org/en/S/PV.426, accessed 15 February 2022.

delegates, who had earlier been invested in supporting the Hyderabadi cause, remained silent.[213]

Despite being the subject of warring commentaries in the *American Journal of International Law*,[214] the Hyderabad matter slowly faded from world memory,[215] leaving Indian officials free to weld the state into the Indian union. In November 1949, the *nizam* issued a *firman* declaring that the Indian constitution would also apply to Hyderabad; this was considered equivalent to the signing of an instrument of accession, completing the process of amalgamating Hyderabad into India.[216]

The Hyderabad case exemplifies the politics surrounding the ability to approach international institutions and thereby the struggle over claims of being an international law subject itself. Early in his consultations with Hyderabad officials, Hersch Lauterpacht advised them not to bother building a legal case on Hyderabad's international status as a state since '[i]f there is a disposition on the part of the members of the Security Council or of the General Assembly to assist Hyderabad and to restrain India, then they will have no difficulty in finding that we are a State. If the tendency is the other way, then they may shield themselves behind the finding that we are not a state.'[217] This view turned out to be prescient when most Security Council members decided to place good relations with India above any concerns about the military invasion of Hyderabad.

Quite apart from indicating the political significance of statehood, scholars have recognized that the Hyderabad dispute was also a key moment for statemaking. Sunil Purushotham focuses on the role played by violence in the process of incorporating Hyderabad into Indian territory to argue that such crises were 'constitutive events through which a new state and the regime of sovereignty emerged'.[218] Taylor Sherman uses the case to trace the multiple strategies that Indian administrators used to manage relations between Hindus and Muslims and suppress a communist rebellion.[219] As the debates before the Security Council demonstrate, the role of violence, which has been carefully documented by scholars, was supplemented by legal arguments. In particular, the Hyderabad

[213] Noorani, *The Destruction of Hyderabad*, (n 160) 265.

[214] See Taraknath Das, 'The Status of Hyderabad During and After British Rule in India', *American Journal of International Law*, 43/1 (1949), 57–72; and Clyde Eagleton, 'The Case of Hyderabad Before the Security Council', *American Journal of International Law*, 44/2 (1950), 277–302.

[215] Even though the issue was last considered in 1949, Pakistan's permanent representative to the United Nations writes to the president of the Security Council every year to retain the 'Hyderabad question' on the list of matters of which the Security Council is seized. The latest communication is Letter from the Permanent Representative of Pakistan to the United Nations to the President of the Security Council, 1 January 2023, S/2023/5, https://digitallibrary.un.org/record/3999365?ln=en, accessed 8 March 2023.

[216] Zubaida Yazdani, 'The End of an Era', in *Hyderabad: After the Fall*, (n 201) 90–94.

[217] Lauterpacht's advice, 5 July 1948, Dep. Monckton Trustees 33, Monckton Papers.

[218] Purushotham, 'Internal Violence', (n 165) 435.

[219] Taylor C. Sherman, 'The Integration of the Princely State of Hyderabad and the Making of the Postcolonial State in India, 1948–56', *The Indian Economic and Social History Review*, 44/4 (2007), 489–516.

controversy demonstrates the significance of the legal idea of territorial sovereignty in the shaping of state space.

Throughout the negotiations to settle the dispute and in their arguments before the Security Council, Hyderabad and India put forth differing visions for South Asia's future, which were predicated on distinct conceptualizations of sovereignty. Hyderabadi officials resisted accession to India by claiming that the state was 'sovereign' and 'independent' after the lapse of British paramountcy. They simultaneously affirmed that the state was willing to negotiate alternative political arrangements to maintain its autonomous status while cooperating with the Indian dominion on matters of common concern. These arguments mirrored those made by the states more generally during the federal debates, during which Hyderabad had been particularly ambivalent about forging close relations with British India at the expense of its autonomy and its link with the Crown. At the heart of Hyderabad's legal case was the idea that sovereignty was divisible: by dividing the exercise of sovereign powers among the Indian and Hyderabadi governments, state advisors aimed to preserve the largest possible measure of state autonomy, including the ability to engage in trade relations with other states and collaborate with Indian authorities only on issues of common concern.

Indian officials, on the other hand, repeatedly articulated a version of sovereignty that privileged the absolute and exclusive control of defined territory. The exercise of centralized control over resources that was necessary for the pursuit of economic development required the consolidation of territory, leaving no space for the existence of semi-autonomous entities such as Hyderabad within territory claimed by India. Consequently, Ramaswami Mudaliar claimed that the invasion of Hyderabad by the Indian army was not an invasion but action to preserve 'law and order', which was within the 'domestic jurisdiction' of India rather than being a matter of 'international concern'. In the aftermath of the chaos and violence of partition, and with the vision of centralized economic planning in mind, it was the articulation of the legal idea of territorial sovereignty during an international dispute that created the notion of a uniform state space and formed the basis of the Indian nation-state.

Conclusion

The emergence of the territorially sovereign nation-state as the established form of political and economic organization in the world was mediated by a variety of historical, social, and cultural factors. Ideas of economic development were particularly influential since a defining trait of anticolonial nationalism was the promise of post-independence progress, which, for many Indian elites, demanded economic planning and a centralized state. Effective planning, however, also required consolidated territory, which the landscape of South Asia, with its maze of legally differentiated territories, did not readily offer. This integrated state space, i.e., the Indian nation-state, did not appear fully formed after independence and partition; it had to be created. Legal ideas such as a specific version of sovereignty that focused on the exclusive control over territory played a key role in the construction of the spatial unity forming the nation-state of India.

Although the concept of sovereignty was not a particularly significant concern for international lawyers in the 1940s, it remained central to debates over decolonization. Given the importance of the princely states in previous debates over the structures of sovereignty in South Asia, it is unsurprising that they remained crucial to the process of postcolonial nation-building. There was, however, a change in those with whom the princes and their advisors debated and negotiated. In earlier years, British officials had been the key constituency with whom the princely states had argued over their legal status. Although anticolonial nationalism played a role in shaping the princes' arguments, they rarely negotiated directly with British Indian politicians. In the years before Indian independence and partition, however, the princes were increasingly pressed to engage directly with political leaders from the Congress and the Muslim League to determine their future in the region.

The princes and the anticolonial nationalists, particularly those belonging to the Congress, differed greatly on what postcolonial South Asia ought to look like. All of them, however, relied on the language of sovereignty to construct these different visions, with their legal arguments being shaped by their political aims and aspirations. Politicians like Jawaharlal Nehru opposed what they saw as the 'Balkanization' of the subcontinent, fearing that a fragmentation of the political system 'would prevent a powerful centre from determining India's profile in the world at large'.[220] Consequently, they relied on the idea of territorial sovereignty to lay the foundations of a centralized nation-state that would exert governmental authority over clearly demarcated territory. By defining sovereignty as territorial and exclusive, Indian politicians and bureaucrats fashioned a distinctively 'national' economic and political space within which the state would exercise control over all persons and resources. The nation's external form was, therefore, closely linked with internal political and economic structures. The princes, on the other hand, continued to define sovereignty as divisible, much as they had during the federal debates. They hoped that this conceptualization of sovereignty would allow for the establishment of political frameworks that would enable the states to simultaneously maintain their autonomy and construct politically and economically beneficial relationships with the new dominions of India and Pakistan as well as the British Crown.

These alternative definitions of sovereignty were repeatedly articulated during negotiations over Indian independence and came to a head in the Hyderabad case

[220] Banerjee-Dube, *A History of Modern India*, (n 62) 456.

before the United Nations. Sovereignty, therefore, was important both for the failed attempt to establish a confederal framework that divided sovereign powers among different entities and for the successful spatialization of the nation, i.e., the construction of the territorially sovereign Indian nation-state. By exploring the assertion of different definitions of sovereignty during the decade of decolonization in South Asia, we can see the key creative role played by law and legal ideas in the construction of the postcolonial order.

Copyright Note

Chapter Seven
Epilogue

In the classic Bollywood thriller *Jewel Thief*, the debonair Dev Anand plays a man pursuing the leader of a gang of thieves from Bombay to the group's hideout in Gangtok in the state of Sikkim. His police commissioner father, played by Nazir Hussain, muses over the thief's cunning and knowledge that 'our police can't do anything there'; he vows to get the Indian government to put pressure on Sikkim to help.[1] His appeals work; the police turn up in the final scenes of the film, but the dialogue bothered me for longer than I care to admit. Why exactly could the Indian police not do anything in Sikkim? Although the issue initially appeared to me to be a legal puzzle about the extent of police jurisdiction in a quasi-federal system, the solution was simple. I had forgotten that the film's release date—1967—was several years prior to Sikkim's annexation by India in 1975.

Before the annexation, the relationship between India and Sikkim had been complex. Through a series of nineteenth-century treaties, the Himalayan states of Nepal, Bhutan, and Sikkim became a buffer zone between British India and the Chinese and Russian empires. In 1899, the British political officer John Claude White effectively took over the administration of Sikkim from the *chogyal* (ruler) Thutob Namgyal. Although internal autonomy was restored to the *chogyal* Tashi Namgyal two decades later, the legal status of the state was left undefined.[2] The 1909 *Imperial Gazetteer of India* listed Sikkim as a 'native state',[3] and it was often treated as one, although in several instances, the British preferred to leave the situation deliberately ambiguous.[4]

The government of independent India signed a standstill agreement with Sikkim in 1947 but did not insist on accession, unlike in the case of the other princely states. Instead, a 1950 treaty outlined India's responsibility for Sikkim's defence, external affairs, and communications, with the state retaining internal autonomy. However, a later exchange of letters provided for the right of the Indian government to intervene in Sikkim's internal affairs for reasons of 'law and order'.[5]

1 *Jewel Thief*, directed by Vijay Anand (Navketan Films, 1967), 1:38:24, https://www.youtube.com/watch?v=eNpWFPH2g3s, accessed 15 February 2022 (translation my own).

2 Jackie Hiltz, 'Constructing Sikkimese National Identity in the 1960s and 1970s', *Bulletin of Tibetology*, 39/2 (2003), 68; and Alex McKay, 'Indian Structures, Sikkimese Processes: On Being Unprepared for the (Indian) Nation', *Asian Ethnicity*, 22/2 (2021), 273.

3 *The Imperial Gazetteer of India*: iv: *The Indian Empire, Administrative* (Oxford: Clarendon Press, 1909), 98.

4 McKay, 'Indian Structures, Sikkimese Processes', (n 2) 273; and Leo E. Rose, 'India and Sikkim: Redefining the Relationship', *Pacific Affairs*, 42/1 (1969), 32.

5 Hiltz, 'Constructing Sikkimese National Identity in the 1960s and 1970s', (n 2) 70.

Sovereignty, International Law, and the Princely States of Colonial South Asia. Priyasha Saksena, Oxford University Press.
 DOI: 10.1093/oso/9780192866585.003.0007

Supplementary arrangements also integrated Sikkim into an effective customs union with India.[6] By the 1960s, there were calls for the revision of the treaty's terms and the *chogyal* Palden Thondup Namgyal expressed the desire for Sikkim to earn 'its "rightful place in the comity of nations"'.[7] This was not to be. In April 1975, two years after popular demonstrations against the undemocratic rule of the *chogyal*, Indian troops entered Gangtok. The *chogyal* was deposed and a heavily disputed referendum backed accession to India.[8]

Sikkim's fate is a reminder of the constructed nature of Indian territory and how the creation of this unified state space continued long after the supposed 'integration' of the princely states into India. In 1951, the French territory of Chandernagore was ceded to India after locals voted overwhelmingly for merger with India. Referendums were also supposed to be held in the territories of Pondicherry, Karaikal, Mahe, and Yanam but these plans were abandoned when India and France failed to agree on the modalities of the vote. Local councils then voted to merge with India without a referendum and France made a *de facto* transfer of administration in 1954, with the cession of formal sovereignty coming in 1956.[9] Although Indian leaders were keen to portray these mergers as 'natural' outcomes, Akhila Yechury has described the uncertainty of the period in which the peoples of these French territories worked their way through multiple options for decolonization.[10] There were also similar debates in relation to the Portuguese territories, Dadra and Nagar Haveli, and Goa and Daman and Diu, which were annexed in 1954 and 1961 respectively.[11] Sikkim was effectively the last piece of the puzzle, although some 'anomalies' remained along the India-Bangladesh border, where both states had enclaves within each other's territory; this situation lasted till the 1974 Land Boundary Agreement was ratified in 2015 to swap the enclaves.[12]

The language of territorial sovereignty underwrote all these moves in the independent Indian government's long quest to create a unified state space that could

[6] Rose, 'India and Sikkim', (n 4) 33–35.

[7] Hiltz, 'Constructing Sikkimese National Identity in the 1960s and 1970s', (n 2) 80.

[8] McKay, 'Indian Structures, Sikkimese Processes', (n 2) 273. For an overview of the complicated politics around the annexation of Sikkim, see Sunaina Kumar, 'Kingdom', *Fifty Two* (16 October 2020), https://fiftytwo.in/story/kingdom/, accessed 15 February 2022.

[9] Jamie Trinidad, *Self-Determination in Disputed Colonial Territories* (Cambridge: Cambridge University Press, 2018), 179–186.

[10] Akhila Yechury, 'Imagining India, Decolonizing *L'Inde Française*, c. 1947–1954', *The Historical Journal*, 58/4 (2015), 1141–1165.

[11] See Quincy Wright, 'The Goa Incident', *American Journal of International Law*, 56/3 (1962), 617–632; and M. N. Pearson, *The Portuguese in India* (Cambridge: Cambridge University Press, 1988), 144–162.

[12] Willem van Schendel, 'Stateless in South Asia: The Making of the India-Bangladesh Enclaves', *Journal of Asian Studies*, 61/1 (2002), 115–147. See also Agreement Between India and Bangladesh Concerning the Demarcation of the Land Boundary between India and Bangladesh and Related Matters, 16 May 1974, https://www.mea.gov.in/Portal/LegalTreatiesDoc/BG74B2547.pdf, accessed 15 February 2022; and Protocol for Exchange of Instruments of Ratification Regarding the India-Bangladesh Land Boundary Agreement, 1974 and Protocol of 2011 to the Land Boundary Agreement, 6 June 2015, https://hcidhaka.gov.in/pdf/PR-II.pdf, accessed 15 February 2022.

form the base for economic self-sufficiency and development. By linking sovereignty with territory, the government of India redefined these areas as constituting the 'domestic' space of the nation, excluding them from the international sphere, and enabling the exercise of governmental authority over them. The Indian constitution, drafted in the aftermath of the terrifying violence of partition,[13] further cemented the fashioning of a strong, centralized postcolonial nation-state, which, as Gyan Prakash argues, also laid the foundation for the suspension of rights during the declaration of an emergency by Indira Gandhi in 1975.[14] The often-violent process of territorializing the nation also had other long-lasting consequences, including on the nature of citizenship. As the importance of consolidated national territory grew, the difference between 'inside' and 'outside' became sharper, with borders becoming ever more significant in defining the nation and creating the problem of the position of minorities within the state.[15] Although India's constitution drafters considered the grant of citizenship based on birth within Indian territory to be 'enlightened' and 'modern',[16] specific groups within the borders of the new state were quickly defined as 'minority' communities and cast as 'aliens' and 'outsiders', even if they had resided in India for long periods of time.[17]

Despite the attempts to create a unified state space, the independent Indian government's espousal of the territoriality of sovereignty was under constant pressure. Elite imaginings of territorial sovereignty had little space to account for 'the complexity of borderland identities'.[18] One significant challenge was the enormous influx of refugees after partition, most of whom had no links with the territory of

[13] On the human cost of partition, see Ritu Menon and Kamala Bhasin, *Borders and Boundaries: Women in India's Partition* (New Delhi: Kali for Women, 1998); Urvashi Butalia, *The Other Side of Silence: Voices from the Partition of India* (Durham, NC: Duke University Press, 2000); Gyanendra Pandey, *Remembering Partition: Violence, Nationalism and History in India* (Cambridge: Cambridge University Press, 2001); Joya Chatterji, *The Spoils of Partition: Bengal and India, 1947–1967* (Cambridge: Cambridge University Press, 2007); Yasmin Khan, *The Great Partition: The Making of India and Pakistan* (New Haven, CT: Yale University Press, 2007); Vazira Fazila-Yacoobali Zamindar, *The Long Partition and the Making of Modern South Asia: Refugees, Boundaries, Histories* (New York, NY: Columbia University Press, 2007); and Neeti Nair, *Changing Homelands: Hindu Politics and the Partition of India* (Cambridge, MA: Harvard University Press, 2011).

[14] Gyan Prakash, *Emergency Chronicles: Indira Gandhi and Democracy's Turning Point* (Princeton, NJ: Princeton University Press, 2019).

[15] Antony Anghie, 'Bandung and the Origins of Third World Sovereignty', in Luis Eslava, Michael Fakhri, and Vasuki Nesiah, eds., *Bandung, Global History, and International Law: Critical Pasts and Pending Futures* (Cambridge: Cambridge University Press, 2017), 551.

[16] Niraja Gopal Jayal, 'Citizenship', in Sujit Choudhry, Madhav Khosla, and Pratap Bhanu Mehta, eds., *The Oxford Handbook of the Indian Constitution* (Oxford: Oxford University Press, 2016), 166.

[17] Itty Abraham, *How India Became Territorial: Foreign Policy, Diaspora, Geopolitics* (Stanford, CA: Stanford University Press, 2014), 69; and Niraja Gopal Jayal, *Citizenship and its Discontents: An Indian History* (Cambridge, MA: Harvard University Press, 2013), 53–56. For more on the relationship between territoriality and citizenship in the South Asian context, see Uditi Sen, *Citizen Refugee: Forging the Indian Nation after Partition* (Cambridge: Cambridge University Press, 2018); and Ornit Shani, *How India Became Democratic: Citizenship and the Making of the Universal Franchise* (Cambridge: Cambridge University Press, 2018).

[18] Elisabeth Leake and Daniel Haines, 'Lines of (In)Convenience: Sovereignty and Border-Making in Postcolonial South Asia, 1947–1965', *The Journal of Asian Studies*, 76/4 (2017), 970–971.

what became India. In response, constitution drafters provided for citizenship to persons who had migrated to India from what had become the state of Pakistan.[19] Another difficulty was posed by the decision to not bestow citizenship to persons of South Asian descent who resided in other countries. Although official state rhetoric effectively abandoned the diaspora who nationalists had courted during the struggle against colonialism,[20] India continued to engage in negotiations with other governments on behalf of overseas Indians even if they were not citizens, complicating the picture on the practices of sovereignty in the postcolonial state.[21]

The former princely states also presented challenges to Indian attempts to classify them as solely domestic concerns. Despite their erasure as separate political entities, the states' erstwhile locations remain productive spaces for movements demanding provincial status within the nation as well as for organized leftwing insurgencies that manage to control spaces unhindered by state control.[22] More significantly, some former states have provided the ground for subnational movements to challenge the Indian state's claims of territorial sovereignty. One prominent campaign involves the Naga people who, during colonial times, were spread across the princely state of Manipur as well as the British territories of Assam, the Naga Hills (an 'excluded area' administered by the governor of Assam), and Burma.[23] The Naga National Council had opposed joining India in 1947 but was overruled by British officials who attached the Naga people to the state of Assam. The Indian government and the Council later disagreed over whether a negotiated agreement provided for the right of the Nagas to claim independence or just more autonomy within India. Some within the Naga movement took up arms and the Indian army was sent to suppress the insurgency, resulting in a violent conflict. A political solution drawn up in 1963 involved carving out the new state of Nagaland from Assam but lying within the Indian union.[24] However, hostilities persisted since many Nagas did not consider the creation of the state to be a complete resolution of their demands.[25] Naga advocates sought international support and were often treated with suspicion by Indian politicians who, as in the Hyderabad case, considered the dispute to be 'an Indian concern, not an international issue'.[26] Much like the

[19] Although the constitution was welcoming of Muslim refugees on paper, their claims were intensely contested in reality. See Jayal, *Citizenship and its Discontents*, (n 17) 51–81.

[20] Joya Chatterji, 'South Asian Histories of Citizenship', *The Historical Journal*, 55/4 (2012), 1049–1071.

[21] Raphaëlle Khan and Taylor C. Sherman, 'Indians and Overseas Indians in Ceylon and Burma, 1946–1965: Experiments in Post-Imperial Sovereignty', *Modern Asian Studies*, 56/4 (2022), 1153–1182.

[22] Eric Lewis Beverley, 'Old Borderlands: Sovereignty and Autonomy in the Hyderabad Deccan, ca. 1800–2014', *Comparative Studies of South Asia, Africa and the Middle East*, 40/3 (2020), 454–467.

[23] Lydia Walker, 'Decolonization in the 1960s: On Legitimate and Illegitimate Nationalist Claims-Making', *Past & Present*, 242 (2019), 241.

[24] Elisabeth Leake, 'At the Nation-State's Edge: Centre-Periphery Relations in Post-1947 South Asia', *The Historical Journal*, 59/2 (2016), 517–523.

[25] Elisabeth Leake, 'Where National and International Meet: Borders and Border Regions in Postcolonial India', *The International History Review*, 44/4 (2022), 856–873.

[26] Walker, 'Decolonization in the 1960s', (n 23) 250–251.

princely states had long attempted to do, the Naga movement has also sought to redraw the boundaries between the domestic and the international, seeking to maintain relationships with the Indian union as well as with the wider world. However, discussions over a long-lasting solution have stalled in recent years because of atrocities committed by Indian armed forces in the region and over Naga demands for a separate constitution and flag.[27]

The position of Jammu and Kashmir, which acceded to India amidst deep controversy, is similarly disputed. Although the state was originally granted a distinct position in the union through Article 370 of the Indian constitution,[28] the government of India soon moved to rename Kashmir's head of state and prime minister as governor and chief minister: all signs of the integration of the state into Indian territory and the removal of symbols of autonomy.[29] Tensions have been exacerbated by the decision of the Narendra Modi government to bifurcate the state into two centrally administered territories in 2019. This removal of the special status altogether was accompanied by extensive press crackdowns, the detention of Kashmiri political leaders, and an increase in the already heavy deployment of armed forces in the region.[30] As both the Naga and Kashmir cases demonstrate, the legal position of several parts of what the government of India considers to be its territory remains contentious. The language of sovereignty provides a means for the negotiation of semi-autonomous relationships with the Indian nation-state while also forming the basis of efforts to fully merge these spaces into the union.[31] Long after the 'integration' of the princely states into India, the doctrine of sovereignty continues to play a critical role in demarcating the boundaries between the domestic and the international spheres.

This history of the disputes over the legal status of the princely states has focused on the attempts of elite actors to carve out a space for themselves in the struggle for power and is specific to the South Asian context. However, it can also provide a basis for investigating the broader role that the doctrine of sovereignty has played

[27] For overviews of the complications surrounding efforts to resolve the situation, see Sanjib Baruah, 'Ending India's Naga Conflict: Facts and Fictions in Postcolonial Sovereignty', *Comparative Studies of South Asia, Africa and the Middle East*, 40/3 (2020), 434–443; and Makepeace Sitlhou, 'Accord', *Fifty Two* (27 November 2020), https://fiftytwo.in/story/accord/, accessed 15 February 2022.

[28] See A. G. Noorani, *Article 370: A Constitutional History of Jammu and Kashmir* (Oxford: Oxford University Press, 2011).

[29] Leake and Haines, 'Lines of (In)Convenience', (n 18) 977.

[30] The abrogation was done through the Jammu and Kashmir Reorganisation Act 2019. See Malavika Prasad, 'Downgraded at the Stroke of a Pen', *The Hindu* (8 August 2019), https://www.thehindu.com/opinion/op-ed/downgraded-at-the-stroke-of-a-pen/article28872213.ece, accessed 15 February 2022; Balu G. Nair, 'Abrogation of Article 370: Can the President Act Without the Recommendation of the Constituent Assembly?', *Indian Law Review*, 3/3 (2019), 254–279; Zaid Deva, 'Basic Without Structure?: The Presidential Order of 1954 and the Indo-Jammu & Kashmir Constitutional Relationship', *Indian Law Review*, 4/2 (2020), 163–198; and 'From Domicile to Dominion: India's Settler Colonial Agenda in Kashmir', *Harvard Law Review*, 134/7 (2021), 2530–2551.

[31] Thomas Blom Hansen uses the example of the Nagas to argue that remnants of 'minor' sovereignty from the colonial period are now seen as intransigent obstacles to the postcolonial nation-state. See Thomas Blom Hansen, 'Sovereignty in a Minor Key', *Public Culture*, 33/1 (2021), 41–61.

in political struggles across the British empire and help us to understand processes of domination and resistance in the contemporary world.[32] The model of divisible sovereignty that British colonial officials articulated in the context of the princely states was consciously exported to other parts of the empire, including the Persian Gulf states, the Malay states, Uganda, and northern Nigeria.[33] And the vision of territorial sovereignty that formed the basis of the Indian nation-state was also the foundation for the globalization of the nation-state form in the middle of the twentieth century. It was repeatedly rearticulated at numerous forums, including, most prominently, the Afro-Asian Conference held in Indonesia in 1955, and became the basis for much of the third world's interventions in international law. The absolutist conceptualization of sovereignty formed the basis of the principles of non-interference and territorial integrity, prized by many newly-independent nations in the mid-twentieth century in their efforts to minimize neo-colonial intervention and build a more equitable international order.[34] The consequences of the crystallization of borders and the emphasis on territorial sovereignty across the world have been familiar: stricter citizenship requirements[35] accompanied by struggles for greater autonomy and independence by subnational movements.[36] Much as it did during the colonial period, sovereignty continues to provide a framework within which to articulate concerns and hammer out potential solutions.

As the long history of debates over the legal status of the princely states demonstrates, sovereignty was a concept that gained multiple meanings over time, as a variety of players attempted to use, shape, and reimagine the idea in different ways to give shape to their often-conflicting visions for imperial and global order. Unravelling the complex history of sovereignty in the colonial context then, can help us to understand the history of the various ways in which individuals have considered ordering the world and their relationships with each other. Arguments about sovereignty were and continue to be a reflection of broader discussions over where the realms of the national and the international lie, i.e., they are debates over

[32] On this point, see Sally Engle Merry, 'Review Essay: Law and Colonialism', *Law and Society Review*, 25/4 (1991), 889–922.

[33] See Ian Copland, *The British Raj and the Indian Princes: Paramountcy in Western India, 1857–1930* (Bombay: Orient Longman, 1982), 298; and Michael H. Fisher, *Indirect Rule in India: Residents and the Residency System, 1764–1858* (Delhi: Oxford University Press, 1991), 459.

[34] See Anghie, 'Bandung and the Origins of Third World Sovereignty', (n 15) 535–551.

[35] Although there were restrictions on movement within the British empire, particularly based on race, decolonization and the emergence of new nation-states led to an explosion in interest in controlling the movement of people and ever-stricter regulation of who could become a citizen. See Sunil Amrith, *Migration and Diaspora in Modern Asia* (Cambridge: Cambridge University Press, 2011), 117–150; and Taylor C. Sherman, 'Migration, Citizenship and Belonging in Hyderabad (Deccan), 1946–1956', *Modern Asian Studies*, 45/1 (2011), 81–107.

[36] For the struggle on the recognition of indigenous rights in Asia, see Hiroshi Fukurai, 'Fourth World Approaches to International Law and Asia's Indigenous Struggles and Quests for Recognition under International Law', *Asian Journal of Law and Society*, 5/1 (2018), 221–231. On the artificiality of borders in Africa, see Makau wa Mutua, 'Why Redraw the Map of Africa? A Moral and Legal Inquiry', *Michigan Journal of International Law*, 16/4 (1995), 1113–1176.

the boundaries of the international; tracing this history is, therefore, key to understanding international law itself.

By focusing on the multiple iterations of concepts like sovereignty by a variety of actors over time, we can understand the crucial role played by conflict and struggle in the creation of the legal architecture of the world. As I have argued in this book, the language of sovereignty was all-encompassing; it was used a means to debate and resolve disputes and continues to be a forum for the negotiation of political power even today. Legal forms and practices, therefore, are political products that arise from the contests of clashing social groups, rather than being timeless and neutral arbiters of social and political disputes; hence, they are contingent and capable of being challenged. Conflict was, and remains, a part of the framework; it is the very essence of legal structures. As a result, international law, and the concept of sovereignty in particular, is a field of conflict, a site of struggle.

Bibliography

Archival Material

Asia, Pacific, and Africa Collections, British Library, London
Crown Representative's Records: Indian States Residencies, IOR/R/2
Crown Representative's Records: Political Department Records, IOR/R/1
Official Publications, IOR/V
Political and Secret Department Records, IOR/L/PS
Proceedings and Consultations, IOR/P
Public and Judicial Department Records, IOR/L/PJ
Records of the Board of Commissioners for the Affairs of India, IOR/F
Tej Bahadur Sapru Papers, IOR Neg 4986–5020
Templewood (Sir Samuel Hoare) Collection, Mss Eur E240
William Lee-Warner Papers, Mss Eur F92

Balliol College Archives, Oxford
Walter Monckton Papers

Lamont Library Microforms, Harvard University
William Henderson Wadhams, *The Reminiscences* (1950), Columbia University Oral History Collection

National Archives of India, New Delhi (NAI)
Foreign and Political Department Records

National Archives of India, Bhopal Regional Office (NAI—Bhopal)
Chamber of Princes Section

Nehru Memorial Museum and Library, New Delhi (NMML)
Federal Papers
Mirza Ismail Papers

United Nations Digital Library
General Assembly Records
Security Council Records

Printed Primary Sources

Aitchison, Charles U., ed., *A Collection of Treaties, Engagements and Sanads Relating to India and Neighbouring Countries*, 14 vols (5th edn, Calcutta: Government of India Central Publication Branch, 1929–1933).

Gopal, S., ed., *Selected Works of Jawaharlal Nehru*, 15 vols (New Delhi: Jawaharlal Nehru Memorial Fund, 1972–1982).

Gopal, S., ed., *Selected Works of Jawaharlal Nehru*, 2nd series, 21 vols (New Delhi: Jawaharlal Nehru Memorial Fund, 1984–1997).

Gwyer, Maurice, and A. Appadorai, eds., *Speeches and Documents on the Indian Constitution, 1921–47*, 2 vols (Bombay: Oxford University Press, 1957).
Kaye, John William, ed., *Selections from the Papers of Lord Metcalfe* (London: Smith, Elder, and Co., 1855).
Keith, A. B., ed., *Speeches and Documents on Indian Policy, 1750–1921*, 2 vols (London: Oxford University Press, 1922).
Khosla, Madhav, ed., *Letters for a Nation: From Jawaharlal Nehru to his Chief Ministers, 1947–1963* (New Delhi: Penguin, 2014).
Mansergh, Nicholas, ed., *The Transfer of Power 1942–7*, 12 vols (London: Her Majesty's Stationery Office, 1970–83).
Palat, Madhavan K., ed., *Selected Works of Jawaharlal Nehru*, 2nd series, 42 vols (New Delhi: Jawaharlal Nehru Memorial Fund, 2012–2019).
Parliamentary Papers: Papers Relating to Oude (London: Harrison and Sons, 1856).
Pirzada, Syed Sharifuddin, ed., *Foundations of Pakistan: All-India Muslim League Documents, 1906–1947*, 3 vols (Karachi: National Publishing House, 1969–1970).
Rao, T. Madhava, *Minor Hints: Lectures delivered to the Maharaja Gaekwar, Sayaji Rao* (Bombay: British India Press, 1881).
Sapru, Tej Bahadur, *Responsa: Selected Legal Opinions*, ed., K. N. Raina (Bombay: N. M. Tripathi Private Limited, 1976).
Sever, Adrian, ed., *Documents and Speeches on the Indian Princely States*, 2 vols (Delhi: B. R. Publishing, 1985).
Singh, Bhupinder, *Public Pronouncements by His Highness the Maharaja Dhiraj of Patiala in connection with the Indian States Committee* (London: Spottiswoode, Ballantyne and Co., 1928).
Speeches by Amin-ul-Malik Sir Mirza M. Ismail, 4 vols (Bangalore: Superintendent at the Government Press, 1930–1942).
Speeches by the Earl of Minto, Viceroy and Governor General of India (Calcutta: Superintendent Government Printing, India, 1911).
The Imperial Gazetteer of India, 26 vols (Oxford: Clarendon Press, 1909–1931).
Tupper, Charles Lewis, *Indian Political Practice: A Collection of the Decisions of the Government of India in Political Cases*, 4 vols (Calcutta: Office of the Superintendent of Government Printing, India, 1895; repr., Delhi: B. R. Publishing, 1974).
Zaidi, Z. H., ed., *Quaid-i-Azam Mohammad Ali Jinnah Papers*, 9 vols (Islamabad: Quaid-i-Azam Papers Project, Culture Division, Government of Pakistan, 1993–2003).

Official Publications

Imperial Conference: Summary of Proceedings (1926)
Indian Annual Register (1930)
Indian Annual Register (1932)
Indian Annual Register (1933)
Indian Annual Register (1937)
Indian Annual Register (1938)
Indian Annual Register (1939)
Indian Annual Register (1947)
Proceedings of the Joint Committee on Indian Constitutional Reform, Vol. I (Part I): Report (1934)
Proceedings of the Meetings of the Chamber of Princes (Narendra Mandal) (1930)

Report of the All-Parties Conference (1928)
Report of the Indian States Committee (1929)
White Paper on Hyderabad (1948)
White Paper on Indian States (1950)

Cases

Empress v. *Keshub Mahajan*, [1882] 8 Cal 985
Nabob of Arcot v. *The East India Company*, 29 ER 544
Nabob of Arcot v. *The East India Company*, 29 ER 841
Statham v. *Statham and His Highness the Gaekwar of Baroda*, [1912] P 92
The East India Company v. *Syed Ally*, 19 ER 417
The Ex-Rajah of Coorg (Veer Rajunder Wadeer) v. *The East India Company*, 54 ER 642
The Secretary of State in Council of India v. *Kamachee Boye Sahaba*, 19 ER 388

Constitutions and Statutes

Code of Criminal Procedure 1872
Constitution of India 1950
Elephants' Preservation Act 1879
Foreign Jurisdiction and Extradition Act 1872
Government of India Act 1858
Government of India Act 1919
Government of India Act 1935
Indian Councils Act 1892
Indian Councils Act 1909
Indian Penal Code 1860
Jammu and Kashmir Reorganisation Act 2019
United Kingdom, Interpretation Act 1889

Treaties

Agreement Between India and Bangladesh Concerning the Demarcation of the Land Boundary between India and Bangladesh and Related Matters, 16 May 1974
Covenant of the League of Nations, 1919
Protocol for Exchange of Instruments of Ratification Regarding the India-Bangladesh Land Boundary Agreement, 1974 and Protocol of 2011 to the Land Boundary Agreement, 6 June 2015

Newspapers

Daily Mail
Morning Post
The Daily Telegraph
The Statesman

The Times
The Times of India

Films

Jewel Thief, directed by Vijay Anand (Navketan Films, 1967), https://www.youtube.com/watch?v=eNpWFPH2g3s, accessed 15 February 2022.

Memoirs and Autobiographies

Butler, Richard Austen, *The Art of the Possible* (London: Hamish Hamilton, 1971).
Campbell-Johnson, Alan, *Mission with Mountbatten* (New York: E. P. Dutton & Co., 1953).
Corfield, Conrad, *The Princely India I Knew: From Reading to Mountbatten* (Madras: Indo-British Historical Society, 1975).
Fitze, Kenneth, *Twilight of the Maharajas* (London: John Murray, 1956).
Ismail, Mirza, *My Public Life: Recollections and Reflections* (London: George Allen & Unwin, 1954).
Laik Ali, Mir, *Tragedy of Hyderabad* (Karachi: Pakistan Co-operative Book Society Ltd., 1962).
Lothian, Arthur, *Kingdoms of Yesterday* (London: John Murray, 1951).
Mason, Philip, *A Shaft of Sunlight: Memories of a Varied Life* (London: André Deutsch, 1978).
Minto, Mary, *India, Minto and Morley, 1905–1910* (London: Macmillan and Co., 1934).
Moon, Penderel, *Divide and Quit* (London: Chatto & Windus, 1961).
Panikkar, K. M., *An Autobiography*, trans. K. Krishnamurthy (Madras: Oxford University Press, 1977).
Sarila, Narendra Singh, *Once a Prince of Sarila: Of Palaces and Tiger Hunts, of Nehrus and Mountbattens* (London: I. B. Tauris, 2008).
Schuster, George, *Private Work and Public Causes: A Personal Record, 1881–1978* (Cowbridge: D. Brown and Sons, 1979).
Setalvad, Chimanlal, *Recollections and Reflections: An Autobiography* (Bombay: Padma Publications, 1946).
Sreenivasan, M. A., *Of the Raj, Maharajas and Me* (New Delhi: Ravi Dayal Publisher, 1991).
Templewood, Viscount, *Nine Troubled Years* (London: Collins, 1954).
Wakefield, Edward, *Past Imperative: My Life in India, 1927–1947* (London: Chatto & Windus, 1966).
Wingate, Ronald, *Not in the Limelight* (London: Hutchinson, 1959).

Secondary Sources

Abbott, Nicholas J., 'A Mulk of One's Own: Languages of Sovereignty, Statehood, and Dominion in the Eighteenth-Century "Empire of Hindustan"', *Itinerario*, 44/3 (2021), 474–501.
Abhyankar, G. R., *Problem of Indian States* (Poona: Aryabhushan Press, 1928).
Ablavsky, Gregory, 'Empire States: The Coming of Dual Federalism', *Yale Law Journal*, 128/7 (2019), 1792–1868.

Ablavsky, Gregory, 'Species of Sovereignty: Native Nationhood, the United States, and International Law, 1783–1795', *Journal of American History*, 106/3 (2019), 591–613.

Abraham, Itty, *How India Became Territorial: Foreign Policy, Diaspora, Geopolitics* (Stanford, CA: Stanford University Press, 2014).

Agnew, John, 'The Territorial Trap: The Geographical Assumptions of International Relations Theory', *Review of International Political Economy*, 1/1 (1994), 53–80.

Aitchison, Charles U., *The Native States of India: An Attempt to Elucidate a Few of the Principles which Underlie their Relations with the British Government* (2nd edn, Calcutta: Office of the Superintendent of Government Printing, 1881).

Aiyar, B. V. Kamesvara, *Sir A. Sashiah Shastri, An Indian Statesman: A Biographical Sketch* (Madras: Srinivasa, Varadachari & Co., 1902).

Aiyer, P. S. Sivaswamy, *Indian Constitutional Problems* (Bombay: D. B. Taraporevala Sons & Co., 1928).

Alexandrowicz, C. H., *An Introduction to the History of the Law of Nations in the East Indies (16th, 17th and 18th Centuries)* (Oxford: Clarendon Press, 1967).

Alexandrowicz, C. H., 'Mogul Sovereignty and the Law of Nations', in David Armitage and Jennifer Pitts, eds., *The Law of Nations in Global History* (Oxford: Oxford University Press, 2017), 62–68.

Alexandrowicz, C. H., 'Some Problems in the History of the Law of Nations in Asia', in David Armitage and Jennifer Pitts, eds., *The Law of Nations in Global History* (Oxford: Oxford University Press, 2017), 76–82.

Alvarez, Alejandro, 'The New International Law', *Transactions of the Grotius Society* 15 (1929), 35–51.

Amrith, Sunil, 'Asian Internationalism: Bandung's Echo in a Colonial Metropolis', *Inter-Asia Cultural Studies*, 6/4 (2005), 557–569.

Amrith, Sunil, *Migration and Diaspora in Modern Asia* (Cambridge: Cambridge University Press, 2011).

Amrith, Sunil, *Unruly Waters: How Mountain Rivers and Monsoons Have Shaped South Asia's History* (London: Allen Lane, 2018).

Anand, R. P., *New States and International Law* (New Delhi: Vikas Publications, 1972).

Anderson, Benedict, *Imagined Communities: Reflections on the Origins and Spread of Nationalism* (London: Verso Books, 1983).

Anghie, Antony, 'Bandung and the Origins of Third World Sovereignty', in Luis Eslava, Michael Fakhri, and Vasuki Nesiah, eds., *Bandung, Global History, and International Law: Critical Pasts and Pending Futures* (Cambridge: Cambridge University Press, 2017), 535–551.

Anghie, Antony, 'Colonialism and the Birth of International Institutions: Sovereignty, Economy, and the Mandate System of the League of Nations', *New York University Journal of International Law and Politics*, 34/3 (2002), 513–634.

Anghie, Antony, *Imperialism, Sovereignty and the Making of International Law* (Cambridge: Cambridge University Press, 2005).

Ankit, Rakesh, 'The Accession of Junagadh, 1947–48: Colonial Sovereignty, State Violence and Post-Independence India', *The Indian Economic and Social History Review*, 53/3 (2016), 371–404.

Anonymous, 'From Domicile to Dominion: India's Settler Colonial Agenda in Kashmir', *Harvard Law Review*, 134/7 (2021), 2530–2551.

Anonymous, 'Kazi Shahabuddin', in *Indian Statesmen: Dewans and Prime Ministers of Native States* (Madras: G. A. Natesan & Co., 1927), 225–232.

Anonymous, 'M.A.N. Hydari', in *Eminent Mussalmans* (Madras: G.A. Natesan & Co., 1926), 491–507.

Anonymous, 'Raja Sir T. Madhav Rao', in *Indian Statesmen: Dewans and Prime Ministers of Native States* (Madras: G. A. Natesan & Co., 1927), 193–224.

Appadorai, A., *Dyarchy in Practice* (London: Longmans, Green and Co., 1937).

Armitage, David, *Foundations of Modern International Thought* (Cambridge: Cambridge University Press, 2013).

Ashton, S. R., *British Policy Towards the Indian States, 1905–1939* (London: Curzon Press, 1982).

Astorino, Samuel J., 'The Impact of Sociological Jurisprudence on International Law in the Inter-War Period: The American Experience', *Duquesne Law Review*, 34/2 (1996), 277–298.

Austin, John, *The Province of Jurisprudence Determined* (London: John Murray, 1832).

Balakrishna, H. G., 'Inaugural Address', in Suryanath U. Kamath, ed., *Studies on Dewan Sir Mirza Ismail* (Bangalore: The Mythic Society, 1998), 1–5.

Balasubramaniam, Uma, *Sayajirao Gaekwad III: The Maharaja of Baroda* (New Delhi: Rupa Publications, 2019).

Bandopadhyay, Sekhar, 'Transfer of Power and the Crisis of Dalit Politics in India, 1945–47', *Modern Asian Studies*, 34/4 (2000), 893–942.

Banerjee-Dube, Ishita, *A History of Modern India* (New Delhi: Cambridge University Press, 2015).

Banerjee, Tarashankar, *Sardar K. M. Panikkar: The Profile of a Historian* (Calcutta: Ratna Prakashan, 1977).

Baruah, Sanjib, 'Ending India's Naga Conflict: Facts and Fictions in Postcolonial Sovereignty', *Comparative Studies of South Asia, Africa and the Middle East*, 40/3 (2020), 434–443.

Basu, Narayani, *V. P. Menon: The Unsung Architect of Modern India* (London: Simon & Schuster, 2020).

Basu, Shrabani, *For King and Another Country: Indian Soldiers on the Western Front, 1914–18* (New Delhi: Bloomsbury, 2015).

Bawa, V. K., *The Last Nizam: The Life and Times of Mir Osman Ali Khan* (New Delhi: Penguin, 1991).

Bayly, C. A., *Indian Society and the Making of the British Empire* (Cambridge: Cambridge University Press, 1990).

Becker Lorca, Arnulf, *Mestizo International Law: A Global Intellectual History, 1842–1933* (Cambridge: Cambridge University Press, 2014).

Bednar, Jenna, 'The Political Science of Federalism', *Annual Review of Law and Social Science*, 7 (2011), 269–288.

Beiter, Benjamin, 'Beyond *Medellín*: Reconsidering Federalism Limits on the Treaty Power', *Notre Dame Law Review*, 85/3 (2010), 1163–1196.

Bell, Duncan, *The Idea of Greater Britain: Empire and the Future of World Order, 1860–1900* (Princeton, NJ: Princeton University Press, 2007).

Bell, Duncan, ed., *Victorian Visions of Global Order: Empire and International Relations in Nineteenth-Century Political Thought* (Cambridge: Cambridge University Press, 2007).

Bell, John, 'Wolfgang Friedmann (1907–1972), with an Excursus on Gustav Radbruch (1878–1949)', in Jack Beatson and Reinhard Zimmermann, eds., *Jurists Uprooted: German-Speaking Émigré Lawyers in Twentieth Century Britain* (Oxford: Oxford University Press, 2004), 517–534.

Bellamy, Carla, 'Alternative Kingdoms: Shrines and Sovereignty in Jaora', *Comparative Studies of South Asia, Africa and the Middle East*, 40/3 (2020), 444–453.

Benton, Lauren, *A Search for Sovereignty: Law and Geography in European Empires, 1400–1900* (Cambridge: Cambridge University Press, 2010).

Benton, Lauren, 'Beyond Anachronism: Histories of International Law and Global Legal Politics', *Journal of the History of International Law*, 21/1 (2019), 7–40.

Benton, Lauren, 'Colonial Law and Cultural Difference: Jurisdictional Politics and the Formation of the Colonial State', *Comparative Studies in Society and History*, 41/3 (1999), 566–574.

Benton, Lauren, 'From International Law to Imperial Constitutions: The Problem of Quasi-Sovereignty, 1870–1900', *Law and History Review*, 26/3 (2008), 595–619.

Benton, Lauren, *Law and Colonial Cultures: Legal Regimes in World History, 1400–1900* (Cambridge: Cambridge University Press, 2002).

Benton, Lauren, and Adam Clulow, 'Protection Shopping Among Empires: Suspended Sovereignty in the Cocos-Keeling Islands', *Past & Present*, 257 (2022), 209–247.

Benton, Lauren, and Lisa Ford, *Rage for Order: The British Empire and the Origins of International Law, 1800–1850* (Cambridge, MA: Harvard University Press, 2016).

Benton, Lauren, and Richard J. Ross, eds., *Legal Pluralism and Empires, 1500–1850* (New York, NY: New York University Press, 2013).

Bentwich, Norman, 'Colonial Mandates and Trusteeships', *Transactions of the Grotius Society*, 32 (1946), 121–134.

Bentwich, Norman, *The Mandates System* (London: Longmans, 1930).

Bergmann, Christoph, 'Confluent Territories and Overlapping Sovereignties: Britain's Nineteenth-Century Indian Empire in the Kumaon Himalaya', *Journal of Historical Geography* 51 (2016), 88–98.

Berman, Nathaniel, '"But the Alternative is Despair": European Nationalism and the Modernist Renewal of International Law', *Harvard Law Review*, 106/8 (1993), 1792–1903.

Beverley, Eric Lewis, 'Frontier as Resource: Law, Crime, and Sovereignty on the Margins of Empire', *Comparative Studies in Society and History*, 55/2 (2013), 241–272.

Beverley, Eric Lewis, *Hyderabad, British India, and the World: Muslim Networks and Minor Sovereignty, c. 1850–1950* (Cambridge: Cambridge University Press, 2015).

Beverley, Eric Lewis, 'Old Borderlands: Sovereignty and Autonomy in the Hyderabad Deccan, ca. 1800–2014', *Comparative Studies of South Asia, Africa and the Middle East*, 40/3 (2020), 454–467.

Bhagavan, Manu, 'A New Hope: India, the United Nations and the Making of the Universal Declaration of Human Rights', *Modern Asian Studies*, 44/2 (2010), 311–347.

Bhagavan, Manu, 'Princely States and the Making of Modern India: Internationalism, Constitutionalism and the Postcolonial Moment', *The Indian Economic and Social History Review*, 46/3 (2009), 427–456.

Bhagavan, Manu, *Sovereign Spheres: Princes, Education, and Empire in Colonial India* (Oxford: Oxford University Press, 2003).

Bhagavan, Manu, 'The Hindutva Underground: Hindu Nationalism and the Indian National Congress in Late Colonial and Early Post-Colonial India', *Economic and Political Weekly*, 43/37 (2008), 39–48.

Bhargava, R. P., *The Chamber of Princes* (New Delhi: Northern Book Centre, 1991).

Bhukya, Bhangya, 'The Subordination of the Sovereigns: Colonialism and the Gond Rajas in Central India, 1818–1948', *Modern Asian Studies*, 47/1 (2013), 288–317.

Birkenhead, Lord, *Walter Monckton: The Life of Viscount Monckton of Brenchley* (London: Weidenfeld and Nicolson, 1969).

Bosco, Andrea, 'Lothian, Curtis, Kimber and the Federal Union Movement (1938–1940)', *Journal of Contemporary History*, 23/3 (1988), 465–502.

Bosco, Andrea, *The Round Table Movement and the Fall of the 'Second' British Empire (1909–1919)* (Newcastle: Cambridge Scholars Publishing, 2017).

Bose, S. K., *Tej Bahadur Sapru* (New Delhi: Government of India, Ministry of Information and Broadcasting, Publications Division, 1978).

Bose, Sugata, *A Hundred Horizons: The Indian Ocean in the Age of Global Empire* (Cambridge, MA: Harvard University Press, 2006).

Bose, Sugata, and Ayesha Jalal, *Modern South Asia: History, Culture, Political Economy* (4th edn, London: Routledge, 2018).

Bottomore, Stephen, '"Have You Seen the Gaekwar Bob?": Filming the 1911 Delhi Durbar', *Historical Journal of Film, Radio and Television*, 17/3 (1997), 309–345.

Boyce, George, 'Federalism and the Irish Question', in Andrea Bosco, ed., *The Federal Idea: The History of Federalism from Enlightenment to 1945*, i (London: Lothian Foundation Press, 1991), 119–138.

Bridge, Carl, *Holding India to the Empire: The British Conservative Party and the 1935 Constitution* (New Delhi: Sterling Publishers, 1986).

Brierly, J. L., *The Law of Nations: An Introduction to the International Law of Peace* (2nd edn, Oxford: Clarendon Press, 1936).

Brierly, J. L., 'The Sovereign State Today', in Hersch Lauterpacht and C. H. M. Waldock, eds., *The Basis of Obligation in International Law and Other Papers* (Oxford: Clarendon Press, 1958), 348–357.

Bryce, James, *The American Commonwealth*, 3 vols (London: Macmillan and Co., 1888).

Buckland, Charles Edward, *Dictionary of Indian Biography* (London: Swan Sonnenschem & Co., 1906).

Bührer, Tanja, 'Intercultural Diplomacy at the Court of the Nizam of Hyderabad, 1770–1815', *The International History Review*, 41/5 (2019), 1039–1056.

Burbank, Jane, and Frederick Cooper, *Empires in World History: Power and the Politics of Difference* (Princeton, NJ: Princeton University Press, 2011).

Burgess, Michael, 'The Federal Plan of the Imperial Federation League 1892: Milestone or Tombstone', in Andrea Bosco, ed., *The Federal Idea: The History of Federalism from Enlightenment to 1945*, i (London: Lothian Foundation Press, 1991), 139–154.

Butalia, Urvashi, *The Other Side of Silence: Voices from the Partition of India* (Durham, NC: Duke University Press, 2000).

Butler, Geoffrey, 'Sovereignty and the League of Nations', *British Year Book of International Law*, 1 (1920–1921), 35–44.

Butler, J. R. M., *Lord Lothian, 1882–1940* (London: Macmillan and Co., 1960).

Callahan, Michael D., *Mandates and Empire: The League of Nations and Africa, 1914–1931* (Eastbourne: Sussex Academic Press, 1998).

Campbell, John, *F. E. Smith, First Earl of Birkenhead* (London: Jonathan Cape, 1983).

Cannadine, David, ed., *Oxford Dictionary of National Biography* (online edn, Oxford: Oxford University Press, 2004).

Case, Holly, 'The Strange Politics of Federative Ideas in East-Central Europe', *The Journal of Modern History*, 85/4 (2013), 833–866.

Cassel, Pär Kristoffer, *Grounds of Judgment: Extraterritoriality and Imperial Power in Nineteenth-Century China and Japan* (Oxford: Oxford University Press, 2012).

Cháirez-Garza, Jesús Francisco, '"Bound hand and foot and handed over to the caste Hindus": Ambedkar, Untouchability and the Politics of Partition', *The Indian Economic and Social History Review*, 55/1 (2018), 1–28.

Chakrabarty, Bidyut, 'Jawaharlal Nehru and Planning, 1938–41: India at the Crossroads', *Modern Asian Studies*, 26/2 (1992), 275–287.

Chambers, Ann, *Ranji: Maharaja of Connemara* (Dublin: Wolfhound Press, 2003).
Charlesworth, Hilary, 'International Law: A Discipline of Crisis', *Modern Law Review*, 65/3 (2002), 377–392.
Chatterjee, Partha, *The Black Hole of Empire: History of a Global Practice of Power* (Princeton, NJ: Princeton University Press, 2012).
Chatterjee, Partha, *The Nation and its Fragments: Colonial and Postcolonial Histories* (Princeton, NJ: Princeton University Press, 1993).
Chatterji, Joya, 'Decolonization in South Asia: The Long View', in Martin Thomas and Andrew Thompson, eds., *The Oxford Handbook of the Ends of Empire* (Oxford: Oxford University Press, 2018), 264–265.
Chatterji, Joya, 'South Asian Histories of Citizenship', *The Historical Journal*, 55/4 (2012), 1049–1071.
Chatterji, Joya, 'The Fashioning of a Frontier: The Radcliffe Line and Bengal's Border Landscape, 1947–52', *Modern Asian Studies*, 33/1 (1999), 185–242.
Chatterji, Joya, *The Spoils of Partition: Bengal and India, 1947–1967* (Cambridge: Cambridge University Press, 2007)
Chen, Li, *Chinese Law in Imperial Eyes: Sovereignty, Justice, and Transcultural Politics* (New York, NY: Columbia University Press, 2015).
Chester, Lucy, *Borders and Conflict in South Asia: The Radcliffe Boundary Commission and the Partition of Punjab* (Manchester: Manchester University Press, 2009).
Chopra, K. N., *Law Relating to the Protection of the Administration of States in India* (Lahore: Universal Book Agency, 1939).
Chudgar, P. L., *Indian Princes under British Protection: A Study of their Personal Rule, their Constitutional Position and their Future* (London: Williams & Norgate Ltd., 1929).
Coates, Benjamin Allen, *Legalist Empire: International Law and American Foreign Relations in the Early Twentieth Century* (Oxford: Oxford University Press, 2016).
Coen, Terence Creagh, *The Indian Political Service: A Study in Indirect Rule* (London: Chatto & Windus, 1971).
Coffey, Donal, '"The Right to Shoot Himself": Secession in the British Commonwealth of Nations', *The Journal of Legal History*, 39/2 (2018), 117–139.
Cogan, Jacob Katz, 'A History of International Law in the Vernacular', *Journal of the History of International Law*, 22/2–3 (2020), 205–217.
Collins, Hugh, 'Law as Politics: Progressive American Perspectives', in James Penner, David Schiff, and Richard Nobles, eds., *Introduction to Jurisprudence and Legal Theory: Commentary and Materials* (London: LexisNexis Butterworths, 2002), 279–333.
Collins, Michael, 'Decolonisation and the "Federal Moment"', *Diplomacy and Statecraft*, 24/1 (2013), 21–40.
Collins, Richard, 'Classical Legal Positivism in International Law Revisited', in Jörg Kammerhofer and Jean D'Aspremont, eds., *International Legal Positivism in a Post-Modern World* (Cambridge: Cambridge University Press, 2014), 23–49.
Collins, Richard, 'The Progressive Conception of International Law: Brierly and Lauterpacht in the *Interbellum* Period', in Robert McCorquodale and Jean-Pierre Gauci, eds., *British Influences on International Law, 1915–2015* (Leiden: Brill Nijhoff, 2016), 437–487.
Condos, Mark, 'The Indian "Alsatia": Sovereignty, Extradition, and the Limits of Franco-British Colonial Policing', *The Journal of Imperial and Commonwealth History*, 48/1 (2020), 101–126.
Condos, Mark, and Gavin Rand, 'Coercion and Conciliation at the Edge of Empire: State-Building and its Limits in Waziristan, 1849–1914', *The Historical Journal*, 61/3 (2018), 695–718.

Cooper, Frederick, *Citizenship between Empire and Nation: Remaking France and French Africa, 1945–1960* (Princeton, NJ: Princeton University Press, 2014).

Copland, Ian, '"Communalism" in Princely India: The Case of Hyderabad, 1930–1940', *Modern Asian Studies*, 22/4 (1988), 783–814.

Copland, Ian, *State, Community and Neighbourhood in Princely North India, c. 1900–1950* (Basingstoke: Palgrave Macmillan, 2005).

Copland, Ian, *The British Raj and the Indian Princes: Paramountcy in Western India, 1857–1930* (Bombay: Orient Longman, 1982).

Copland, Ian, 'The Dilemmas of a Ruling Prince: Maharaja Sayaji Rao Gaekwar and "Sedition"', in Peter Robb and David Taylor, eds., *Rule, Protest, Identity: Aspects of Modern South Asia* (London: Curzon Press, 1978), 28–48.

Copland, Ian, 'The Hyderabad (Berar) Agreement of 1933: A Case Study in Anglo-Indian Diplomacy', *The Journal of Imperial and Commonwealth History*, 6/3 (1978), 281–299.

Copland, Ian, 'The Other Guardians: Ideology and Performance in the Indian Political Service', in Robin Jeffrey, ed., *People, Princes and Paramount Power: Society and Politics in the Indian Princely States* (Delhi: Oxford University Press, 1973), 275–305.

Copland, Ian, 'The Princely States, the Muslim League, and the Partition of India in 1947', *The International History Review*, 13/1 (1991), 38–69.

Copland, Ian, *The Princes of India in the Endgame of Empire, 1917–1947* (Cambridge: Cambridge University Press, 1997).

Corbett, P. E., 'What is the League of Nations?', *British Year Book of International Law*, 5 (1924): 119–148.

Corbett, P. E., 'World Order—An Agenda for Lawyers', *American Journal of International Law*, 37/2 (1943), 207–221.

Cornish, William, 'International Law', in William Cornish et al., eds., *The Oxford History of the Laws of England*, xi: *1820–1914: English Legal System* (Oxford: Oxford University Press, 2010), 255–277.

Craven, Matthew, and Rose Parfitt, 'Statehood, Self-Determination, and Recognition', in Malcolm D. Evans, ed., *International Law* (5th edn, Oxford: Oxford University Press, 2018), 177–226.

Crawford, James, *Brownlie's Principles of Public International Law* (9th edn, Oxford: Oxford University Press, 2019).

Crawford, James, 'Public International Law in Twentieth-Century England', in Jack Beatson and Reinhard Zimmermann, eds., *Jurists Uprooted: German-Speaking Émigré Lawyers in Twentieth-Century Britain* (Oxford: Oxford University Press, 2004), 681–708.

Curtis, Lionel, *Dyarchy* (Oxford: Clarendon Press, 1920).

Curtis, Lionel, *The Problem of the Commonwealth* (Toronto: The Macmillan Company of Canada Ltd., 1916).

Daly, Samuel Fury Childs, 'A Nation on Paper: Making a State in the Republic of Biafra', *Comparative Studies in Society and History*, 62/4 (2020), 868–894.

Darwin, John, *The Empire Project: The Rise and Fall of the British World-System, 1830–1970* (Cambridge: Cambridge University Press, 2011).

Das, Santanu, *India, Empire, and First World War Culture: Writings, Images, and Songs* (Cambridge: Cambridge University Press, 2018).

Das, Taraknath, *Sovereign Rights of the Indian Princes* (Madras: Ganesh & Co., 1924).

Das, Taraknath, 'The Status of Hyderabad During and After British Rule in India', *American Journal of International Law*, 43/1 (1949), 57–72.

d'Aspremont, Jean, 'Critical Histories of International Law and the Repression of Disciplinary Imagination', *London Review of International Law*, 7/1 (2019), 89–115.

Datla, Kavita Saraswathi, 'Sovereignty and the End of Empire: The Transition to Independence in Colonial Hyderabad', *Ab Imperio*, 3 (2018), 63–88.

Datla, Kavita Saraswathi, 'The Origins of Indirect Rule in India: Hyderabad and the British Imperial Order', *Law and History Review*, 33/2 (2015), 321–350.

Day, Jenny Huangfu, 'The Enigma of a Taiping Fugitive: The Illusion of Justice and the "Political Offence Exception" in Extradition from Hong Kong', *Law and History Review*, 39/3 (2021), 415–450.

De, Rohit, 'Between Midnight and Republic: Theory and Practice of India's Dominion Status', *International Journal of Constitutional Law*, 17/4 (2019), 1213–1234.

de Campos-Rudinsky, Jordan, 'James Bryce and Parliamentary Sovereignty', *Modern Intellectual History*, 19/3 (2022), 734–756.

Deva, Zaid, 'Basic Without Structure?: The Presidential Order of 1954 and the Indo-Jammu & Kashmir Constitutional Relationship', *Indian Law Review*, 4/2 (2020), 163–198.

Devji, Faisal, 'The Minority as Political Form', in Dipesh Chakrabarty, Rochona Majumdar, and Andrew Sartori, eds., *From the Colonial to the Postcolonial: India and Pakistan in Transition* (New Delhi: Oxford University Press, 2007), 85–95.

Devji, Faisal, *Muslim Zion: Pakistan as a Political Idea* (Cambridge, MA: Harvard University Press, 2013).

Dicey, A. V., 'Federal Government', *Law Quarterly Review*, 1/1 (1885), 80–99.

Dicey, A. V., *Introduction to the Study of the Law of the Constitution* (8th edn, London: Macmillan and Co. 1915).

Dirks, Nicholas, *The Hollow Crown: Ethnohistory of an Indian Kingdom* (Cambridge: Cambridge University Press, 1987).

Donaldson, Megan, 'The League of Nations, Ethiopia, and the Making of States', *Humanity: An International Journal of Human Rights, Humanitarianism, and Development*, 11/1 (2020), 6–31.

Duara, Prasenjit, 'The Cold War and the Imperialism of Nation-States', in Richard H. Immerman and Petra Goedde, eds., *The Oxford Handbook of the Cold War* (Oxford: Oxford University Press, 2013), 86–101.

Eagleton, Clyde, 'The Case of Hyderabad Before the Security Council', *American Journal of International Law*, 44/2 (1950), 277–302.

Elden, Stuart, 'Contingent Sovereignty, Territorial Integrity and the Sanctity of Borders', *SAIS Review of International Affairs*, 26/1 (2006), 11–24.

Elias, T. O., *Africa and the Development of International Law* (Leiden: A. W. Sijthoff, 1972).

Ellinwood Jr., Dewitt Clinton, 'The Round Table Movement and India, 1909–1920', *Journal of Commonwealth Political Studies*, 9/3 (1971), 183–209.

Eslava, Luis, Michael Fakhri, and Vasuki Nesiah, eds., *Bandung, Global History, and International Law: Critical Pasts and Pending Futures* (Cambridge: Cambridge University Press, 2017).

Eslava, Luis, and Sundhya Pahuja, 'The State and International Law: A Reading from the Global South', *Humanity: An International Journal of Human Rights, Humanitarianism, and Development*, 11/1 (2020), 118–138.

Faruqui, Munis D., 'At Empire's End: The Nizam, Hyderabad and Eighteenth-Century India', *Modern Asian Studies*, 43/1 (2009), 5–43.

Feaver, George, *From Status to Contract: A Biography of Sir Henry Maine 1822–1888* (London: Longmans, 1969).

Fejzula, Merve, 'The Cosmopolitan Historiography of Twentieth-Century Federalism', *The Historical Journal*, 64/2 (2021): 477–500.

Fisher, H. A. L., *James Bryce: Viscount Bryce of Dechmont, O. M.*, 2 vols (London: Macmillan and Co., 1927).
Fisher, Michael H., 'Diplomacy in India, 1526–1858', in H. V. Bowen, Elizabeth Mancke, and John G. Reid, eds., *Britain's Oceanic Empire: Atlantic and Indian Ocean Worlds, c. 1550–1850* (Cambridge: Cambridge University Press, 2012), 249–281.
Fisher, Michael H., *Indirect Rule in India: Residents and the Residency System, 1764–1858* (Delhi: Oxford University Press, 1991).
Fitzmaurice, Andrew, 'Liberalism and Empire in Nineteenth-Century International Law', *American Historical Review*, 117/1 (2012), 122–140.
Foray, Jennifer, 'A Unified Empire of Equal Parts: The Dutch Commonwealth Schemes of the 1920s–40s', *The Journal of Imperial and Commonwealth History*, 41/2 (2013), 259–284.
Friedmann, Wolfgang, 'International Law and the Present War', *Transactions of the Grotius Society*, 26 (1940), 211–233.
Fukurai, Hiroshi, 'Fourth World Approaches to International Law and Asia's Indigenous Struggles and Quests for Recognition under International Law', *Asian Journal of Law and Society*, 5/1 (2018), 221–231.
Gaekwad, Fatehsinhrao, *Sayajirao of Baroda: The Prince and the Man* (London: Sangam, 1989).
Gandhi, M. K., *The Indian States' Problem* (Ahmedabad: Navajivan Press, 1941).
Gandhi, Rajmohan, *Modern South India: A History from the 17th Century to Our Times* (New Delhi: Aleph Book Company, 2018).
Getachew, Adom, 'Securing Postcolonial Independence: Kwame Nkrumah and the Federal Idea in the Age of Decolonization', *Ab Imperio*, 3 (2018), 89–113.
Getachew, Adom, *Worldmaking After Empire: The Rise and Fall of Self-Determination* (Princeton, NJ: Princeton University Press, 2019).
Ghatak, Subrata, 'Gandhian Economic Thought and the Economic Policy of the Indian National Congress', in Mike Shepperdson and Colin Simmons, eds., *The Indian National Congress and the Political Economy of India 1885–1985* (Aldershot: Avebury, 1988), 282–290.
Ghosh, Durba, *Gentlemanly Terrorists: Political Violence and the Colonial State in India, 1919–1947* (Cambridge: Cambridge University Press, 2017).
Gilmartin, David, *Empire and Islam: Punjab and the Making of Pakistan* (Berkeley, CA: University of California Press, 1988).
Gilmartin, David, 'Partition, Pakistan, and South Asian History: In Search of a Narrative', *Journal of Asian History*, 57/4 (1998), 1068–1095.
Giovanopoulou, Afroditi, 'Pragmatic Legalism: Revisiting America's Order After World War II', *Harvard International Law Journal*, 62/2 (2021), 325–374.
Glennon, Michael J., and Robert D. Sloane, *Foreign Affairs Federalism: The Myth of National Exclusivity* (Oxford: Oxford University Press, 2016).
Godsmark, Oliver, 'Fragmented Sovereignty, *Ḍakaitī* (Banditry), and "Criminal Tribe" in a "Minor" State of Late Colonial India', *The Historical Journal*, 66/2 (2023), 435–458.
Goldsmith, Jack, 'Federal Courts, Foreign Affairs, and Federalism', *Virginia Law Review*, 83/8 (1997), 1617–1716.
Gong, Gerrit, *The Standard of 'Civilization' in International Society* (Oxford: Clarendon Press, 1984).
Gorman, Daniel, 'Lionel Curtis, Imperial Citizenship, and the Quest for Unity', *The Historian*, 66/1 (2004), 67–96.
Gorman, Mel, 'Sir William O'Shaughnessy, Lord Dalhousie, and the Establishment of the Telegraph System in India', *Technology and Culture*, 12/4 (1971), 581–601.

Goswami, Manu, 'Imaginary Futures and Colonial Internationalisms', *American Historical Review*, 117/5 (2012), 1461–1485.

Goswami, Manu, *Producing India: From Colonial Economy to National Space* (Chicago, IL: University of Chicago Press, 2004).

Grant Duff, Montstuart Elphinstone, *Sir Henry Maine: A Brief Memoir of his Life, with Some of his Indian Speeches and Minutes*, ed., Whitley Stokes (New York: Henry Holt & Co., 1892).

Green, L. C., 'Georg Schwarzenberger (1908–1991)', *American Journal of International Law*, 86/2 (1992), 341–342.

Haines, Daniel, 'A "Commonwealth Moment" in South Asian Decolonization', in Leslie James and Elisabeth Leake, eds., *Decolonization and the Cold War: Negotiating Independence* (London: Bloomsbury, 2015), 185–202.

Haksar, K. N., and K. M. Panikkar, *Federal India* (London: Martin Hopkinson Ltd., 1930).

Haksar, K. N., *Indian States and the Federation* (Bombay: D. B. Taraporelava Sons & Co., 1937).

Haksar, K. N., 'Intimate Glimpses', in K. N. Raina and K. V. Gopala Ratnam, eds., *Tej Bahadur Sapru: Profiles and Tributes* (Chandigarh: Tej Bahadur Sapru Commemoration Volume Committee, 1971), 109–115.

Halberstam, Daniel, 'Federalism: Theory, Policy, Law', in Michael Rosenfeld and András Sajó, eds., *The Oxford Handbook of Comparative Constitutional Law* (Oxford: Oxford University Press, 2012), 576–608.

Hall, William Edward, *International Law* (Oxford: Clarendon Press, 1880).

Hammoudi, Ali, 'The International Law of Informal Empire and the "Question of Oman"', *Third World Approaches to International Law Review*, 1 (2020), 121–151.

Hansen, Thomas Blom, 'Sovereignty in a Minor Key', *Public Culture*, 33/1 (2021), 41–61.

Hardiman, David, 'Baroda: The Structure of a 'Progressive' State', in Robin Jeffrey, ed., *People, Princes and Paramount Power: Society and Politics in the Indian Princely States* (Delhi: Oxford University Press, 1973), 107–135.

Harrington, Jack, *Sir John Malcolm and the Creation of British India* (Basingstoke: Palgrave Macmillan, 2010).

Harvie, Christopher, 'Ideology and Home Rule: James Bryce, A. V. Dicey and Ireland, 1880–1887', *English Historical Review*, 91/359 (1976), 298–314.

Hazard, John N., Louis Henkin, and Oliver J. Lissitzyn, 'In Memoriam: Wolfgang Gaston Friedmann, 1907–1972', *American Journal of International Law*, 67/1 (1973), 102–103.

Herzog, Don, *Sovereignty RIP* (New Haven, CT: Yale University Press, 2020).

Higgins, A. Pearce, 'The Late Doctor T. J. Lawrence', *British Year Book of International Law*, 1 (1920–21), 231–234.

Higgins, Rosalyn, *The Development of International Law Through the Political Organs of the United Nations* (London: Oxford University Press, 1963).

Hiltz, Jackie, 'Constructing Sikkimese National Identity in the 1960s and 1970s', *Bulletin of Tibetology*, 39/2 (2003), 67–83.

Hobsbawm, Eric, *Nations and Nationalism since 1790* (Cambridge: Cambridge University Press, 1990).

Hobsbawm, Eric, *The Age of Empire: 1875–1914* (New York: Pantheon Books, 1987).

Hogben, William Murray, 'The Foreign and Political Department of the Government of India, 1876–1919: A Study in Imperial Careers and Attitudes', PhD thesis, University of Toronto, 1973.

Holbrook, Carolyn, 'Anzac, Empire and War: Australian Nationalism and the Campaign for Imperial Federation', *Australian Historical Studies*, 52/1 (2021), 45–62.

Holdsworth, W. S., 'The Indian States and India', *Law Quarterly Review*, 46/3 (1930), 407–446.

Hooja, Rima, *Crusader for Self-Rule: Tej Bahadur Sapru & the Indian National Movement* (Jaipur: Rawat Publications, 1999).

Hudson, Manley O., 'The Prospect for International Law in the Twentieth Century', *Cornell Law Quarterly*, 10/4 (1925), 419–459.

Hussain, Nasser, *The Jurisprudence of Emergency: Colonialism and the Rule of Law* (Ann Arbor, MI: University of Michigan Press, 2004).

Ikegame, Aya, *Princely India Re-imagined: A Historical Anthropology of Mysore from 1799 to the Present* (London: Routledge, 2013).

Imlay, Talbot C., 'International Socialism and Decolonization during the 1950s: Competing Rights and the Postcolonial Order', *American Historical Review*, 118/4 (2013), 1105–1132.

Inagaki, Haruki, 'The Rule of Law and Emergency in Colonial India: The Conflict between the King's Court and the Government in Bombay in the 1820s', PhD thesis, King's College, London, 2016.

Jackson, Simon, 'Diaspora Politics and Developmental Empire: The Syro-Lebanese at the League of Nations', *Arab Studies Journal*, 21/1 (2013), 166–190.

Jacobs, Ellen, '"An Organizing Female with a Briefcase": Barbara Wootton, Political Economy and Social Justice, 1920–1950', *Women's History Review*, 16/3 (2007), 431–446.

Jagannathan, Shakunthala, *Sir C. P. Remembered: A Granddaughter's Reminiscences* (Mumbai: Vakils, Feffer & Simons Ltd., 1999).

Jain, M. P., *Outlines of Indian Legal History* (5th edn, Bombay: N. M. Tripathi, 1990).

Jalal, Ayesha, *The Sole Spokesman: Jinnah, The Muslim League and the Demand for Pakistan* (Cambridge: Cambridge University Press, 1985).

Jayal, Niraja Gopal, 'Citizenship', in Sujit Choudhry, Madhav Khosla, and Pratap Bhanu Mehta, eds., *The Oxford Handbook of the Indian Constitution* (Oxford: Oxford University Press, 2016), 163–179.

Jayal, Niraja Gopal, *Citizenship and its Discontents: An Indian History* (Cambridge, MA: Harvard University Press, 2013).

Jeffrey, Robin, 'A Sanctified Label—"Congress" in Travancore Politics, 1938–48', in D. A. Low, ed., *Congress and the Raj: Facets of the Indian Struggle, 1917–47* (2nd edn, New Delhi: Oxford University Press, 2004), 435–472.

Jeffrey, Robin, *The Decline of Nayar Dominance: Society and Politics in Travancore, 1847–1908* (London: Chatto & Windus for Sussex University Press, 1976).

Jenks, C. Wilfred, 'Some Constitutional Problems of International Organizations', *British Year Book of International Law*, 22 (1945), 11–72.

Jenks, C. Wilfred, 'The International Labour Organisation as a Subject of Study for International Lawyers', *Journal of Comparative Legislation and International Law*, 22/1 (1940), 36–56.

Jenks, C. Wilfred, 'The Significance Today of Lorimer's "Ultimate Problem of International Jurisprudence"', *Transactions of the Grotius Society*, 26 (1940), 35–65.

Jhala, Angma Dey, *Courtly Indian Women in Late Imperial India* (London: Pickering & Chatto, 2008).

Jhala, Angma D., 'The Malabar Hill Murder Trial of 1925: Sovereignty, Law and Sexual Politics in Colonial Princely India', *The Indian Economic and Social History Review*, 46/3 (2009), 373–400.

Jones, J. Mervyn, 'State Succession in the Matter of Treaties', *British Year Book of International Law*, 24 (1947), 360–375.

Kale, Sunila S., 'Structures of Power: Electrification in Colonial India', *Comparative Studies of South Asia, Africa and the Middle East*, 34/3 (2014), 454–475.

Kalmo, Hent, and Quentin Skinner, 'Introduction: A Concept in Fragments', in Hent Kalmo and Quentin Skinner, eds., *Sovereignty in Fragments: The Past, Present and Future of a Contested Concept* (Cambridge: Cambridge University Press, 2010), 1–25.

Kamat, Manjiri N., 'Border Incidents, Internal Disorder and the *Nizam*'s Claim for an Independent Hyderabad', in Waltraud Ernst and Biswamoy Pati, eds., *India's Princely States: People, Princes and Colonialism* (London: Routledge, 2007), 212–223.

Kawashima, Koji, *Missionaries and a Hindu State: Travancore, 1858–1936* (Delhi: Oxford University Press, 1998).

Kayaoğlu, Turan, *Legal Imperialism: Sovereignty and Extraterritoriality in Japan, the Ottoman Empire, and China* (Cambridge: Cambridge University Press, 2010).

Kaye, John William, *The Life and Correspondence of Charles, Lord Metcalfe*, 2 vols (London: Smith, Elder & Co., 1858).

Kaye, John William, *The Life and Correspondence of Major-General Sir John Malcolm*, 2 vols (London: Smith, Elder & Co., 1856).

Keen, Caroline, *An Imperial Crisis in British India: The Manipur Uprising of 1891* (London: I. B. Tauris, 2015).

Keene, Edward, 'The Treaty-Making Revolution of the Nineteenth Century', *The International History Review*, 34/3 (2012), 475–500.

Keith, A. B., *A Constitutional History of India, 1600–1935* (2nd edn, London: Methuen & Co., 1937).

Keith, A. B., *The Constitution, Administration and Laws of the Empire* (New York: Henry Holt & Company, 1924).

Keith, A. B., *The Governments of the British Empire* (London: Macmillan and Co., 1935).

Keith, A. B., *The Sovereignty of the British Dominions* (London: Macmillan and Co., 1929).

Kendle, John, *The Round Table Movement and Imperial Union* (Toronto: University of Toronto Press, 1975).

Kennedy, David, 'International Law and the Nineteenth Century: History of an Illusion', *Quinnipiac Law Review*, 17/1 (1997), 99–136.

Kennedy, David, 'Speaking Law to Power: International Law and Foreign Policy—Closing Remarks', *Wisconsin International Law Journal*, 23/1 (2005), 173–182.

Kennedy, David, 'The Disciplines of International Law and Policy', *Leiden Journal of International Law*, 12/1 (1999), 9–133.

Kennedy, David, 'The Move to Institutions', *Cardozo Law Review*, 8/5 (1987), 841–988.

Kennedy, David, 'When Renewal Repeats: Thinking Against the Box', *New York University Journal of International Law and Politics*, 32/2 (2000), 335–500.

Kerr, Philip, 'The Only Road to International Peace', in Philip Kerr and Lionel Curtis, *The Prevention of War* (New Haven, CT: Yale University Press, 1923), 49–76.

Khan, Raphaëlle, and Taylor C. Sherman, 'Indians and Overseas Indians in Ceylon and Burma, 1946–1965: Experiments in Post-Imperial Sovereignty', *Modern Asian Studies*, 56/4 (2022), 1153–1182.

Khan, Shafa'at Ahmad, *The Indian Federation: An Exposition and Critical Review* (London: Macmillan and Co., 1937).

Khan, Yasmin, *The Great Partition: The Making of India and Pakistan* (New Haven, CT: Yale University Press, 2007).

Khilnani, Sunil, *The Idea of India* (New Delhi: Penguin, 1997).

Khorakiwala, Rahela, *From the Colonial to the Contemporary: Images, Iconography, Memories, and Performances of Law in India's High Courts* (Oxford: Hart Publishing, 2019).

Koskenniemi, Martti, 'Hersch Lauterpacht', in Jack Beatson and Reinhard Zimmermann, eds., *Jurists Uprooted: German-Speaking Émigré Lawyers in Twentieth-Century Britain* (Oxford: Oxford University Press, 2004), 601–662.

Koskenniemi, Martti, *The Gentle Civilizer of Nations: The Rise and Fall of International Law, 1870–1960* (Cambridge: Cambridge University Press, 2001).

Koskenniemi, Martti, *To the Uttermost Parts of the Earth: Legal Imagination and International Power, 1300–1870* (Cambridge: Cambridge University Press, 2021).

Kostal, R. W., *A Jurisprudence of Power: Victorian Empire and the Rule of Law* (Oxford: Oxford University Press, 2005).

Kudaisya, Medha, '"The Promise of Partnership": Indian Business, the State, and the Bombay Plan of 1944', *Business History Review*, 88/1 (2014), 97–131.

Kumar, Mohan, *Sir Tej Bahadur Sapru: A Political Biography* (Gwalior: Vipul Prakashan, 1981).

Kumar, Sunaina, 'Kingdom', *Fifty Two* (16 October 2020), https://fiftytwo.in/story/kingdom/, accessed 15 February 2022.

Kumarasingham, Harshan, ed., *Constitution-Making in Asia: Decolonisation and State-Building in the Aftermath of the British Empire* (London: Routledge, 2016).

LaCroix, Alison, *The Ideological Origins of American Federalism* (Cambridge, MA: Harvard University Press, 2010).

Lahiri Choudhury, Deep Kanta, *Telegraphic Imperialism: Crisis and Panic in the Indian Empire, c. 1830–1920* (New York: Palgrave Macmillan, 2010).

Lambert-Hurley, Siobhan, *Muslim Women, Reform and Princely Patronage: Nawab Sultan Jahan Begam of Bhopal* (London: Routledge, 2007).

Landauer, Carl, 'From Status to Treaty: Henry Sumner Maine's *International Law*', *Canadian Journal of Law and Jurisprudence*, 15/2 (2002), 219–254.

Landauer, Carl, 'J. L. Brierly and The Modernization of International Law', *Vanderbilt Journal of Transnational Law*, 25/5 (1993), 881–918.

Lauterpacht, Elihu, *The Life of Sir Hersch Lauterpacht* (Cambridge: Cambridge University Press, 2010).

Lauterpacht, Hersch, 'International Law and Colonial Questions, 1870–1914', in Elihu Lauterpacht, ed., *International Law: Being the Collected Papers of Hersch Lauterpacht, ii: The Law of Peace* (Cambridge: Cambridge University Press, 1975), 95–144.

Lauterpacht, Hersch, *International Law and Human Rights* (London: Stevens & Sons, Ltd., 1950).

Lauterpacht, Hersch, 'Sovereignty and Federation in International Law', in Elihu Lauterpacht, ed., *International Law: Being the Collected Papers of Hersch Lauterpacht, iii: The Law of Peace* (Cambridge: Cambridge University Press, 1977), 5–25.

Lauterpacht, Hersch, 'The Doctrine of Non-Justiciable Disputes in International Law', *Economica*, 24 (1928), 277–317.

Lauterpacht, Hersch, *The Function of Law in the International Community* (Oxford: Clarendon Press, 1933).

Lauterpacht, Hersch, 'The Grotian Tradition in International Law', *British Year Book of International Law*, 23 (1946), 1–53.

Lauterpacht, Hersch, 'The Law of Nations and the Punishment of War Crimes', *British Year Book of International Law*, 21 (1944), 58–95.

Lauterpacht, Hersch, 'The Law of Nations, the Law of Nature and the Rights of Man', *Transactions of the Grotius Society*, 29 (1943), 1–33.

Lauterpacht, Hersch, 'The Mandate Under International Law in the Covenant of the League of Nations', in Elihu Lauterpacht, ed., *International Law: Being the Collected Papers of Hersch Lauterpacht*, iii: *The Law of Peace* (Cambridge: Cambridge University Press, 1977), 29–84.

Lauterpacht, Hersch, 'The Nature of International Law and General Jurisprudence', *Economica*, 37 (1932), 301–320.

Lauterpacht, Hersch, 'Westlake and Present Day International Law', *Economica*, 15 (1925), 307–325.

Lavin, Deborah, *From Empire to International Commonwealth: A Biography of Lionel Curtis* (Oxford: Oxford University Press, 1995).

Lavin, Deborah, 'Lionel Curtis and Indian Dyarchy', in Andrea Bosco, ed., *The Federal Idea: The History of Federalism from Enlightenment to 1945*, i (London: Lothian Foundation Press, 1991), 193–210.

Lawrence, T. J., *The Principles of International Law* (Boston, MA: D. C. Heath & Co., 1895).

Leake, Elisabeth, 'At the Nation-State's Edge: Centre-Periphery Relations in Post-1947 South Asia', *The Historical Journal*, 59/2 (2016), 509–539.

Leake, Elisabeth, 'Where National and International Meet: Borders and Border Regions in Postcolonial India', *The International History Review*, 44/4 (2022), 856–873.

Leake, Elisabeth, and Daniel Haines, 'Lines of (In)Convenience: Sovereignty and Border-Making in Postcolonial South Asia, 1947–1965', *The Journal of Asian Studies*, 76/4 (2017), 963–985.

Lee, Ivan, 'From Reciprocity to Territoriality: Extradition, the Opium War, and the Idea of British Sovereignty in Hong Kong, 1842–44' *Law and History Review*, 40/3 (2022), 437–458.

Lee-Warner, William, *The Life of the Marquis of Dalhousie*, 2 vols (London: Macmillan and Co., 1904).

Lee-Warner, William, *The Native States of India* (London: Macmillan and Co., 1910).

Lee-Warner, William, 'The Native States of India: A Rejoinder', *Law Quarterly Review*, 27/1 (1911), 83–89.

Legg, Stephen, 'An International Anomaly? Sovereignty, the League of Nations and India's Princely Geographies', *Journal of Historical Geography* 43 (2014), 96–110.

Legg, Stephen, 'Dyarchy: Democracy, Autocracy, and the Scalar Sovereignty of Interwar India', *Comparative Studies of South Asia, Africa and the Middle East*, 36/1 (2016), 44–65.

Legg, Stephen, 'Imperial Internationalism: The Round Table Conference and the Making of India in London, 1930–1932', *Humanity: An International Journal of Human Rights, Humanitarianism, and Development*, 11/1 (2020), 32–53.

Legg, Stephen, 'Political Lives at Sea: Working and Socialising To and From the India Round Table Conference in London, 1930–1932', *Journal of Historical Geography*, 68 (2020), 21–32.

Leonard, Zak, 'Law of Nations Theory and the Native Sovereignty Debates in Colonial India', *Law and History Review*, 38/2 (2020), 373–407.

Lewis, Malcolm M., 'The International Status of the British Self-Governing Dominions', *British Year Book of International Law*, 21 (1922–23): 21–41.

Lobban, Michael, 'English Approaches to International Law in the Nineteenth Century', in Matthew Craven, Malgosia Fitzmaurice, and Maria Vogiatzi, eds., *Time, History and International Law* (Leiden: Martinus Nijhoff Publishers, 2007), 65–90.

Long, Roger D., and Ian Talbot, eds., *India and World War I: A Centennial Assessment* (London: Routledge, 2018).

Louis, Wm. Roger., and Ronald Robinson, 'The Imperialism of Decolonization', *The Journal of Imperial and Commonwealth History*, 22/3 (1994), 462–511.

Low, D. A., 'Sir Tej Bahadur Sapru and the First Round Table Conference', in D. A. Low, ed., *Soundings in Modern South Asian History* (Canberra: Australian National University Press, 1968), 294–329.
McClenaghan, Tony, *For the Honour of My House: The Contribution of the Indian Princely States to the First World War* (Warwick: Helion and Company, 2019).
McGuinness, Margaret E., 'Three Narratives of *Medellín v. Texas*', *Suffolk Transnational Law Review*, 31/2 (2008), 227–246.
McKay, Alex, 'Indian Structures, Sikkimese Processes: On Being Unprepared for the (Indian) Nation', *Asian Ethnicity*, 22/2 (2021), 272–289.
McLeod, John, *Sovereignty, Power, Control: Politics in the States of Western India, 1916–1947* (Leiden: Brill, 1999).
MacMunn, George, *The Indian States and Princes* (London: Jarrolds Publishers, 1936).
McNair, Arnold, 'Aspects of State Sovereignty', *British Year Book of International Law*, 26 (1949), 6–47.
McNair, Arnold, 'International Law in Practice', *Transactions of the Grotius Society*, 32 (1946), 154–165.
McNair, Arnold, 'The Need for the Wider Teaching of International Law', *Transactions of the Grotius Society*, 29 (1943), 85–98.
McQuade, Joseph, 'Beyond an Imperial Foreign Policy?: India at the League of Nations, 1919–1946', *The Journal of Imperial and Commonwealth History*, 48/2 (2020), 263–295.
Magnuson, William, 'The Domestic Politics of International Extradition', *Virginia Journal of International Law*, 52/4 (2012), 839–902.
Maine, Henry Sumner, *Ancient Law* (London: John Murray, 1861).
Maine, Henry Sumner, *International Law* (London: John Murray, 1888).
Maine, Henry Sumner, *Lectures on the Early History of Institutions* (London: John Murray, 1875).
Maine, Henry Sumner, 'The Conception of Sovereignty and Its Importance in International Law', *Papers of the Juridical Society* (1855), 26–45.
Malcolm, John, *Memoir of Central India*, 2 vols (2nd edn, London: Kingsbury, Parbury, & Allen, 1824).
Mamdani, Mahmood, *Citizen and Subject: Contemporary Africa and the Legacy of Late Colonialism* (Princeton, NJ: Princeton University Press, 1996).
Mamdani, Mahmood, *Define and Rule: Native as Political Identity* (Cambridge, MA: Harvard University Press, 2012).
Mandala, Vijaya Ramadas, 'The Raj and the Paradoxes of Wildlife Conservation: British Attitudes and Expediencies', *The Historical Journal*, 58/1 (2015), 75–110.
Manning, William Oke, *Commentaries on the Law of Nations* (London: S. Sweet, 1839).
Manor, James, 'Gandhian Politics and the Challenge to Princely Authority in Mysore, 1936–47', in D. A. Low, ed., *Congress and the Raj: Facets of the Indian Struggle, 1917–47* (2nd edn, New Delhi: Oxford University Press, 2004), 405–434.
Mantena, Karuna, *Alibis of Empire: Henry Maine and the Ends of Liberal Imperialism* (Princeton, NJ: Princeton University Press, 2010).
Mantena, Karuna, 'On Gandhi's Critique of the State: Sources, Contexts, Conjectures', *Modern Intellectual History*, 9/3 (2012), 535–563.
Mantena, Karuna, 'Popular Sovereignty and Anti-Colonialism', in Richard Bourke and Quentin Skinner, eds., *Popular Sovereignty in Historical Perspective* (Cambridge: Cambridge University Press, 2016), 297–319.
Mantena, Rama Sundari, 'Anticolonialism and Federation in Colonial India', *Ab Imperio*, 3 (2018): 36–62.

Marglin, Jessica M., 'Extraterritoriality and Legal Belonging in the Nineteenth-Century Mediterranean', *Law and History Review*, 39/4 (2021), 679–706.
Mayaram, Shail, *Resisting Regimes: Myth, Memory and the Shaping of a Muslim Identity* (New Delhi: Oxford University Press, 1997).
Mayne, Richard, John Pinder, and John C. de V. Roberts, *Federal Union: The Pioneers: A History of the Federal Union* (Basingstoke: Macmillan, 1990).
Mazower, Mark, *Governing the World: The History of an Idea* (London: Allen Lane, 2012).
Mazower, Mark, *No Enchanted Palace: The End of Empire and the Ideological Origins of the United Nations* (Princeton, NJ: Princeton University Press, 2009).
Medhi, Abhilash, 'Infrastructural Contingencies and Contingent Sovereignties on the Indo-Afghan Frontier', *Modern Asian Studies*, 54/6 (2020), 1949–1986.
Mehrotra, S. R., 'Imperial Federation and India, 1868–1917', *Journal of Commonwealth and Comparative Politics*, 1/1 (1961), 29–40.
Mehta, Mohan Sinha, *Lord Hastings and the Indian States* (Bombay: D. B. Taraporevala Sons & Co., 1930).
Menon, A. Sreedhara, *Triumph and Tragedy in Travancore: Annals of Sir CP's Sixteen Years* (Kottayam: Current Books, 2001).
Menon, Ritu, and Kamala Bhasin, *Borders and Boundaries: Women in India's Partition* (New Delhi: Kali for Women, 1998).
Menon, V. P., *The Story of the Integration of the Indian States* (New York: Macmillan, 1956).
Menon, V. P., *The Transfer of Power in India* (Princeton, NJ: Princeton University Press, 1957).
Merry, Sally Engle, 'Review Essay: Law and Colonialism', *Law and Society Review*, 25/4 (1991), 889–922.
Metcalf, Barbara D., and Thomas R. Metcalf, *A Concise History of Modern India* (2nd edn, Cambridge: Cambridge University Press, 2006).
Metcalf, Thomas, *Ideologies of the Raj* (Cambridge: Cambridge University Press, 1995).
Metcalf, Thomas, *Imperial Connections: India in the Indian Ocean Arena, 1860–1920* (Berkeley, CA: University of California Press, 2007).
Metcalf, Thomas, *The Aftermath of Revolt: India, 1857–1870* (Princeton, NJ: Princeton University Press, 1964).
Miller, Bradley, *Borderline Crime: Fugitive Criminals and the Challenge of the Border, 1819–1914* (Toronto: University of Toronto Press, 2016).
Mishra, Pankaj, 'Exit Wounds', *New Yorker* (13 August 2007), https://www.newyorker.com/magazine/2007/08/13/exit-wounds, accessed 15 February 2022.
Mohr, Thomas, 'The Statute of Westminster, 1931: An Irish Perspective', *Law and History Review*, 31/4 (2013), 749–791.
Montgomery-Hyde, H., *Walter Monckton* (London: Sinclair-Stevenson, 1991).
Moore, R. J., *Escape from Empire: The Attlee Government and the Indian Problem* (Oxford: Clarendon Press, 1983).
Moore, R. J., *Making the New Commonwealth* (Oxford: Clarendon Press, 1987).
Moore, R. J., *The Crisis of Indian Unity, 1917–1940* (Oxford: Clarendon Press, 1974).
Morefield, Jeanne, '"An Education to Greece": The Round Table, Imperial Theory and the Uses of History', *History of Political Thought*, 28/2 (2007), 328–361.
Morton-Jack, George, *The Indian Empire At War: From Jihad to Victory, The Untold Story of the Indian Army in the First World War* (London: Little, Brown, 2018).
Moyn, Samuel, 'Fantasies of Federalism', *Dissent* (Winter 2015), https://www.dissentmagazine.org/article/fantasies-of-federalism, accessed 15 February 2022.

Moyn, Samuel, 'From Aggression to Atrocity: Rethinking the History of International Criminal Law', in Kevin Jon Heller et al., eds., *The Oxford Handbook of International Criminal Law* (Oxford: Oxford University Press, 2020), 341–360.
Mukherjee, Mithi, *India in the Shadows of Empire: A Legal and Political History, 1774–1950* (New Delhi: Oxford University Press, 2010).
Muldoon, Andrew, *Empire, Politics and the Creation of the 1935 India Act* (Farnham: Ashgate, 2009).
Mutua, Makau wa, 'Why Redraw the Map of Africa? A Moral and Legal Inquiry', *Michigan Journal of International Law*, 16/4 (1995), 1113–1176.
Naik, Priya, 'The Case of the "Other India" and Indian IR Scholarship', *Third World Quarterly*, 35/8 (2014), 1496–1508.
Nair, Balu G., 'Abrogation of Article 370: Can the President Act Without the Recommendation of the Constituent Assembly?', *Indian Law Review*, 3/3 (2019), 254–279.
Nair, Janaki, *Mysore Modern: Rethinking the Region under Princely Rule* (Minneapolis, MN: University of Minnesota Press, 2011).
Nair, Neeti, *Changing Homelands: Hindu Politics and the Partition of India* (Cambridge, MA: Harvard University Press, 2011).
Nehru, Jawaharlal, *The Discovery of India* (Calcutta: The Signet Press, 1944; New Delhi: Oxford University Press, 1989).
Nicholson, A. P., *Scraps of Paper: India's Broken Treaties, Her Princes, and the Problem* (London: Ernest Benn Limited, 1930).
Noel-Baker, Philip, *The Present Juridical Status of British Dominions in International Law* (London: Longmans, 1929).
Noorani, A. G., *Article 370: A Constitutional History of Jammu and Kashmir* (Oxford: Oxford University Press, 2011).
Noorani, A. G., 'Of a Massacre Untold', *Frontline* (3 March 2001), https://frontline.thehindu.com/other/article30159646.ece, accessed 22 June 2022.
Noorani, A. G., *The Destruction of Hyderabad* (London: Hurst & Company, 2014).
Nuckolls, Charles W., 'The Durbar Incident', *Modern Asian Studies*, 24/3 (1990), 529–559.
Oakley, Ann, *A Critical Woman: Barbara Wootton, Social Science and Public Policy in the Twentieth Century* (London: Bloomsbury Academic, 2011).
O'Malley, L. S. S., *The Indian Civil Service, 1601–1930* (2nd edn, London: Frank Cass, 1965).
Oliver, Peter C., '"Dominion Status": History, Framework and Context', *International Journal of Constitutional Law*, 17/4 (2019), 1173–1191.
Oppenheim, Lassa, *International Law: A Treatise*, i: *Peace*, 3rd edn, ed. Ronald F. Roxburgh (London: Longmans, Green and Co., 1920).
Orford, Anne, *International Law and the Politics of History* (Cambridge: Cambridge University Press, 2021).
Owen, Nicholas, *The British Left and India: Metropolitan Anti-Imperialism, 1885–1947* (Oxford: Oxford University Press, 2007).
Palmer, Julian, *Sovereignty and Paramountcy in India* (London: Stevens and Sons, 1930).
Pandey, Gyanendra, *Remembering Partition: Violence, Nationalism and History in India* (Cambridge: Cambridge University Press, 2001).
Pandey, Gyanendra, *The Construction of Communalism in Colonial North India* (Delhi: Oxford University Press, 1990).
Panikkar, K. M., *An Introduction to the Study of the Relations of Indian States with the Government of India* (London: Martin Hopkinson, 1927).
Panikkar, K. M., *His Highness the Maharaja of Bikaner: A Biography* (London: Oxford University Press, 1937).

Panikkar, K. M., *Inter-Statal Law: The Law Affecting the Relations of the Indian States with the British Crown* (Madras: University of Madras, 1934).

Panikkar, K. M., *The Indian Princes in Council: A Record of the Chancellorship of His Highness the Maharaja of Patiala* (Humphrey Milford: Oxford University Press, 1936).

Panikkar, K. M., 'The Native States and Indian Nationalism', *The Modern Review*, 25/1 (1919), 37–44.

Paolini, Rita, 'An Indian Student in Oxford During World War I: Kavalam M. Panikkar Between Nationalism and Princely States', *Monde(s)*, 9 (2016), 59–74.

Papanek, Hanna, 'Purdah: Separate Worlds and Symbolic Shelter', *Comparative Studies in Society and History*, 15/3 (1973), 289–325.

Parasher, Tejas, 'Federalism, Representation, and Direct Democracy in 1920s India', *Modern Intellectual History*, 19/2 (2022), 444–472.

Parfitt, Rose, '*Empire des Nègres Blancs*: The Hybridity of International Personality and the Abyssinia Crisis of 1935–36', *Leiden Journal of International Law*, 24/4 (2011), 849–872.

Parry, Clive, 'The Legal Nature of the Trusteeship Agreements', *British Year Book of International Law*, 27 (1950), 164–185.

Patil, S. H., *The Congress Party and Princely States* (Bombay: Himalaya Publishing House, 1981).

Pearson, M. N., *The Portuguese in India* (Cambridge: Cambridge University Press, 1988).

Pedersen, Susan, 'Back to the League of Nations', *American Historical Review*, 112/4 (2007), 1091–1117.

Pedersen, Susan, *The Guardians: The League of Nations and the Crisis of Empire* (Oxford: Oxford University Press, 2015).

Phadnis, Urmila, *Towards the Integration of Indian States, 1919–1947* (Bombay: Asia Publishing House, 1968).

Phillimore, Robert, *Commentaries Upon International Law*, 4 vols (Philadelphia, PA: T&JW Johnson, 1854–1861).

Pillai, G. Paramaswaran, 'Raja Sir T. Madava Row', in *Representative Men of Southern India* (Madras: Price Current Press, 1896), 33–48.

Pillai, Sarath, 'Fragmenting the Nation: Divisible Sovereignty and Travancore's Quest for Federal Independence', *Law and History Review*, 34/3 (2016), 743–782.

Pinder, John, 'Prophet Not Without Honour: Lothian and the Federal Idea', *The Round Table*, 72/286 (1983), 207–220.

Pitts, Jennifer, *Boundaries of the International: Law and Empire* (Cambridge, MA: Harvard University Press, 2018).

Pitts, Jennifer, 'Empire and Legal Universalisms in the Eighteenth Century', *American Historical Review*, 117/1 (2012), 92–121.

Prakash, Gyan, *Another Reason: Science and the Imagination of Modern India* (Princeton, NJ: Princeton University Press, 1999).

Prakash, Gyan, *Emergency Chronicles: Indira Gandhi and Democracy's Turning Point* (Princeton, NJ: Princeton University Press, 2019).

Prasad, Malavika, 'Downgraded at the Stroke of a Pen', *The Hindu* (8 August 2019), https://www.thehindu.com/opinion/op-ed/downgraded-at-the-stroke-of-a-pen/article28872213.ece, accessed 15 February 2022.

Prasad, S. N., *Operation Polo: The Police Action Against Hyderabad, 1948* (Delhi: Historical Section, Ministry of Defence, Government of India, 1972).

Purcell, Kate, 'On the Uses and Advantages of Genealogy for International Law', *Leiden Journal of International Law*, 33/1 (2020), 13–35.

Purushotham, Sunil, 'Federating the Raj: Hyderabad, Sovereign Kingship, and Partition', *Modern Asian Studies*, 54/1 (2020), 157–198.
Purushotham, Sunil, 'Internal Violence: The "Police Action" in Hyderabad', *Comparative Studies in Society and History*, 57/2 (2015), 435–466.
Purushotham, Sunil, 'Sovereignty, Federation, and Constituent Power in Interwar India, ca. 1917–39', *Comparative Studies of South Asia, Africa and the Middle East*, 40/3 (2020), 421–433.
Putra, Kerala, *The Working of Dyarchy in India, 1919–1928* (Bombay: D. B. Taraporevala Sons and Co., 1928).
Raghavan, Srinath, *War and Peace in Modern India* (Basingstoke: Palgrave Macmillan, 2010).
Rai, Mridu, *Hindu Rulers, Muslim Subjects: Islam, Rights, and the History of Kashmir* (Princeton, NJ: Princeton University Press, 2004).
Rainau, Mircea, '"A Mass of Anomalies": Land, Law, and Sovereignty in an Indian Company Town', *Comparative Studies in Society and History*, 60/2 (2018), 367–389.
Rajagopal, Balakrishnan, *International Law from Below: Development, Social Movements, and Third World Resistance* (Cambridge: Cambridge University Press, 2003).
Ramusack, Barbara, 'Congress and the People's Movement in Princely India: Ambivalence in Strategy and Organization', in Richard Sisson and Stanley Wolpert, eds., *Congress and Indian Nationalism: The Pre-Independence Phase* (Berkeley, CA: University of California Press, 1988), 377–403.
Ramusack, Barbara, *The Indian Princes and their States* (Cambridge: Cambridge University Press, 2004).
Ramusack, Barbara, *The Princes of India in the Twilight of Empire: Dissolution of a Patron–Client System, 1914–1939* (Columbus, OH: Ohio State University Press, 1978).
Ranadive, R. K., *The Legal Rights of the Indian States and of their Subjects, or The Truth About the Indian States* (Baroda: The Good Companions, 1950).
Rao, R. Venkoba, 'Sir Manubhai N. Mehta', in *Ministers in Indian States* (Trichinopoly: Wednesday Review Press, 1928), 13–14.
Ray, Reeju, 'Interrupted Sovereignties in the North East Frontier of British India, 1787–1870', *Modern Asian Studies*, 53/2 (2019), 606–632.
Resnik, Judith, 'Law's Migration: American Exceptionalism, Silent Dialogues, and Federalism's Multiple Ports of Entry', *Yale Law Journal*, 115/7 (2006), 1564–1671.
Rice, Stanley, *Life of Sayaji Rao III Maharaja of Baroda*, 2 vols (London: Oxford University Press, 1931).
Robinson, Rowena, 'Planning and Economic Development: Ambedkar versus Gandhi', in Biswamoy Pati, ed., *Invoking Ambedkar: Contributions, Receptions, Legacies* (Delhi: Primus Books, 2014), 59–71.
Robson, Laura, 'Capitulations Redux: The Imperial Genealogy of the Post-World War I "Minority" Regimes', *American Historical Review*, 126/3 (2021): 978–1000.
Rodrigues, Mario, *Batting for the Empire: A Political Biography of Ranjitsinhji* (New Delhi: Penguin Books, 2003).
Rose, Leo E., 'India and Sikkim: Redefining the Relationship', *Pacific Affairs*, 42/1 (1969), 32–46.
Rosenboim, Or, 'Barbara Wootton, Friedrich Hayek and the Debate on Democratic Federalism in the 1940s', *The International History Review*, 36/5 (2014), 894–918.
Rubin, Gil, 'From Federalism to Binationalism: Hannah Arendt's Shifting Zionism', *Contemporary European History*, 24/3 (2015), 393–414.
Ruggie, John, 'Territoriality and Beyond: Problematizing Modernity in International Relations', *International Organization*, 47/1 (1993), 139–174.

Saksena, Priyasha, 'Jousting Over Jurisdiction: Sovereignty and International Law in Colonial South Asia, c. 1858–1950', SJD dissertation, Harvard University, 2018.
Sarila, Narendra Singh, *The Shadow of the Great Game: The Untold Story of India's Partition* (London: Constable, 2006).
Sarkar, Sumit, *Modern India, 1885–1947* (Delhi: Macmillan India, 1983).
Sarkar, Sumit, *Modern Times: India, 1880s–1950s, Environment, Economy, Culture* (Ranikhet: Permanent Black, 2014).
Satia, Priya, 'Risking a Colonial Anticolonialism', *European Journal of International Law*, 32/3 (2021), 1017–1026.
Schwarzenberger, Georg, *Power Politics* (London: Jonathan Cape, 1941).
Schwarzenberger, Georg, 'The "Aid Britain" Bill and the Law of Neutrality: Some Reflections on the Scope of the Functional Approach to International Law', *Transactions of the Grotius Society*, 27 (1941), 1–29.
Scobbie, Iain, 'Hersch Lauterpacht', in Bardo Fassbender and Anne Peters, eds., *The Oxford Handbook of the History of International Law* (Oxford: Oxford University Press, 2012), 1179–1184.
Seaman Jr., John T., *Citizen of the World: The Life of James Bryce* (London: I. B. Tauris, 2006).
Sen, D. K., *The Indian States, Their Status, Rights and Obligations* (London: Sweet and Maxwell, 1930).
Sen, Dwaipayan, '"No matter how, Jogendranath had to be defeated": The Scheduled Castes Federation and the Making of Partition in Bengal, 1945–1947', *The Indian Economic and Social History Review*, 49/3 (2012), 321–364.
Sen, Satadru, *Migrant Races: Empire, Identity and K. S. Ranjitsinhji* (Manchester: Manchester University Press, 2004).
Sen, Uditi, *Citizen Refugee: Forging the Indian Nation after Partition* (Cambridge: Cambridge University Press, 2018).
Sender, Henny, *The Kashmiri Pandits: A Study of Cultural Choice in North India* (Delhi: Oxford University Press, 1988).
Sergeant, Philip W., *The Ruler of Baroda: An Account of the Life and Work of the Maharaja Gaekwar* (London: John Murray, 1928).
Shani, Ornit, *How India Became Democratic: Citizenship and the Making of the Universal Franchise* (Cambridge: Cambridge University Press, 2018).
Shankar, Devika, 'A Slippery Sovereignty: International Law and the Development of British Cochin', *Comparative Studies in Society and History*, 64/3 (2022), 820–844.
Sharafi, Mitra, 'The Marital Patchwork of Colonial South Asia: Forum Shopping from Britain to Baroda', *Law and History Review*, 28/4 (2010), 979–1009.
Sherman, Taylor C., 'Migration, Citizenship and Belonging in Hyderabad (Deccan), 1946–1956', *Modern Asian Studies*, 45/1 (2011), 81–107.
Sherman, Taylor C., 'The Integration of the Princely State of Hyderabad and the Making of the Postcolonial State in India, 1948–56', *The Indian Economic and Social History Review*, 44/4 (2007), 489–516.
Simma, Bruno, and Carsten Hoppe, 'From *LaGrand* and *Avena* to *Medellín*—A Rocky Road Toward Implementation', *Tulane Journal of International and Comparative Law*, 14/1 (2005), 7–60.
Simpson, Thomas, 'Bordering and Frontier-Making in Nineteenth-Century British India', *The Historical Journal*, 58/2 (2015), 513–542.
Sinclair, Guy Fiti, 'C. Wilfred Jenks and the Futures of International Organizations Law', *European Journal of International Law*, 31/2 (2020), 525–542.
Singh, Dharmjit, *Lord Linlithgow in India, 1936–1943* (Jalandhar: ABD Publications, 2005).

Singh, Gajendra, 'India and the Great War: Colonial Fantasies, Anxieties and Discontent', *Studies in Ethnicity and Nationalism*, 14/2 (2014), 343–361.

Singh, Geetashree, 'Colonising Elephant Hunting in Assam (1826–1947)', *Indian Historical Review*, 47/2 (2020), 313–329.

Singh, Gurmukh Nihal, *Indian States and British India: Their Future Relations* (Benaras: Nand Kishore & Bros., 1930).

Singh, Hira, *Colonial Hegemony and Popular Resistance: Princes, Peasants, and Paramount Power* (New Delhi: Sage Publications, 1998).

Singh, Prabhakar, 'Indian Princely States and the 19th-century Transformation of the Law of Nations', *Journal of International Dispute Settlement*, 11/3 (2020), 365–387.

Singh, Prabhakar, 'Of International Law, Semi-colonial Thailand, and Imperial Ghosts', *Asian Journal of International Law*, 9/1 (2019), 46–74.

Singha, Radhika, *The Coolie's Great War: Indian Labour in a Global Conflict, 1914–1921* (London: Hurst, 2020).

Sinha, Sachidananda, *Dyarchy in Indian Provinces in Theory and Practice* (London: East India Association, 1926).

Sitlhou, Makepeace, 'Accord', *Fifty Two* (27 November 2020), https://fiftytwo.in/story/accord/, accessed 15 February 2022.

Slinn, Judy, *Clifford Chance: Its Origins and Development* (Cambridge: Granta Editions, 1993).

Slobodian, Quinn, *Globalists: The End of Empire and the Birth of Neoliberalism* (Cambridge, MA: Harvard University Press, 2018).

Sluga, Glenda, *Internationalism in the Age of Nationalism* (Philadelphia, PA: University of Pennsylvania Press, 2013).

Smith, Leonard V., 'Sovereignty Under the League of Nations Mandates: The Jurists' Debates', *Journal of the History of International Law*, 21/4 (2019), 563–587.

Smith, Simon C., *British Relations with the Malay Rulers from Decentralization to Malayan Independence, 1930–1957* (Kuala Lumpur: Oxford University Press, 1995).

Smith, Wilfred Cantwell, 'Hyderabad: Muslim Tragedy', *Middle East Journal*, 4/1 (1950), 27–51.

Sohal, Amar, 'Ideas of Parity: Muslims, Sikhs and the 1946 Cabinet Mission Plan', *South Asia: Journal of South Asian Studies*, 40/4 (2017), 706–722.

Somervell, D. B., 'The Indian States', *British Year Book of International Law*, 11 (1930), 55–62.

Spear, Percival, 'Obituaries: Professor L. F. Rushbrook Williams', *Asian Affairs*, 10/1 (1979), 113–114.

Steinle, Stephanie, 'Georg Schwarzenberger (1908–1991)', in Jack Beatson and Reinhard Zimmermann, eds., *Jurists Uprooted: German-Speaking Émigré Lawyers in Twentieth Century Britain* (Oxford: Oxford University Press, 2004), 663–680.

Stern, Philip, 'Bundles of Hyphens', in Lauren Benton and Richard J. Ross, eds., *Legal Pluralism and Empires, 1500–1850* (New York, NY: New York University Press, 2013), 19–48.

Stern, Philip, 'Company, State, and Empire: Governance and Regulatory Frameworks in Asia', in H. V. Bowen, Elizabeth Mancke, and John G. Reid, eds., *Britain's Oceanic Empire: Atlantic and Indian Ocean Worlds, c. 1550–1850* (Cambridge: Cambridge University Press, 2012), 130–150.

Stubbings, Matthew, 'British Conservatism and the Indian Revolt: The Annexation of Awadh and the Consequences of Liberal Empire, 1856–1858', *Journal of British Studies*, 55/4 (2016), 728–749.

Sundaram, Lanka, 'The International Status of India', *Journal of the Royal Institute of International Affairs*, 9/4 (1930), 452–466.

Sundararajan, Saroja, *Sir C. P. Ramaswamy Aiyar* (New Delhi: Allied Publishers, 2002).

Sundarlal, Pandit, and Qazi Muhammad Abdulghaffar, 'A Report on the Post-Operation Polo Massacres, Rape and Destruction or Seizure of Property in Hyderabad State', in Omar Khalidi, ed., *Hyderabad: After the Fall* (Wichita, KN: Hyderabad Historical Society, 1988), 95–115.

Sylvest, Casper, *British Liberal Internationalism, 1880–1930: Making Progress?* (Manchester: Manchester University Press, 2009).

Sylvest, Casper, 'International Law in Nineteenth-Century Britain', *British Year Book of International Law*, 75 (2005), 9–70.

Sylvest, Casper, 'James Bryce and the Two Faces of Nationalism', in Ian Hall and Lisa Hill, eds., *British International Thinkers from Hobbes to Namier* (New York, NY: Palgrave Macmillan, 2009), 161–180.

Talbot, Ian, *A History of Modern South Asia: Politics, States, Diasporas* (New Haven, CT: Yale University Press, 2016).

Talbot, Ian, 'Planning for Pakistan: The Planning Committee of the All-India Muslim League 1943–46', *Modern Asian Studies*, 28/4 (1994), 875–889.

Thakurdas, Purushottamdas, et al., *Memorandum Outlining a Plan of Economic Development for India* (Harmondsworth: Penguin, 1945).

Thane, Pat, 'Barbara Wootton (1897–1988): Pioneering Social Scientist, Feminist and Policymaker', *Women's History Review*, 23/5 (2014), 793–798.

Thompson, E. P., *Whigs and Hunters: The Origin of the Black Act* (London: Allen Lane, 1975).

Thompson, Edward, *The Life of Charles, Lord Metcalfe* (London: Faber and Faber, 1938).

Thompson, Edward, *The Making of the Indian Princes* (London: Oxford University Press, 1943).

Travers, Robert, 'A British Empire by Treaty in Eighteenth-Century India', in Saliha Belmessous, ed., *Empire by Treaty: Negotiating European Expansion, 1600–1900* (Oxford: Oxford University Press, 2015), 132–160.

Travers, Robert, 'Constitutions, Contact Zones, and Imperial Ricochets: Sovereignty and Law in British Asia', in H. V. Bowen, Elizabeth Mancke, and John G. Reid, eds., *Britain's Oceanic Empire: Atlantic and Indian Ocean Worlds, c. 1550–1850* (Cambridge: Cambridge University Press, 2012), 98–129.

Travers, Robert, *Ideology and Empire in Eighteenth-Century India: The British in Bengal* (Cambridge: Cambridge University Press, 2007).

Trinidad, Jamie, *Self-Determination in Disputed Colonial Territories* (Cambridge: Cambridge University Press, 2018).

Tulluch, H. A., 'Changing British Attitudes Towards the United States in the 1880s', *The Historical Journal*, 20/4 (1977), 825–840.

Tupper, Charles Lewis, 'India and Sir Henry Maine', *Journal of the Society of Arts*, 46 (1898), 390–405.

Tupper, Charles Lewis, *Our Indian Protectorate: An Introduction to the Study of the Relations between the British Government and its Indian Feudatories* (London: Longmans, Green and Co., 1893).

Unterman, Katherine, *Uncle Sam's Policemen: The Pursuit of Fugitives Across Borders* (Cambridge, MA: Harvard University Press, 2015).

Vachha, P. B., *Famous Judges, Lawyers and Cases of Bombay: A Judicial History of Bombay During the British Period* (Bombay: N. M. Tripathi Private Ltd., 1962).

Vadi, Valentina, 'International Law and Its Histories: Methodological Risks and Opportunities', *Harvard International Law Journal*, 58/2 (2017), 311–352.

Vagts, Detlev F., 'International Law in the Third Reich', *American Journal of International Law*, 84/3 (1990), 661–704.

van Meersbergen, Guido, 'The Diplomatic Repertoires of the East India Companies in Mughal South Asia, 1608–1717', *The Historical Journal*, 62/4 (2019), 875–898.

van Schendel, Willem, 'Stateless in South Asia: The Making of the India–Bangladesh Enclaves', *Journal of Asian Studies*, 61/1 (2002), 115–147.

Varadachariar, N. D., *Indian States in the Federation* (Humphrey Milford: Oxford University Press, 1936).

Vaughan, Chris, 'The Politics of Regionalism and Federation in East Africa, 1958–1964', *The Historical Journal*, 62/2 (2019), 519–540.

Visvesvaraya, M., *Planned Economy for India* (Bangalore: Bangalore Press, 1934).

Wagner, Kim A., *Amritsar 1919: An Empire of Fear and the Making of a Massacre* (New Haven, CT: Yale University Press, 2019).

Walker, Lydia, 'Decolonization in the 1960s: On Legitimate and Illegitimate Nationalist Claims-Making', *Past & Present*, 242 (2019), 227–264.

Wempe, Sean Andrew, 'A League to Preserve Empires: Understanding the Mandates System and Avenues for Further Scholarly Inquiry', *American Historical Review*, 124/5 (2019), 1723–1731.

Wertheim, Stephen, 'The League of Nations: A Retreat from International Law?', *Journal of Global History*, 7/2 (2012), 210–232.

Wertheim, Stephen, 'The League That Wasn't: American Designs for a Legalist–Sanctionist League of Nations and the Intellectual Origins of International Organization, 1914–1920', *Diplomatic History*, 35/5 (2011), 797–836.

Westlake, John, *Chapters on the Principles of International Law* (Cambridge: Cambridge University Press, 1894).

Wheare, K. C., *The Statute of Westminster, 1931* (Oxford: Clarendon Press, 1933).

Wheatley, Natasha, 'Mandatory Interpretation: Legal Hermeneutics and the New International Order in Arab and Jewish Petitions to the League of Nations', *Past & Present*, 227 (2015), 205–248.

Wheatley, Natasha, 'New Subjects in International Law and Order', in Glenda Sluga and Patricia Clavin, eds., *Internationalisms: A Twentieth-Century History* (Cambridge: Cambridge University Press, 2016), 265–286.

Wheatley, Natasha, 'Spectral Legal Personality in Interwar International Law: On New Ways of Not Being a State', *Law and History Review*, 35/3 (2017), 753–787.

Wilde, Simon, *Ranji: The Strange Genius of Ranjitsinhji* (London: Aurum Press, 1999).

Wilder, Gary, *Freedom Time: Negritude, Decolonization and the Future of the World* (Durham, NC: Duke University Press, 2015).

Wilkinson, Callie, 'Weak Ties in a Tangled Web? Relationships between the Political Residents of the English East India Company and their Munshis, 1798–1818', *Modern Asian Studies*, 53/5 (2019), 1574–1612.

Witt, John Fabian, 'Anglo-American Empire and the Crisis of the Legal Frame (Will the Real British Empire Please Stand Up?)', *Harvard Law Review*, 120/3 (2007), 754–796.

Wood, John R., 'Indian Nationalism in the Princely Context: the Rajkot Satyagraha of 1938–9', in Robin Jeffrey, ed., *People, Princes and Paramount Power: Society and Politics in the Indian Princely States* (Delhi: Oxford University Press, 1978), 240–274.

Wootton, Barbara, *Socialism and Federation* (1941), https://federalunion.org.uk/socialism-and-federation/, accessed 17 March 2021.

Wright, Quincy, *Mandates Under the League of the Nations* (Chicago, IL: The University of Chicago Press, 1930).

Wright, Quincy, 'The Goa Incident', *American Journal of International Law*, 56/3 (1962), 617–632.

Wylie, Francis, 'Federal Negotiations in India 1935–9, and After', in C. H. Philips and Mary Doreen Wainwright, eds., *The Partition of India: Policies and Perspectives, 1935–47* (Cambridge, MA: M. I. T. Press, 1970), 517–526.

Yahaya, Nurfadzilah, 'Class, White Women, and Elite Asian Men in British Courts During the Late Nineteenth Century', *Journal of Women's History*, 31/2 (2019), 101–123.

Yazdani, Zubaida, 'The End of an Era', in Omar Khalidi, ed., *Hyderabad: After the Fall* (Wichita, KN: Hyderabad Historical Society, 1988), 90–94.

Yazdani, Zubaida, and Mary Chrystal, *The Seventh Nizam: The Fallen Empire* (London: The Author, 1985).

Yearwood, Peter J., *Guarantee of Peace: The League of Nations in British Policy, 1914–1925* (Oxford: Oxford University Press, 2009).

Yechury, Akhila, 'Imagining India, Decolonizing *L'Inde Française*, c. 1947–1954', *The Historical Journal*, 58/4 (2015), 1141–1165.

Zachariah, Benjamin, *Developing India: An Intellectual and Social History, c. 1930–50* (Delhi: Oxford University Press, 2005).

Zamindar, Vazira Fazila-Yacoobali, *The Long Partition and the Making of Modern South Asia: Refugees, Boundaries, Histories* (New York, NY: Columbia University Press, 2007).

Zastoupil, Lynn, 'J. S. Mill and India', *Victorian Studies*, 32/1 (1988), 31–54.

Zhu, Yuan Yi, 'Suzerainty, Semi-Sovereignty, and International Legal Hierarchies on China's Borderlands', *Asian Journal of International Law*, 10/2 (2020), 293–320.

Zubrzycki, John, *The Last Nizam: An Indian Prince in the Australian Outback* (Sydney: Macmillan, 2006).

Index

For the benefit of digital users, indexed terms that span two pages (e.g., 52–53) may, on occasion, appear on only one of those pages.